The Creation of the French Royal Mistress

The Creation of the French Royal Mistress

From Agnès Sorel to Madame Du Barry

TRACY ADAMS AND CHRISTINE ADAMS

The Pennsylvania State University Press
University Park, Pennsylvania

Library of Congress Cataloging-in-Publication Data

Names: Adams, Tracy, 1959– author. | Adams, Christine,
    1962– author.
Title: The creation of the French royal mistress : from
    Agnès Sorel to Madame Du Barry / Tracy Adams
    and Christine Adams.
Description: University Park, Pennsylvania : The
    Pennsylvania State University Press, [2020] |
    Includes bibliographical references and index.
Summary: "Explores the sociogenesis and development
    of the French royal mistress, examining the careers
    of nine of the most significant holders of that title
    between 1444 and the final years of the ancien
    régime"—Provided by publisher.
Identifiers: LCCN 2019055814 | ISBN 9780271085975
    (cloth) | ISBN 9780271085982 (paperback)
Subjects: LCSH: France—Kings and rulers—
    Paramours—History. | France—Court and
    courtiers—History.
Classification: LCC DC36.3 .A33 2020 | DDC
    352.23092/2 [B]—dc23
LC record available at https://lccn.loc.gov/2019055814

The Pennsylvania State University Press is a member of
the Association of University Presses.

It is the policy of The Pennsylvania State University
Press to use acid-free paper. Publications on uncoated
stock satisfy the minimum requirements of American
National Standard for Information Sciences—
Permanence of Paper for Printed Library Material,
ANSI Z39.48–1992.

FOR TANGUY LE DOUJET (1951–2013)
"IN PERPETUUM, FRATER, AVE ATQUE VALE."

CONTENTS

Semiformalized extraconjugal relationships have always been a fixture of human social life. However, these relationships have taken very different shapes. The life of a concubine in the Edo castle had little in common with that of a Venetian courtesan, and neither had much in common with the life of an ancient Greek hetaira. The powerful French royal mistress, too, was a recognized extraconjugal social position with its own defining features, most notably the important political work that it included. Like kings or queens, royal mistresses existed across Europe and demonstrated certain commonalities, but, like the king or queen of France, the position was also particular to that kingdom, evolving along with other social structures, events, and personalities into a unique institution.

In what follows we offer an overview of the role of the royal mistress as it developed in France, tracing the careers of nine of its most powerful holders. As anyone who has worked on royal mistresses is aware, these women have come down to us embedded in networks of legend, verifiable information, and fantasy that are often difficult to disentangle: Agnès Sorel was "officially designated" as royal mistress; Diane de Poitiers was raised by Anne of France; Louis XIV allowed his mistresses no political influence; Madame de Pompadour procured young women to entertain Louis XV at the Parc-aux-Cerfs. Following an anecdote to its source is already a daunting task, and assessing whether that source is credible even more so. Probable biases and motives have to be acknowledged as well as the relative proximity of the source to its object. On the one hand, eyewitnesses, like ambassadors, do not always understand what they are watching. On the other, oral traditions sometimes convey truthful information across the centuries. Although in this study we are often unable to pronounce on whether a particular anecdote is true, we have always cited our sources.

When we cite a secondary source for an anecdote, the primary source is available in the secondary source. In the rare cases where we have searched fruitlessly to locate a source, we have acknowledged that.

Because the sources change so dramatically across the centuries, it is important to say a few words about these. One of our arguments is that a precondition for the mistress as the position developed in France was the presence of resident ambassadors, who, by recognizing the importance of these women for their unparalleled access to the king and soliciting them for information and help, both reflected reality in their reports and helped reify the position. But these men arrived in France only under François I, who reigned from 1515 to 1547. The tenure of Agnès Sorel, therefore, although important for the tradition of the French royal mistress, was very different from the tenures of those who followed her. The sources for Agnès are limited almost exclusively to chronicles, which means that they are sparse relative to her successors.

The sources chronicling the career of Anne de Pisseleu d'Heilly, the Duchess of Étampes, mistress of François I, raise a special set of issues. Many of the ambassador letters dealing with her remain unedited, making work on her more time-consuming and materially more difficult than work on her successors. We would like to acknowledge the invaluable work of David Potter and François Nawrocki in the archives relevant to Anne de Pisseleu's period. Their studies make possible work on her in a survey like this one. Instead of reading through literally thousands of pages of painful-to-decipher script, we can head immediately to the spots that these scholars have already identified and work outward from there. Although we have personally examined the archival sources cited here and translated them ourselves, we located those related to Anne in the first place by following Potter and Nawrocki's leads. We would also like to acknowledge the research of Robert Knecht, Cédric Michon, Jonathan Reid, and Kathleen Wilson-Chevalier, each of whom, in a different way, has brought the reign of François I and the tenure of Anne to life.

From Diane de Poitiers on, most of the primary sources are edited. The sources relative to Diane and Gabrielle d'Estrées are manageable in number. A new issue arises, however, with the mistresses of Louis XIV and XV: an explosion of information. It is quite simply impossible to create a succinct chapter that takes account of all the ambassador reports, memoirs, and histories related to these women. In these cases, we have undoubtedly omitted points that could have been discussed, especially information about other mistresses that would have been interesting to include.

A word about the names: we have opted for the names by which the women are most commonly known. The exception is the Duchess of Étampes, to whom we refer as Anne, because her career is intertwined with that of Diane de Poitiers, whom no one calls "Poitiers." For a small bit of consistency, then, we refer to these women as Anne and Diane. As always, we fretted over the particle "de." Chronicler Jacques-Auguste de Thou, for example, is given as "Thou" according the Bibliothèque nationale de France's list of international approved forms, but historians call him "De Thou." Analogies do not work: one finds De Gaulle under "d," not "g." We have tried to be consistently inconsistent in such cases. As for alternating between "of" and "de," we have tried to use the former when the reference is to territory, the latter when it forms part of a last name.

Translations, of which there are many in a study like this, are our own, except where indicated.

Finally, we owe thanks to many colleagues who have helped us realize this project. We first acknowledge the Netherlands Institute for Advanced Studies, then in Wassenaar, for a grant that allowed us to hold a colloquium called "Female Beauty Systems Throughout the Centuries" in November 2013. This project grew out of that colloquium. We also gratefully acknowledge a grant from the Herzog August Bibliothek in Wolfenbüttel, which gave us the chance to work through some of this material. A special thanks to Jill Bepler and the wonderful staff at that fabulous institution. We would further like to thank the colleagues who gave us a chance to present and discuss the material that follows: Amy Nelson Burnett and the Medieval and Renaissance Center at the University of Nebraska, Lincoln; Cynthia Brown and the Medieval Studies Center at the University of California, Santa Barbara; Deborah McGrady and the Departments of French, English, Medieval Studies, and Women, Gender, and Sexuality, University of Virginia; Zrinca Stahuljak and the UCLA Center for Medieval and Renaissance Studies (CMRS), UCLA; Charles-Louis Morand-Métier and the Departments of French and Medieval Studies at the University of Vermont; Anna Klosowska and the Miami University Summer French program in Dijon; and Ginny Blanton and Kathy Krause and the Departments of English and French at the University of Missouri, Kansas City. Others provided useful and generous feedback, including Jeroen Duindam, Bill Egginton, Jody Enders, Bob and Elborg Forster, Chuck Holden, Colin Jones, Tom Kaiser, Karen Offen, Orest Ranum, and Kathleen Wilson-Chevalier. A special thanks to Angus Kennedy for providing on short notice a source that we could not get our hands on! Many thanks as well to our editor Ellie Goodman and the rest of the team at Penn State University Press for all their help. Most of all, we want to acknowledge the pleasure of working on the book together. During long walks, we gradually formulated the theoretical framework that serves as the basis for this project. And because our areas of scholarly expertise are different but complementary, it is a book that neither of us could have completed separately.

A huge thanks to our families, Glenn, Danny, and Elise, and Paul, Sylvie, and Julia, for their constant support. Finally, we dedicate this book to our beloved and much-missed Tanguy, in memory of the evenings, filled with food, wine, and conversation, that stretched into the early hours of the morning. Here, finally, is that book we talked so much about!

Introduction
What Was It About France?

Frederick the Great, discussing the ruinous propensity of German princelings to imitate Louis XIV in book 10 of his 1740 *Antimachiavel*, put the
French royal mistress on a par with the Versailles court and the French
army in the list of outrageously expensive items that the princelings coveted.
"There is not a cadet of a cadet line," he scoffed, "who does not imagine
himself as a sort of Louis XIV: he builds his Versailles, he has his mistresses,
he leads his army."[1] Christoph Wieland, writing three decades later, accords
the royal mistress a similar role. The enthralling Alabanda, who keeps the
eyes of King Azor averted from the misery of his people, can only be a
comment on the extraordinary position of the French royal mistress in her
setting of unimaginable opulence.[2] What was evident to these German
eyes remains so: whether one found the French royal mistress fabulous or
appalling, she was a constituent element of the king's grandeur. No one
today would underestimate the importance of her splendor for bolstering
the monarchy. But in addition to her visual role, she was a politician. True,
not every royal mistress wielded clout. Contemporaries such as the Duke
of Luynes distinguished between real and temporary holders of the role.
Even if the rumor that Madame de Pompadour was installed at Versailles
was true, "she was only a fling [*passade*], not a mistress," Luynes asserted,
incorrectly, as it happens.[3] However, the most powerful mistresses rivaled
the king's closest advisers in terms of influence.

This study explores the sociogenesis and development of the position
in France, examining the careers of nine of its most significant holders:

Agnès Sorel, Anne de Pisseleu d'Heilly, Diane de Poitiers, Gabrielle d'Estrées, Françoise Louise de La Baume Le Blanc, Françoise Athénaïs de
Rochechouart de Mortemart, Françoise d'Aubigné, Jeanne-Antoinette Poisson, and Jeanne Bécu.[4] Although kings had always had extraconjugal sexual
partners—some of them powerful, such as Alice Perrers or Jane Shore—only
in France did the royal mistress become a tradition, a quasi-institutionalized
political position, generally accepted if always vaguely scandalous. And yet
the position has been studied only in popular narrative histories intended
to titillate.[5] Other powerful female roles central to royal family life, such as
the queen, the queen's entourage, and the female regent, an unofficial role
once considered somewhat illegitimate, have received serious attention in
recent years, as have individual mistresses.[6] However, the important and
enduring position of French royal mistress per se has not been explored.

The study's point of departure is a simple question: What was it about
France? We would like to be very specific about our approach to this question. The creation of the role could be examined from any number of valid
and enlightening perspectives. For example, it could be approached through
a psychoanalytic lens, to hypothesize about the hidden emotional reasons
why the role emerged when it did. Or it could be examined within the
context of the *Querelle des femmes*, that long-term debate over the merits
and faults of women, which corresponds, chronologically, to the appearance of the powerful royal mistress in France. However, given our own
critical inclinations, we have opted to examine the intellectual, emotional,
and physical environment that made emergence of the role possible.

We take as the basis of our analysis Fernand Braudel's three-part schema
of history, which differentiates long- from medium-term structures and
both of these from short-term events, and, in this introduction, we initi-
ate the study by applying the schema to the period between 1450 and
1540. Agnès Sorel, often considered to be the first significant French royal
mistress, died in 1450; around 1540 Anne de Pisseleu d'Heilly, the Duchess of Étampes (1508–1580), begins to appear in ambassador reports as a
central figure in court politics. As we will see in chapter 1, although indirect
evidence attests to Agnès's political influence, it was not widely recognized
during her own time. In contrast, no one doubted Anne de Pisseleu's power.
Between these two dates, then, something occurs that makes it possible for
the king's mistress to be taken seriously as a political adviser. We trace the
convergence of structures and events in France during the period in question that allowed this to happen, first exploring a long-term structure that
was a precondition for the position, a particular idea of gender already in

place by the period that we are exploring. *Conditio sine qua non* for the royal mistress, this notion of gender also formed the basis for female regency, and, because this notion of gender is articulated in treatises on female regency, we start by examining how this slightly earlier and more familiar role was conceptualized. But if the same assumptions about gender support both roles, the royal mistress does not derive from the female regent. Rather, the royal mistress is a female version of the royal mignon, a medium-term structure originating in the mid-fifteenth century. Therefore we turn next to the mignons, or favorites, groups of young men associated directly with the king, who eventually admitted women among their number—although only one at a time.[7] But under what circumstances was this role opened to women? To conclude our discussion of the convergence of structures that permitted the development of the royal mistress, we examine the position in the context of another long-term structure, the widely discussed theatricalization of the royal court under François I (b. 1494, r. 1515–47), which produced an environment within which women took part in "a vital system of communications through which messages [were] transmitted, channels opened up; they investigate[d] possibilities through talking to the right people, before men, by now confident of success, [made] more direct overtures."[8]

The role of powerful royal mistress became imaginable with the intersection of these structures. Still, it had to be activated by an intelligent and charismatic woman associated with a king willing to be advised by women. In other words, the position's realization depended on what Braudel describes as particular events layered on top of the structures that we examine in this introduction. These events form the content of the following chapters in which we examine the individual careers.[9]

A PARTICULAR IDEA OF GENDER

Although queens had earlier served as regents, under Isabeau of Bavaria (1371–1435) and Anne of France (1461–1522) a genuine preference for female regents took hold. Ordinances promulgated by the mad king Charles VI (b. 1368, r. 1380–1422) on behalf of Queen Isabeau reveal the logic behind this preference. Fearing that he would die prematurely after his earliest psychotic breakdowns in 1392 and 1393, the king settled what would happen in the case of his death, awarding regency of the realm ("government, guard and defense") to his brother, Louis of Orléans (1372–1407), and guardianship of the young king to his queen, Isabeau, aided by his uncles.[10] But Louis's primacy led to rivalry with the royal uncles, each side accusing the other of wanting to usurp the throne. Hoping to lessen the possibility of civil war, Charles VI abolished regency altogether in an ordinance of 1403, stipulating instead that in the event of the king's death, his heir would succeed immediately, whatever his age.[11] Minus a regent, the queen mother, as guardian, would hold the reins of power, although her minor son "officially" ruled.[12] The advantage of this scenario was that unlike a male regent—say, the minor king's paternal uncle—the queen would prioritize not her own career but the welfare of her son. As Charles VI's ordinance asserts, a mother "has a greater and more tender love for her children, and, with a soft and caring heart, she takes care of and nourishes them more lovingly than any other person, no matter how closely related."[13]

But maternal instinct was not the only basis for female preference. Here we need to consider the conception of gender underwriting the preference—that is, a long-established assumption that women were legally inferior to men but politically as capable as them. A number of conceptions of gender coexisted in late medieval and early modern France. However, this paradoxical one was particularly significant in shaping the experience of sexual difference among the nobility and therefore in supporting female regency. The conception undergirded feudal law, which allowed women to wield authority in the absence of a husband, son, or brother, but *only* under such circumstances.[14] Political theoretician Christine de Pizan (1365–1431) gives the first self-conscious articulation of the principle, foregrounding the "natural" differences between men and women while insisting that women could perform as well as men in all things. As she recounts in her *Livre de la mutacion de fortune* of 1402, when her husband died she took over his role, metamorphosing into a man.[15] True, women were excluded from certain positions by God's viceroy Nature, Christine admits.[16] Her father had hoped to pass his precious "stones" of astrological and medical knowledge on to a son. But Christine was a girl, resembling her father in all things: manner, body, and face. Only her "sexe" was different, and, for this reason, she could not inherit her father's riches, although she could have done the job.[17] Or, as a treatise on natural law of 1601 asserts, female modesty and the virtue particular to the sex, not any intellectual disadvantage, render reigning or commanding "souverainement" inappropriate for women.[18]

This idea that women were fit for all jobs but legally restricted from taking on certain ones except when there was no man to do it was common across Europe. What was unique about France, however, was the vision's instantiation in the so-called Salic Law, which was elaborated over the course of the fifteenth century. True, the Salic Law excluded women from succession to the throne under any circumstances. But it implicitly allowed them to govern as regents. Indeed, by making them legally incompetent to succeed and therefore unable to usurp the throne, it created a tendency to favor them as regents. In this way, it gave a legal basis to the assumption that the queen mother was the safest choice for regent—set out in Charles VI's regency ordinances—and further enhanced the advantage that she already enjoyed by virtue of her presumed maternal instinct. That the Salic Law was understood in this way is clear from seventeenth-century regency treatises. Pierre Dupuy (1582–1651) sets out what we might call the "safety" argument in his *Traité des régences et des majorités des rois de France*, first printed in 1655: "The principal reasons for this choice [of queen as regent] are based on . . . the natural affection of a mother for her children and [the fact] that there can be no suspicion of any danger for the princes committed to their care." He then references the Salic Law, writing that "women, by virtue of their sex, are less capable of invading the State [*Estat*] of their children than any other person" for the reasons that "by the law of the State [*Estat*], they are excluded from the royalty; that it is impossible to imagine that it would even enter their minds to try to achieve such a thing; that they cannot be helped by anyone at all, not possessing this basic requirement; that they cannot act on their own, but [only] through others, in all the principal acts of their administration and particularly in acts of war and affairs of great resolve."[19] Robert Luyt in 1652 states the point still more forcefully: "Queens have normally been preferred in this choice to all Princes of the Blood and other lords, religious or secular, for the same reason, that we do not need to fear that they would usurp the crown, because they are precluded from doing so by the fundamental Law of this monarchy."[20]

The Salic Law, then, paradoxically created an opportunity for female authority. But it created a very particular conception of authority, forcing female regency to be imagined as a sort of open secret in which the king—a child—reigns, although it is in fact his mother who does the work. As Lucien Bély observes, a very young prince such as Charles IX did not manage European affairs. In reality, the Guises and, especially, regent Catherine de Médicis wrote the letters carried by French envoys, signed by the young monarch.[21] And yet Dupuy's treatise insists, as we saw above, that female regents could not act on their own. Scholarship on female regency such as Katherine Crawford's *Perilous Performances* describes how the queen mother "performed" her maternity to cover her governing.[22] We will return to this notion of the open secret.

Another aspect of the paradox is central to how female governance was imagined, although it is never explicitly stated in regency treatises. Although Christine de Pizan precedes the heyday of the Salic Law, she voices, as we have seen, the principle on which it was founded. We noted that for Christine a powerful woman was always a substitute, like Christine herself metamorphosing into a man. Equally important here, however, she also constructed female power as the necessary supplement to male power. In the *Livre de la cité des dames* of 1405, Christine describes gender differences as complementary. "God wanted men and women to serve him differently, and to help each other and give each other mutual aid, each according to his manner," explains the allegorical character Reason, "and he thus created the two sexes to be of different natures, as necessary to the accomplishment of the tasks."[23] In her *Livre des trois vertus*, Christine explains that men are reactive because they are hot, whereas women are moist, cold, and peaceful, and therefore integral to maintaining order. When war threatens the kingdom, writes Christine, the princess is "the means of peace and harmony." She works "to avoid war because of the trouble that can arise from it." She explains to warring lords that "if they would like to make amends or make suitable reparations, she would happily make an effort to try to find a way to pacify her husband."[24] But Christine saves her clearest formulation of female power as the necessary supplement to the male version for her final known work, the *Ditié de Jehanne d'Arc*, which, proclaiming the recent victories of the French over the English, recalls that Charles VII (b. 1403, r. 1422–61) would not have prevailed had it not been for Joan of Arc: "And you Charles, King of France, seventh of that noble name, who have been involved in such a great war before things turned out at all well for you, now, thanks be to God, see your honour exalted by the Maid who has laid low your enemies beneath your standard."[25] Joan was required for Charles's victory.

If the Salic Law was at times bolstered by misogynistic arguments, the principle of female exclusion was imaginable without recourse to such arguments, simply on legal grounds, common notions about maternal instinct and female modesty, and the traditional view of men and women as complementary, equally necessary, components of a whole (the absent or minor king could not rule without his mother). We return now to the official royal mistress, whose role was based on the same assumptions about gender. As

Françoise Autrand has noted with reference to the fifteenth century, "In the western Christian model, power has a feminine side ('face')."[26] True, for most great lords, this feminine aspect of their authority was represented by their wives. The queen of France undoubtedly played a crucial role in the configuration of royal power, representing mercy in the eyes of the public. However, with few exceptions, she was foreign, inevitably raising suspicions of prior loyalty and, among courtiers, the need for another, more secure way to access the king. In contrast with the queen, the royal mistress was always French and utterly devoted to the king.

THE MIGNON OR FAVORITE

But this role was difficult to represent. The monarchy was structured on the model of the family.[27] Female regency, as we have seen, fit into the already-existing framework of feudal law. In contrast, the official royal mistress could not be slotted into a social or legal structure. The rise of the royal mignons, or favorites, as they came to be called from the middle of the sixteenth century, offered a conceptual framework.[28] A mid-term structure (that is, recurring but not fundamental), the favorite was also common across Europe, although the role took very different forms. Arlette Jouanna dates the rise in France of these young men of the mid-level provincial nobility who pledged themselves directly to the king, without the intermediary of one of the Princes of the Blood or great lords of the realm, to the reign of Henri III (b. 1551, r. 1574–89).[29] The court favorite, the "parvenu-turned-power-broker," in John Adamson's apt words, "whose promotion violated the axioms of the aristocratic honour code," was the antithesis of ancient nobility.[30]

   It is important to note that although from a modern perspective the form of power represented by the mignons may look like a self-evident feature of any rather loosely organized political system, it is culturally specific, arising only under certain circumstances.[31] In France as elsewhere, it was linked to the absence of a strict division between "formal" and "informal" power. But in France it was also directly proportional to the king's ability to circumvent the claims of the great lords of the realm, who had their own political agendas and who made significant demands in return for their loyalty. As the polity came to be overtly constructed as "absolutist," the king became the only openly recognized political actor. Although, as Hillay Zmora and others warn, early modern French monarchs "were a great deal less mighty than the term 'absolutism' suggests," a superficial adherence to the structures of absolutism allowed the king to grant extensive political involvement to the courtiers of his choice.[32] Serving entirely at the king's pleasure and answerable to no one else, the mignons contested "the influence exercised by the great lords of the realm," which, from the king's perspective, made them all the more valuable.[33] Entirely dependent on the king, they had no agenda except to maintain him in power. The king's relationship to them was one of dilection, his gifts to them signs of his favor or grace, not of obligation.[34] The mignons would always lack any official definition or designation *for their particular role*, but they helped define the power of the king, serving as beloved advisers bound to him alone, living in his proximity.[35] They served as a "contact zone between court society, the kingdom, and the prince," forming "a screen that masked or represented the king."[36]

These descriptions of the mignons apply equally well to royal mistresses. Like the mignons, they were entirely devoted to the king but only more so. The similarity is no accident. Arlette Jouanna and Nicolas Le Roux show that the mignons reached their apogee under Henri III, but, significant for the history of the royal mistress, the category first appears just as Agnès Sorel begins her rise. The term "mignon" dates, according to Philippe Contamine, to the early fifteenth century.[37] Chronicler Thomas Basin situates the appearance of groups of flattering young men who, loved by Charles VII, attracted grace and favor to themselves and a "little woman" called "the lovely Agnès" in the same time frame.[38]

However, the court society that Agnès Sorel inhabited had no means of imagining, much less representing, her role, as we show in chapter 1. For this reason, she cannot be considered an official royal mistress in the same sense as the others studied here. Some crucial elements were missing. For one, Charles VII's court was less brilliant than the ones to follow. The "King of Bourges" was for many years locked out of Paris, and when his kingship was finally recognized, he had no desire to move to that city. His court did not include, at least to the same degree, the vibrant artistic cultural life with contingents of women that would provide later royal mistresses with a flexible "cover" for political activity. In the decades following Agnès's death, the female presence at court became increasingly visible, as Anne of Brittany (1477–1514), queen first of Charles VIII (b. 1470, r. 1483–98) and then Louis XII (b. 1462, r. 1498–1515), organized the queen's household, the *maison de la reine*, which expanded significantly during her reign.[39] Just as men held official positions in the king's household, women began to solicit positions in the queen's household to acquire social capital as well as financial remuneration; the high-ranking *charges* of the queen's *dame d'honneur* and the *surintendante* conferred both status and power.[40] These women could become influential patrons.[41] Female courtiers flourished in the absence of any strict distinction between formal and informal power, operating within the framework of family and court networks that valued women as mediators and brokers.[42] They could arrange marriages, arbitrate problems, and negotiate positions for their families and friends.[43]

And still, there were limits. Although mistresses posed no particular problem, occupying a recognized, if rather negative, position in the courtly social imaginary, it was a different matter to imagine one as royal adviser. How did Anne de Pisseleu d'Heilly come to be recognized as a political actor?

THE COURT AS A STAGE

No separate space for a politically powerful king's lover existed at the court of Charles VII. Chronicler Georges Chastellain describes Agnès as an intruder, usurping the queen's role. Marie of Anjou was forced to suffer a "tramp, a little servant of low birth, being and living in intimacy every day with [the queen]; having [Agnès's] quarter in the king's hotel, better maintained and outfitted than [the queen's] own . . . having all royal honors and services for [Agnès], *as if she were the queen*."[44]

In contrast, contemporaries did not understand Anne to be intruding into the space of Queen Eleonore of Austria but to be inhabiting a parallel space of her own.[45] Structured as an open secret, Anne's political activity was strategically ignored except by a select few in very restricted arenas. Or, to put it slightly differently, François I's court provided Anne with different spaces for enacting contradictory roles without denouncing her as a liar, a fraud, or a prostitute. Her primary roles, which she performed in public, were to serve in the queen's entourage and the household of the royal daughters, conforming in these cases to courtly hierarchy. As the king's mistress she performed numerous other "wifely" tasks for a greatly reduced audience. Finally, she performed the roles of royal adviser and diplomat before a still more reduced audience. Although it was clear to many that she was the king's mistress and clear to some that she served as one of his principal political advisers, as we will see, her behavior was impeccable, supported by a complicit court. Catherine de Médicis explains in a letter of 1582 that the key to Anne's success and that of Anne's successor, Diane de Poitiers, was that everyone behaved as if nothing were happening, as if all were "honorable." Comparing the flagrant behavior of her son-in-law, Henri of Navarre, to that of her discreet late husband, Catherine avers that nothing would have angered King Henri II more than had she, as queen, kept ladies who spoke openly about such things as his impregnating Janet Fleming.[46]

This handling of the royal mistress's political activity as open secret must be seen within the context of—indeed, as the product of—a much-discussed phenomenon, "a particular psychological disposition, a certain *habitus*, organized around a constitutive theatricality," which becomes particularly evident under François I.[47] This theatricalization, which we might think of, most fundamentally, as an awareness of oneself and others as performing various roles, is evident in many phenomena beyond the exercise of discretion described by Catherine. Perhaps most obvious, the lives of early modern French kings and courtiers were played out before an audience. "Different from the Spanish monarchs or Austrian emperors who led a secluded existence," writes Benedetta Craveri, "the French kings passed the entire day in public, conversing familiarly with the great lords of the realm, and the humblest courtiers could approach them."[48] Visitors understood court life as a show and expected to be dazzled. In a treatise on kingship first presented to the young François I in 1519, Guillaume Budé describes crowds watching "as at a spectacle of honor" and a "theater of nobility."[49]

Contributing to the perception of the court as theater was the appearance of the resident ambassador in France. Ambassadors, of course, had always existed. But under François I they became a fixture, often remaining for years. Like other visitors, these men observed French court festivals with amazement. In 1539 Antonio Bendidio produced for the Duke of Mantova a minutely detailed account of a magnificent Epiphany performance involving the crowning of a certain lady of the queen, Madame Lestrange, as Queen of the Bean ("Regina della fava"), a custom unfamiliar to him. Bendidio described the sable-lined robes in which this queen was clad and the procession and the feasts and performances that followed, apologizing for writing at such length: he was afraid of trying to convey accurately the splendor in "few words."[50] However, representatives of sometimes hostile governments were not merely gaping; they were scouring and recording for their lords the gestures and conversations of the participants in such festivals. Their lords relied on such information to guess from afar what the king of France was up to. Every quarrel and every alliance between courtiers was potentially significant, and, knowing this, courtiers strove to control their outward appearances.

Baldassare Castiglione's *The Courtier*, begun in 1508, published in 1528, and translated into French in 1538, articulated its renowned descriptions of self-consciousness in this same context. Successful courtiers were actors—that is, highly self-aware beings who gave the appearance of being entirely spontaneous—practicing "in all things a certain nonchalance which conceals all artistry and makes whatever one does seem uncontrived and effortless."[51] An increased attention to the distinction between surface appearance and profounder meaning also manifested itself in a growing interest in deciphering symbols and in masks; collections of love poems dedicated to women whose identities remain debated, along with *ballets de cour* that celebrated the exploits of real individuals through dance allegories, demonstrate that this attention encompassed an appreciation for the play between persona and the individual human being.[52]

This theatrical atmosphere, where strategic dissimulation was both a high-stakes political activity and a source of pleasure, permitted the royal mistress to flourish as a political actor. Possessing privileged access to information and power, she was sought after for advice and mediation by ambassadors seeking advantage for their own lords, in a society itself embedded in the larger environment of the constant contest for territorial domination among François I of France, Henry VIII of England (b. 1491, r. 1509–47), and Charles V, the Holy Roman Emperor (1500–1558, r. 1519–56). Although the birth of what is today known as *raison d'état*, the principle that all is moral in the struggle to promote national interest, is typically dated to Richelieu, in their relentless struggle for preeminence these three monarchs employed all means necessary to further their own causes, and their ambassadors competed to keep one step ahead of their competitors. In such a setting, a powerful royal mistress was an invaluable mediator, for the French king because she was the most solicitous of his interests, and for his opponents because she was closer to the king than even his most intimate advisers.

Certainly earlier courts had always been highly ritualized, and courtiers had always dissimulated. But the difference was that during the sixteenth century, courtiers began to recognize themselves as actors and to think explicitly and at length about how to manipulate the forms of courtly ritual for advantage. To return to the schema of long-term historical structures that we evoked earlier, the theatricalization of court life must be regarded as part of a profound shift often understood as a movement from a God- to a

human-centered universe or the emergence of subjectivity. Modern scholars have largely abandoned the notion of a medieval/Renaissance divide,
seeing more continuity than rupture, but it is not controversial to note
major differences when one compares the art, literature, and theater of,
say, the early fourteenth century with late sixteenth-century counterparts.
William Egginton, himself following Heidegger, approaches these differences as evidence of a shift as one in the perception of space, from what
Egginton calls space that was already meaningful or present to "theatrical spatiality." Sometime around the onset of what we think of as the early
modern period, he writes, the medieval perception of space as full, "thickly
laden with figures and impressed with meaning, capable of transmitting
influences between bodies and distinctly unfit for housing sharp distinctions
between the real and imaginary," yielded to one emptied "of this plenitude,
of its meaningful attachment to places and emblems."[53] In Egginton's analysis, the paradigm of the shift to theatrical spatiality is the theater itself,
which, around the early seventeenth century in France, starts to reflect the
more general development beginning in the early fifteenth century of different techniques for representing three-dimensional space. As Josette Féral
observes, "stage-related theatricality" is only possible in the first place because
a "transcendental structure whose general characteristics are assumed by the
theater" already exists.[54] The new consciousness can be perceived in a variety
of forms, including the development in art and literature of an embodied
point of view through the figure of an internal spectator.[55]

To sum up, the position of official royal mistress became possible when
the notion of gender that posited women as men's intellectual equals if
legal inferiors was actualized in a relationship of dilection modeled on
the relationship between the king and his mignons; however, the position
would not be widely recognized until the courtly environment offered the
royal mistress a theatrical means of representing her role in a way that was
understood and accepted by her spectators, at least by those in the know.
Although Agnès Sorel appears during the same period as the mignons, and
although the king's relationship with her was based on dilection, contemporaries describe her only as the king's best-loved mistress, never as the
equivalent in influence of one of his mignons. Anne, in contrast, attained
the status of royal favorite, her courtly contemporaries recognizing different versions of her at different times and in different places. Thanks to this
shift in perception, François I was in a position to create the official royal
mistress by fiat, Anne herself to take up the challenge, and foreign ambassadors to work with her.

THE CREATION OF THE OFFICIAL ROYAL MISTRESS

Even in France not all kings had powerful mistresses, for it was the king who ultimately determined whether to grant a woman the trust and influence accorded women such as Diane de Poitiers or Madame de Montespan. The role remained dormant when an individual king's personality or personal situation precluded his relying on a woman not related to him. Louis XI seems to have held women in contempt except for his daughter, Anne of France; Louis XII was too emotionally engaged with his queen, Anne of Brittany, to turn to a mistress; the three sons of Catherine de Médicis, François II, Charles IX, and Henri III, preferred to rely on their mother's counsel rather than seek the advice of a different woman, and although Louis XIII appears to have fallen madly in love with at least two different young women, he seems to have been more passionately attracted to men than women and relied on powerful father figures, such as the Duke of Luynes and Cardinal Richelieu, for political guidance.[56]

This means that with the necessary conditions operative, the rest of the story must be explained in terms of chains of events and individual characteristics and personalities.[57] The chapters of this study build on the foundation established in this introduction to trace the trajectory of the position as it developed over time. In chapter 1 we distinguish the role of Agnès Sorel from that of her successors. Given the lack of evidence, it is difficult to discuss the details or even the general nature of Agnès's political role with any certainty, except to say that she was perceived as too powerful during her own time, victim of an unknown assassin who gave her a massive overdose of mercury. Her importance as the founder of a genealogy of royal mistresses, however, is beyond dispute, beginning with Jean Fouquet's iconic depiction of the lactating Virgin with Agnès's face, commissioned by Étienne Chevalier. Painted shortly after Agnès's death, this Virgin-Agnès mediates between the kneeling Chevalier and the divine in an analogy of Agnès's courtly role. The figure also collapses eroticism and maternity in a way that will never again be possible. Agnès provides an ideal for future mistresses, but only after her death. Living women will be unable to embody such an ideal. Still, writings about later holders of the position will point back to Agnès as the founder of the tradition.

Chapter 2 deals with the first official French royal mistress whose unique role was recognized by contemporaries, Anne de Pisseleu d'Heilly, the Duchess of Étampes, mistress of François I. Since Agnès's reign, a transformation in court life had occurred, which Egginton's argument about the shift to theatrical spatiality helps articulate. In the newly theatrical world of François I, an abundance of female roles suggested by the decorations at Fontainebleau offered women new ways to perform their paradoxical role, and the increasing valorization of dissimulation allowed their political activity to be tacitly accepted. Moreover, Anne's function, treated as an open secret, was imagined as complementary not only to the king's role but also to the queen's: as embodiment of an alliance with a foreign dynasty and mother of the royal heir, Queen Eleonore of Austria, who was the sister of the king's great rival, Emperor Charles V, was always an outsider, regarded with suspicion, whereas Anne was the center of court life and the king's most devoted servant.

But whereas Anne did little to represent herself in any memorably specific way, her successors availed themselves of the newly available imagery. The huntress Diana was a prominent figure at Fontainebleau, and this goddess remained a constant tool in the repertory of images for self-representation among the mistresses to follow. In chapter 3 we examine Diane de Poitiers, Seneschale of Normandy and Duchess of Valentinois, mistress of dauphin and later King Henri, who often occupied the royal court with the Duchess of Étampes and who, according to a long tradition, was her jealous rival. Diane's role, like Anne's, was imagined not as rivaling but as complementing that of Henri II's queen, Catherine de Médicis. Diane's role, like Anne's, was structured as an open secret. Along with the Guise brothers and the Connétable Anne de Montmorency, she was recognized as one of Henri II's most trusted advisers and courted for her access to the king. But different from Anne, a mythology based on the huntress grew up around Diane. Although it is important to distinguish between depictions of the historical Diane—that is, depictions representing her own features—and more general references to the huntress, Diane drew on the enormous body of literary and visual references to this figure to articulate her job as political adviser to the king.

The forceful presence of Queen Catherine de Médicis obviated any possibility of a mistress on par with an Anne de Pisseleu or Diane de Poitiers during the reigns of her three sons. The next powerful royal mistress was Gabrielle d'Estrées, subject of chapter 4. Only seventeen when she first caught the eye of Henri IV, Gabrielle began her career as an influential advocate for her family and friends, imagined by them as an Agnès Sorel, the king as a besotted Charles VII. Gabrielle quickly become a central political adviser. To her detriment, however, the king, who had failed to produce an heir during his nearly twenty-year marriage to Queen Marguerite, fixed on Gabrielle as a potential queen after the marriage was annulled. The strongly negative reaction to this idea demonstrates the mutual exclusivity of the roles of queen and mistress. It appears that Henri IV had already decided to bow to the wishes of his advisers and people and marry Marie de Médicis when the pregnant Gabrielle suffered an attack of what may or may not have been eclampsia and died in agony. Modern historians, little inclined to credit rumors of poisoning, take for granted that she died of natural causes. But her sudden death—described by her contemporaries as divine intervention—solved too many difficult problems for assassination to be dismissed as a possibility.

Chapter 5 moves to the court of Louis XIV, where the politically astute and decorative official mistress became a fixture of court society. Although for his predecessors one mistress stands out among the others as the most powerful, for Louis XIV (and Louis XV as well) the choice is less clear. Under Louis XIV in particular the job was sought by competitors. Louis XIV's mother, Anne of Austria, who served as regent during Louis's youth, occupied a central role at court until her death in 1666, and, while still young, Louis began to seek out women who could play an equally influential role. Louise de La Vallière, Louis's first recognized mistress, was content to stay in the background. But such a companion could not satisfy an older and more confident king. Françoise Athénaïs de Rochechouart de Mortemart, Marquise de Montespan, filled the role of official mistress during the prime of Louis's reign. Possessing all the qualities that La Vallière lacked, Montespan was uniquely suited to play the role of unofficial queen at Louis's court, performing with theatrical flair and ensuring that the French royal court was the most cultured and admired in the world. Although she was eventually replaced by the pious and sober Marquise de Maintenon, who would become Louis's wife, Montespan is synonymous with the king's glory years.

Louis XIV famously claimed that he allowed his mistresses no political influence—even though his courtiers clearly recognized the hollowness of that claim—but his assertions of sole political authority preserved the open secret of the mistress's role during his reign. However, the status of open secret became increasingly difficult to maintain, as we see in chapter 6, when in 1745 Louis XV installed Jeanne-Antoinette Poisson, later the Marquise de Pompadour, in the position. Earlier mistresses had always had a reason for being at court. Pompadour was there only at the request of the king, her family belonging to the financial bourgeoisie. Still, by drawing on the existing scripts to justify and solidify her purpose at the court,

Pompadour established herself as a central political actor and intermediary between the king and his courtiers, famously entertaining requests for favors at her morning toilette. Her political role continued and even expanded after her sexual relationship with the king was finished, ending only with her premature death at the age of forty-two. But this too-visible exercise of influence gave a disgruntled public a target for its unhappiness with royal policies (especially the catastrophe of the Seven Years' War). Louis XV's final mistress, Jeanne Bécu, the Countess Du Barry, dealt the role's mystique its death blow by depriving the open secret definitively of its secrecy. The pornographic *libelles* that attacked both her and the king served to undercut the legitimacy of the French monarchy in the years leading up to the Revolution of 1789. The memory of Du Barry's perceived rapaciousness, as well as her identification with royalist politics, led to her execution in 1793 under a new political system that championed political transparency as well as the exclusion of women from politics altogether.

The last chapter reflects on the final "royal mistress" of France, Queen Marie Antoinette, whose execution preceded Du Barry's by less than two months. As Carolyn Harris has discussed in her recent study, this unfortunate queen's fervent attempts to create a companionate marriage based on genuine intimacy caused her to be treated as a mistress in political *libelles*, explicitly compared to Du Barry. Like Gabrielle d'Estrées, the queen collapsed two roles that the French wished to keep distinct. The mistress was by definition an actor of many roles and also seductive and loving toward the king. The queen was meant to be different. As the urban bourgeoisie, influenced by the philosophies of Rousseau, called the nobility out for its deceitful ways, Marie Antoinette, a queen who behaved like a mistress, received the brunt of their outrage. To make the situation still more difficult, she also embodied the problems inherent to French queenship, representing a foreign competitor.

The position of the official royal mistress ended with the monarchy and did not reemerge with the Restoration. The politics of the modern age did not allow a woman to occupy the position that royal mistresses had under the ancien régime. And yet many French men and women continued to celebrate the ability of women to exercise influence as an open secret under the cover of charm and beauty—the notion of sexual difference as complementary, rooted, as we have seen, in the Middle Ages, continuing its long tradition.[58] What Mona Ozouf has referred to as the "French singularity," the presumably uniquely French construction of the relationship between the sexes, harks back to Christine de Pizan by way of courtly gallantry, as a social system that allows attractive women immense power if they exercise it surreptitiously.[59] Even today certain strains of French feminism imagine women and men to be fundamentally and naturally different but mutually necessary, living in harmonious complementarity and enacting their relationships through gallant conversation.[60] The complementary notion of gender has only ever been operative for elite women, and certainly it has been idealized. But it has exerted significant influence in France from the Middle Ages until the present. The official royal mistress is perhaps the most representative example or limit case of the French singularity.

CHAPTER I

The Beginning of a Tradition

Agnès Sorel

In that season (which was the year 1440), the Duchess of Burgundy, grandly accompanied . . . came from Châlons to Champagne . . . and the queen spoke to her honorably and intimately; because they were both aging princesses and beyond gossip. I think that they suffered from the same malady which is called jealousy, and they often told each other their secret sorrows. . . . And, in truth, their suspicions seemed to have been warranted, for the king had recently raised up a poor girl, a gentlewoman called Agnès Sorel, and put her in a position of such triumph and power that her station might be compared to that of the great princesses of the kingdom. And certainly she was one of the most beautiful women I have ever seen; and she has brought much good to the kingdom of France. She brought before the king young men-at-arms and excellent companions, by whom the king has since been well served.

—OLIVIER DE LA MARCHE, *Les Mémoires de Messire Olivier de La Marche*

Tradition holds that Agnès Sorel rose "in golden glory like a phoenix from the ashes of dark centuries" to wield "political influence over country and king."[1] Charles VII laid eyes on her for the first time in 1443 and, within a year, set her up in a household that upstaged the queen's. For six years, he showered her with gifts and accorded her unprecedented political influence. She then abruptly died of a massive overdose of mercuric chloride.

Historians often regard Agnès as the first "official" mistress of a French king. A recent study explains that "in 1444, Agnès Sorel became the first officially designated French royal mistress, when the forty-year-old king Charles VII (1422–1461) selected this extraordinarily beautiful twenty-two-year-old young woman as his mistress. When he presented her to his court and gave her a position within it, he defined a new role for women and defined a new practice for French kings. This recognition . . . gave her a quasi-official status." One would want to know in what sense Agnès was the first "officially designated" French royal mistress and what the author's source for the claim is. But it is not footnoted. Later in the text we read that during a "joyous entry" of the same year the king "publicly designated Agnès Sorel as the first official royal favorite."[2] Once again, there is no footnote.

Such impasses are common in the scholarship on Agnès. Any discussion of Agnès's significance during her lifetime, then, must begin by returning to the sources to see what they actually say. Relative to the other royal mistresses, her career is sparsely evidenced. A handful of documents record the king's donations to her and others on her behalf, and some mentions in court records are suggestive of her political influence. The physical evidence of her tomb and bones is also significant. We will return to these. But because the resident ambassador did not yet exist, we have none of the detailed letters of daily court life that fill in so much of what we know about the careers of later mistresses, and the genre of the memoir that brings to life the intrigues of later courts did not yet exist. The main source of information on Agnès is the chronicle, which we explore in the first section of this chapter. It is important to recognize that chronicles do not necessarily give an accurate picture of Agnès's role. Still, they do make clear that the attention the king paid her was perceived as extraordinary, the position he awarded her far above what she deserved.

"AND CERTAINLY SHE WAS ONE OF THE MOST BEAUTIFUL WOMEN I HAVE EVER SEEN"

A search of all known chronicle references to Agnès turns up no mention of any official designation, nothing to suggest that during her lifetime she was recognized, either publicly by the king or implicitly by her contemporaries, as anything more than Charles VII's sexual partner, let alone as the holder of a recognized role. Indeed, chroniclers seem not to know what to make of the fact that the daughter of Jean Sorel, officer of the Count of Clermont, Charles I of Bourbon, and seigneur of Coudun near Compiègne—a woman with no dynastic claim to power—had gotten herself set up in great estate within the space of a few months and maintained favor until her death.[3]

Cited above, the earliest mention of her by eyewitness Olivier de La Marche offers nothing precise, no joyous entry or public acknowledgment. Describing a trip of Isabelle of Portugal, Duchess of Burgundy, to Châlons in June 1445, La Marche observes only that "the king had recently raised up a poor girl, a gentlewoman called Agnès Sorel, and put her in a position of such triumph and power that her station might be compared to that of the great princesses of the kingdom."[4]

Completely contradicting La Marche's account, Jean Chartier insists that Agnès was not the king's mistress at all. In his continuation of the *Grandes Chroniques de France*, official chronicle of the French royal house from 1437 until Charles VII's death in 1461, Chartier claims to have examined, under oath, courtiers associated with Agnès. The result of his investigation? There was no affair. First, the king had never stopped sleeping with the queen; second, the queen, not the king, had been responsible for Agnès's large entourage; third, the king saw Agnès only in groups and was never seen to touch her below the chin; fourth, although she had a child, it was never claimed by the king; fifth, she was very charitable; sixth, when she heard of the calumnies spoken against her, she was overcome by a flux in the stomach and died. Except for the point that Charles VII did not acknowledge Agnès's child, each point is either true or partly true, but Chartier draws a false conclusion, asserting that it was "not plausible [*vraisemblable*] that the king conducted himself in such a way."[5]

La Marche and Chartier are outliers among the chroniclers, the former in his positive evaluation that Agnès brought much good to the kingdom, the latter in his claim that she was nothing special to the king. Other chroniclers fall between, recognizing Agnès as the king's specially favored mistress and expressing ambivalence about her. Thomas Basin, observing that the king had as his "delight" or "darling" "quite a beautiful little minx" popularly known as the "belle Agnès," remarks on Charles VII's excessive libido and mentions that Agnès was not faithful, either.[6] Georges Chastellain writes that the king, madly in love, spent vast sums on Agnès and that never was a princess more beautifully outfitted, adding that for this reason many murmured against her and the king as well.[7] For Jacques Du Clercq, the king "took up with a young woman."[8] Some chroniclers refer to Agnès as the king's concubine. For Robert Gaguin, who is reading Chartier, the pomp of her lifestyle and sudden promotion of her family raised suspicions of adultery or concubinage; for Pope Pius II, she was one of the king's concubines.[9]

In their references to Agnès's status with the king and the riches this brought her, the chroniclers make clear that they believed her career to be unprecedented. True, several French kings fathered illegitimate children by unknown women, and the names of a handful of mistresses have survived: Marie de Breuillet for Louis VI; Biette Cassinel for Charles V; Odette de Champdivers for mad Charles VI.[10] But Agnès seemed to the chroniclers to be in a different category, and they felt the need to account for her astounding rise. The explanation that they latched onto, that the king was madly in love with her, is pure question begging, in the sense that it simply repeats what needed to be explained.[11] Residue of the Fall and automatic reaction to beauty, lust was the default explanation for irrational political behavior; Agnès therefore must have been astonishingly beautiful.[12] Only Chastellain—the single chronicler who does not refer to her beauty—and La Marche seem to have witnessed Agnès with their own eyes.[13] Although some, such as Basin, theoretically might have seen her, given their itineraries and use of expressions such as "they say," they seem to rely on hearsay. True, the Melun Diptych, as we will see, might be regarded as proof of her genuine beauty. But the reality of her beauty (and how beautiful can a person actually be?) was not the point. Rather, reducing the complicated situation to a madly desiring king, the chroniclers put the relationship into a framework that they understand. Their withering references to Agnès's cousin, Antoinette de Magnelais, with whom the king comforted himself after Agnès's death, take on special interest within this explanatory framework. Chastellain and Du Clercq, neither of whom has anything good to say about Agnès, hold Antoinette in real contempt, characterizing her as a procurer presiding over a harem of beautiful young women. These young women constantly followed the king, who in return maintained them in grand style.[14] Du Clercq recounts how Antoinette solicited a lovely, innocent, and reluctant young woman named Blanche Rebreuves to join her company. Blanche, the chronicler observes, was horrified by the life at court but was forced by her family to present herself there. Rumor had it that after spending a bit of time with Antoinette, Blanche, too, entered into the "very good graces" of the king.[15] Although the two chroniclers cannot dredge up anything really terrible to write about Agnès herself, they attack her by attacking her family.

Although the story of an old man's lust leading him astray is an ancient one, the devotion that the king showed Agnès, as we will demonstrate, setting her up like a queen and listening to her advice, suggests an attachment beyond the physical, which he, like all kings, would have had no end of opportunities to indulge far less expensively and scandalously. We suggest, then, that although his contemporaries had no vocabulary or conceptual framework for making sense of what was happening, Agnès achieved power by slotting into a position that had recently achieved a sort of potentiality with the rise of the mignons and by advising the king, who trusted her. Charles VII's own personality was crucial and especially suited to help realize such a position, because he had been surrounded all his life by politically active women. His own mother, Isabeau of Bavaria, helped govern the kingdom after his father, Charles VI, became insane, as we saw in the introduction. Then in 1413, at age ten, the future king entered the household of his fiancée's mother, the formidable Yolande of Anjou.[16] Joan of Arc was another important figure at a turning point in Charles VII's career. It is not surprising that Charles VII called on a woman for political support after the death of Yolande in 1442.

AGNÈS'S CLOUT

As we have seen, Agnès's presence at court and her lavish lifestyle were noted by chroniclers. But given the dearth of direct evidence about the degree of her political involvement, the nineteenth-century French historians who first assembled all the sources on her held differing opinions about it. Auguste Vallet de Viriville saw Agnès as Charles VII's mentor, writing that in contrast with later "maîtresses en titre," Agnès joined the king in "a supreme union of two individual sympathies" that "became an essential cause of stability" and a "measure of the peace in the state."[17] Countering this argument was Gaston du Fresne de Beaucourt, who asserted that she "exercised no influence over politics" and was convinced that she could not have been born until at least 1422.[18] He explained that for her to have coached the reputedly timid Charles VII into a warrior, she would have had to enter his life in the 1430s, that is, before the events that marked his turn to "manliness": before he broke away from the powerful Georges de La Trémoille, who was forced from the king's private council in 1433; concluded the Peace of Arras with the Burgundians in 1435; made his famous appearance on the walls of Montereau in 1437; or restored Pontoise in 1441.

Modern scholars of medieval and early modern women are looking for something different from either Vallet de Viriville or Fresne de Beaucourt. As we will see, we now know that Agnès was born in about 1422, confirming the basis for Fresne de Beaucourt's claim that "before Agnès and without Agnès, the king of Bourges had vanished, and the king of France dramatically ascended in all his glory and power."[19] But despite this, recent scholarship on female power leads to the opposite conclusion from Fresne de Beaucourt. He dismisses Agnès's influence as "only intimate," disclosing "itself uniquely in courtly intrigue . . . in certain favors, certain rapid promotions, noticed by contemporaries."[20] For modern scholars, this is the very definition of power. Recent studies of mediating queens, female regents, and royal mistresses argue that having power means access to the king or his proxies and the ability to achieve status and gifts for oneself and one's friends. "These forms of power may have been unstable, uncertain, and transient, just as they were for most men below the level of the monarch, but they were no less effective and real," writes Susan Broomhall, "and they made meaning and authority both for those within the court and those beyond it in geography, culture, and time."[21]

Agnès's ascent was quick. Raised by Isabelle of Lorraine, second wife of René of Anjou, from a very young age, Agnès appears for the first time in a 1444 list of Isabelle's servants, making a lowly ten livres per year.[22] Knowing that Isabelle and René visited Saumur in Anjou at the same time as the king during the summer of 1443, scholars assume that Charles VII met Agnès during the visit.[23] By 1444 he had already gifted her with the Château de Beauté.[24] In addition to this royal property, in 1446 the king awarded her the châtellenie de la Roquecezière in Rouergue. In 1447 she received a pension of 3,000 livres. Issoudun and Vernon-sur-Seine were given to her in 1449. When she died, Charles had a magnificent tomb erected to enclose her heart at Jumièges, where she had expired, and another for her body in Notre-Dame de Loches. Agnès herself made important gifts to a number of foundations, further proof of her wealth and an indication of her charitable nature.[25] Her four brothers entered the king's household, two as *écuyers d'honneur*, two as archers in the royal bodyguard.[26] Her mother was awarded a lifelong pension. A series of five letters written by her personally to solicit favors for others demonstrates her role as mediator.[27] Also, complaints about Agnès's too-magnificent lifestyle attest to her status. Chastellain reports that after Agnès transferred to the queen's service, Marie d'Anjou daily had to endure the presence of her husband's young mistress to avoid discord and to safeguard her own estate (presumably because the king let no attack on his mistress go unavenged).[28] Du Clercq remarks that Agnès's estate was greater than that of the saintly queen.[29]

Still, Charles VII's generosity does not necessarily mean that Agnès participated in politics. For that, we turn to other evidence, indirect but suggestive. For one thing, her horrendous death indicates that someone thought her important enough to want to dispose of her. In late 1449 or early 1450, Agnès crossed some 350 kilometers of frozen landscape between Loches in the Loire valley and the abbey at Jumièges in Normandy, heavily pregnant, to join the king who was reconquering the province from the English.[30] Normally an aristocratic woman would have been expected to lie in for four to six weeks before giving birth.[31] Why did Agnès undertake the arduous journey at such a time? Chartier reports that she had come "to warn the king and tell him that some people wanted to betray him and deliver him into the hands of his old enemies the English."[32] Although the king "did nothing but laugh," according to Chartier, surely Agnès must have believed him to be in real danger to have traveled so far under such conditions.[33]

Shortly after her arrival, Agnès was struck with a flux in the stomach, according to Chartier, and died in the throes of agony on 11 February 1450.[34] Childbirth? Chartier does not mention a baby, claiming, as we have seen, that chagrin at the gossip about her made her sick.[35] However, in 2005 forensic specialist Philippe Charlier and his team examined Agnès's exhumed remains, recording the bones of a fetus among them. But childbirth was not the cause of death, he discovered; rather, Agnès died of a massive overdose of mercury.[36] Charlier ruled out death from mercury poisoning caused by long-term exposure through cosmetics or treatment for worms, because the extremely high level of mercury in her hair "is not compatible with a long survival, and the poisoning would have been acute, preceding death by 48 to 72 hours."[37] To relativize the degree of the overdose, the normal dose of mercuric chloride as a treatment for worms was roughly the size of the head of a pin, usually taken in a crumb of bread, whereas she would have needed to swallow something like a teaspoon full of the drug, ten thousand times the normal dose, to account for the level of mercury in her remains.[38] Charlier's conclusion: "Thus Agnès Sorel's poisoning has been confirmed by an investigation worthy of the best detective (or historical?) novels. No one can say whether the poisoning was voluntary or not. But a perfect suspect exists: Robert Poitevin, the king's physician and one of the three executors of her will, who would have had access to the drugs and could have transformed them into poison. Vile crime? We are waiting for historians to solve the mystery and unmask the guilty party."[39]

Surely, attended by Poitevin, Agnès could not have been given such a dose by accident.[40] Nothing suggests a suicide. And yet historians, especially recent ones, seem strangely reluctant to assume that Agnès was assassinated, influenced perhaps by the modern tendency to dismiss conspiracy theories as paranoid fantasies. However, in premodern court politics conspiracy was common, "a perfectly rational way of understanding a court-centred political culture."[41] Poisoning too was relatively common, in fact and in perception.[42]

But what would have been the motive for killing the king's mistress? Some context will be useful. It seems that someone or some group of people was trying to rid Charles VII of his most intimate circle of advisers. Between 1448 and 1452, Charles VII's three closest favorites fell, although only Agnès was assassinated: first Pierre de Brézé, seneschal of Anjou and Poitou in the service of the king from 1437 and head of his government from 1443, then Agnès in 1450, and finally Jacques Coeur, master of the mint, in 1452.[43] The stories of the falls of Pierre and Agnès are clearly linked to the dauphin Louis; we will return to Jacques Coeur, whose fall is more tenuously linked to this figure. The king had always had an extremely conflictual relationship with the dauphin, especially after the young man led an armed uprising known as the Praguerie against his father in 1440.[44] Although they reconciled, the king remained wary of his son, who was dissatisfied with the authority his father allotted him and who regarded his father's gatekeepers as obstacles to his own advancement. A collection of depositions analyzed by Fresne de Beaucourt shows Louis's servants claiming in 1446 that the dauphin had been hatching a plot to oust Pierre and then take over the government himself.[45] Among the related depositions, one claims that the reason for Louis's animus toward Pierre was that the dauphin believed that the seneschal was "destroying everything with the help of Agnès, through whom he held the king in subjection."[46] That plot went nowhere. But then, in 1447, Pierre was caught in an elaborate plot of his own, trying to turn the king definitively against the dauphin. To carry it out, Pierre had engaged the assistance of Guillaume Mariette, a courtier-spy and officer at the dauphin's court.[47]

The plot can be reconstructed from the record of Mariette's 1448 trial, which is included among the *pièces justificatives* appended to Fresne de Beaucourt's edition of the chronicle of Mathieu d'Escouchy, continuator of Monstrelet's chronicle. The trial record includes *mémoriaux*, that is, instructions from Pierre, whom Chastellain will later describe as "legendary for his way with words" (le plus bel parlier de son temps), taken down in writing by Guillaume. Pierre's flair for the dramatic is on display throughout the *mémoriaux*, which amount in many places to a sort of script for how Guillaume was to surreptitiously cause trouble between the king and the dauphin by reporting carefully selected bits of information to the Duke of Burgundy and the king.[48] Agnès, too, is implicated in this plot, mentioned at crucial points in the *mémoriaux* as a sure means of influencing the king.

The trial record shows that Guillaume was arrested initially in October 1447, in Bourges, seat of Charles VII's government, on an unrelated charge, but that he was soon discovered to be carrying the aforementioned mémoriaux in his boots. Imprisoned, Guillaume quickly escaped. However, the king and the dauphin were determined to discover what he had been up to, and several months after his escape, he was rearrested by the dauphin's men, interrogated, and moved to Paris for the trial.[49] According to the record, Guillaume initially claimed that the mémoriaux were not his and that he had discovered them, abandoned, on the road (3:267–68). After being tortured, however, he admitted that they were notes that Pierre had dictated (3:301–2).

Sifting through the record reveals a tortuous story of Guillaume, at the instigation of Pierre, being instructed to feed the Duke of Burgundy information about how badly the duke was viewed at the royal court and elsewhere. Guillaume was to warn the duke that the power dynamic at the royal court had changed and that Pierre was out to destroy him: there was bad blood between the dauphin and Pierre, who now had the king's ear. Guillaume was to add that the shift of power at the royal court was being helped along by Agnès, "from whom Pierre has whatever he wants" (3:268). As Guillaume recounts after his confession in the later pages of the trial record, he was to gain the duke's confidence by bad-mouthing Pierre. Guillaume would be able to extract information about the dauphin from the duke (3:307).

Besides the Duke of Burgundy, Guillaume was to speak to the king. Guillaume explains that Pierre coached him in exactly what to say, with Pierre playing the role of the king.[50] Guillaume was to tell the king of the dauphin's plans to overthrow him and say that the dauphin was determined to present a good face to Pierre in order to usurp the throne and destroy Pierre. Guillaume was also to explain to the king that the dauphin had the support of most of the council and that they got along well with Pierre, who suspected nothing of the plot (3:307). Furthermore, Guillaume was to speak to the dauphin, telling him things sure to upset him.[51] He was to report that Pierre hated him and advocated against him to the king. Pierre, Guillaume was to say, had informed the king that the dauphin believed that the king was behaving so badly that he, the dauphin, was going to put things in order and chase Agnès away.

In short, the trial record demonstrates that Pierre was a schemer and Agnès, whom he treated as an accomplice, a reliable means of exerting power over the king. Pierre's confidence in her influence is reflected in the code name given to her in Guillaume's correspondence: Helyos, the sun, an image evoking a brilliant and powerful presence (3:320).

Predictably, the revelation of the mémoriaux caused trouble for Pierre, forcing him to answer questions before the king's commissaries.[52] He requested the opportunity to defend himself.[53] It appears that Agnès aided Pierre in his defense because the Bourgeois of Paris's journal records that during the time when Pierre's trial would have been in process, Agnès herself made a trip to Paris.[54] Although the author does not explain the reason for the trip, the timing is surely no coincidence, nor is the fact that the king exonerated Pierre, who was soon back at court.[55] Still, if Pierre got himself a reprieve in the Mariette case, his career seems to have foundered after Agnès's death. Although just before her fateful trip to Normandy, Pierre had been made seneschal of that duchy, once she was gone he no longer served as the head of government. Pierre Bernus remarks that one "cannot help but see a correlation between the favor of [Pierre] and that of the mistress, which developed, as mathematicians say, one as a function of the other."[56] The dauphin initially threw Pierre in prison on mounting the throne in 1461.[57]

A motive for Agnès's murder, then, is that, in the eyes of the dauphin, she and Pierre wielded too much power over the king and they were plotting against him. A further motive might be that Louis was afraid that his father would renounce the queen and marry Agnès, displacing him from succession. Such things had happened before. Charles VII and Marie of Anjou were second cousins, which theoretically precluded their marriage. Marriage within the prohibited degree was an entirely political game, which meant that even first cousins could marry if the pope was favorable. More important here, even long-term marriages could sometimes be annulled.[58] It should also be noted that in 1445, the king had cleared his wife's Anjou family out of the government, which, in addition to Agnès's presence, may have suggested to the dauphin that still more sweeping change was coming.[59] Although no historical evidence suggests that Charles VII ever contemplated disinheriting his son, he certainly had strong reasons to wish him gone, as we have seen. It was not as if the throne was secure in the mid-fifteenth century. Henry VI of England had been considered king of France by a portion of the French and the Burgundians until 1435. Whatever the king himself felt, the dauphin may have feared that his father would disinherit him.

True, the first evidence of Louis's attitude toward Agnès shows him courting her favor, itself an acknowledgment of her influence with his father.

In 1444 he presented her with tapestries that he had confiscated during an expedition against the Count of Armagnac. But Louis's relationship with the king and thus with those most able to influence him worsened from that point on.[60] As for Agnès specifically, the dauphin began to hate her: Aeneas Sylvius Piccolomini, diplomat for Emperor Frederick III (and later Pope Pius II), writes that the cause of the animosity between Charles VII and the dauphin was Agnès, whom Louis had chased with his sword, wanting to kill her.[61] Aliénor of Burgundy, author of the renowned volume on Burgundian court etiquette from 1484 to 1491, also asserts that Louis had been chased from court by the king because of some conflict of which Agnès was said to be the cause.[62] Moreover, we find rumors that Louis poisoned Agnès in Jean Le Clerc's interpolation recounting the reign of Charles VII in the *Chronique Martiniane*. Le Clerc writes that some said that the father's hatred for his son was caused by the death of "la belle Agnès," who died of poison, although the author adds that he does not know himself whether the dauphin was actually accused of the poisoning.[63] The editor of the interpolation, Pierre Champion, notes that Le Clerc relied on Chartier's chronicle for the years after 1447, adding that when not copying from this chronicle or from that of Du Clercq, "he reports the memories of Jacques and Antoine de Chabannes on the reign of Charles VII."[64] The story of Agnès's death is one of the points at which Le Clerc must have turned to a different source, because his account is nothing like Chartier's. Du Clercq initially reports only that it was said that Agnès had been poisoned, although he does not say by whom. Several pages later, he reports that in 1456 Antoine de Chabannes was sent by the king along with a great many armed men to seize the dauphin and bring him to his father. Du Clercq claims that he did not know the motive behind the order, reporting that some said that it was because the dauphin had destroyed the Dauphiné through heavy taxation, but others said that it was because he had killed Agnès.[65] At this point, he cites the narrative of Enguerrand de Monstrelet, who also claims that he did not know whether the dauphin had been justly accused.[66]

Returning to Jacques Coeur, it is necessary to consider the doctor Poitevin again. Coeur was brought down on charges of financial malfeasance and was never restored. However, before those charges, his downfall had been sought through the clearly specious accusation that he had poisoned Agnès. To exonerate their father, Jacques Coeur's children claimed that Poitevin had told them that Agnès could not have been poisoned because she had given birth to a live child, which would have impossible had she

THE BEGINNING OF A TRADITION

been poisoned. Poitevin testified, they reported, that "the said lady before her death had a child who lived for six months, which is clear proof that she was never poisoned."[67] But, as noted above, Charlier reports that the bones of a fetus were discovered in the urn bearing Agnès's remains, and no other source reports a live birth. Under the circumstances, Poitevin's claim of the impossible live birth of a child who went on to live for six months seems suspicious, all the more so now that we know that Agnès was indeed poisoned, whether deliberately or by accident. In this context, it is worth recalling that Poitevin, the king's primary doctor, was also the dauphin's primary doctor ("premier phisicien des Roys Charles et Louys").[68] Poitevin is the ideal suspect, as Charlier notes, and what better way for the doctor to deflect any attention from himself than by claiming that Agnès gave birth to a living child, making death by poisoning impossible?[69]

Did Louis have the king's too-influential mistress murdered? There is no proof. Our point is not to insist that Louis XI was behind the assassination, although it is indisputable that Pierre and Agnès were targets of the dauphin's wrath. Still, there might be other motives that we will never know of. Agnès was surrounded by people during her final days. For example, Pierre de Brézé's wife was there.[70] Nothing indicates such a thing, but could she have been jealous of her husband's close association with Agnès? Or did one of Agnès's ladies have a grudge against her? What we do want to stress is that Agnès's death looks like a murder. No one doubts the political motivation behind the falls of Pierre and Jacques, and had either of them died abruptly with massive amounts of mercury detected in their remains by a modern forensic specialist, historians would assume that they had been victims of a political assassination. When we discover today through an autopsy that a body contains ten thousand times the normal amount of a drug such as sleeping pills, safe when taken as recommended, we do not insist that the death was purely accidental. On the contrary, we assume that it was deliberate.

AGNÈS'S AFTERLIFE AND THE CREATION OF THE FIRST FRENCH ROYAL
MISTRESS

The evidence necessary to assess Agnès's political power with certainty is lacking. However, her career served as an inspiration for future kings and their mistresses, her image summoned to bestow legitimacy and glamour until revolutionaries wiped out the last trace of the role with the execution of Madame Du Barry in 1793. In this discussion of Agnès's afterlife, we examine her image in the decades just after her death. Some of its elements were culled, and others passed down to the sixteenth century and beyond to contribute to the tradition of the French royal mistress.[71]

The young woman whose story we have just recounted may seem like an unlikely inspiration for future royal mistresses. However, her immortalization as the Virgin of Jean Fouquet's Melun diptych explains the phenomenon to a large extent.[72] This important early purveyor of her image was probably painted just after Agnès's death as a donor portrait, commissioned by Étienne Chevalier, Agnès's friend and one of the three executors of her will. The panels, each 36 by 32 inches, depict, on the left, Chevalier flanked by his patron saint, Étienne or Stephen, and, on the right, Agnès-cum-Virgin with child.[73] They hung together over Chevalier's tomb in the collegiate church Notre-Dame de Melun, some forty miles southeast of Paris, until 1773, when the canons sold them to raise money for repairs.[74]

In contrast with contemporary chroniclers, who could not articulate the relationship between Agnès and the king in any but the terms of overwhelming lust, Fouquet's lactating Virgin-Agnès visually harmonizes the sacred and the erotic. Her cape is trimmed with ermine, a symbol of purity. We know from Agnès's will that she owned ermine-trimmed clothing.[75] The crisp linen on which the baby Jesus sits is likewise meaningful. In contemporary portraits of the Virgin we often see white cloth, which Christine de Pizan links to femininity, writing that it gives women pleasure, "which is neither ugly nor unrefined, but honest and decent. So she will make sure that she has beautiful, delicate linen, abundant to decorate and well wrought; she will keep it white and sweet smelling."[76] Discussing the *Madonna lactans*, Megan Holmes explains that as realism became more prominent, the genre became more dangerous—that is, likelier to arouse erotic feelings—and one begins to notice "formal devices that worked to restabilize religious meanings." Among these was a technique applied to the diptych of interrupting the realistic depiction of the female body: "the Virgin's bare breast was rendered non-integral, detached from her body, jarring dissonantly with the greater degree of naturalism" cultivated in other parts of the painting.[77] With the Virgin-Agnès's strangely spherical breast, Fouquet seems to acknowledge his duty to short-circuit erotic appeal.

And yet the overall effect is erotic. Erik Inglis describes the "frisson of the [painting's] explicit and self-aware position on the border between the sacred and the profane."[78] More specifically, Miri Rubin writes of the

Virgin-Agnès that "although her eye is downcast, the whole effect is courtly, celestial and other-worldly . . . nonetheless personal and enticing," and Margaret Miles notes more generally that in "a society in which a woman's milk was a practical, emotional, social, and religious issue, the nursing Virgin was likely to have evoked an intimate and volatile mixture of danger and delight."[79]

The Virgin-Agnès mediates a relationship between the observer, who is actually a participant rather than mere observer given the religious nature of the painting, and the sacred reality that it represents; more precisely, it illustrates such a mediation taking place between Chevalier and God via the Virgin-Agnès. The image thus reflects in a sacred register the principal function of the royal mistress, who was the mediator par excellence, the person whose goodwill was more valuable than any other courtier because of her special access to and influence with the king. Although Agnès had detractors and enemies, no other royal mistress would be so praised for luminous goodness. She seems to have been genuinely loved by many, in a way that her successors, with the possible exception of Gabrielle d'Estrées, were not. As we have seen, her donations appear to have been substantial.

The Melun diptych was widely known and cited. François Avril mentions a rondel in a church window in the Musée Fenaille in Rodez depicting a lactating Virgin with child, as well as several examples of the motif in Books of Hours illustrated by painters with connections to the artistic communities of the Tourangeau.[80] The painting's fame in the first years of the sixteenth century is attested by the painter Gaultier de Campes, who made a trip to Melun specifically to view it.[81] In addition, Fouquet's depictions of the young woman, as we will see, inspired a number of sixteenth- and seventeenth-century copies, although no trace of the Virgin remains in these. This is not surprising, because as a model for the political royal mistress more generally, the Virgin was not an option. Living mistresses could not have drawn on Virgin imagery to authorize their positions. The one-off representation of a royal mistress in the Melun diptych seemed acceptable after the death of Agnès, or so its very existence suggests, but the case is exceptional, emphasizing her uniqueness, the limited possibilities for representing women in her world, and Chevalier's great affection for and connection to Fouquet. Queens— that is, women whose positions were sanctioned by their place within the family—associated themselves with the Virgin. Italian painters also seem to have applied the features of their courtesan models to depictions of sacred and profane women.[82] But as a consciously wielded strategy of self-representation by political royal mistresses, this was out of the question. It never happened again.

Other traces from the early years suggest that Agnès's reputation was mixed during her lifetime. The scant evidence that we have of opinion beyond courtly circles hints that she was viewed negatively, to the extent that anyone knew about her at all. King Charles VII had fled Paris during the Burgundian attack of 1418 and never again lived there, residing primarily in Bourges. His romantic liaisons were therefore less obvious than they might have been had he lived in Paris. Still, the Bourgeois of Paris's description of Agnès's trip to Paris at the time of Brézé's trial suggests that she was known by reputation among the Parisians, because the Bourgeois refers to her disapprovingly as the "amie" of the king, who "was called and had herself called the belle Agnès." The Parisians did not take to her, he writes, and they "did not do her the honor that her great pride demanded," which caused her to aver that she would never have set foot in Paris had she known how she would be treated. Then she left, "living in sin as before."[83]

Among religious figures, Agnès's reputation was mixed. On the one hand, as noted above, the chronicler Chartier made a point of proclaiming her innocence with regard to Charles VII. Nor did Pope Nicolas V have any problem with Agnès. A letter from him conceding to his "beloved daughter in Christ noblewoman Agnès Sorel" the right to travel with a portable altar to keep up her prayers shows no discomfort with her position.[84] The epitaph on her massive marble tomb at Loches proclaimed her charity toward the Church and the poor.[85] On the other hand, regarding that same tomb, the author of the eighteenth-century *Grand dictionnaire historique* suggests that the religious hierarchy at Loches did not entirely approve. Despite her generous gifts to Notre-Dame de Loches, including a golden crucifix and a silver image of Mary Magdalene, the canons tried to persuade King Louis XI to let them move the enormous tomb, supposedly because it got in their way during Mass.[86] Perhaps assuming that Louis XI would be favorable toward their request because of his aversion to Agnès (an assumption all the more natural if any among them believed that he had had her assassinated), they were disappointed when the king scolded them for trying to displace someone who had given so copiously to them.

Feelings toward Agnès within courtly circles were also mixed. We have seen that chroniclers decried her too large and elaborate entourage, but she had close friends among the king's intimates. Also, her own family tradition embraced the young woman's relationship with the king. Two of Agnès's daughters married into families that cultivated her positive image.

First, then, a word on these daughters. In addition to the child who did not survive Agnès's abrupt death, Agnès bore the king three daughters who lived to adulthood, all of whom were married by their half-brother, King Louis XI, to courtiers or sons of courtiers who had served Charles VII. The eldest, Marie, was married to Olivier de Coëtivy, brother to Prégent, the admiral of France; the second, Charlotte, to Jacques de Brézé, son of Pierre; and the youngest, Jeanne, to Antoine, son of admiral of France Jean de Bueil.[87] Olivier de Coëtivy, Pierre de Brézé, and Jean de Bueil were among the conspirators who overthrew La Trémoille in 1433, making Charles of Anjou the king's closest adviser; uniting their families with the king's natural daughters verifies Agnès's continued stature.

One of Agnès's daughters, Charlotte, met a tragic end, discovered *in flagrante delicto* with an officer and slain by her husband. Louis XI imprisoned his brother-in-law, an unusual move for such a case.[88] Charlotte was related through marriage to Diane de Poitiers, through Charlotte's son, Louis de Brézé, who married Diane. Not surprisingly, Diane seems never to have mentioned the relationship. The families of the two other daughters passed on a positive tradition of Agnès. Marguerite, daughter of Agnès's eldest daughter, Marie, owned a Book of Hours containing an illustration of Bathsheba ogled by David, which James Kren has associated with Agnès. This Bathsheba, standing at the window of a structure that recalls the Sainte-Chapelle, looks modestly downward, different from other contemporary depictions. A different bas-de-page David repents, gazing up at Bathsheba. Kren speculates that in the eyes of Marguerite, the depiction "honoured the controversial Agnès's position as object of royal desire."[89] Another intimation of a family tradition is found in the *Jouvencel*, composed in the first years of the 1460s by Jeanne's father-in-law, Jean de Bueil.[90] The reference occurs in a scene where a group of lovely young women accompanies the queen to postdinner entertainment in the king's chambers. One of the young women, associated by tradition with Agnès, addresses the king, urging him to take arms. The king replies that all had already been won by Jouvencel. Still, the young woman persists, telling the king that "great kings are involved in great affairs."[91]

A further indication of a family tradition is a series of frescoes that would have been painted shortly after Agnès's death. The frescoes are described in a 1778 article in the periodical *Bibliothèque universelle des romans*.[92] The article, examining Agnès's portrayal in histories of Charles VII, views her sympathetically, asserting, for example, that even the queen supported the love affair. It claims that the queen, understanding that the king was not in love with her, decided that she could only offer him the counsel of "reason." The author goes on to explain that, despite Agnès's gentle character, the young woman aroused the jealousy and hatred of the dauphin Louis, who was rumored to have had her killed. But what is most interesting about the article is the description of a series of frescoes depicting Agnès's life, which the author claims to have seen. These frescoes decorated the walls of the Château de la Guerche, which had once belonged to relatives of Agnès, although, according to the author, the owner of the castle at that time was one of the editors of the periodical, the Marquis de Paulmy d'Argenson (whose father we will encounter in chapter 6), explaining how the author knew about the frescoes.[93] The frescoes trace a narrative in which the beautiful Agnès initially refuses a shower of royal gifts but eventually gives in, because everything conspired to push her into the arms of the king, who required her gentle guidance to learn the lessons of love and, later, valor. The author describes the frescoes as illustrations of "this beautiful person" in the midst of "different ornaments and allegorical figures related to the different situations of her life." Agnès is kidnapped, like Ganymede, and boasts in a Latin device that she gave herself only to the "king of the birds."[94] The author gives no date for the frescoes but writes that legend has it that the castle was a frequent trysting spot for Charles VII and Agnès, becoming the property in 1450 of André de Villequier, husband of Antoinette de Maignelais.

CONCLUSION

At the early modern French court, female qualities were distributed across the queen and the mistress, who occupied important but clearly differentiated positions: a maternal figure, on the one hand, in contrast with a more intellectual, political, and sexual one, on the other. We see this division of duties already beginning to form with Agnès, although in a negative way. Chastellain indignantly opposes the saintly queen to the royal mistress. The queen was sorely tested by Agnès's presence, but she suffered in exemplary fashion "the conduct of her husband regarding his dissolute life with women, such as no one of her time had to bear to such an extent," specifically, "to obtain peace and keep her estate secure and whole, she had suffered a ribald, poor servant of low birth, associating daily with her and seeing her have her own quarters in the king's hotel, in better order and better appointed than her own and with a larger company of women than her own, and seeing the seigneurs and nobility and the king himself seeking her out; and having royal estate and services for herself."[95]

Chastellain criticized Agnès for her social transgression, for occupying a position higher than that to which she was entitled. The function and boundaries of her role were still undefined, her relationship with the king illegible within the terms available to her contemporaries, although at least one chronicler, Olivier de la Marche, granted her the positive ability to attract worthy young men to the king's service. But she was more often taken as evidence of the king's personal lack of continence, which his contemporaries associated, in turn, writes Franck Collard, with the lack of order at court and respect to the queen.[96] The king never lived it down. Even in the last year of his life, he was said to be "continually under the domination of women, a situation about which there are many complaints."[97] Agnès herself seemed ambivalent about her role, taking steps to mitigate her guilt and frame herself positively. In 1444 she donated to the chapter of Loches a statuette of Mary Magdalene made of silver and covered with gold: "In honor and reverence of Saint Mary Magdelene, the noble mademoiselle de Beaulté has given this image in the church of the château of Loches, in which image is enclosed one rib and some hairs of the said saint."[98] Mary Magdalene reappears in Chartier's description of Agnès's deathbed, where, quoting Agnès's Augustinian confessor, the chronicler notes that during her last hours, Agnès spoke frequently of that saint as a "great sinner in sin of the flesh" and also called the Virgin Mary to her aid.[99]

But if the image of the reconciled sinner Mary Magdalene furnished Agnès with comfort on her deathbed, as an outlet for expressing both her penitence and confidence that she would be forgiven, the saint had multiple images that would have served Agnès with positive imagery during her lifetime. Contemporary iconography portrayed Mary Magdalene as an educated woman, a lover of books. For Agnès, an association with Mary Magdalene may have given her a way of representing herself next to the queen's Virgin Mary.[100] And despite Chastellain's contempt, Agnès embodied traits that allowed her, in the opinion of some, to transcend the disapprobation that normally would have been associated with a woman not related to the king living with him in high estate. Product of the same construction of gender that made the Virgin's mediation and access to God an emblem of female power—of the same set of attitudes that produced the Salic Law, which paradoxically created an unofficial and yet potentially powerful role for the queen mother as regent—the role of royal mistress would eventually share with female regency the potential for power along with its restrictions, and, like female regency, it would require a woman to integrate a number of conflicting images into a coherent representation of power.

The positive strain of the legend that developed around Agnès influenced mistresses to come. The space for royal mistress existed *in potentia*, and Agnès helped realize the role, even though it would not be fully acknowledged and articulated until François I came to power, bringing a new reservoir of imagery and narrative—the full range of classical mythology, including, most important, the story of the huntress Diana— for interpreting court life. "Images are formed by the cultural system they represent, but they also partake in the formation of this system, a formation that works as an ideological authorization," writes Lena Liepe. "This means that images should be interpreted not only as mere illustrations reflecting historical processes; they are in themselves historical processes that contribute to the culturally defined self-comprehension of an epoch."[101] In contrast with Charles VII, for François I, being surrounded by women implied no weakness. A strong libido would become a positive element of his identity and his mistresses visible proof of his grandeur.

CHAPTER 2

A Tradition Takes Hold

Anne de Pisseleu d'Heilly

[Masks] were used at banquets or festivals
In the olden days, but only for entertainments;
Not everyone wore one. But
Today no one does not wear one,
Everyone wants to act and color his ruse,
Dissimulate, under counterfeit language:
But it is not surprising if we take advantage of masks
Because everyone falsifies his own face.

—LA PERRIÈRE, *Théâtre des bons engins*

A sketch of Agnès Sorel in the album known today as the Aix or Mont-mor collection of 1526 demonstrates that her legend continued to grow. On the back of the sketch, a short poem allegedly penned by François I, a king equally renowned as soldier and lover, lauds Agnès for having inspired Charles VII to drive the English out of France. The album, composed of crayon drawings of the royal family and prominent courtiers, also includes, along with the drawing of Agnès, sketches of Anne of France, who had died in 1522, and Mary Tudor, who although still alive had had no connection with the French court since her short marriage to Louis XII in 1515. Commissioned in 1526 by queen mother Louise of Savoy (1476–1531), the album instigated a vogue for the genre among courtiers. Some of these albums still exist today.[1]

Alexandra Zvereva hypothesized recently that Louise's purpose in having commissioned the album would have been to reaffirm the French court's grandeur after the royal army's demoralizing defeat by the troops of Habsburg emperor Charles V at Pavia in 1525 and to assert that despite the king's imprisonment in Spain, his court was holding steady.[2] But why the portrait of a long-dead royal mistress among members of the royal entourage? Zvereva suggests that Agnès's portrait served to justify the position at court (and in the album) of the king's favorite mistress at the time, Madame de Chateaubriant, Françoise de Foix, and also to "recall the role that women could play in affairs of State."[3] Zvereva's first point is well taken, although, to be clear, when the album was created, the king had not seen Françoise in many months, and, if she had been the first highly visible royal mistress after Agnès, she was not the woman who would realize the possibilities of the position.[4] That would be left to her successor, Anne de Pisseleu d'Heilly, subject of this chapter.[5] Moreover, Agnès was known as an inspiration for Charles VII but not as a political player, as we have seen. We would therefore modify Zvereva's second point slightly, proposing that Louise's intention would have been to acknowledge the role of royal mistress as a positive but limited one.

Louise's portrait in the Aix album—although long ago removed—visually asserted her primacy, following just after the king, and contemporary witnesses suggest that she would not have tolerated another powerful woman in her ambit.[6] After the death of her husband, Charles of Angoulême, in 1496, she dedicated her life to raising her daughter, Marguerite, later queen of Navarre (1492–1549), and son, her "Caesar," twice serving as his regent.[7] She wielded political force even when she held no official function. Cardinal Louis of Aragon observed that she accompanied her son and Queen Claude everywhere and exercised "absolute power" over them.[8] In a letter to Cardinal Wolsey, an unnamed clerk repeats a comment by the pope that the French king could not be trusted until he was no longer ruled by Louise and the seigneur de Bonnivet, admiral of France.[9] In 1521 ambassador to France William Fitzwilliam writes to Wolsey that in case of conflict Wolsey should apply to Louise, because "when the king would stick at some points, and speak very great words, then my Lady would qualify the matter"; the king is so "obeisant" to her that he refuses nothing that she requires him to do.[10] A year later, Holy Roman Emperor Charles V notes that the king "spends his time in the chace with the Cardinal of Lorraine, leaving everything to his mother, the Admiral and the Chancellor."[11] After Pavia, when Louise governed the realm for her imprisoned son, a number of English ambassadors report that the Parlement in Paris was challenging her rule.[12] However, Louise retained control, declaring to the magistrates that it was beneath her to seek vengeance, but had she not been regent they would have not gotten away with such effrontery.[13]

As for the relationship between Louise and Anne, Brantôme mentions that tradition held that Louise chose her for her son. "I have heard it said and I believe to be true," he announces, "that Madame the Regent had taken [Anne] with her as one of her ladies and produced her for the king François on his return from Spain, in Bordeaux, which lady he took for his mistress and left the aforementioned Madame de Chateaubriand."[14] Anne, of course, remained in Louise's shadow. But even after the queen mother's death in 1531, she did not rise immediately. François I's boyhood friend the Connétable Anne de Montmorency (1493–1567) was the principal royal adviser from the time of Louise's death until his own downfall. Already in August 1527, Henry VIII's ambassador to France, Anthony Brown, describes Anne as the maiden favored by the king.[15] However, she is not a political player. Then suddenly in around 1539 she steps onto the stage of diplomacy, ally of the king's sister, Queen Marguerite of Navarre, highly influential with François I, and sought after by foreign ambassadors.

In what follows, we explore what happened between Louise's death and Anne's rise before moving to an examination of Anne's career. Compared to Agnès's story, Anne's is richly documented. Unlike Agnès, Anne was barely mentioned by contemporary chroniclers. We discuss this omission in chapter 3. However, ambassadors' letters, many of them unfortunately unedited and therefore difficult to access, detail her political activity.

THE FIRST POLITICAL ROYAL MISTRESS: THE EARLY POLITICAL CONTEXT

We begin by laying out the political situation that formed the context for Anne's rise. From his succession until his death, François I was driven by a personal imperative to recover his Italian lands, particularly Milan, and he spent his career allying himself with whomever he believed likely at a given moment to help him achieve his goal.[16] Although Emperor Charles V and Henry VIII of England were his primary allies/enemies, Muslim Ottoman emperor Suleiman I the Magnificent (b. 1494, r. 1520–66), the pope, and the German Protestant princes also played roles in his strategies. He saw Milan as his birthright, inherited from his great-grandmother, wife of Louis I of Orléans (1370–1407), Valentina Visconti (1368–1408). François

I's immediate predecessor, Louis XII, grandson of Valentina, had dislodged
Lodovico Sforza from rule. In 1512 the French were in turn routed by the
Swiss, who restored Sforza rule with Lodovico's son, Massimiliano. Soon
after François I ascended the throne in 1515, he led the French to retake
Milan in the battle of Marignano and imprisoned Massimiliano. But the
French were driven out by Charles V in 1522 and forced to return Milan
to Francesco II Sforza. François I lost Milan definitively in 1525, when his
troops were defeated by Charles V's army at Pavia and he himself taken
prisoner. Although his sister negotiated his return to France in 1526, he was
forced to send his two oldest sons, dauphin François and Henri, to Spain
as hostages while he carried out the terms of the treaty.[17]

Anne, whose eventual rise would be intimately tied to these dreams of
recovering Milan, presumably met François I for the first time when she
accompanied Louise as a lady-in-waiting to greet the returning king, as
we have seen. In addition to Brantôme, other late sources such as Scévole
and Louis de Sainte-Marthe's *Histoire généalogique de la Maison de France*,
first published in 1612, record that on that occasion the king fell in love at
first sight with "this young lady of excellent beauty."[18] When and how Anne
entered Louise's entourage in the first place is unknown, but, like Agnès
and all political royal mistresses until the reign of Louis XV, her presence
at court was justified by her family's status. The Pisseleus were relatively
important in Picardy, having acquired the lordship of Heilly, near Amiens,
and other territories that brought in a sizeable income.[19] Picardy was in
the process of shifting loyalty from Burgundy to France during Anne's
childhood, and her family served François I. In 1523 some of her brothers
helped establish the king's legion in Picardy, and in 1524 her father became
an officer at the royal court.[20] It is not clear in which direction the family
influence worked initially—that is, who got whom installed.

On his return to France the king declared his agreement with Charles V
null and void because it had been carried out under duress; then he founded
the League of Cognac against the emperor with the Milanese, the Venetians, and the pope. In summer 1529 Louise, accompanied again by Anne,
traveled to Cambrai to resolve the resulting conflict, helping negotiate
what has become known as "the Ladies' Peace."[21] This accord stipulated the
king's marriage to the emperor's sister, Eleonore, and the return of the royal
sons. Tensions between the king and the emperor, however, would soon
resume. In the meantime, Louise's death in 1531 deprived the king of his
most trusted and devoted counselor and theoretically might have provided
an opening for Anne's rise. However, this was not the case, although Anne

remained at court in the entourage of royal princesses Madeleine and Marguerite, the king's affection for her visible to all.[22] A scandalized letter from diplomat Francis Bryan to Henry VIII recounts that during the new queen Eleonore's entrance into Paris, the king and Anne were among the spectators gathered in Paris to greet her. Already things between the king and queen were going very badly, Bryan notes: they had not lain together once in four nights, and the king spoke very little to her, barely ever leaving Anne. Most shocking of all, throughout the entry, François I "toke [Anne] and sett hyr before Hym in a opyn wyndow, and ther stode devysyng with her 2 long howrys in the syght and face of all the peple; whych was not a lytyll marvelyd at of the beholdders."[23] In a concrete show of favor, the king married Anne in 1532 to Jean de Brosse and made the pair the Duke and Duchess of Étampes.[24]

Louise's death, then, did not bring Anne's rise; instead, "the hour of Anne de Montmorency" had sounded. Montmorency, companion in arms to the king, had served him as grand master of France since the return from captivity in 1526, attaining the status of principal royal counselor in 1531. In this role Montmorency had a clearly formulated political philosophy for helping the king reclaim Milan, one that Thierry Rentet describes as "equilibrium." Montmorency's motto, "Je maintiendrai" (I will hold steady), Rentet observes, announces the privileging of balance between opposing forces.[25] Brute military conquest would never achieve the king's primary goal of recovering Milan, Montmorency believed, because if the Milanese were conquered, they would turn to the emperor for aid.

The king's enthusiasm for Montmorency's philosophy ebbed and flowed, tested in particular when Francesco II Sforza died heirless in November 1535 and Charles V refused to offer a daughter or a niece with the duchy as dowry to Prince Henri. Placing Milan in the hands of the French king was unacceptable to Charles V, and Henri's position as second in line to the throne created too great a risk, although the emperor hinted that he might consider such an arrangement for the king's youngest son, Charles of Orléans. Already mistrustful, François I became truly alarmed when Charles V captured Tunis in 1535 and then landed in Sicily to work his way up the Italian peninsula.[26] A pro-war faction skeptical of Montmorency's approach then crystallized around Philippe de Chabot, Admiral de Brion, also a companion of the king from boyhood. Brion's and Montmorency's rivalry is attested from the early 1530s, and in 1535–36 Montmorency briefly lost favor to his competitor as François I determined to answer Charles V's aggressions with military action.[27] The French invaded Savoy in January, ostensibly to recover lands wrongly seized by Charles III of Savoy, brother-in-law of Charles V, but in fact as an unofficial declaration of war. In response, the imperial army took Piedmont, defeating the admiral, and invaded Provence in July. The French army attempted to take Milan for Prince Henri but failed, and war broke out in earnest in 1536. In June 1536 the king recalled Montmorency, giving him command of the entire army, with Prince Henri the nominal leader.[28] Their military success, which earned Montmorency the position of connétable, created a lasting bond between the two.[29]

This close relationship widened the quarrel between Brion and Montmorency by bringing another group into the struggle: those associated with the prince, including his mistress, Diane de Poitiers. The quarrel was further complicated by the notoriously difficult relationship between the king and Henri. When the dauphin François died abruptly in 1536 and Henri became heir to the throne, the relationship between the king and Henri further deteriorated, as we will see.[30]

Montmorency's power was reinforced with the Truce of Nice in July 1538 between France and the empire. A personal meeting between the king and emperor at Aigues-Mortes followed. With peace restored, hope for the return of Milan was renewed. The emperor's daughter would marry Prince Charles, bringing Milan with her; the emperor's son Philip would marry François I's daughter, Marguerite. François I would abandon alliances with Henry VIII and the Turks. In addition, François I allowed Charles V to cross through France on his way to Ghent to suppress warring cities in Flanders.[31] But he waited in vain for the marriage between his son and the emperor's daughter, and in April 1540 the emperor changed course, offering, along with his niece, not the duchy that the king so coveted but the Low Countries, Burgundy, and the Charolais. In October Charles V invested his own son Philip with Milan.

Montmorency's policy again looked like a failure, and, furious, François I turned on him once more.[32] Around this point, Anne begins to appear in ambassador reports as a full-blown political figure, Montmorency's misplaced faith in the emperor giving her an opportunity to convince the king that she was better equipped to promote his interests than the ideological connétable. And yet as abrupt as the written sources make her appearance seem, it did not emerge out of the blue but had been prepared over the preceding decade.

THE COURT OF FRANÇOIS I AS THEATER

We noted in the introduction that François I's court was perceived by observers as a sort of theater. This sense of theatricality, we suggest, along with the vision of gender that we have laid out, was a historical precondition for a politically powerful royal mistress as the role developed in France.

The perception of court life as theater was to a large extent a function of the presence of resident ambassadors, who became a fixture in France with the reign of François I.[33] These men spent their days observing courtiers to glean intelligence that would allow their lords to make informed decisions and trying to make contact with the king and his intimates to promote their lord's interests. Their presence transformed court life. As historian of diplomacy Lucien Bély writes, "Little by little [the ambassador's] arrival became a spectacular event in court life, and rules developed throughout Europe to add splendor to the ceremony. The foreign ambassador observed the country and the court in the land in which he was stationed. He informed his master. But he also judged the manners of the king and his intimates, and this foreign gaze resulted in tighter order and magnificence. In particular, the royal apartments became a series of rooms through which the ambassador progressed when he was received before reaching the throne or the king's chambers."[34] Ambassadors were both actors and audience. A good ambassador, writes Ellen R. Welch, "needed a strong repertoire of performance skills"; he had to be able to "deliver good speeches and carry himself with grace in the elaborate ceremonies of diplomacy" and "dissimulate as well as any actor—to tell lies or at least conceal knowledge—in order to gather intelligence for his master."[35] In his study of Annecy-born Eustache Chapuys, imperial ambassador to the court of Henry VIII, Richard Lundell adds playwright to the list of the ambassador's roles, in reference to the carefully prepared reports the ambassador sent to his lord. Chapuys "report[s] facts, as best he can gather and corroborate, as well as rumors, particularly in cases when those rumors fit with a larger narrative that seems plausible. . . . The documents 'speak' from the standpoint of Chapuys. Not only does he report facts, but also he writes himself in as the central actor. His voice is that of the narrator."[36]

Conversely, the knowledge that ambassadors were writing reports, "carefully prepared statement[s] of the political situation . . . filling in the background with special attention to the character and motive of the important persons and faction," caused courtiers to carefully guard their words, actions, and even facial expressions.[37] As we detail in the following section, politics at the French court were factional, success at them depending on a gift for dissimulating one's own motives and correctly gauging those of one's opponent. Political actors therefore performed for at least two separable audiences: foreign ambassadors and other courtiers with whom they were in constant competition for influence. Dissimulation was therefore a way of life, implying "a range of techniques for safeguarding one's secrets by rendering them unreadable or invisible to others," as Jon R. Snyder describes it. Dissimulating language, "as artificial as a highly stylized work of art," provided a cover for the talented courtier, who not only "relied on probing psychological self-critique" but "sought to scrutinize with equal rigor the motives and abilities of all those participating in the conversation as well."[38]

The unofficial ways in which information circulated allowed women to participate in court politics in ways that would no longer be possible when diplomatic procedure came to be codified and fully professionalized.[39] Women who had close access to power through family or sentimental ties were highly prized, and their value was reflected and enhanced by artistic renovations in the French royal palaces beginning in the 1530s, when an abundance of striking visual examples of new female functions appeared in art commissioned by the king. This imagery helped the royal mistress, her interlocutors, and her audiences symbolize her role. Citing Norbert Elias, Robert van Krieken insists on the significance of such symbolism, defining "agency" as the "strategic seizure" of opportunities but not the "actual creation of those opportunities." These are limited by the "specific structure of the society and the nature of the functions" that exist within the society.[40] François I's art was a significant factor in the creation of new opportunities for female action, and Anne seized those opportunities.

The female imagery was framed by the king's visual assertions of his absolute right to extend grace wherever he saw fit. From the time of François I's return from Spain, writes Janet Cox-Rearick, the "character of his patronage of architecture changed, the number and complexity of the commissions he gave dramatically expanded, and he began to use architecture for political ends—as a means to power."[41] Kathleen Wilson-Chevalier explains that in this the king followed a pattern "established earlier in Italy by the Este, Gonzaga, Medici, Montefeltro and the like," that is, a pattern of reflecting one's glory through one's chateau.[42] To control the meaning of the events both triumphant and demoralizing of his reign, the king enlisted artists to decorate Fontainebleau in particular with imagery from classical antiquity and mythological imagery, inviting Rosso Fiorentino (1494–1540) to move from Florence to Fontainebleau in 1530. Rosso Fiorentino was soon followed by Francesco Primaticcio (1504–1570).

Earlier kings had been represented as biblical monarchs such as David. Classical allusions had not been completely absent from the visual references surrounding François I's immediate successor, Louis XII, who had been declared higher than "Theseus, Jason, Hercules, and all the Greeks and Romans" in Lyon after defeating the Venetians in 1509.[43] Still, when François I's rival, Charles V, began to represent his exploits with the use of classical imagery under the influence of foreign merchants, a new way of representing monarchy emerged. Already for Charles V's 1515 entry into Bruges, the Italian merchants living there commissioned three triumphal arches "in which personifications of vices, represented as monsters, were conquered by mythological heroes, as well as a fountain with three female figures bent over a basin, with rosewater, red wine, and white wine flowing from their breasts."[44] François I, too, began to be represented in mythological imagery. Jupiter greeted the young king when he entered Rouen in 1517, the god's destruction of the giants performed to promote, allegorically, the crusade that he was being urged to lead following the capture of Milan in 1515.[45]

In fact, the king had long been associated with classical and mythological figures, including the ubiquitous regenerating salamander, and the manuscripts that he would have known as a boy and young man also associated him with figures from mythology.[46] A 1510 manuscript of prognostications opens with a full-page illumination depicting Louise/Latona attacked by the dragon, Python. Python has just received an arrow in the side, fired on by Latona's son, François/Apollo, who stands with bow still drawn, and his sister, Marguerite/Diana, holding his arrows.[47] The 1520 work of Jean Thenaud, the king's Franciscan almoner, "Troys résolutions et sentences," rejects in the form of a dream vision astrological prognostications of a terrible flood that, according to astral conjunctions, was scheduled to hit the world in 1524, but it opens with a paean to François I, whose spirit is described as integrating a superabundance of gifts from the spiritual and angelic world with the qualities of Jupiter, Phoebus, Venus, Mercury, Mars, Diana, and Saturn.[48]

But the use of classical imagery exploded at Fontainebleau, the stage on which the king performed his kingship.[49] A number of primary sources claim that the king himself brought the imagery to life when he revealed for guests the ways in which it glossed his own exploits.[50] Margaretha

Rossholm Lagerlöf notes that only the king fully understood the meaning of the images, "products of an artist skilled in 'inventions' of the classical heritage and keen to render the concepts and narratives in bewildering, unexpected ways."[51] For the king's sister, Marguerite, Fontainebleau without the king was an empty theater, a lifeless backdrop. "Your walls, without you," she writes, "are just a dead body."[52]

During the 1530s, Rosso Fiorentino and Primaticcio redecorated the Galerie François I, the long gallery leading from the king's apartments to the chapel of the Trinitaires, and the Galerie d'Ulysse, where sixty paintings illustrated the adventures of the famous traveler. Although the Galerie d'Ulysse was demolished in 1739, the Galerie François I still exists, its seven facing bays showcasing a still perplexing iconographic program. Modern art historians agree that a definitive interpretation of the mythological references is not possible, but in a general sense it is clear that the program begins with mythological tales representing themes of war and destiny and culminates in the glorification of the king.[53]

More easily grasped by visitors would have been the meaning of the imagery that would have confronted them as they entered the chateau through what was then the main entrance, the Porte Dorée. Here Primaticcio drew on the *Iliad* to gloss the king's exploits and his familial struggles as well, creating images that affirmed the king's authority "in the face of threats of feudal resurgences," writes Wilson-Chevalier—that is, the court factions that we have mentioned. These tensions included the conflicted relationship with his son Henri, which became still more strained with the dismissal of Montmorency.[54] The culminating *Iliad* scene, decorating the vault, shows Zeus putting his house back in order, a vivid reminder of who was in charge: Vulcan, Zeus's insubordinate son, has been struck by a thunderbolt.[55]

Alongside references to the king's primacy, sexual imagery held a central position in the Porte Dorée, with sexually explicit scenes such as Primaticcio's two-part depiction of the bawdy comedy of Omphale, Hercules, and Faunus from Ovid's *Fasti* adorning the walls. In the first painting, Omphale dresses her warrior in her own diaphanous clothing, and in the second, Hercules ejects from bed the visibly aroused Faunus, who has mistaken the warrior for Omphale.[56] Representations of erotic encounters still decorate the Galerie François I itself (although many of these "adult"-themed works have since been removed).[57] Despite a tendency to collect religious paintings and portraits early in his reign, François I later showed a distinct preference for the erotic. After 1530, Cox-Rearick notes, the king's "commissions and acquisitions increasingly included painting and sculpture of secular, often erotic, subjects." She cites a letter to the king that reveals his wide-spread image as connoisseur of women. The donor of Costa's *Venus with a Cornucopia* writes that "this picture comes before a great and good judge of bodily beauty—especially of women."[58] Henri Zerner remarks on the "explosive expressiveness of the human body in its full splendor" at Fontaine-bleau, adding that "it would have been hard to avoid the feeling that one was faced with a conception of existence completely different from that passed down by preceding generations." Old principles were challenged, he continues, by "something serious and almost painful in the evocation of sensuous pleasure."[59] Nude sculptures placed throughout the palace picked up the erotic themes. One prominent example should have been (it was never actually installed) Cellini's *Nymph of Fontainebleau*. This bronze relief represented the legend that gave Fontainebleau its name—that is, the story of the spring, personified as the nymph, discovered during a hunt by the royal hound Bliaud. Originally intended to crown the Porte Dorée, this depiction of a reclining nude, who looks very much like the huntress Diana with her arm around a stag's head, ended up adorning Diane de Poiters's Anet.[60] We will return to this bronze relief.

François I was a soldier, trained as a boy in the art of warfare along with friends who would accompany him throughout his life. But the Fontaine-bleau program reveals that an equally integral element of his identity were erudition, culture, and sexuality. He infused his warrior ethos with riches drawn from ancient culture, where women were constantly present in an abundance of guises. Describing the emphasis on the feminine at Fontaine-bleau as a redefinition-in-progress of rivalrous manliness, Wilson-Chevalier writes that women, "conflated with culture, were being placed at the centre of the civilizing function assigned to the king's court," where they compli-cate traditional notions of the warrior.[61]

Indeed, Lagerlöf notes that Fontainebleau was a "world of female power—a Venus world dominated by sensual pleasures, water, and fertile lands and woods with springs, fruits and animals" where the "slender naked female figure recurring as the nymph, as Venus and as symbol of pleasure is the characteristic visual sign of the place and the style of its imagery."[62] According to a story recounted by the ambassador from Ferrara, Alfonso Calcagnino, the king himself associated Anne with Venus. While visiting a foundry to view some new bronzes, the ambassador observed the arrival of the king, Anne, and some other courtiers. The king motioned toward a Venus, mentioning her perfect figure, at which Anne smiled and left the room to warm herself.[63]

More than Venus, however, the huntress Diana would seem to be an obvious choice for decoration. But the presence at court of Diane de Poiters, mistress of Prince Henri, as we have seen, made any association with the huntress impossible. Not surprisingly, under François I's program, Diana appears most often in stories in which she does not predominate. One example is a fresco in the baths depicting the story of Jupiter, Callisto, and Diana. Jupiter, exuding the heat of life, puts Juno and Diana in their places with Venus at his side, a visual image that might be read as a comment on the king's tense relationship with his son, via the image of a subdued Diana, surely a reference to Diane de Poitiers.[64] And the story of Cellini's nymph, mentioned above, offers another example of a devaluation of Diana. It is not clear whether the nymph was imagined as a Diana figure from the outset, or only when the relief was dispatched to Anet, probably in the early 1550s. In any case, one wonders why the nymph never graced the spot over the Porte Dorée intended for it. Katherine Marsengill argues that Anne, seeing the finished nymph, rejected it as too evocative of Diana and refused to let it be mounted in the chateau's entry. In addition, Anne demanded that Cellini's commission be revoked and reassigned to Primaticcio. Cellini left the court in disgrace in 1545.[65] Marsengill hypothesizes that Anne's dislike of Cellini, documented by the artist in his autobiography, stems from this incident, although Cellini himself appears to have had no idea why she had turned against him.[66]

With the disgrace of Montmorency, Anne was installed in the connétable's former apartments, which were then magnificently redone for her with paintings illustrating episodes from the life of Alexander.[67] The painting of *Apelles Painting Alexander and Campaspe* depicts Alexander and his mistress entwined in a sexually explicit embrace, undoubtedly a reference to the king and Anne. However, the king's right to authorize marriages and conduct love affairs with whomever he chose is reflected in another of the images, Alexander marrying Campaspe to Apelles (we recall that François I married Anne to Jean de Brosse, elevating the couple to the Duke and Duchess of Étampes) and himself marrying Roxanne in another. Another image of Alexander with the Amazon queen Thalestris, showing her climbing into his bed, seems to speak to the nature of Anne's political role: not the king's equal, she is nonetheless a formidable match.

The overarching lesson of the Alexander program (in fact, of the entire Fontainebleau program), argues Wilson-Chevalier, was to announce that "one man alone controlled all."[68] Not that biblical associations ever vanished from kingly iconography. But classical figures introduced a wider range

of female models into the discourse of power than their religious counterparts, the king distributing gifts to his concubines, among others. Here we
rejoin Le Roux's discussion of favor, of the king who showered gifts, like
grace, on whomever he pleased.[69]

For women at court, the effect of the decoration was to be confronted
with new ways of imagining their roles, far beyond the Virgin and saints.
These holy entities existed in real space, their iconography serving in a
literal sense as conduits to the divine. Their inherent reality meant that,
except for the exceptional Agnès, no mistress could reasonably be associated
with them. In the theatrical world of Fontainebleau with its burgeon-
ing of heroes, gods, and goddesses, it was possible for Anne to enact new
paradoxical roles, ranging from the chaste to the erotic, exercising political influence in one sphere unseen by those for whom she performed the
innocuous role of the king's extraconjugal sexual partner in another and
the decorous one of governess to the royal children or lady-in-waiting to
the queen in another.

THE OFFICIAL ROYAL MISTRESS AND FACTIONAL POLITICS

By 1539–40, ambassadors routinely include Madame d'Étampes along with
other highly ranked members of the court—the king, the queen, Montmorency, the queen of Navarre, the dauphin, the dauphine—whose words,
activities, and relationships they analyze for their lord and whom they
court on his behalf.[70] What most interests ambassadors in the earliest
letters is her relationship with Montmorency, which they interpret as part
of a larger intrigue—that is, the struggle for primacy between Montmorency and Brion, a quarrel that involved numerous groups of courtiers, as
we have seen, and ultimately had to do with whether the king would go
to war with the emperor. The quarrel would continue until Montmorency's definitive fall in the summer of 1541 and encompass the struggle over
the marriage between the Duke of Cleves and Jeanne of Navarre, daughter
of Marguerite and Henri of Navarre. Ambassadors recognized the direct
impact that this strife had on François I's decisions regarding Charles V and,
as we will see, Henry VIII.[71] Anne, whose correspondence shows her to be
still soliciting Montmorency's good will in 1536, hitches her own attempt
to bring down Montmorency to this preexisting quarrel, allying herself
with Brion and his supporters. This alliance also reinforced her relationship with Marguerite of Navarre, with whom she had been friendly since

at least as early as 1537. Marguerite herself had had a fraught relationship with the connétable over the years. In 1533 she told the English ambassador, the Duke of Norfolk, that she had little faith in getting the king to work on returning the half of Navarre that had been ceded to the Spanish while Montmorency was "in authority," adding that he will not long remain if she can "impeach it" and that "few of the nobles will be sorry."[72] She supported the admiral against the connétable during the connétable's temporary fall from grace in 1536, and she definitively supported the admiral as of 1540.[73] Furthermore, the quarrel made enemies of Anne and the dauphin and his mistress, Diane de Poitiers, a point that we will explore in detail at the end of this chapter.

To frame the following discussion, we note that Anne's political activity has often been described as incoherent and Anne herself as a flighty interloper in the male business of politics. We hope to show in what follows that in her political actions nothing distinguishes her from her male counterparts. Court factions resembled neither modern political parties nor social cliques.[74] Factions formed around a central dispute—in the case at hand, around the long-standing rivalry between Brion and Montmorency over their competing desires for supremacy, or, to put it slightly differently, over their incompatible strategies for dealing with the emperor. In 1540 Montmorency, himself on shaky ground, spearheaded an effort to get Brion investigated for fraud. Begun by the chancellor Poyet in August 1540, the investigation resulted in the admiral's conviction in February 1541.[75] In general, other quarrels then formed around the central one, with different players joining in when they thought that to do so might further a cause of their own. Factional players changed tactics with shifts in the situation— Marguerite of Navarre and Montmorency switched sides with noticeable frequency, as did François I, Henry VIII, and the emperor—leading to an impression of constant treachery. But such side-switching is quite simply the inevitable result of factional politics, which is, by definition, the spontaneous formation of groups to promote results in the absence of overarching institutions formally invested with the authority to arbitrate. Nothing like a political ideology of the type that unites members of a modern political party and determines their response to issues motivates members of factions. As for the perception of factions as social cliques, it is even more difficult to find evidence of friendship as a motivating factor. Despite the well-known language of love that marks exchanges of the period, decisions were in a strange way also fundamentally impersonal, motivated by family interest.

Anne's place among the factions was recorded and taken seriously by ambassadors stationed at the French court. In a letter of 17 February 1540 to Henry VIII, the Duke of Norfolk reports meeting with Marguerite of Navarre, who, because of her evangelical religious leanings, tended to be sympathetic to the English king. Norfolk, who was trying to lure François I away from the emperor and into an alliance with the English king, describes how Marguerite, whose wiliness was well known to contemporaries, laid out his best chance for success. The pro-imperial Montmorency was still influential with the king, who therefore remained favorable toward the emperor. And yet Marguerite, whom Norfolk reports to be an avowed enemy of the connétable, predicts Montmorency's fall and attests to Anne's rise, counseling Norfolk to "make a great trust in" the connétable: it would not "as yet avail to strive against him." Rather, Norfolk should court Chancellor Guillaume Poyet, "who was in great credit with the King and easily won with fair words," and, in addition, "try and win Madame d'Estampes" because the king, "if a thing were fixed in his head, would hardly let it be plucked out, and the persons who had most influence with him against [Montmorency's] mind are Madame d'Estampes and the Cardinal of Lorraine."[76]

Norfolk then describes himself responding that it seems strange to him to "seek anything at such a woman's hand," to which Marguerite replies that she is only advising Norfolk to do what she herself did.[77] He followed up on the advice, reporting to Henry VIII six days later that he and Wallop, received by François I in his bedchamber, learned from the king himself that Marguerite had been correct: the king had no intention of breaking with the emperor. Still, Norfolk adds that he also "had this day a good time with the Queen of Navarre and Madame d'Estampes and trusts good will come of it."[78] Henry VIII, obviously convinced by Norfolk of Anne's clout, replies in a letter of 5 April to Wallop that Wallop should tell François I that he has sent Madame d'Étampes a couple of palfreys, as she had requested.[79]

By April 1540 ambassadors to England accord Anne the same respect they do Marguerite, whose stature they had recognized since the early 1520s. On 8 April, Wallop describes to Cromwell his attempts to extract information about "the King's pleasure" from Anne and Marguerite. Assuring Cromwell that he, Wallop, can accurately read expressions, he also notes that he will be in a better position to discern François I's feelings toward Montmorency on the king's return. In the meantime, Brion, along with the queen of Navarre and "Madame d'Estampes will be ready to hasten [Montmorency's] fall."[80] The remainder of the letter announces that Montmorency's assurances about the return of Milan to François I are looking less likely: a message has arrived from the emperor, according to Wallop's informant, confirming that the long-sought marriage between Prince Charles and a daughter of the emperor might be coming but "under such abominable conditions as Wallop's informant will not write." Ten days later, Wallop reports on a further meeting with Marguerite during which he set out the case for François I sending a representative to Henry VIII in England to discuss the former's "whole mind and desire" regarding the emperor.[81] Marguerite agreed that it was a good idea, suggesting that Wallop first try to arrange a meeting between the monarchs in Calais, after which it might be possible to bring François I to England. Most of all, she believed that "these things could best be managed by Madame d'Estampes, for if she herself intervened she would be thought partial." Marguerite was eager not to seem too inclined toward the Protestant king, but Anne, although she had similar religious leanings, as we will see, was extremely discreet about them, therefore seeming more impartial.

The emperor's ambassadors found Anne's rise to be worthy of extensive reporting as well. In August 1540, in the face of Montmorency's vulnerability, the emperor seems to have instructed François Bonvalot, Abbé de Saint-Vincent, to court Anne, for the ambassador replies, "Respecting my keeping on good terms with [the chancellor Poyet], the cardinal de Tournon, and Madame d'Étampes . . . I am doing my best according to Your Majesty's instructions." He adds that he has had some difficulty, because the "Chancellor and the lady are not much attached to Your Majesty or Your ministers." He does not have personal knowledge of the reason for Anne's antagonism, he reports, but it is said to be that "when Your Majesty passed through this kingdom [to go to Flanders] you did not make so much of her as she expected, which has hardened her heart."[82] In that same letter he reports that although the connétable still has the king's favor, it is not growing, and that although he has many enemies who "are continually striving to unseat him," they have not yet succeeded.[83]

The emperor then helped deepen Montmorency's disgrace on 11 October 1540, confirming the anti-Montmorency faction's suspicions that he had no intention of delivering Milan: as we have seen, Charles V invested his own son Philip with the duchy.[84] Nonetheless, François I forced Montmorency to linger at court, intending, Robert Knecht reasons, to maximize his humiliation.[85] Wallop writes to Henry VIII in November that the connétable had asked the king's permission to withdraw, to which the king, with "water" streaming from his eyes, demanded whether he had not been a good lord to Montmorency. As Wallop recounts the drama, the king professed to still love the connétable; indeed, he said, "I can fynd but one fawlt in you, whiche is, 'that you love not those that I do.'" Wallop adds that the king was referring to "Madame d'Estampez." Montmorency attempted to make amends, courting Anne. The following Monday before departing for his home for Christmas, he went to take his leave of her, before she was even out of bed. From this, Wallop surmised, "theye ar now agreed."[86] Wallop misinterpreted the situation. Reconciliation had been not effected, and Anne continued to maintain the upper hand. In December 1540 papal nuncio Hieronimo Dandino reports that "madama di Tampes" was without exception the most powerful influence on the king.[87]

Italian ambassadors followed the developing story with the same interest. Carlo Sacrati wrote to Duke of Ferrara, Ercole d'Este, on 12 February 1541 that he had been told that "Madama di Tampes" and many others who support the cause of Brion now hate the connétable and have told the king that he is out of his mind ("pazzo") and that they hope to see him enter into disgrace with His Majesty. On 14 February Sacrati recounted a vivid drama performed the day before for the king in hopes of securing the pardon of Brion, convicted as we have seen the previous August. After departing Fontainebleau, the king had gone to see the admiral's wife and brought her back to court. Later, as he entered Anne's chambers, Brion's wife fell to her knees crying, "Sire, have pity and mercy on my husband," a cry repeated four or five times with increasing humility and passion by the other ladies.[88] The visibly shaken king was further accosted on his way out by one of Brion's granddaughters, who threw herself at his feet and kissed them. The ploy wrought the intended effect. Brion was restored, although his health was not robust enough to take over Montmorency's position on his own. Instead, François I set up a triumvirate of Brion, Cardinal Tournon, and the maréchal Claude d'Annebault, all of them Anne's allies, at least at that moment.[89]

Intertwined with the Brion-Montmorency struggle and providing the final reason for Montmorency's permanent exile from court was the marriage between the king's niece, Jeanne, daughter of Marguerite and Henri of Navarre, and the Duke of Cleves. The king's intent was to cement a French alliance with Protestant German lords against the emperor, meaning that the wedding in itself was a glaring sign of the failure of the policy that Montmorency had fought so vigorously to promote.[90] The machinations surrounding the marriage offer glimpses of Marguerite and Anne working together at various points to manage the marriage plans and, in the process, discredit the connétable. Although it is difficult ever to be sure of the motives at play, it seems that in addition to her other reasons for hating Montmorency, Marguerite resented his interference in her plans for her daughter's union.[91] In December 1540 Marguerite proclaimed to papal nuncio Dandino in a long and tearful discussion her contempt for the connétable, who had nearly gotten her and her husband chased from court.[92] The connétable had revealed to the king that Marguerite had first sought to marry Jeanne to the emperor's son and then, without the consent of the king, the Duke of Cleves. Proof of a long-term falling-out between Marguerite and Montmorency over that issue is the fact that between December 1539 and June 1547, Marguerite did not address a single letter to the connétable.[93]

Marguerite expressed different attitudes about her feelings toward the proposal to marry her only living child, heir to the throne of Navarre, to the minor prince William of Jülich-Cleves-Berge, either because she changed her mind or because she was trying to hide what she felt, or possibly both. Some historians assume that she was genuinely equivocal. David Potter writes that she was "intensely reluctant that the marriage of William and her daughter should proceed but still keen to encourage a Protestant alliance."[94] In contrast, Pierre Jourda sees her ambivalence as deliberate, assuming that both Marguerite and Henri of Navarre initially pretended to agree to the marriage contract to gain time because they had no immediate means of resisting the king, but that they also maintained contact with Charles V's ambassadors, harboring the "secret design" of pulling out should the need arise.[95] Certainly Henri of Navarre never genuinely supported the Cleves marriage. Hoping to recover the Spanish half of Navarre, he desired a match between his daughter and the emperor's son Philip to bring about this reunification. Possibly without Marguerite's knowledge, the king of Navarre also plotted to have his daughter "kidnapped" by Charles V's son and married to him, although the plot was not carried out.[96] Rouben Cholakian also emphasizes Marguerite's clever dissimulation, arguing that the queen coached her daughter to defy the king by refusing to marry the Duke of Cleves. In any case, Marguerite was inevitably torn between the interests that had become hers through marriage and those that bound her to her brother, and the king was well aware of this.

The primary sources are difficult to decipher because in her exchanges with ambassadors on the matter, Marguerite so clearly strives not to give too much away. Wallop reports to Henry VIII in December 1540 that Marguerite had disclosed to him that she and her husband had not yet resigned themselves to the marriage, stating that they "would not be hasty, but learn first how the Duke stands with the Emperor."[97] In that same conversation, Wallop notes that Anne revealed that the king's daughter, rather than Jeanne, might marry the Duke of Cleves. Wallop immediately follows up with Marguerite, who reports that such a rumor indeed circulates but no one knows for sure whether it is true. A dispatch of June 1541 from the emperor's spy, Juan Martinez Descurra, suggests that a union with the king's daughter was a real possibility, reporting that several of François I's most trusted counselors, including Anne, opposed the Cleves-Navarre marriage. They objected that the French kingdom would be surrounded by enemies should the Duke of Cleves one day became king of Navarre through his wife and then ally with the emperor. Moreover, they claimed that it was not right to marry a girl against the wishes of her parents. As a solution, the trio proposed that the king's own daughter, who was older, be offered to the duke instead.[98] Descurra further reports that the queen and king of Navarre felt secure that the king would heed his counselors.

But if the king listened to the advice, he did not follow it, and, as we have seen, the marriage took place in June 1541. Given the bride's young age, however, it was decided that consummation would not yet occur, and, from that moment on, both Anne and Marguerite ceased to openly resist, and perhaps even embraced, the marriage. In October 1541 Marguerite's secretary Frotté, counted Anne among those supporting the marriage, writing that those in favor were the "king, Tournon, Admiral Chabot, Chancellor Poyet, Annebault, the chancellor of Alençon," and Anne, "who is entirely for Monseigneur [of Cleves]."[99] Marguerite's positive attitude toward her new son-in-law, whether sincere or manufactured, is plain in the long series of letters that she wrote him. Not that it mattered in the end: the king turned against the Duke of Cleves after learning in 1543 that he had surrendered to the emperor, invalidating the French-Cleves alliance, and the marriage was annulled in 1545.

As for Montmorency, the marriage of the little Jeanne to the Duke of Cleves in June 1541 marked the end of his tenure at court. His humiliation reached its peak when the small bride, wearing her golden crown, violet satin mantle trimmed in ermine, and two skirts of gold and silver decorated with precious stones, refused to walk up the aisle, either because she was "too heavily loaded down with the weight of her apparel or just wanted to raise one last objection."[100] The king directed Montmorency to haul the girl to the altar as the stupefied guests gawked at the once proud man performing a task so "little appropriate and honorable."[101] According to Brantôme, the connétable, after having "served as a spectacle for all," bid "adieu" to François I's court for good, saying that his "credit had run out."[102]

Anne, on the other hand, was firmly established in her position. With Montmorency gone, she had managed to get the greatest obstacle to her ability to influence the king dismissed from court. Admittedly, her ascension had also been facilitated by François I's worsening health, a point we emphasize because the scenario recalls the gravely ill king's dependence on his mother and sister during his Spanish captivity. While he lay near death, his sister had traveled to Spain to care for him and his interests, the French kingdom administered by Louise. Anne would now fulfill a similar role. The king's ill health becomes a subject of discussion again in late 1539. Henry VIII's ambassador Edmund Bonner, writes on 18 October 1539 that the "French king has been diseased, and has not come abroad for four or five days."[103] On 10 November a different source observed that the king "hathe [been sore] sycke, so that no man wolde warrant hym lyfe . . . cutt and bladders takyn owt of hym, that y[e should mar]vell to here."[104] Despite periods of reasonable health during which ambassadors noted his sanguine appearance, the king deteriorated during the following years, possibly suffering from syphilis. Intelligence from the imperial ambassador reveals in 1545 that he was suffering from fevers that "troubled him several times, and came on suddenly without any premonition, lasting on one occasion for five days." Moreover, it was "discovered that he had a gathering under the lower parts, which distressed and weakened him so much that he could not stand."[105]

The king's ongoing physical ailments deepened his dependence on Anne. In a missive of 1542 meant to reprove, Dandino writes that the king was "completely in the thrall of Madame d'Étampes, who . . . makes the king believe that he is God on earth and that no one can harm him, and that anyone who tells him differently has his own agenda."[106] Dandino's criticism, however, captures the essence of the political royal mistress: Anne tirelessly praises and protects the king, promoting his interests above all others, her loyalty recalling that of the single-mindedly devoted Louise.

RUSE AND POLITICS

Anne came to Marguerite's aid in a quarrel with the king instigated by Montmorency regarding Jeanne's marriage. We noted that Marguerite had proclaimed her hatred of Montmorency to papal nuncio Dandino; Dandino also reported in the same letter that Marguerite had avowed that Anne had much helped her at a time when she needed it, and for this reason, she remained Anne's slave and spoke of her like a goddess.[107] Marguerite too looked out for Anne when the chance arose. Besides Montmorency's fall, the queen of Navarre helped bring about that of royal chancellor Poyet, close ally of Montmorency. Poyet, we have seen, facilitated the removal of Brion from his position in 1541, a ploy that Anne had managed to have reversed. This same Poyet, referring to Anne's intervention in a different matter, grumbled to Marguerite in 1542 that women (meaning Anne) were not content to impose their will but were now telling magistrates (Poyet) how to do their job. Marguerite relayed the comment to her brother; Poyet found himself in prison.[108] It seems as if the women also joined forces to return Cardinal Tournon to the king's good graces by means of a play: "The Cardinal of Turnon is restored to favour," writes William Paget in 1542, "by Madame d'Estampes and the queen of Navarre, who lately played a farce before him, in which the players were the King's daughter, Madame d'Estampes, Madame de Nevers, Madame Montpensier, and Madame Belley."[109]

Beyond their political usefulness to each other, the women were drawn together by their shared religious beliefs. It is indisputable that later in her life Anne was Protestant, described by the English envoy Thomas Hoby in 1566 as "a grave, godlie, wise, sober and courteious lady, one of the staies of the refourmed religion in Fraunce," and welcoming Protestant leaders in her castle at Challuau in 1576.[110] True, it is not known how or when she first "converted" nor how deep her commitment was early on.[111] Jonathan Reid writes that the sources show that "during the period 1540–1546 an evangelical faction, whose anchor had long been Marguerite, continued to operate at court. Its major figures were Admiral de Brion, the Du Bellay brothers, and less reliably, madame d'Étampes."[112] But if Anne had to be yet more discreet about her beliefs than Marguerite, who could always retire to Nérac when the situation required, the 1540s offered more opportunity for her to promote religious reform with Marguerite. Throughout the mid-1540s, Reid documents, Marguerite and Anne were in close secret contact with the English, professing their support for the religious cause and striving to bring peace between Henry VIII and François I. By 1545, St. Mauris wrote to Charles V that Protestants at the French court were receiving great favor because Madame d'Étampes "inclines to the Lutheran discipline," and Queen Eleonore maintained the same.[113]

These secret negotiations with the English are of special interest in understanding Anne's political activity in the last years of her tenure. The three-way competition for allies among François I, the Protestant king Henry VIII, and the Catholic emperor caused the final years of François I's reign to degenerate into incessant and catastrophically expensive warfare, but Anne, favoring Reform, supported an alliance with the English throughout.[114] She has been characterized as outstandingly conspiratorial and flighty during this time, as one who "vaguely favoured an English rather than an imperial alliance" and whose "role in court politics under Francis I was essentially capricious, with changes of alignment according to the whim of the moment."[115] Contemporary reports are partly responsible for the impression. Nicolas Villey, seigneur de Marnol, remarked that all her life she had been "flighty and unstable."[116] Also, in 1545, Venetian ambassador Marino Cavalli reports that she abruptly shifted from supporting peace with the English to pushing for war, all because she knew that the blame for the continuing war would fall on the shoulders of the Admiral Annebaut, "whom [Anne] wishes to crush completely."[117] As we have tried to make clear, a glance at French politics during the sixteenth century shows that Anne was not uniquely changeable. As for the latter, Cavalli's assertion, not supported by other sources, is most likely a case of an ambassador's misunderstanding tactics. Anne, on the one hand, and Annebaut and Tournon, on the other, struggled for primacy in the mid-1540s, but nothing suggests that she suddenly turned pro-war against the English.[118]

An examination of Anne and Marguerite's reactions toward the Treaty of Crépy as recorded in contemporary sources makes the point that motives that seem incoherent often mask an underlying strategy. The women's positions seem at first glance to make no sense. And yet, although the machinations surrounding the Treaty of Crépy cannot be definitively interpreted, if we impute a couple of strategic lies to the women, their positions begin to fall into place. In May 1543 Henry VIII, having agreed with Charles V to invade France within the year, sent François I an ultimatum threatening war, and on 22 June it was declared. Wallop crossed the Channel to Calais with an army of five thousand men to defend the Low Countries. In response, William of Cleves joined the French and invaded Brabant. However, Cleves's support did not last long, for he surrendered to the emperor in September 1543.[119] Skirmishing with imperial troops in northern Italy led to the French victory at the battle of Ceresole on 11 April 1544, but François I still did not manage to regain Milan, forced to send troops from Italy to Picardy, which the English and Charles V had just invaded.[120]

Charles V, struggling to manage religious turmoil in the empire, eventually asked Henry VIII to continue the fight without him or to allow him to make a separate peace with France, and, without waiting for the reply, he concluded the Peace of Crépy with the French on 18 September 1544.[121] The treaty, sealed with an agreement of marriage between the king's younger son, Charles, and a niece of the emperor, brought a temporary lull and hope of regaining Milan by diplomatic means. Among other things, Prince Charles was to choose between Charles's daughter Mary (with the Netherlands and Franche-Comté as a dowry) and his niece Anna (Milan). François I would contribute the duchies of Bourbon, Châtellerault, and Angoulême and relinquish his claims to the territories of the Duchy of Savoy. But most interesting here, the treaty contained a secret appendix, presumably known only to François I and Charles V, in which the king promised to help the emperor support the church, specifically, the Council of Trent; make no separate peace with the English; and contribute to the war effort that Charles V was planning against the Protestant Schmaldkaldic League, which had formed in 1531 against him.[122] We will return to this secret appendix.

The dauphin was violently opposed to the treaty, arguing that the power it would award Prince Charles would lead to instability when Henri took the throne.[123] At Fontainebleau in December Henri signed a protestation against the ratification of the treaty, witnessed by the Guise brothers, his close friends.[124] As for Anne, she favored the treaty; indeed, she has been accused of being a traitor for pushing to settle with the emperor to the disadvantage of the French. Somehow the goal that the king had been seeking for years, installing a member of the royal family as the Duke of Milan, is transformed into an act of treachery? The argument has long been laid to rest.[125] And yet her support for settling with the emperor might seem odd given that she had backed Marguerite in secret dealings with the English to bring about, through an alliance, "the greatest benefit that ever came to Christendom" since at least 1542.[126] It also seems odd that Marguerite of Navarre supported the Peace of Crépy, writing a long and enthusiastic letter to the king to congratulate him and, later that year, an *étrenne* praising the peace and comparing her brother to Solomon.[127] She expresses pleasure that peace throughout Christendom was near, and, although she does not mention it, she must have rejoiced that Milan might after all finally be returned to the French.[128] She even encloses a small figure of Solomon with her letter. She could have sent an insincere congratulatory letter without a poem and figure of Solomon had she been interested only in appearance.

Although Marguerite and Anne would have rejoiced at the end of a ruinous war, if they were aware of the secret appendix, the treaty would have been anathema to everything they were working for. Nor did their secret contact with the English end with the treaty, whatever its secret appendix stipulated. Reid writes that the sources show that during the entire period from 1540 to 1546 "an evangelical faction, whose anchor had long been Marguerite, continued to operate at court."[129] Post-treaty, during the summer of 1545, they made contact with Protestant educator-diplomat Johannes Sturm to arbitrate between England and France.[130] François I vetted the plan, and representatives convened in October. However, before the mediation began, the sudden death of Prince Charles on 9 September 1545 undid the basis for the Treaty of Crépy. The devastated king allowed the mediation to continue, but it led nowhere. Therefore, a secret mission, led by Sturm but sent by Marguerite and Anne, solicited Paget with a new plan for an English-French alliance against the emperor, one based on their common hatred of the pope.[131]

To return to the secret appendix, was it kept hidden from Marguerite and Anne so that they were unaware of the terms as they quietly worked to bring the Reform to France? Or did they know about it from the beginning and also that it would never be honored? In other words, had François I told them that he had only agreed to it as a ruse? It would not be the first time: as we have seen, he had reneged on the Treaty of Madrid, which had secured his release from his captivity in Spain, nearly as soon as he had landed on French soil by refusing to turn Burgundy over to the emperor. And if the king was aware of and condoned Marguerite and Anne's secret negotiations with the English in this case, once again, it would not be the first time that he had sent women to negotiate on his behalf specifically so that he could disclaim the results if necessary. A report on the Ladies' Peace of 1529, brokered by Louise and Charles V's aunt, Marguerite of Austria, lists among the reasons for Louise and Marguerite's carrying out the negotiations the fact that François I had many allies who would have to be consulted if he were to enter negotiations with Charles V, which meant in practical terms that peace would never be achieved. However, if Louise negotiated, the king of France could always claim to his allies later that he had had no idea what she was doing and blame everything on her.[132] Did he encourage Marguerite and Anne to work secretly with their English counterparts for the same reason?

Anne's capriciousness looks like a ruse if we assume that she and Marguerite knew exactly what they were doing, whether or not they were

authorized by the king. And aware or not of the secret treaty, their continued contact with the English meant that they sought to protect the Reform
while bowing to the necessity for peace with the emperor. Unfortunately for
them, the Treaty of Ardres, or Camp, between François I and Henry VIII
in the summer of 1546 restored peace, but it did not create the religious
union they had promoted.[133] Marguerite and Anne continued to insist to
their English interlocutors that François I could be coaxed into breaking
with the pope if Henry VIII would make the first move.[134] When the two
kings died in 1547, however, Henry VIII in January, François I in March,
one was Protestant while the other remained Catholic.

ANNE AND DIANE DE POITIERS: A JEALOUS RIVALRY?

In addition to being charged with capriciousness, Anne frequently has been
cast as a jealous competitor in a personal rivalry with Diane de Poitiers,
mistress of Prince Henri.[135] Diane often resided at the royal court at the
same time as Anne, present there at times from the 1520s until the death of
Henri II in 1559, and Anne from the early 1520s until the death of François
I in 1547. Modern historians, following a path traceable ultimately to the
chronicler François-Eudes de Mézeray (1610–1683), have described the court
as a "theater for rivalry between the leading court ladies," the women as "two
favorites" who would "come up against each other in a series of intrigues."[136]
Even her evangelical beliefs have been attributed to her rivalry with Diane,
Desgardins writing that "it seems probable that Anne de Pisseleu became
a Protestant out of her hatred for Diane, ardent Catholic."[137]

This image of Anne and Diane engaged in a frenzied catfight has a
venerable tradition immortalized by Francis Decrue de Stoutz (1854–1928),
whose volumes on Montmorency remain indispensable. Decrue blames
court factionalism under François I on this rivalry, asserting that the women
"transmit[ted] their mutual hatred to their royal lovers." More profoundly,
he theorizes, the mistresses emblematized a struggle between a fresh new
court and a tired old one, Anne supporting the new through Charles, "the
brilliant duke of Orléans and Angoulême" and younger brother of Henri,
against Diane and "the severe Dauphin."[138] Montmorency supported the
dauphin but neglected the interests of Charles, continues the historian,
failing to push the emperor on his promise to cede the Milanais to this
prince. The emperor, seeing the battle lines and wishing to stir up trouble,
invested his own son with Milan, giving François I the excuse he needed

to eject Montmorency. Decrue's conclusion: "the real reason for [Mont-morency's] disgrace was the hatred of the former court for the new one, the jealousy between the king's lover and the Dauphin's."[139]

And yet it is difficult to understand why anyone would attribute Mont-morency's fall, the difficult father-son relationship, and even the emperor's cession of Milan to his own son Philip to Anne and Diane's mutual jealousy when such compelling explanations for the course of events exist, as we have tried to show. Surely the attribution reverses the cause and effect: far from creating factionalism, Anne and Diane's relationship was a function of the factions into which they were drawn by virtue of Anne's attachment to the king and Marguerite of Navarre and Diane's to the dauphin. Factionalism, already fueled by the collection and circulation of secret information, gave Anne and Diane opportunities for exercising influence in the first place. Many contemporaries remark on the antipathy between Anne and the dauphin Henri, between Anne and Montmorency, and, more generally, between the rival factions. But the animus between the women is always explained as the result of their allegiance to opposing parties, not personal jealousy. A well-known anecdote about Anne remarking that she was born the same day that Diane was married may be apocryphal, traceable to 1627, nearly one hundred years after the fact.[140] True, we have noted that Anne rejected the Nymph of Fontainebleau, apparently unwilling for Diane's avatar to preside over the space she ruled: as mistress of the king, she preceded the mistress of the dauphin. But at stake was power, not personal jealousy.

Anne and Diane appear together only rarely in sources. However, the dauphin's antipathy toward his father's mistress receives abundant comment and would inevitably have shaped Diane's attitude toward Anne.[141] In September 1541 William Howard reports to Henry VIII that the "Dolphyn has no great affection to the Admiral [de Brion], because of his familiarity with Madame de Estampes, 'which the Dolphyn favoureth in no wise.'"[142] Dandino too mentions the bad blood, remarking that same year that Prince Charles loves the sister of Admiral de Brion's wife, Madame de Montpen-sier, and hates the admiral's adversary [Montmorency]; "the dauphin dares not offend Diane, his lady, who is related to the connétable." Anne helps as much as she can, Dandino affirms, and "with dexterity behaves wisely, but everyone knows that the connétable hates her and that she hates the connétable." Dandino further notes that the dauphin had ordered the dauphine Catherine not to talk to Anne.[143] Yet another report of 1543 observes that the dauphin seconded an insult directed at Anne by Charles V's "gentilzhommes" who called her a "meschante putain."[144]

The few mentions of Anne and Diane's testy relationship by ambassadors suggest political, as opposed to personal, animosity centered around
the connétable. In February 1542 Marnol writes to Charles V of a confron-
tation between the dauphin and Anne that had to do with a relative of
Diane, for whom the dauphin has "more respect than for anyone else in
the world." Anne went tearfully to the king, who became sick with anger.
Marnol continues that Anne will never stop until she destroys Diane's
credit and authority, not only because of her hatred but also because of
the secret intelligence between Montmorency and Diane.[145] Another anecdote of 1544 related by Ferrarese ambassador Giulio Alvarotti has Diane
being chased from the court by the king. Although initially the ambassador did not know why, a few days later he learned from a reliable source
that the dauphin, who was with the army at the front in Boulogne, had
written to the king that he had been advised to request that the Admiral
Annebaut be replaced. The king and Anne assumed that the request had
come from Diane, angling to have Montmorency sent to replace Annebaut. Alvarotti concludes the letter by observing that "the king and Anne
were saying terrible things about [Diane]. Also, the king chased her from
court, either on his own, or at the demand of Madame d'Étampes, great
friend of [Annebaut]."[146] When the dauphin returned, he demanded Diane's
unconditional return, and when the king refused, he departed the court
for Anet. Adrien Thierry points to a letter from Henri II to Diane written
shortly after François I's death, reminding her, as a sign of his devotion,
that he had taken her side against the king.[147]

Such traces of overt antagonism between Anne and Diane, then, seem
to demonstrate political rather than personal rancor, a result of the factions
with which they were involved. Those making the case for a jealous rivalry
have further perceived traces in court literature dating from the late 1530s
and early 1540s. In his collection of short *étrennes* of 1538 for the ladies
of the court, Clément Marot indicates great admiration for Anne, dedi-
cating two flattering pieces to her, awarding her the golden apple for her
beauty, and praising her complexion. But in Diane's *étrenne* he claims only
to have heard that she had had less fun in her youth than she was having
in middle age ("au printemps / qu'en autonne"). This is surely a reference
to her autumn-spring relationship with Henri.[148] A poem also published
in 1538 viciously scorns Diane's aged face and heavily applied cosmetics.[149] Referring to this poem, Desgardins writes that the rivalry "became
so impassioned that the Duchess of Étampes inspired Jean Voulé, poet
from Champagne, author of a calumnious publication against Diane."[150]

Such writings, Thierry asserts, "originated in the hatred of the Duchess of Étampes for Diane de Poitiers: inspired and remunerated by the jealous mistress of François I, they could not do otherwise than express the emotions that animated her."[151] A frequent claim that Anne "commissioned" such verses against Diane sometimes footnotes Guiffrey's edition of Diane's letters.

However, when we trace the footnote, we see that Guiffrey writes nothing about commissioning verses.[152] We suggest that this insulting literature is more interesting for what it suggests about perceptions in the late 1530s of Anne as a participant in Reformist circles and Diane as a conservative Catholic than for anything it reveals about the women's personal relationship. The examples cited were composed by known Reformist sympathizers. Marot's religious affiliation requires no further explanation. The second poem, too, was composed by a known Reformist, Jean Voulé, Voultré, or Visagier, friend of Marot, part of the circle of Rabelais and Dolet.[153] Given this context, the poems, especially Anne and Diane's *étrennes*, could be interpreted as an evocation of the contrast between the young, regenerative power of the Reformed religion and the deception of the old one. The 1540 dedication of Charles de Sainte-Marthe, himself part of the same circle, of his *Poésie françoise* to Anne strengthens the impression that she was perceived as a religious ally, as does Marguerite of Navarre's dedication of her love debate poem, "La Coche," to Anne.[154]

CONCLUSION

The importance of the mistress was enhanced by the fact that from the time of Queen Eleonore, during whose tenure Anne reached her apogee, the queens of France were foreign-born, with one exception: Marguerite de Valois, who, as we will see, had problems of her own. Monique Cottret notes that between the queen and mistress, "the jobs were divided up, the queen [taking on] reproduction and representation, the mistress arts and letters and hostessing court life."[155] To this we would add that because there was no risk of a prior commitment to a foreign dynasty with the mistress, unlike the queen, in the absence of an influential queen-mother, the mistress was the king's most faithful and intimate adviser. True, a royal marriage was the material proof of an alliance. But alliances did not always endure. Eleonore was the sister of the French king's bitter enemy, and François I seemed to take pleasure in humiliating her. As for Eleonore's successor, Catherine de Médicis, she suffered from knowing that she was perceived by many as a foreigner and an unworthy match for a French prince.[156] Later, when Henri II became king, the mistrust continued. For example, when the king left Catherine regent during a military expedition to Italy in 1552, she was initially overjoyed, but she quickly discovered to her chagrin that she was forced to share the charge with Annebaut.[157]

Still, the role was always unofficial, an open secret performed only before certain audiences. As we noted in the introduction, Catherine de Médicis remarked that as far as Anne was concerned, all was honorable. We see Anne in 1538 accompanying the queen on a trip to visit the emperor, her brother, who had come to sign the Treaty of Nice, in neighboring Ville-franche. Cardinal Siguenza bears witness to the status of Anne's position at that event as an open secret and Queen Eleonore's role in promoting that status. He reports back to the empress in Spain that some of the ladies "of the Queen's suite, and among them one called Madame Estampa, the Queen's trainbearer, went to the dwelling of the High Commander, others to that of the duke of Mantua (Frederico Gonzaga) and other lords, where supper, dancing, music, and other entertainments had been prepared for them beforehand. It is reported that king Francis has declared himself the 'cavalier servente' of the above-mentioned lady, and that queen Leonor, far from being jealous, is very glad of it, thinking that it is only a fit of courtly gallantry on his part."[158] This cannot possibly have been true. Although the queen may not have been jealous, surely she knew that the relation-ship between the king and Anne was more than a "fit of courtly gallantry." But everyone behaved as if "all was honorable."

In a trip to the Netherlands in 1544, Anne is the only lady allowed to share the queen's litter.[159] Even at the height of her power, in 1546, we find Anne waiting on the queen, presenting herself to the world as Eleon-ore's servant. At the baptism of Elisabeth or Isabelle, daughter of Prince Henri and Catherine, we see "the Queen, whose train was borne by Mme. d'Étampes as lady of honour, and who was followed by Mme. Marguerite of France, the Princess d'Albret and Mme. de Vendome walking together."[160]

The kings of France from Charles VI through Henri II relied on a woman as a close adviser, with the exception of Louis XI. For Charles VI it was his queen, Isabeau of Bavaria; Charles VII, first his mother-in-law, Yolande, then his mistress, Agnès Sorel; Louis XI seems to have held women in contempt except his daughter, Anne of France; Charles VIII, his sister, Anne of France; Louis XII, his queen, Anne of Brittany; François I, his mother, Louise of Savoy, then Anne; Henri II, Diane. As we see in the next chapter, the trend continued. The role of official royal mistress, then, must be seen within this more fundamental context of the royal tendency to rely on a female adviser, itself a function of the gender ideology that constructed women as equals in competence but inferiors in law, and, because of this very inferiority and the inability of women to assume power for themselves, as the most loyal and therefore best choice for intimate political advisers. The role was always controversial, viewed as a positive, or at least practical, reality by those able to take advantage of the access that the role of mistress offered. On the other hand, given the ambivalence of her status, she was an easy target for accusations of treachery.

CHAPTER 3

Diane de Poitiers

Epitome of the French Royal Mistress

By this Diana was meant Madame the Duchess of Valentinois, who was worthy of love, because, beyond her beauty, she was a very competent and generous lady, and she had a great and generous heart; and, also, she descended from one of the greatest and oldest houses of France, that of Poitiers and Lusignan, from which came many generous people of both sexes, as evidenced by Melusine, and this Duchess of Valentinois; being as she was and so generous, she could not help but counsel, preach, and persuade the king, of all great, lofty and generous things.

—PIERRE DE BOURDEILLE BRANTÔME, *Memoires*

Anne fell and Diane rose with the death of François I on 31 March 1547.[1] Despite the old king's plea that his successor look kindly on Anne, Henri II sent her and much of the previous administration packing almost as soon as the royal body was cold.[2] Having left the court shortly before the king's death, Anne later sent a servant to the chateau of Saint-Germain-en-Laye to inquire about her usual rooms and pay her respects to the new king. Henri II had the servant informed that he was turning allocation of the rooms over to Queen Eleonore, whom Anne had treated very badly, and that he wanted to hear nothing about Anne or her family.[3] Anne retreated to Brittany where her husband was "gouverneur."[4]

Montmorency, on the other hand, was recalled, and by 28 May ambassadors were reporting that he controlled access to the new king. On hearing that François I had died, Duke Cosimo I of Florence sent ambassador Giambattista Ricasoli to France to pay his regards and suss out the new situation. Ricasoli quickly discovered that all business went through the connétable, informed of this by the new queen, Catherine, herself.[5] Giulio Alvarotti, writing to the Duke of Ferrara on 8 July, describes negative attitudes toward the connétable who "pretends to know everything and that the other people governing know nothing. He is still more insolent than before and makes himself odious to men, women, and everyone else in the world, because he always speaks with great arrogance and won't listen to anyone."[6] Somehow Henri II noticed none of this, Alvarotti continues, claiming that the king let himself be governed by his "maestro."

Montmorency was an immensely powerful man with an extensive clientele, and he was clearly appreciated by François I and Henri II. But contemporary testimony suggests that he was perceived as condescending by anyone who tried to deal with him as an equal. In February 1542 Marnol had written to Charles V of Montmorency's overweening pride. Although the connétable had been exiled in the summer of 1541, as we have seen, Marnol reports that when the king began to have second thoughts about sending him away, Anne reanimated his anger, informing him that the connétable had been saying that he had no doubt that he would soon be recalled by the king to continue his services, because the affairs of the kingdom could not be managed without him. In fact, the connétable did not at all regret his exile, because he knew that the honor and reputation that his recall would bring would more than equal the pain of his dismissal and that his enemies would be greatly shamed by it.[7] Although Anne admittedly was not an unbiased source and may have been lying, the claim appeared plausible to the king, who knew Montmorency well. Moreover, her assertion is compatible with a 1540 report by Wallop to Henry VIII that nobody much liked Montmorency, the "said Cunstable not liking the mynischement of a parte of this his auctorite, and havyng many ennemyes in the Court to hyndre hym."[8] Writing several years later, Venetian ambassador Lorenzo Contarini reports that the connétable "is not well liked at court, almost all of the important courtiers belonging to [Diane's] faction, among them the entire House of Guise."[9]

However, in his new post, Montmorency would be forced to share his power. First, the Guise family was also in the ascendant.[10] Patriarch Claude (1496–1550) had been made Duke of Guise by François I. But although this intimate of Montmorency had lost some of the king's favor with the connétable's fall and had even withdrawn to Burgundy, his sons, childhood companions of Prince Henri, rose with the new king. The eldest son, François, had already been made governor of the Dauphiné by François I. Charles, cardinal and archbishop of Reims, crowned the new king.

Second, Montmorency would have to deal with Diane, who completed the circle of intimates of the king. The new king showered her with signs of favor. Three of her nephews became bishops. Her son-in-law Henri-Robert de La Marck, Duke of Bouillon, became a maréchal of France and governor of Normandy. Her status is demonstrated in the hierarchical list of court notables carried by papal envoy Michele della Torre, who arrived at the French court on 19 September 1547: the king is followed immediately by Princess Diane of France, followed by the queen; the dowager queen, Eleonore; the king's sister, Marguerite; the Duchess of Guise; and Diane. Diane was followed by Marguerite of Navarre.[11] Moreover, the king's attachment to her was remarked on by ambassdors; according to imperial ambassador Jean de St. Mauris, he was "more inclined with affection toward her than the late king had been toward Madame d'Estampes," and after any negotiation with an ambassador, he "returned immediately to her to give her an account of what had happened."[12] In June St. Mauris wrote that the king was Diane's "slave," complaining that between her, the connétable, and the Guises, no one could get near enough to the king to let him know what was going on outside of the court.[13] On 8 October 1548, the king made Diane the Duchess of Valentinois, guaranteeing that her title would be commensurate with her new status.[14]

Anne had risen to power in royal palaces adorned with images of active women from classical mythology. This new valorization of women was an important part of the process by which a royal mistress became imaginable as a political adviser. However, Anne left no program of self-representation, no collection of visual or textual references to particular figures, by means of which she may have controlled her image. She enacted her role as an open secret, and it was accepted as such by the ambassadors who dealt with her, but she did not express her role through an aesthetic program. Diane's renown, in contrast, rests in part on wide-ranging representations that drew on the imagery of Diana the huntress. In what follows, then, we rely heavily on a different type of evidence than that which we used in chapters 1 and 2. Like Anne, Diane is mentioned in ambassador reports, although not with anything like the same frequency. As we will see, Henri II consulted her after each of his dealings, but she tended not to make herself as available as Anne had. Like Anne, she is almost absent from chronicles. In contrast with Anne, however, a rich trove of sources documents the ways in which she was visually represented. We begin by discussing the historical context within which Diane rose to prominence. We then turn to an examination of how she was represented and how she represented herself.

"NOTHING UNSEEMLY"

Diane is assumed to have been born in 1499 to a family tracing its ancestors to the twelfth-century Dauphiné.[15] Daughter of Jean de Poitiers, Seigneur de Saint Vallier, and Jeanne de Batarnay, she is often said to have been raised by Anne of France, although no record of this exists.[16] This Anne, later Duchess of Bourbon, served as regent for her younger brother, King Charles VIII, and a number of young women who became politically powerful, including Marguerite of Austria, Louise of Savoy, and Philippa of Guelders, resided at different times at her court. At fifteen, Diane was married to the fifty-five-year-old Louis de Brézé, seigneur of Anet, grand seneschal and later governor of Normandy. That their wedding was celebrated in the hôtel of the Bourbons in Paris and attended by King François I and Queen Claude attests to the couple's lofty position.[17] They had two daughters: Françoise, who would marry Robert IV de La Marck, was born in 1518, and Louise, who would marry Claude of Lorraine, Duke of Aumale, may have been a few years younger. Diane did not spend all of her time at Anet but also served in the household of Louise of Savoy, in whose accounts for 1515 she is mentioned under "Dames et demoiselles," earning 35 livres; in accounts for 1522 (the only others available), she receives 300.[18]

In 1524 Diane's father, Jean de Poitiers, was sentenced to death for conspiring with the rebellious connétable Charles of Bourbon, who had been married to Anne of France's daughter, Suzanne, heir to the Bourbon territories. After Suzanne's death, Louise of Savoy claimed these territories, and the outraged Charles allied with Emperor Charles V and fled, with the support of Jean de Poitiers.[19] Diane, coached by her father, begged the queen mother to intervene with the king to spare him, while her husband appealed to François I directly.[20] The interventions were successful. However, they spawned the persistent legend that Diane offered her "virtue" to the king in exchange for her father's life. The story of Diane's bargain has been disputed by historians since the nineteenth century, on the ground that it was propagated by Protestants, who hated her; that her husband the seneschal would not have tolerated his wife's adultery; and that Diane was a virtuous woman who would never have done such a thing.[21] In assessing the legend's probability, it is important to distinguish among several different rumors purporting a relationship between Diane and the king. The first was floated during Diane's lifetime. An entry in the journal of the anonymous Bourgeois of Paris mentions a rumor that the actual reason for Jean de Poitiers's plight was that he had threatened to kill the king for having raped ("violée") one of his daughters.[22] A second version, not necessarily connected to Diane's plea on her father's behalf, is the simple assertion that she had had a liaison with François I. This is recorded by Contarini in 1552.[23] A third version, that she sold her matronly chastity, was circulated by, among others, Brantôme, who claims that he had heard that a certain young woman had saved her father who was already on the scaffold when the news of his pardon came.[24] Descending, the father thanked his daughter's "bon con," which had saved him. This version, then, has no written history until Brantôme, and there is no particular reason to believe it, although, as is often the case with Brantôme, we cannot know whether the oral history on which he relied was accurate, pure fantasy, or some of both. The early defenses of Diane against Brantôme were put forth on the basis of her impeccable reputation, an approach that modern historians would not find convincing in itself, particularly given the circumstances. After all, a young woman of impeccable reputation might very well sell herself to save her father. But there is no real evidence.

As for Diane's first meeting with her prince, it was probably just after the return of the boy from his imprisonment in Spain, at the coronation or one of the entries for Queen Eleonore.[25] Henri's devotion to a woman twenty years his senior is often attributed to his traumatic imprisonment. This early misery is assumed to be one of the reasons for a lack of love toward his father. As we saw in the previous chapter, several sources comment on the tense father-son relationship. A legend holding that the king approved Diane as a mentor for the sad boy derives from "additions" by historian Jean Le Laboureur (1623–1675) to the memoirs of Michel de Castelnau (1520–1592), a soldier and ambassador to the English court. Le Laboureur, adding a section on the person and death of Henri II, writes that when François I "expressed to [Diane] his displeasure at the lack of vivacity Prince Henri showed, she told [the king] that [Henri] needed to fall in love and that she wanted to make [Henri] her galant. The king, who shared his affection between her and the Duchess of Étampes, consented; but although the Court lived extremely licentiously at that time, it appears that nothing unseemly took place between [Diane and Henri]."[26] Closer to the event, the first eyewitness reports of the relationship from the Venetian ambassador to the French court, Marino Cavalli, support Le Laboureur, also denying any physical relationship between the two. Describing the twenty-eight-year-old dauphin, Cavalli writes: "He is not at all a womanizer; his own wife was sufficient; for conversation, he seeks that of [Diana], who is 48 years old. He has a genuine tenderness for her; but it is said that there is nothing lascivious in it and that this affection is like that between a mother and son; it is held that this lady has undertaken to instruct, correct and counsel M. le Dauphin, and to push him to all action worthy of him."[27]

Whatever the exact nature of the relationship, Diane, widowed in 1531, was central to Henri's family life, attending not only to the prince but also to the wife to whom Cavalli refers, Catherine de Médicis. The 1533 marriage between the young pair was arranged by François I and Pope Clement VII, Catherine's ward and great-uncle, to seal an alliance to further mutual goals against the emperor.[28] There had been opposition to this alliance at the French court, the Médicis being regarded as upstarts by some. But Diane was devoted to the bride, possibly because they were closely related: Diane, like Catherine, descended from the La Tour d'Auvergne family.[29] Also important for Diane, one imagines, was that the young Catherine, born in 1519, was malleable, as a second wife might not be. Therefore Diane took care to see that the couple reproduce to avoid Catherine's being sent back to Italy. Contarini reports that she often sent Henri to sleep with his wife.[30]

Little is known about Diane's presence at court during the life of François I. As discussed in the previous chapter, ambassador letters place her in the dauphin's faction, but no other records of her there exist. As Susan Broomhall notes, "the bulk of Diane's extant letters . . . concern the period of her acknowledged political influence, during the reign of Henri II from 1547 to 1559," with nothing from the years immediately before.[31] However, her presence during the reign of Henri II is reasonably well documented and appears to have been controversial. That Montmorency, the Guise brothers, and Diane were perceived to be running the government did not win them universal approval. Writes Gaspard de Saulx-Tavannes, "King Henri had the same weaknesses as his predecessor, a feeble mind, and it could be said that the reign was not his but the connétable's, Madame de Valentinois's, and Monsieur de Guise's."[32]

And yet the trio was never harmonious, even from the beginning. St. Mauris, writing on 10 August 1547, ignores Diane while noting the bad blood between the men: "The Constable is all powerful in this Court at present but there is bitter jealousy on the part of the Guises, who bear secret enmity to him, and many obstacles are thrown in the Constable's way."[33] But contemporaries agree that from the beginning of the reign, Diane allied with the Guises.[34] Her son-in-law, the third Guise son, Claude, is reported by Saulx-Tavannes to have had the foresight still during the reign of François I to "covertly win over Diane de Poitiers by proposing a marriage between her older daughter and [his son Claude] Monsieur d'Aumale." The marriage between Louise de Brézé and Claude had taken place in 1546.[35]

Indeed, the reign began with a proxy duel between the Guises and Diane, on the one hand, and Montmorency, on the other, played out in the single combat between Guy Chabot, baron de Jarnac, and François de Vivonne, seigneur de la Châtaigneraie. The hatred between the young men had resulted from an insulting comment that Châtaigneraie allegedly made about Jarnac, an insinuation that there was something indecent about the relationship between Jarnac and his stepmother. Jarnac "gave him the lie" (at least according to some versions of the story), a response normally requiring a duel. Châtaigneraie, older and more experienced, was heavily favored to prevail.[36] But Jarnac was married to the Duchess of Étampes's sister Louise, and François I refused to permit a duel in which Anne's relative was sure to be killed. When Henri II ascended the throne, however, the challenge was renewed, historian Desgardins hypothesizing that the intention was to impose another form of "persecution against the Duchess of Étampes."[37] The new king and Diane of course supported Châtaigneraie, and, according to the chronicler Jacques-Auguste de Thou, the Guises supported him as well, because of the king. Montmorency, in contrast, De Thou stresses, was behind Jarnac but could not show it, afraid of offending the king. He therefore enlisted Charles de Gouffier de Boisy, grand écuyer, to declare himself for Jarnac.[38]

To the amazement of all, on 10 July 1547, before an enormous crowd, the underdog Jarnac defeated his boastful opponent with a maneuver that has become known as the "coup de Jarnac," a surprise slice of the sword, in this case, to the back of Châtaigneraie's leg. The cut severed a tendon, rendering Châtaigneraie immobile. The wound was not necessarily fatal, but, refusing to surrender, Châtaigneraie bled to death.[39] De Thou concludes the entry with these ominous words: "It was noticed that the end of [Henri II's] reign corresponded only too justly to its bloody beginnings. He had failed in his duty, authorizing a real and serious combat, and the Heavens saw to it that he would be killed himself in a joust amidst applause and public entertainment."[40]

Throughout Henri II's reign, Montmorency and the Guises would vie to control policy toward war against the English and the emperor. Montmorency promoted peace, as he always had, in contrast with the bellicose Guises, whose goal was "to deal with the German princes and cities, in

order to directly attack the emperor in the kingdom of Naples and the Milanais."[41] Their rivalry would come to a head with the defeat of the French
army under the connétable by the combined English and imperial forces
along with the connétable's capture at the disastrous battle of Saint Quentin, in Picardy, as we will see.[42]

The story of Diane's tenure is, to a large exent, one of how she managed
these colleagues. Alvarotti reports in early 1548 that while Charles of Guise
was traveling in Italy drumming up support for war against the emperor,
Montmorency tried first to distance François of Guise from the court so
as to have unobstructed access to the king.[43] Diane, however, objected. In
response to this failure, Montmorency had the king sign a letter requiring
Charles of Guise to remain in Rome. Furious, Diane protested to the king,
who in turn called in Montmorency to reproach him. Despite the years of
favoring Montmorency while Anne did everything possible to keep him
from returning to court, Diane appears to have disliked him as bitterly
as her predecessor had. Once the new king had reestablished Montmorency as connétable and principal adviser, she found him to be as much of
a barrier as had Anne. Montmorency, for his part, perhaps made wary by
his experience with Anne, did his best to drive a wedge between Diane and
the king, his intrigue shading into the burlesque, as an anecdote recounted
by Contarini reveals.

> [Montmorency and Diane] are enemies to the king's great displea-
> sure. The enmity began years ago, although it only became very
> open last year when Madama realized that the connétable had
> plotted to have the king fall in love with a governess of the little
> queen of Scotland, a lovely lady, and thereby take his love away
> from her; and as it went, the governess became pregnant by the
> king; which bothered Madama so much that she lamented greatly,
> and the king excused himself, and for a long time Diane and the
> connétable did not speak. Finally at the insistence of the king they
> made up, but in fact they still hate each other as much as ever, so
> much that there are now two factions at court.[44]

Although we have only Contarini's word for Montmorency's scheming, as
we saw earlier, Henri II did indeed have a child with Janet Fleming.

Diane's political activity, as Susan Broomhall's analysis of the duchess's
correspondence demonstrates, was extensive, as was her involvement, from
a distance, in the king's wars.[45] In contrast with Anne, she was powerful

in her own right before her tenure as official royal mistress because she was the widow of the seneschal of Normandy. Nonetheless, Diane's own letters and ambassadors' reports about her confirm a difference between her and Anne's styles, Diane's appearing more deliberately equivocal. Her political approach is reflected, as we detail at the end of this chapter, in her multilayered visual self-representations. However, we first consider in the following section how her position was imagined by contemporaries, focusing in particular on her place in some royal entries, which, celebrating the ascension of Henri II and his queen, Catherine, also included the political royal mistress, in veiled but unmistakable terms.

DIANE AND DIANA

The status of Diane's political activity as an open secret seems more carefully constructed than Anne's, the nature of her relationship with the king remaining a mystery to this day. As we have noted, contemporaries remarked on the age difference, and an aura surrounded her personal appearance, which she was said to have preserved through the aid of potable gold and other drugs. Brantôme reports that at sixty-six she looked just as she always had, her skin very white although she wore no makeup.[46] Her youthful appearance cannot be confirmed, but an examination of her hair by Joel Poupon and Philippe Charlier revealed that it contained five hundred times the normal level of gold. They explain that very white skin and teeth and fragile hair and bones are effects of chronic gold poisoning.[47] Even beyond her ingestion of potable gold, Diane's enigmatic ways continue to fascinate, her bizarrely equivocal self-representation meriting attention.

We have seen that during the 1530s the atmosphere of the royal court was transformed by artistic programs that sexualized and feminized some of its spaces. Simply standing in rooms decorated with gorgeously colored, erotically posed men and women must have directed the attention of at least some courtiers to themselves as sexual creatures. Such awareness must have been heightened by the flagrantly obvious codpieces—visible even in portraits of the austere Henri II himself—that remained popular until the last decades of the sixteenth century.[48] Initially these were patches intended to cover the "indecent" male parts left too exposed by mid-fifteenth-century short tunics over tights, but by the early sixteenth century men of the court sported enormous protuberances just beneath their short jackets.

Still, it was not as if women were suddenly free to indulge openly in affairs. Their sexual behavior remained subject to stringent codes. Prostitutes were prostitutes; courtly ladies were another category, required to maintain an appearance of decency. Brantôme jokes about the double bind created by the competing discourses, relating the story of a "great lady" who told some of her beautiful friends that God had done her a favor in making her ugly, because had she been beautiful, she would have been a whore, just like they were. His wry conclusion: only beautiful, chaste women are worthy of praise.[49] Others, however, approached the paradox seriously, as a problem of representation that required women to "speak sex and display sexuality—without losing 'honor,'" or, in the words of Claude Chappuys, librarian and chamberlain to the king, to be "nymphs in body, goddesses in manner."[50] The neo-Platonist Castiglione in book 3 of *The Courtier* offers counsel to ladies for maintaining this delicate balance:[51]

> The lady who is at Court should properly have, before all else, a certain pleasing affability whereby she will know how to entertain graciously every kind of man with charming and honest conversation, suited to the time and the place and the rank of the person with whom she is talking. And her serene and modest behaviour, and the candour that ought to inform all her actions, should be accompanied by a quick and vivacious spirit by which she shows herself free from boorishness; but with such a virtuous manner that she makes herself thought no less chaste, prudent and benign than she is pleasing, witty and discreet.

That narrator admits that the courtly lady is forced to "observe a certain difficult mean, composed as it were of contrasting qualities."[52]

Such a double bind, of course, was nothing new. What was different was that from the 1530s court women found new ways to represent and manage it, and that this sort of reconciliation was particularly important for the royal mistress, who more than any other required a means of exuding a sort of chastity that was not literally sexual chastity but rather strength or independence and power. Christian chastity of the sort offered by female saints, in other words, was not a viable option. The huntress, in contrast, was associated with chastity, but no one would have dared test her, and she offered women a way to manage the dichotomous feminine imagery.[53] We have seen that even had Anne been interested in availing herself of Diana imagery, she could not easily have done so. Diane, however, took advantage of the figure for her self-representation. As Françoise Bardon has noted, Diana was a multivalently meaningful figure who "existed before Diane [de Poitiers]—timid, still associated with the forest, even in her artifices." But Diana also embodied several potentially contradictory qualities, supplying raw material for enacting a well-developed, complex character. Bardon observes that the "great innovation that the artists of Fontainebleau bring to the theme of Diana is this: to an erudite and ancient tradition they will substitute a decorative and modern esthetic. At Fontainebleau, the theme comes to life, it enters into history, in the city, it becomes French. We sense that Diane of Anet could not have existed without this renovation—this passage from erudite mythology into living mythology."[54]

Diane's assumption of the aura of Diana was a collaborative production, carried out by her audiences and herself, as we can see in the royal entries with which Henri II's reign began. During the fourteenth century, northern Europeans had begun to celebrate the accession of a new king (or queen) with spectacular entries, harking back to the classical age, into the cities of the realm.[55] Although early on these affairs had been relatively uncomplicated processions directed by city dignitaries to offer gifts to the new ruler, who in return confirmed their privileges, they became increasingly magnificent, especially near the end of the fifteenth century.[56] In addition to parades of civic dignitaries to welcome the prince and splendid royal processions, the guilds began to construct pageants where plays were performed. Especially pertinent to our discussion, in France the trend in the direction of increasingly elaborate productions also saw a growing tendency toward mythological themes. Poet Maurice Scève's illustrated official description of the entry of Henri II and Catherine into Lyon in 1549 demonstrates a yet more advanced state in the development of the royal mistress, with the citizens of Lyon actively collaborating with the king to honor her, right in front of the queen.[57] One of the many entertainments offered during the entry was a play featuring Diana the huntress. An enclosed field decorated with tufts and trees descending from a chateau offered a space for the play. As the king approaches the field, he is greeted first by stags and does accompanied by the sound of horns. Suddenly, the huntress and her companion nymphs appear, the lower parts of their legs visible beneath their rich clothing. The huntress approaches the king to present him with a humble lion, representing Lyon, and a poem. During the queen's entrance the same Diana made a similar presentation.[58]

Ordinary townspeople presumably watched the scene simply as a pleasant tale, and Scève draws no attention to the connection between the

huntress of the play and the king's mistress, as we would expect, omitting
any mention of the real Diane.[59] In fact, "Diana the chaste / the white
moon" was associated early in France with queens, notably with Eleonore
in 1533 during her entry into Rouen, writes Edith Karagiannis-Mazeaud.[60]
Karagiannis-Mazeaud, citing Lecoq, also notes that in the entry of Louis
XII's second queen, Mary of England, Diana represented France, alongside Phebus, representing the king, and the Stella maris, representing
Queen Mary herself.[61] Theoretically, then, Queen Catherine might have
been honored by the Diana play. So much the better that the meaning be
equivocal. However, those closely associated with the royal court could
not have missed the reference. In his description of the event, the ambassador of the Duke of Mantova, Giorgio Conegrani, records the king and
"Madama la gran Seniscialla" slipping off to take a ride in a gondola on
the river together. For those in the know, the connection would have been
obvious.[62] Brantôme remarks in his discussion of the festival that the play
of Diana and her nymphs was much appreciated by the king and also by
Diane de Poitiers, who forever afterward loved the Lyonnais.[63]

   This entry, with its homage to Diane under the figure of the huntress
Diana, reproduces the place that the official royal mistress now held in
the social imaginary. Central to the royal entourage, Diane's status as official royal mistress, like Anne's before her, was both perfectly evident and
obscured, an open secret. She lived in plain sight at court, like an actress
playing at Diana peacefully cavorting with the nymphs in a play that
could be understood in multiple ways. To finish this section we would like
to explore a few points about Diane's image. The topic has already been
expertly researched.[64] However, we would like to emphasize the image's
theatricality: the ways in which Diane drew on its different aspects to enact
different roles, public and private, and the consciousness of contemporaries of Anet as a theater in which Diane carried this out.

   Diane's authority was intertwined with that of the king, with whom
she shared everything from court entertainment to politics, and yet she
retained a status (mother? lover?) so ambiguous that to this day historians
disagree about it. However, we suggest that the question that fascinated
nineteenth-century historians (did they or did they not?) is beside the
point. The salient issue is Diane's flagrant but deliberately opaque centrality to every aspect of the king's life, the carefully constructed "open secret"
of her position. Although the images most closely associated with Diane—
her widow's colors of black and white and her moon associated with the
huntress Diana—were also central to Henri II's personal imagery, for

which reason it has been proposed that the king adopted them to demonstrate his love for Diane. Thierry Crépin-Leblond shows that their shared half-crescent moon can be traced to Valois heraldry and imperial imagery.[65] Moreover, Henri II's well-known insignia of an H with two interlocking Ds can also be read, theoretically, as an H with two Cs (standing for Catherine), although it should be noted that contemporaries seem to have favored the former interpretation. Among other descriptions, we find in Scève's book of the entry into Lyon details of an obelisk in the shape of a pyramid past which the procession marched. One of the obelisk's decorations was the "figure [chiffre] of the said Seigneur, which are two Ds and Hs interlaced and crowned."[66] Still, the very essence of the symbolism is that it was always ambiguous, susceptible to conflicting interpretations. Diane was both faithful widow and the king's mistress, lady of Anet and king's adviser. It depended on the audience.

Similar was Henri and Diane's use of Amadis of Gaul literature. François I, presumably having encountered the romance in Spain, commissioned Nicolas d'Herberay des Essars to compose a translation of the cycle, which then contained eight books. Essars dedicated book 1 of his work to Charles of Angoulême in 1540 and the seven subsequent books to military leaders. But the romance took a different turn, writes Marian Rothstein, when Jacques Gohory, composer of book 11, dedicated his own work to Diane.[67] Lauding Diane's attachment to the "Lucine deity" by which she attracts all the best spirits to her, Gohory explains that he is addressing his book with the heroine he has created, Diane de Guindaye, to Diane. The adventures of Agesilan, descendant of the hero Amadis of Gaul, who pursues the beautiful Diane de Guindaye, mirror those of the original hero and heroine, Amadis and Oriana, the perfect knight and his lovely lady. As Rosana Gorris Camos writes, "A profound affinity exists between [Gohory's] reading of Diana and the incarnation of the myth in a strange and contradictory historical person surrounded by legends, austere and inaccessible, a lady who inspired reverence by her obvious fidelity to the memory of her husband but at the same time imposed the 'deference of an Amadis' on her lover."[68]

As for Anet, contemporary poets "evoked the splendor that impressed all of their contemporaries and contributed to the poetic creation of the grand mansion, to the true creation of the myth of Anet." By the time of the king's death, Anet had become as much topos in court celebration as a real place, writes Jean Balsamo.[69] Diana the huntress reigned there. As we have seen, Cellini's nymph of Fontainebleau, now imagined as Diana with her stag, finally made its way to Anet after the death of François I. Under the renovations of royal architect Philibert de l'Orme, the bronze relief was mounted over the chateau's principal portal, which bears the date 1552.[70] In addition, the magnificent white marble Diane d'Anet, now at the Louvre, once graced a large fountain at the chateau.

A long debate surrounds the relationship between the many representations of Diana the huntress and Diane de Poitiers. Are any of the many portrayals of the goddess from Diane's lifetime actually portraits of her? Patricia Zalamea writes that excepting "the Diane of Anet fountain sculpture and a medal that shows Diane de Poitiers on the obverse and an image of Diana trampling Cupid on the reverse, few of the presumed depictions of Diane as Diana can be firmly connected to her. None of the so-called mythological portraits of Diane de Poitiers are documented."[71] We do not wish to enter the complex discussion of whether any of the many images associated with Diane actually represent her features—that is, resemble the real human being. Our point is simply that the huntress, with her rich and often contradictory interpretations, offered women of the court a model for self-representation. A woman named Diane was particularly well placed to inspire the association.

DIANE AS POLITICAL ACTOR

What do politics look like when carried out by such an equivocal actor? Diane's political activity was criticized by some, overtly acknowledged by a select few, and discreetly ignored by most. Historian Father Jean Lestocquoy refers to this game of ignoring while acknowledging, writing that the papal nuncio ordinarily spoke of the king's "favorite" with "a thoroughly diplomatic politeness," adding that had a nuncio not presented himself to the royal mistress he quickly would have become persona non grata and remained without influence.[72]

Similar, Contarini reports a 1551 conversation among courtiers about whether Henri II loved Montmorency or Diane better. The courtiers' answer, the ambassador recounts, was Diane.[73] Why? The king, they concluded, loved the connétable because he was useful, whereas he loved Diane for herself alone, "per vero amore." To be loved for oneself alone, a reflection of the Ciceronian ideal of true friendship as disinterested, seems flattering to Diane on the one hand. On the other, the pronouncement is bewildering. Contarini explains that Diane had counseled the king when he was dauphin, even lending him money. However, when he became king, she no longer took part in state affairs, although he spent an hour and a half with her each evening after dinner discussing everything that had happened that day. If Diane was receiving daily ninety-minute briefings on what was going on in the royal council (and, presumably, reacting to the briefing), surely she was taking part in state affairs, as an adviser, and surely she was as useful to him in this capacity as the connétable was and as she herself had been earlier, when she presided over his transformation from awkward youth into prince. And surely the courtiers knew this.

One example of Diane's political participation will clarify her process. Despite the Treaty of Crépy in 1544, followed by the Treaty of Ardres on 7 June 1546, temporarily halting hostilities with the English, Henri II's reign, like his father's, was marked to the end by warfare. Henri II declared war against Charles V in 1551, allying with German Protestant princes with the 1552 Treaty of Chambord.[74] But if Henri II was buoyed by the successful siege of Metz, the French army's 1553 invasion of Tuscany was not successful. Joining with the Sienese against the Florentines, led by Cosimo de Médicis and Charles V, the French and their allies were defeated at the battle of Marciano in August 1554.[75] Charles V abdicated from various parts of his empire during 1555–56, dividing the empire into the Spanish Empire, including the Netherlands, which he ceded to his son Philip II of Spain, and the Holy Roman Empire, which he ceded to his brother Ferdinand I.[76] From then on Henri II's attention turned to the Netherlands. His army under Montmorency was defeated at Saint Quentin in 1557, Montmorency himself taken prisoner.[77] In that same year, the English retook Calais. The Guises, indefatigable and normally successful men of war, declared themselves ready to continue the fight.[78] Henri II nonetheless, to the Guises' fury, signed the Peace of Cateau-Cambrésis with Queen Elizabeth on 2 April 1559 and with Philip II on 3 April, thereby renouncing any claim to Italian lands.[79] To seal the accord, Philip II would marry Henri II's daughter, Elisabeth of Valois. We will return to this marriage.

The immediate lead-up to the Peace of Cateau-Cambrésis offers a particularly clear glimpse of Diane's political work. Always the peacemaker, Montmorency, from his prison, had urged the king to seek an accord, to which, in at least one example, Diane and Henri II replied in a joint letter. This, as Broomhall remarks, "rendered the intertwined political and emotional relationship of Henri and Diane entirely explicit through both its material and textual representation."[80] An examination of the manuscript shows that in the first lines of the letter, Diane sends her thanks to the connétable for a recent missive; the king then takes up the pen, in mid-sentence, to thank him for detailed news on the peace negotiations already under way; Diane, for her part, finishes the letter, once again taking up the pen in mid-sentence. They both sign the letter in their own hand. "That Montmorency should be the recipient of the only known example of this material demonstration of power may be significant: he was widely understood to be Diane's greatest rival for the affection and influence of the King at this period," writes Broomhall.[81] Although Diane had shifted support from the Guises, she was making clear to Montmorency that her words and the king's were interlaced, distinguishable but inextricably connected.

Still, the king had not yet determined to seek peace. A dispatch by Venetian ambassador Giovanni Michiel sheds further light on Diane's involvement in the king's final decision. The connétable had already been released from captivity when Michiel wrote on 15 November 1558 that it was true that

> all persons think it improbable that the King will in any way alter his first conditions, which are moreover openly blamed by many persons, and more especially by the favourers and dependents of the Guise family, as dishonourable; but I am nevertheless told on the best authority, that the Constable having lately written an autograph letter to his Majesty, and another, in accordance with it, to the Duchess of Valentinois, knowing what her influence can effect with the King, and above all at present, when there is an open rupture and enmity between her and [Charles] Cardinal of Lorraine, she being so united with the Constable that they are one and the same thing, the Duke de Guise is therefore much afraid lest the King's intense desire for the agreement, he being thus persuaded by the Duchess, and also by the Constable, on the two occasions when he came hither, will cause his Majesty at any rate to accept the conditions of King Philip.[82]

Turning a still sharper lens on Diane, Cardinal Trivultio writes on 16 November that she had gone out riding after hunting with the king, who was still determined not to settle. But when the pair returned, Henri II had changed his mind, and the hope of peace had been revived.[83] Diane, like Henri II, had received letters from Montmorency, and, after long discussion, she had persuaded the king of the wisdom of seeking peace.[84] One would like to know how the Guises responded to Diane's undermining of their plans. Happily, the reaction of Queen Catherine, also in favor of maintaining a French interest in Italy, was recorded by Giulio Alvarotti. The evening of the king's resolution, Diane entered the chamber of the queen and found her engrossed in a book. When Diane asked what she was reading, the queen replied that it was a book about the kingdom and that she was finding that in every period scurrilous women ("donne putane") had been behind kings' decisions.[85]

It is a sad irony that this peace, which ended years of strife between France and the empire, should have been the indirect cause of the king's premature death. The wedding between Philip II and the king and queen's daughter Elisabeth, stipulated in the Peace of Cateau-Cambrésis, was scheduled for 4 July 1559, but it was preceded by festivities, including a joust at the Hôtel des Tournelles on the Place des Vosges on 30 June. As he competed, the king received splinters just above his right eye from the shattered lance of an opponent. Although he seemed initially to be on the road to recovery, on 4 July blood poisoning set in, and he died on 10 July. Diane was not admitted to his room during the entire time of his agony, a preview of her fate at the hands of Queen Catherine.[86]

Although both Anne and Diane were acknowledged as genuine political players by court faction members, officers, and ambassadors, their *modi operandi* were different. Each performed different characters depending on the audience. Diane, however, seems to have invested major effort in cultivating a personal image that was at once coherent and multivalent, permitting conflicting interpretations, which she apparently performed very effectively. Encouraging identification with the attributes of a figure popular before her birth, she defined visually and aesthetically the role of official royal mistress beyond anything that Anne had attempted.

CONCLUSION

Two versions of power, which we might imagine as leonine and vulpine, had existed throughout the Middle Ages in varying relationships. Early versions of the duality, say, Marie de France's fables or the stories of Renard, tended to valorize the lion while admitting, sometimes with admiration, the fox's skill. A number of popular binaries were negotiated through this pair: the lion was associated with the masculine, the sun, and the king (the Valois emblem was a sun), and the fox with the feminine, the moon, and the mistress. Traditionally, the king and queen together symbolized harmony, the uniting of transparent strength and gentle mercy, as we see in coronation ritual and royal entries. But during the course of the sixteenth century this duality became inadequate to represent kingly power. As the culture of dissimulation developed, the king's force came to be doubled by the mistress's cleverness; to put it another way, the sun that represented the king remained, but it was supplemented by a screen or mask that both revealed and concealed the "truth" that royal power depended on dissimulation. As Machiavelli so famously noted, rendering positive what Cicero had deemed negative, "The lion cannot protect himself from traps, and the fox cannot defend himself from wolves. One must therefore be a fox to recognize traps, and a lion to frighten wolves."[87]

We conclude this chapter by returning to the quotation with which we began, Brantôme's reflection on a quatrain mocking Henri II for being governed by Diane, telling him that he is nothing but wax—that is, soft and susceptible to the impressions of others. In typical Brantôme fashion, the memoirist pretends to defend Henri II by praising Diane's great generosity: Who would not listen to her? Along the way he casually links Diane to Melusine, mentioning that both descended from the great and ancient House of Poitiers and Lusignan. Brantôme does not expand on the similarities between these cousins, but Melusine's great claim to fame was her hidden life, her weekly transformation into a serpent from the waist down. The secret was discovered one day by her husband spying on her in her bath. But although he was shocked, he initially remained silent, and life continued as normal. It was only when one evening in a bad moment he exposed his wife's secret to a group of guests that their accommodation came to an end. As soon it was articulated, the arrangement became public and had to be dealt with. Outed, Melusine leaped to the windowsill and flew off into the night.

Like her famous relative, Diane expended an enormous amount of energy in concealing what was obvious to all. She, the king, and the queen, along with all the courtiers, were complicit in the secret, remaining silent about their arrangement, at least in public. Unlike her famous relative, her open secret held together throughout her lifetime. As long as no one spoke of it, all was well, all was "honorable."

CHAPTER 4

Gabrielle d'Estrées

Never the Twain Shall Meet

[I] made it clear to [Henri IV] that he would expose France to everything that he wanted to avoid, and, worse, that legitimating the children that he had had with [Gabrielle d'Estrées] would mean that the elder, incontestably born from a double adultery, would be inferior to the second, who had only the shame of a single adultery; and that both [would be inferior] to those whom his mistress would later have after becoming his legitimate wife; which, because they would never be able to establish their estate, could not fail to become an endless source of conflict and war.

—MAXIMILIEN DE BÉTHUNE, duc de Sully, *Oeconomies*

Diane's tenure at the royal court ended with Henri II's sudden death. In a letter of 12 July 1559, Venetian ambassador Giovanni Michiel describes the government shake-up following the king's demise. Among the many changes, he notes, the new king, François II, had informed Diane de Poitiers that she was from then on "to remain in retirement, and live as far from the Court as possible, enjoying however all her property and revenues in security, without fear of molestation."[1]

But by 1559 the role of political royal mistress was established in the French social imaginary, even though it would lie dormant until assumed in 1591 by Gabrielle d'Estrées (1573–1599), mistress of King Henri IV (r. 1589–1610). None of the three kings who followed Henri II, his sons François II (r. 1559–60), Charles IX (r. 1559–74), or Henri III (r. 1574–89), was in a position to raise a mistress to power. François II, fifteen when he assumed his one-year reign, was controlled by the Guises, relatives of his young wife, the future Mary, Queen of Scots.[2] The young king's "faculties were such," writes Stuart Carroll, that although he was no longer a minor, "regency was a possibility." However, Queen Catherine, an obvious choice for regent, ceded to the Guises, sharing their priorities: high on "conquest in Italy," low on "religious persecution."[3] In any case, one imagines that the Guises would not have tolerated a powerful mistress, even if the little king had lived long enough to try to install one.

François II's successor, Charles IX, married to Elisabeth of Austria in 1570, possessed at least one mistress, Marie Touchet.[4] But only ten at his ascension, he relied on Queen Catherine, his regent, continuing to do so after his majority as he struggled to contain the bloody Religious Wars, which, beginning in 1562, would rage intermittently until 1594. Under different circumstances, Marie might have become a powerful political mistress; later in life, at least, she displayed an aptitude for ruse, getting her own daughter Henriette de Balzac d'Entragues set up as the mistress of Henri IV following the death of his beloved Gabrielle d'Estrées, the subject of this chapter. When Marie's daughter caught the eye of Henri IV, Marie and her husband "sold" the king their daughter's "virtue." Henri IV's exasperated superintendent of finances, Maximilien de Béthune, Marquis of Rosny and later Duke of Sully (1560–1641), recounts that Henriette was first granted 1,000 écus but then claimed to be unable to find a private spot in which to consummate the relationship, because her parents watched her so closely. Money was not enough for the Balzac d'Entragues: in addition, they requested that the king write a letter promising to marry Henriette, which he did. However, he added that the wedding would take place only after the birth of a son.[5] Henriette's son was stillborn, and the king married Tuscan princess Marie de Médicis.[6] Marie Touchet, then, seems to have grown into a person capable of intrigue, but, as a young woman up against Catherine, she could not have competed.

As for Henri III, none of his mistresses was powerful. He selected his own bride, Louise of Lorraine or Vaudémont, after which the queen mother reasserted her primacy. Even chroniclers referred to Catherine as the "queen" and Louise as the "young queen," and Brantôme remarks that neither Henri III nor his mother liked women of their court who stuck their minds or noses into state affairs.[7]

The official royal mistress reappears under Henri of Navarre, Henri IV of France, whose situation lent itself to the installation of one. After the heirless Henri III's premature death at the hands of an extremist Catholic assassin in August 1589, the Valois throne passed to the House of Bourbon, headed by Protestant leader Henri of Navarre.[8] But in the midst of the Religious Wars, the Catholics did not recognize his claim. Although Henri of Navarre was the closest male relative to Henri II, the men were only indirectly related, and Henri IV was threatened by pretenders throughout his reign.[9] In August 1589 he held much of the south and west of the kingdom, while the ultraconservative Catholic League, originally formed in 1576 by Henri I, Duke of Guise (assassinated in 1588, Duke Henri was the son of Duke François, previously mentioned as nemesis of the Connétable Montmorency under King Henri II), held the north and east. September 1589 found him attempting to wrest Normandy from the league. Defeating their army under Charles of Mayenne, brother of Henri I of Guise, in the battle of Arques, he continued on through Normandy. Still, his claim to the throne meant nothing without overwhelmingly Catholic Paris, and taking the city seemed impossible. Henri of Navarre, or Henri IV, therefore, was a king without a royal court.

In the atmosphere of constantly looming betrayal—the king avoided numerous assassination attempts, receiving a superficial cut on the upper lip from the knife of would-be killer Jean Chastel, a young Jesuit, in 1594—a loyal female companion would have seemed especially desirable.[10] No woman close to the king fit the description. Although married since 1572 to a French queen, Marguerite, daughter of Henri II and Catherine, he did not live with her, for a number of reasons; the most important was a history of mistrust dating back to the Saint Bartholomew's Day Massacre of 1572, when their wedding catalyzed a series of rampages that spread from Paris throughout the kingdom. Marguerite writes in her memoirs that she had no idea what was happening in the first days of violent chaos after her marriage, and, although a devout Catholic, she initially supported her husband.[11] However, her relationship with him complicated those with her family, particularly with her brother Henri III.[12] The political situation in France pulled the couple in directions too distant for Marguerite to be a reliable companion. After breaking and reconciling with Henri of Navarre, she eventually allied with the Guises to plot against both him and her brother.[13] As for the other women in his family, Henri IV's mother, queen of Navarre Jeanne d'Albret (1528–1572), daughter of Marguerite of Navarre and Henri d'Albret, had been a forceful Protestant activist, raising her son and her daughter, Catherine, to be Huguenots. But she had been dead for years when her son ascended the throne. The king was close to his sister, but he would convert to Catholicism in 1593 to appease the majority of the kingdom, and Catherine's absolute commitment to her religion became a problem between them.

For Henri IV, then, mistresses, of whom he had many, were especially important for moral support and political advice. Like François I, this king was renowned as much as a lover as a warrior. Katherine Crawford describes him as doubly competent, the "'Vert Galant' whose sexual exploits contrasted sharply with his immediate predecessor's sexual incompetence and the 'Hercule Gaulois' who labored tirelessly to restore his war-ravaged kingdom," noting that he "embraced both figures as aspects of his image."[14]

And yet in 1589, overwhelming any desire for female solace was Henri IV's need to produce an heir. In contrast with François I's marriage, Henri IV's to Marguerite was childless; it is not clear how many offspring the Vert Galant produced before the birth of his son César in 1594 with Gabrielle, but none was legitimized. Fatherhood, therefore, assumed the highest priority during the first years of his reign. In addition to fulfilling the practical need for a son to carry on the Bourbon line, Crawford argues that the symbolism was crucial because the painfully obvious lack of a son could be read as a sign that Henri IV was doomed in the way of his Valois predecessors. Because "he had not broken the pattern of royal reproductive failure or allayed the panoply of gender and sexual anxieties attached to it, Henry was susceptible to many of the same charges of weakness created by the reproductive failure that marked the previous reign."[15]

In what follows, we examine the tenure of Henri IV's most renowned partner, Gabrielle d'Estrées, an exemplary mistress and near-queen, to suggest that her career reinforced the formation of the role of official royal mistress in the strongest possible way, along the lines established by Anne and Diane: she would eventually be defined against the queen, demonstrating that the two roles incarnated distinct functions. But we begin by considering the status of the political royal mistress at the time that Henri IV and Gabrielle commenced their liaison. The story of Agnès Sorel enjoyed increased circulation during the 1570s, which, coinciding with the apogee of Queen Catherine's power, suggests that Anne's and Diane's tenures were deliberately not incorporated into the image of the official royal mistress. A different model was being sought. In reaching back to Agnès for authority, those interested in presenting the role in a positive light eschewed the model of political player in favor of one of a sweet-natured blond beauty capable of inspiring a king to greatness.

Our sources for Gabrielle, like those for Anne and Diane, include ambassadors' letters. However, important once again are contemporary and near-contemporary chronicles. The king's attempts to make Gabrielle his queen were a matter of interest for the kingdom, bringing to her an attention that had not been accorded her immediate predecessors.

THE REAPPEARANCE OF THE POLITICAL ROYAL MISTRESS

In his article "Anne de Pisseleu d'Heilly," David Potter draws attention to Montaigne's complaint about the failure of contemporary memoir writers to discuss the king's mistress. In "On Books," Montaigne criticizes the Du Bellay brothers' work for excluding all mention of the exiles from court of Connétable Anne de Montmorency and Admiral de Brion, and ignoring Madame d'Étampes altogether: "Sometimes a man might embellish or hide secret actions," Montaigne concedes, "but to completely hide something that everyone knows to be true, and, particularly, things that have public effects of great significance, is an unpardonable fault."[16] The essayist concludes that anyone looking for serious information on the reign of François I will have to look elsewhere. Montaigne is surely correct. And yet in complaining about Anne's absence, he identifies precisely the mechanism that allowed her to exercise power, the open secret that we have been discussing. She participated in factional politics, dealt with diplomats, and helped make political decisions by managing her activity as an open secret. Guillaume Du Bellay and his brother Jean, allied with Anne for several years, were of course aware of her significance.[17] In remaining silent they respected her secret.

Such silence was widespread. Although, as we have seen, the correspondence of ambassadors and diplomats from this period leaves no doubt as to Anne's centrality to politics, chroniclers ignore her. Indeed, information on her in any source during Montaigne's active years as a writer, roughly 1570–92, was scarce. Neither Jean du Tillet's *La Chronique des Roys de France* (1549), nor the *Journal d'un bourgeois de Paris sous le règne de François Premier*, which covers 1515–36 and circulated in manuscript form, mentions her. In the anonymous *Cronique du roy Françoys*, she appears just once, accompanying Marguerite de Navarre in a cortège for Anne de Montmorency's installation as connétable.[18] In the ten years following her death Diane de Poitiers was equally little mentioned. But beginning with the 1575 publication of the vituperative *Discours merveilleux de la vie, actions et desportemens de Catherine de Médicis* in which Catherine is the pimp, the "maquerelle," who procures Diane for Henri II, Diane entered a period of very negative publicity.[19] How much Montaigne knew about Anne and Diane, or whether he assumed that they deserved praise or blame, then, would have depended on his oral sources and the pamphlets he was reading.

But in contrast with the poverty of information on Anne and the defamation of Diane, during the last decades of the sixteenth century—that is, during the reigns of Charles IX and Henri III—references to Agnès Sorel appear in both imagery and texts. François Avril writes that the crayon portraits in the album collections discussed in the previous chapter "created a fashion, and the memory of Agnès Sorel long continued to haunt imaginations," sparking numerous copies into the seventeenth century. Queen Catherine owned a collection of such crayon portraits containing Agnès's portrait.[20] As for a written tradition, a poem of 1573 addressed to a "Seigneur Sorel" by Pléiade member Jean-Antoine de Baïf proclaims that the honored Sorel "race" had been brightened by the beauty so desired by a great king. Agnès was famous, he writes, for her love and care for King Charles, which resulted in her death. The poem acclaims Agnès for having motivated the love-drunk king to take up arms and drive the English from France. In the end, the king's "virtue flamed up / from the same torch that had extinguished it," that is, from his desire for his mistress. But, the poem continues, with the English defeated in Normandy, the king retired for the winter to Jumièges, where Agnès suddenly appeared with the news of a conspiracy being hatched against him.[21] Although the poem does not directly claim that she had been assassinated for this, its last lines are oddly vague. Perhaps Baïf hesitated to float rumors that might have been awkward in royal circles. He was, after all, a close associate of Queen Catherine, herself intimately involved in religious feuding and palace intrigue.

In any case, although the tradition of Agnès's warning the king that his life was in danger never became an important component of her legend, the Bordelais Bernard de Girard, Seigneur du Haillan (1535–1610), who was named historiographer of France by Charles IX and maintained the role under Henri III and IV, continues the legend of the young woman's arousing the king's sense of valor in the *Histoire générale des roys de France*, first published in 1576. Brantôme follows Haillan's passage nearly word for word in his own collection of stories about the ladies of the French court.[22]

> We have the very pretty example of the Belle Agnès who, seeing King Charles VII so enamored of her and worrying about nothing else but making love to her and seeming soft and cowardly,

not caring about his own kingdom, said to him one day that when she had been just a girl an astrologer had predicted that she would one day be loved and served by one of the most valiant and courageous kings in Christendom, and that when the king had done her the honor of loving her she had thought that he was that valorous king who had been predicted; but seeing him soft with little interest in his affairs she realized that had been wrong and that he was not that courageous king; rather that one was the king of England, who was skilled with arms and was taking many beautiful cities right before the king of France's eyes. Therefore, she said to the king, I'm going to find him, because he is the one the astrologer meant. These words hurt the heart of the king so that he began to cry, and, from then on, taking courage, he chased the English from the kingdom.[23]

No such positive tradition attached to Anne or Diane. Although the continuation of Haillan's history, published first in 1627, and Brantôme's remarks on the love lives of the French kings, composed sometime between 1594 and 1616, refer briefly to them, both were written too late to tell us anything about the manner in which or to what degree these mistresses had been absorbed into the image of the political royal mistress available to Henri IV and Gabrielle. Henri IV was very much aware of Agnès, however. Avril believes that he may have been the force behind the new portraits of her, noting that as crayon copies of her became more distant from the exemplar, they grew ever less attractive until a return to the sources was deemed necessary. At the king's instigation, painters took the Melun diptych as a model, Avril explains, citing two paintings associated with the chateaux of Versailles and Mouchy. In addition, supervising construction of a new portrait gallery of the kings and queens of France in the Louvre, Henri IV may have sent Jacques Bunel to copy the Melun diptych for presentation there, Avril suggests. In any case, the king offered to buy Agnès's portrait from the church for 10,000 livres.[24] Obviously his offer was refused, given the continued presence of the painting in the church. But his son, the dauphin who became Louis XIII, was also sent to marvel at it, according to Jean Héroard, journalist of the dauphin's youth.[25]

Henri IV's interest in Agnès as a model mistress is also noted in the memoir of royal secretary Jules Gassot, according to which the king not only appreciated Agnès's beauty but imagined the young woman and Charles VII's relationship as a gloss on his own love affairs. Gassot describes the king comparing his passion for Gabrielle and other mistresses to Charles VII's for Agnès, writing that "[the king] never got tired of such loves, saying that King Charles VII with the belle Agnès, his love had conquered his kingdom."[26] The genealogy of the official royal mistress that was being constructed, then, was founded on Agnès's absolute devotion and beauty.

WHO WAS GABRIELLE D'ESTRÉES?

In November 1590 Henri IV camped his troops near the castle of Coeuvres near Compiègne, about 100 kilometers northeast of Paris.[27] Coeuvres was the home of the Estrées family, Antoine, Françoise, and their two sons and six daughters.[28] Antoine had served Henri III and, after Henri III's assassination, Henri IV.[29] Gabrielle's mother, Françoise Babou de La Bourdaisière, model for Ronsard's Astrée, had been lady-in-waiting to the girl who would become Mary, Queen of Scots.[30] In his gossipy *Historiettes*, Gédéon Tallemant des Réaux (1619–1692) remarks on the dubious reputation of Françoise and her daughters, recounting that they had been dubbed the seven capital sins.[31]

During Henri IV's stay, grand écuyer of France Roger de Saint-Lary, Duke of Bellegarde, favorite of Henri III and then Henri IV, piqued the king's interest with stories of the beauty of his beloved, the seventeen-year-old Estrées daughter Gabrielle—or so we learn from the multiply authored and reworked set of texts known as *L'histoire des amours de Henri IV* (The story of the loves of Henri IV).[32] These texts reflect youthful memories of Louise-Marguerite of Lorraine, Princess of Conti (1588–1631), who became a close friend of Marie de Médicis, Henri IV's queen after Gabrielle's death.[33] The stories are certainly fictionalized but, where the facts can be verified, seem generally to reflect reality. As for the emotions and motivations they attribute to the characters, these may or may not represent an oral history that bears at least some resemblance to reality. Like Brantôme's stories of court life, they must be received with caution, but even where they are not true, they represent court gossip and are, for this reason, worthy of interest. In any case, the Princess of Conti's stories are the source of the anecdotes about Henri IV and Gabrielle's first encounters; according to these, Gabrielle, herself in love with Bellegarde, was not at all pleased when the king took one look at her and fell head over heels in love. Royal attention was an obstacle to the happiness that she was expecting to share with Bellegarde. Still, the king somehow managed to win over the golden-haired young woman of "extreme beauty."[34] Just under one year later, Henry Unton, an English diplomat whom Henri IV allowed to accompany him on campaign, reports that the king was on the way to Compiègne because he was in love with the governor's daughter, "who hath verie greate power over him."[35] By 1592 Théodore Agrippa d'Aubigné (1552–1630) notes that the king had already long ago fallen in love with Gabrielle and that he was known to slip away from battle to visit her.[36]

Historians have pointed out that the Estrées family, whom they generally describe as morally lax and venal, took advantage of Henri IV's infatuation by convincing the king in April 1591 to lay siege to Chartres, where the family had territory to regain from the Catholic League, rather than continuing through Normandy, which the Protestants had nearly retaken at the time of Henri III's death.[37] Thus the king returned government of Chartres to the husband of Gabrielle's aunt, Isabelle Babou de la Bourdaisière, Marquise de Sourdis, and her lover, the Count of Chiverny, regained charge of the region and his position as chancellor.[38] In August 1591 the king besieged Noyon, which he returned to Gabrielle's father.

The king's enchantment with Gabrielle is amply attested by the king himself in his many letters to her, which, beginning in 1593, offer a rich store of information on his feelings toward his mistress.[39] Still, if the depth of the king's attachment is indisputable, much about the young woman herself remains difficult to discern. The one characteristic that appears repeatedly in contemporary references is amiability. Accounts of Anne and Diane leave no such impression, stressing instead their political acumen. Gabrielle is different, but it is difficult to know whether her sweetness was spontaneous or strategic. Unton avers that she was known to be simple and of limited intelligence in a letter to Queen Elizabeth of 1596.[40] Théodore Agrippa d'Aubigné, in contrast, observes that the lovers ("amies") of kings had always brought the hatred of courtiers down on themselves, either because they got in the way or because they caused those who did not adore them to lose favor. He marvels that Gabrielle, whose extreme beauty suggested nothing of the lascivious, was able to live more as a queen than a concubine for so many years and yet make so few enemies.[41] Louise-Marguerite's *L'histoire des amours de Henri IV* represents Gabrielle in a similarly positive light. After the king had made her a duchess, "seeing herself in a positon of such dignity and high expectations, she behaved so courteously and so decorously that those who did not want to like her could not hate her: she presided over everything at court, but with a great sweetness, and she obliged everyone as much as she could. . . . And she lived with such gravity and restraint that it seemed that she had never moved from the Company of the Vestals, her clothes and actions representing only a perfect modesty."[42]

Sully offers a more layered portrait, painting Gabrielle as a tool in the hands of Isabelle and Chiverny but, at the same time, artificial, wont to stage emotional acts for effect. Commenting on her folly in letting it be known that she expected to be the next queen, he adds that she may have been smothered by ambition—or badly advised. But he does not leave the reader with an impression of a naïve teenager, his observations adding up to a picture of a young woman who was both manipulated by her scheming relatives and possessed of a sort of instinctive talent for dissimulation. In a long anecdote centered on what he believes to have been the inappropriate use of public funds to finance a gala baptism for her and Henri IV's son Alexandre, Sully describes Gabrielle condescendingly rebuffing Sully himself when he enters her chamber to inform her that the festival will not be fully reimbursed. Gabrielle then turns on the tears when the king materializes to support the superintendent. According to Sully, Gabrielle began to sob and to try to kiss the king's hands, while the king dismissed the tears as an act and Gabrielle herself as "full of artifice."[43] How much credence to lend Sully's take on the incident? Gabrielle's modern and unflattering biographer, Raymond Ritter, follows the superintendent's lead, writing that "however dim, Gabrielle was a woman."[44]

And yet Gabrielle, like all courtiers, would have spent most of her life dissimulating. What would it even mean to be accused of being "full of artifice" in such a context? Indeed, recent readers would probably be inclined to accept Sully's portrait of her as both congenial and scheming—in other words, as a successful courtier. It is worth noting that Sully has Henri IV bring the discussion to a close by ordering Gabrielle to continue to exercise her "same sweetness of spirit."[45] She seems to have been a dissimulator but a pleasant one.

Still, as historians recognized already in the nineteenth century, neither Sully's *Mémoire des sages et royales oeconomies d'estat* nor his *Mémoires* can be taken as straightforward information about the people he describes. First, Sully's memoirs were not actually written by Sully. Near the middle of the eighteenth century, writes nineteenth-century historian Adrien Desclozeaux, the Abbé de l'Ecluse des Loges created the work out of the *Mémoire des sages et royales oeconomies d'estat*, and under the abbé's pen, "the narrative took on a completely different aspect." Gone were the "bitter censures, the implacable resentments." As for the *Mémoire des sages et royales oeconomies d'estat*, Decloxeaux and others have compared the letters that Sully included in this work with the originals where possible and discovered that the superintendent had a propensity for changing them to make himself look more intimate with the king and more important than he was.[46] The safest way to approach Sully's accounts of Gabrielle, then, is to be on the watch for possible bias in his own favor while looking for the ring of truth, just as we do with other problematic sources, such as Louise-Marguerite of Lorraine, Brantôme, or indeed any modern character witness.

Examining the collected evidence, we suggest that the picture that emerges is of a very young woman—relative to Anne and Diane, she was painfully inexperienced when she began her rise—with a genuine gift for conflict resolution invited into a no-win situation by a much older king who should have known from the beginning that he could not actually deliver on his promise of marriage. It is easy enough from a modern perspective to feel sympathy for a king who wanted to live as the husband of the woman and the father of the children he loved. Moreover, Henri IV's humor, which reverberates, like his favorite expression for swearing, "ventre saint-gris," through the written traces of his speech, along with his willingness to compromise on his religious views for the sake of peace, makes him attractive to modern readers. The king arouses all the more compassion for falling victim, like his predecessor, to a fanatical Catholic, this one named Jean-François Ravaillac, in 1610.[47] But in all ways exponentially more powerful than Gabrielle, he did her no favor in cultivating her to be the future queen.

THE OFFICIAL ROYAL MISTRESS

In Unton's letter to Queen Elizabeth, cited above, the diplomat quotes the king as claiming that Gabrielle never intervened in political affairs.[48] This is patently untrue, yet it adheres to the construction of the political royal mistress's work as an open secret, like Anne and Diane, modeled ultimately on Agnès Sorel. In this section we discuss the young woman's career as official royal mistress.

Gabrielle's tenure began in typical fashion when she was married in 1592 to Nicolas d'Amerval, sire de Liancourt. With few exceptions, the official mistress was married. This gave her a household of her own, which meant a certain amount of security while the king continued to enjoy access to her. If the king arranged the marriage, the "complacent and venal" husband was richly rewarded.[49] But Gabrielle's marriage differed from others in being temporary. Supported by Henri IV, she requested an annulment in August 1594, just after the birth of her and the king's first child, César. The speedy termination raises questions.[50] Was it actually Henri IV who had arranged the marriage—or had it been imposed by Antoine d'Estrées to separate his daughter from Henri IV, as the king himself seems to hint in a letter of 26 June 1593, and as Gabrielle seems to confirm during the annulment proceedings, which she instigated on 27 August 1594?[51] In the summer of 1592, Gabrielle's mother had been murdered under scandalous circumstances. Tallement des Réaux relates how she left her husband to take up residence with the much younger Yves d'Allègre in his chateau in Issoire, only to be stabbed to death, along with Yves, in in the middle of the night by irate townspeople. Tallement des Réaux hastens to note the political motivation of the murders: the rebels, taking the side of the Catholic League, rose up against Yves and Françoise, royalists—that is, supporters of Henri IV.[52] Nonetheless, Antoine may have reacted to the dishonor of his family by trying to restore a bit of decorum among the family members he could control. Desclozeaux proposes a similar scenario, drawing on the annulment proceedings to argue that Gabrielle's father married his daughter to get her out of the hands of Henri IV, but that the bridegroom, who was impotent, sexually and in a more general sense as well, was quite simply unable to fulfill the task assigned him.[53] In contrast, Henri IV's recent biographer, Jean-Pierre Babelon, sees the king as deciding that a "complacent husband" needed to be found for Gabrielle.[54] Vincent J. Pitts, too, argues for the king's involvement in the arrangement, hypothesizing that the Estrées and Henri IV collaborated in marrying Gabrielle to Amerval to "provide her with some respectability."[55] Ritter assumes Gabrielle herself to have been in on the game as well, along with her father and the king.[56]

If the king was involved, why did he so quickly change his mind? We will return to this important question in the following section. For the moment, we simply observe that during her first years with the king, Gabrielle behaved and was treated like a normal official royal mistress. In his correspondence to her, the king manifests passion and the faith that he put in her. In 1593 or 1594, likely alluding to her continuing fancy for Bellegarde, he begs her to be happy with just one servant, assuring her that she has the power to change him, that she is wrong if she believes that anyone could serve her more faithfully than he.[57] In October 1595 (or perhaps 1597) he affirms that they love each other very well: as for women, no one loves better than she, and as for men, no one is his equal in knowing how to love.[58] Nor is it surprising that he would cling so tightly to a woman with no divided loyalty, whose only interest was to promote his, considering the trouble that his marriage to the Catholic Marguerite of Valois had caused for both parties. In contrast with the nightmarish set of problems that marriage into the House of Valois had occasioned, Gabrielle's simple, steadfast support, whatever he did, would have been a consolation. His conversion to Catholicism is one example. Undertaken on 25 July 1593 at the cathedral of Saint-Denis, the ritual brought him into good standing with the Catholic Church (his excommunication would be lifted in 1595), but it was reviled by Protestants, of course, and also many Catholics who regarded it as insincere (it was, in fact, his second conversion). Contemporaries and near contemporaries, even those who disliked Gabrielle, regarded her as entirely supportive or even a principal force behind the conversion.[59] Mézeray inserts the young woman's blandishments into a narrative that he borrows partly from Sully, enumerating the arguments that had persuaded Henri IV of the necessity of conversion. The nobility was already reproaching Henri IV for the long war; other reasons included the extreme lack of money, the disapproval of his best men, his pity for the misery of his people, the prodding of some ministers of his cabinet, and the advice of his closest friends, as well as, according to Mézeray's account, Gabrielle's caresses. Furthermore, "Gabrielle represented to him that unless he became a Catholic he would have to spend, unfortunately, the rest of his life weighted down with arms, tired, amid conflict, danger, traps, far from rest, from the pleasures of hunting, love, good spirit, game, and all that makes life sweet."[60]

True, not everyone approved of Gabrielle's influence in this case. Protestant Aubigné laments that she was the "last instrument who did more than all."[61] In the early days of their love affair, writes Aubigné, she had been Protestant, trusting only servants who celebrated the Lord's Supper and followed the Reform. She preached constantly the faithfulness of those people and declaimed daily against tyranny, which was her term for what the king had to suffer from the Catholics who served him, "exhorting this prince to persevere in his faith." Then it became clear that only the pope could annul the king's first marriage. At that point she began to employ her great beauty and the best hours of the days and nights to put forward her arguments in favor of conversion.[62] Not a positive development, in Aubigné's eyes.

With the newly Catholic king safely crowned on 27 February 1594, Gabrielle continued to watch over how he enacted his religious beliefs, ensuring that he maintained appearances, at least. Relaxing with a lute player and friends after dinner one night in March 1597, the king spontaneously joined in when the group began to sing Psalm 78. The vigilant Gabrielle gently covered his mouth to remind him that singing the psalms was a Protestant practice. The king immediately fell silent.[63]

Like other official mistresses, Gabrielle served the king as a diplomat, most notably during negotiations to reconcile with the Catholic League. She was approached in the first instance by the league's leader, the Duke of Mayenne, Charles of Lorraine, son of François, Duke of Guise, prominent in Henri II's administration. Through the intermediary of a close friend, the duke requested that Gabrielle plead his case to the king. Defending such a good cause, she was informed, would bring her the favor of the pope and the French, and the affection of the Catholics. In return for her successful mediation, the duke promised that he would support her son's succession to the throne. De Thou recounts:

> The Duke of Mayenne, having nothing left to hope from the Spaniards, had [Gabrielle] asked by the President Jeannin to mediate with the king to make peace and to employ at the same time her credit on behalf of the princes of the Catholic party. . . . The Duke offered her at the same time his services and promised this ambitious woman, in his own name and the name of his party, to defend against everyone and to place on the throne, despite the princes of the Royal House, the children she had had with the king, if this prince named them his successors.[64]

Gabrielle persuaded the king to enter into negotiations, and an agreement was drawn up in January 1596. Mayenne was invited to come to Gabrielle's chateau at Monceaux to make public submission. With her sister Diane, Gabrielle traveled to Monceaux to supervise preparations on 30 January.[65] The next day Mayenne arrived at noon and was helped to dismount from his horse (apparently he was a very large man). Gabrielle, waiting at the front door, received him and directed him to the king's room. The duke bowed low three times and prepared to kneel and kiss the king's foot, but Henri IV graciously raised and embraced him. Peace was restored.

Gabrielle also participated in the Edict of Nantes, which, signed on 13 April 1598, brought an end to the Religious Wars. The last of the league holdouts had been Philippe-Emmanuel of Lorraine, Duke of Mercoeur, brother of Henri III's queen, who had established a final stronghold in Brittany. In November the duke, knowing that the king was not willing to negotiate with him, approached Gabrielle with an offer to marry his daughter to César, explaining that his spouse the duchess was prepared to come to Gabrielle to seal the agreement.[66] At roughly the same time, the king's counselor and governor of Saumur, Huguenot Philippe de Mornay, seigneur du Plessis, solicited Gabrielle to intercede to soften Henri IV toward peace.[67] Henri IV entered Brittany at the head of an army, and on 20 March 1599 Mercoeur surrendered to the king. Their agreement included the marriage of César to Mercoeur's daughter and a large payment to the duke. Gabrielle's interactions with the duchess are detailed by De Thou.[68]

When she was solicited by Pierre Séguier, president of the Parlement of Paris, to use her influence to convince the king to back down on the 1598 Edict of Nantes offering tolerance to Protestants, she "put him off" (*l'esconduit*), saying that the king was right. After all, the Protestants were good servants of the king, whereas the Leaguers, she reminded Séguier, had taken arms against the king. When the Protestant Duke of Bouillon, Maréchal of France, heard about this response, he paid Gabrielle a personal visit to thank her.[69]

Gabrielle, then, was an exemplary political royal mistress, and she reaped the benefits typical of the royal favorite. The king elevated her first to Marquise of Monceaux in 1595 and then Duchess of Beaufort in 1597.[70] We have noted some of the favors granted members of her family. In addition, she received generous pensions, territories, and regency of César's territories.[71]

Gabrielle might well have remained comfortably in her position. But the king required a legitimate heir, and, against all precedent, he began to think of marrying his mistress. At first blush, it is difficult to see how he could have even contemplated the idea. Beyond the problem that both were already married, by the sixteenth century, as Fanny Cosandey has explained, European royalty formed a genuine caste, with admission jealously regulated.[72] However, in the king's eyes, it appears that such a marriage seemed possible because his historical context imbued the relationship with a special divine significance. The affair, embedded in the period of Henri IV's reunification of a kingdom that, although still divided, achieved relative peace with the king's conversion, had been blessed with healthy offspring. This elevated it above the king's many passionate but ultimately insignificant relationships. In addition, Inès Murat suggests that Gabrielle's talent for pacification made her an ideal companion for Henri IV at this point in his career.[73] Even more compelling, based on what they had accomplished together, Henri IV imagined that he and Gabrielle shared a providential destiny. As for the guaranteed disapproval of his subjects, with an internal—if shaky—peace in place, the king initially seems to have believed that he had little to gain from an alliance with an exterior power. His more immediate interest was in demonstrating his own power, which meant, above all, producing an heir.

FROM OFFICIAL ROYAL MISTRESS TO QUEEN?

Henri IV had already resolved in about 1592, soon after beginning his affair with Gabrielle, to divorce Marguerite. Setting aside a childless queen was not a problem if the choice for the new queen was deemed appropriate. The normal procedure would have been for him to leave Gabrielle in place as his official royal mistress while shopping for a bride from one of the European dynastic houses. A number of candidates existed, including Marie de Médicis, niece of the grand duke of Tuscany, whom the king had already approached in the first years of the 1590s.[74]

But Henri IV did not follow normal procedure. Just after the registration of Gabrielle's divorce, he recognized her son, César, as his heir.[75] In his letter of legitimation, registered with the Parlement of Paris on 3 February 1595, his assertion of divine favor regarding the birth is striking. The king begins the letter by recalling that none of his predecessors had ever had to deal with a situation like his: a desolated state in quasi-inevitable ruin. And yet through the grace of God and much hard work he had raised the state to its former shape and dignity. For this reason he wants all the more to found a lineage that will remain after him. Still, he continues, "because God has not yet permitted that we have [children] in a legitimate marriage, the queen our legitimate spouse having been separated from us for ten years, we wanted, as we waited for Him to deign to give us children who could legitimately succeed to this crown, to seek to have them elsewhere, in some worthy and honorable spot. . . . Concerning this matter, having recognized the great grace and perfections, as much intellectual as physical, of our very dear and most beloved lady Gabrielle d'Estrées, we have for the past few years tried this."[76] The king then explains that he had pursued Gabrielle and asserted his authority over her and that, after a long struggle, she had condescended to obey and comply, and it had pleased God to give them a son. He would use similar language to announce the birth of his second son, their third child,

Alexandre, writing, "God has given me this day a son who will be no less beautiful than my son of Vendôme."[77]

On 24 February 1595, three weeks after legitimating César, Henri IV wrote Mornay, asking him to begin working on an annulment of his marriage with Marguerite: "Take care of, I ask you, this affair, with your usual dexterity and diligence."[78] The king can only have been thinking of marrying Gabrielle at this point: the timing cannot be coincidence. Normally the birth of an illegitimate child would not cause a king to start thinking about marrying the child's mother. Bastard children regularly formed part of the extended royal household.[79] But Philippe Hurault, Count of Chiverny, stresses the importance of fertility for Henri IV, relating that the king told him that Gabrielle's ability to bear children was a tremendous asset (in addition to César, later Duke of Vendôme [1594–1665], she would bear two more children, Catherine-Henriette of Bourbon [1596–1663] and Alexandre, Knight of Vendôme [1598–1629], and she would die giving birth to a fourth), and Sully reports that in 1596 the king mentioned Gabrielle's fertility among qualities he demanded in a wife. Presenting Sully with a list of the things that he hoped to accomplish during his reign, the king included, along with allowing the two religions to subsist and being delivered from his first wife, a marriage with a woman of appropriate birth who was of sweet and complacent humor, who loved him and whom he could love, and would give him children soon enough that he would still have time to instruct them, turning them into brave, gallant, and skilled princes.[80] Although he does not name Gabrielle, it is clear to whom he refers.

Henri IV's closest and most sympathetic advisers desperately wanted him to divorce and remarry—but not Gabrielle. Far from guaranteeing a peaceful transition of power on Henri IV's death, such a marriage would create chaos, they believed.[81] The succession would be contested by, among others, Henri IV's heir, Henri II of Bourbon, Prince of Condé. This Henri was the son of the king's paternal cousin Henri I, victim of poisoning possibly at the hand of his own wife, himself son of Henri IV's paternal uncle Louis of Bourbon.[82] Other claims would be pressed as well, it was feared. Indeed, claims would later be pressed even against Henri IV's legitimate son with Marie de Médicis.[83]

But the king began to treat Gabrielle as queen in public, seemingly to adjust his people to the idea. He had already accorded her a central position in his entry into Paris after his coronation on 15 September 1594. Pierre L'Estoile describes the scene:

It was eight o'clock at night when His Majesty crossed the Bridge of Notre Dame, accompanied by a large number of cavalry and surrounded by the magnificent nobility. The king, smiling broadly and happy to see the people crying "Vive le Roi" so happily, kept his hat in his hand, principally to salute the ladies and young misses at the windows; among them, he greeted three very pretty ones who were dressed in mourning. . . . [Gabrielle] preceded the king by a short distance in a magnificent covered litter bedecked with pearls and precious stones so luminous that they obscured the light of the torches; and she wore a gown of black satin betassled in white.[84]

Diane de Poitiers's central but carefully obscured presence in Henri II's entry into Lyon suggests that the presence of the royal mistress in such an event was no surprise. However, the openness with which Gabrielle participated, preceding even the king, was unprecedented.

In addition, in November 1594 Francesco Bonciani, secret agent in Paris for the grand duke of Tuscany, had already mentioned the king's passionate attachment to Gabrielle, noting that it seemed strange to him that Henri IV should be the prey of the duchess with so little concern for appearances. On 28 December Bonciani writes to the grand duke that the king cannot live an hour without Gabrielle, although in affairs of state he does not allow her to govern. By 8 February he remarks that no one speaks any longer of the annulment—the king is so enamored of Gabrielle that he is not thinking in terms of marriage, as if he were pleased with the life that he was leading.[85] Over the course of the year, the ambassador continues to note how amazed the court is at the besotted king's lack of attention to his job.

And yet all along, Bonciani notwithstanding, the king seems to have been thinking of marriage: to Gabrielle. Signs, large and small, of Henri IV's intention to marry her abound. Sometime between 1593 and 1598, he inserts a poem in a letter to her asking her to share his crown.[86] A painting of Gabrielle "en Diane" by Ambroise Dubois, recently returned to the Louvre, is also suggestive of his plans. Although we associate Diana with Diane de Poitiers—that is, the royal mistress—mythological themes were very fluid, and Marie de Médicis would also adopt Diana, among other goddesses, as an emblem. A Diana gallery would be installed at Fontainebleau during that queen's reign, a gallery that may or may not have been begun for Gabrielle.[87] Another piece of evidence is a copy of an earlier painting by Clouet, possibly representing Diane de Poitiers as Diana bathing with her nymphs while observed by a man on horseback, dressed in Henri II's colors of black and white. The copy exchanges Gabrielle for Diane with Henri IV as the man on horseback.[88] A coin with the head of Henri IV on one side and Gabrielle on the other, struck in 1597, also bears witness to the seriousness of his intent.[89] Gabrielle began to occupy the position of queen in public, waited on by the bowing and scraping Duchess of Guise, eating what took her fancy with one hand while holding the other out to be kissed by the king, reports L'Estoile.[90]

Resistance to the prospect of Gabrielle as queen surged. In 1596 Bonciani asserts that it would be a good thing if the Estates General were to assemble and force Henri IV to put some order back in his life. After all, France was now at war with Spain, the people desired peace, and the king needed to get down to the business of making it.[91] About the baptism of the couple's daughter, Catherine-Henriette, that same year, De Thou describes "sensible people" expressing outrage that a mere "bastard" was receiving such a lavish ceremony.[92] Malicious pamphlets blaming Gabrielle for current problems were circulating widely.[93] L'Estoile reports that on 10 July 1597, when the king elevated his mistress from the Marquise of Monceaux to Duchess of Beaufort, the woman who had been called the "Duchess of Filth" from then on became known as the Duchess of Beaufort. In late 1598 someone who had heard that the king intended to marry Gabrielle planted a poem in the royal bed that complained sarcastically that a little "lead and wax" could legitimize the son of a whore.[94]

Despite all, Henri IV seemed committed to his plan. De Thou recounts that during an informal meeting with papal legate Cardinal Alexandre de Médicis, the king supplicated the cardinal to intercede with the pope for the annulment that would allow him, the king, to produce a legitimate male heir. However, during a "digression," the king began to praise Gabrielle, letting slip his intention to marry her, which he had intended to keep secret. Alarmed, the cardinal immediately begged leave to return to the pope. Realizing his error, Henri IV sent Nicolas Brûlart de Sillery as a diplomat to Rome, instructing him, at least according to De Thou, to pretend that the king "had changed his mind regarding Gabrielle d'Estrées" so as to obtain the annulment.[95]

And yet at about this same time, Gabrielle began to sense that something was not right. She could not have helped but know that most of the court regarded the proposed marriage as a disaster. Heightening her distress, she had presentiments of doom. Pierre de L'Estoile reports in the winter of 1599 that the king and she, in bed together, each had a dream, each remarkable given what actually happened, and told each other: the said Duchess dreamed that she was watching a great fire coming toward her and could not escape; and having awoken with a great start wanted to wake the king up, but, he, tired from hunting, told her to leave him alone, which she did, and, getting up quietly, she went into her dressing room to cry to one of her ladies-in-waiting whom she loved dearly. When she returned to bed, the king dreamed that he saw her die and, waking up, recounted his dream to her, and she told the king hers. Already a long time before, having been convinced by fortune-tellers that she would not live long, she had often gone off alone to cry. One of them had told her that she would be on the verge of achieving her desire, but that a small child would prevent her from it.[96]

Her intuition that she would never wear a crown was sadly accurate. Henri IV had indeed changed his mind. Just before Easter, the king, allegedly wanting to win the approval of the Parisians for his future bride, decided that the pair should respect morality by living apart over Holy Week.[97] He would stay at Fontainebleau while she returned to Paris. But Gabrielle was beside herself. Convinced that she was seeing her deepest fears confirmed, she broke down, entreating the king not to leave her.[98] He remained obdurate; Gabrielle departed. On Wednesday of Holy Week, she recovered her equilibrium and went to dine in the gorgeous hotel of the Florentine Sebastiano Zametti, or Zamet as he was known to his French friends, a fabulously wealthy self-made financier and tax farmer who enjoyed cordial relations with the king and Gabrielle.[99] Sources report that after eating a type of lemon called a poncire at Zamet's hotel, she fell ill. Initially she rallied. On Thursday, however, after Mass, she once again became sick, going into labor late in the afternoon. Seized with wild convulsions that contorted her body and distorted her face in such a way as to terrify her attendants, she agonized until five o'clock on the morning of Saturday, 10 April, when she died. Henri IV started out for Paris when news of her illness reached him, but on receiving word en route to her bedside that she had died, he turned back to Fontainebleau. In fact, the information of her death, coming in a letter written by Guillaume de Fouquet, seigneur de La Varenne, was false at the time of its writing. Gabrielle was not yet dead at the time that the king was informed that she was.[100]

THE ASSASSINATION OF GABRIELLE D'ESTRÉES?

The king was wild with grief. And yet the evidence makes clear that at some time during the course of his slowly unfolding plan to make his official mistress his queen, something had shaken his confidence that the marriage was ordained by God.

Light has been shed on the king's complex emotional state by Belgian historian Jacques Bolle, who in 1955 published an odd little work called *Pourquoi tuer Gabrielle d'Estrées?* Possibly because it was constructed as a sort of police investigation rather than a straightforward historical study, the book slumbered for decades.[101] And yet Bolle's research is crucial for piecing together Gabrielle's story. In the afterword, Bolle explains that the diplomatic correspondence between France and Tuscany collected by Canestrini and Desjardins (which we have called *Négociations diplomatiques* in the footnotes) was culled of several important letters.[102] Most striking, Bolle observes, is the note at the bottom of page 365 in volume 5 of *Négociations diplomatiques*, explaining that in a letter of 2 December 1598 Bonciani expresses alarm at the great evil that could come from the crazy love of the king for Gabrielle. This is striking because in the *Négociations diplomatiques* that letter is followed by a silence of nearly one year from Bonciani; his next letter is dated November 1599. However, Mediceo, Filza 461 of the Medici archives in Florence, Bolle affirms, contains more than two dozen ciphered letters for that period from Bonciani and Jacopo Guicciardini, a Florentine knight who had served as intermediary between Henri IV's camp and the grand duke of Florence.[103] Bolle and his collaborator Corti deciphered these and other pertinent coded letters not known to Canestrini and Desjardins.

Of particular interest are several letters that testify that Henri IV was negotiating a marriage with Marie de Médicis even as he was making plans for his marriage to Gabrielle. In a letter of 18 January 1599, Bonciani worries that Henri IV is playing Ferdinand for a dupe: "It's important that you keep your eyes open because it is clear that you are dealing with sneaky people" (12). And yet a letter of 22 February 1599 about Marguerite, heretofore amenable to an annulment, describes her backing out because she does not want to see the king married to Gabrielle, that infamous tramp ("cette décriée bagasse")—which, Bonciani adds, did not displease the king—and shows the agent beginning to think that Marie de Médicis will be the next queen of France (13).[104] Bonciani next notes that the king has made promises to Gabrielle that he will not keep and goes on to speak about Marie's dowry (13). By March, writes Bolle, "Bonciani no longer doubts the reality of the marriage between Henri IV and the Princess Marie. He speaks of it like something that has been decided; apparently he had received serious guarantees concerning the subject" (29). On 9 March Bonciani writes that he has spoken to Sully, and the king says that if the pope does not want to deal with the affair because of possible tension between the Spaniards and the Italians, he, worried about his reputation, wants the Italians to let him know how to marry the princess (29–30). In short, one month before Gabrielle's death, Henri is making plans to marry Marie de Médicis.

In addition to showing that Henri IV was already negotiating a state marriage while Gabrielle was still alive, Bolle proposes that Gabrielle died at the hands of an assassin. However, the perpetrator, he claims, was none of the obvious suspects—that is, a member of the Florentine contingent acting on behalf of the grand duke. Zamet, who would have been the best placed to do Gabrielle in, had too much to gain from Gabrielle's ascension, so Bolle eliminates him as a suspect. Moreover, as Bolle points out, had the Florentine contingent been behind the assassination, surely they would not have carried it out in the home of a prominent Florentine (110). Finally, the grand duke's gold was supporting the French court. True, Ferdinand wanted to marry his niece to the French king. But if this did not work out he would simply take his money elsewhere—specifically, to the emperor, Rodolphe II (111). Ferdinand occupied the position of strength vis-à-vis the French. Thus Bolle looks for someone outside of the Florentine "camarilla," opting for the king's right-hand man, La Varenne.

But before zeroing in on La Varenne, Bolle describes the dismay that reigned at court in the days before Gabrielle's death:

> The ministers and dignitaries of the French court were much more affected than the Florentines by the ambition of Gabrielle d'Estrées. Riled, they weighed the options on all sides and were angered to see the king inclining toward the solution that would mean penury for the Court of France.
>
> A unanimous sentiment made itself felt. . . . It was the phenomenon of moral contagion often observed in the collective psychology. (111)

Then taking note of the collective relief that followed Gabrielle's death, Bolle hypothesizes that it was only natural that a member of the crowd would assume the responsibility to act for the greater good. La Varenne, he claims, was the one: a man who had shown himself ready to take the initiative over his long career in the service of the kingdom, and who, as we have seen, had prematurely announced the death of Gabrielle. But for Bolle, La Varenne was less an assassin than an instrument of the will of the entire court. Gabrielle was killed, "inexorably, by the force of a general intrigue; the real plot was born of Sully's exhortations, the clergy's representations, Marguerite's letters, and, finally, we bitterly regret to say, the pitiful feebleness of the king, converting his illicit arrangement into the longing for an heir, with falsely juvenile tears, with an astounding aptitude for double dealing" (115).

There is something to Bolle's argument. The court does indeed seem to have been cheered by Gabrielle's opportune demise. De Thou describes the courtiers' barely concealed relief: "The entire court went into mourning, and the event seemed to cause much sadness, but at bottom, the Princes and Seigneurs experienced a secret joy, regarding the death of this lady as a happy circumstance that God presented to the king so that he could get married and have legitimate heirs who would strengthen the crown, which he could not have done had Gabrielle lived."[105]

CONCLUSION

That Agnès Sorel was poisoned matters, bearing on her political importance. Whether Gabrielle's tragic death was planned or natural is less significant for understanding her tenure. The crucial point is that Henri IV had been convinced to back out of the marriage with her, conforming at the eleventh hour to expectations, but, apparently unable to tell her, he left her adrift in a sea of anxiety.

Kathleen Wellman proposes that had Henri IV held out and married Gabrielle, he would have changed the nature of royal marriage, which, as we have been discussing, brought together members of often adversarial houses.[106] This is certainly possible, had the transition of power after his death gone smoothly. A scene from Sully's so-called *Mémoires* supports Wellman's suggestion, revealing the very good reasons a king would want to choose his own bride. Henri IV has approached Sully for advice on choosing a queen, confessing his great fear that any woman from an important family would be more devoted to those members than to him. He hesitates to marry Louise of Guise because of the "too-great passion that she demonstrates for her House, and especially for her brother, which might give rise to the desire to elevate them to my detriment and still more to that of my children if ever regency of the state should fall into her hands."[107] We have noted the problems of attribution regarding the *Mémoires*, but the point is well taken, whoever made it. Had Henri IV chosen Gabrielle as his queen and all had gone well, the need for a royal mistress would have been obviated, revising the nature of the royal marriage. But something changed the king's mind, and he made a state marriage, which it appears he would have done with or without Gabrielle's death. The possibility of a new version of marriage evaporated. Given the result, we suggest, the turmoil created by Henri IV and Gabrielle's near miss only strengthened the distinction between the roles of queen and mistress, because, as we will see in what follows, they remain entirely different roles through subsequent reigns, until the cataclysmic demise of the ancien régime.

We cannot close a chapter on Gabrielle without discussing the notorious portrait known as *Gabrielle d'Estrées and One of Her Sisters*, which is believed to represent her in a bathtub with another woman who has never been definitively identified. The painting is housed today in the Louvre. As we have seen, other portraits representing Gabrielle exist. Still, *Gabrielle d'Estrées and One of Her Sisters* is the most mysterious and controversial of the images associated with her, as much for its opaque symbolism as for its erotic subject matter. In the foreground we see seated in a bathtub a brunette woman and a blond, presumed to be Gabrielle. The brunette delicately extends her left thumb and index finger to touch the tip of the blond's breast. The blond woman holds a ring with her thumb and index finger of her left hand. In the background we can make out a red-haired woman sewing, a mirror above a fireplace reflecting the lower part of an outstretched body, and a catafalque covered in green.

These are the symbols to be deciphered. Wolfram Fleischhauer's fictionalized but erudite story of his own search to solve the mystery of this painting's meaning offers an ingenious and satisfying interpretation of these symbols. Fleischhauer's hero, speaking to a history professor, proposes that a disgruntled artist, his commission to paint Gabrielle having been reneged on, decides to reveal the royal mistress's darkest secret. The secret was sure to upset the king even though Gabrielle was already dead when the painting was undertaken. The hero hypothesizes that although the blond is certainly Gabrielle (her pallor signifying that she is no longer living) holding the symbol of her marriage promise between her fingers, the woman beside her cannot reasonably be interpreted as her sister.[108] No, she can only be the dark-haired Henriette de Balzac d'Entragues, and the painting can only be intended to reveal that the father of Gabrielle's fourth child was not Henri IV. The delicate, intimate little gesture of Henriette, who will also try and fail to marry the king, indicates Gabrielle's pregnancy. But the king was undergoing surgery on his venereal-diseased sexual regions in October 1598, the moment when the child would have been conceived. The lower half of the body reflected in the mirror therefore belongs to Bellegarde, who spent time at Monceaux with Gabrielle in October 1598: he was the real father of the baby who would die with Gabrielle. The red-haired woman in the background represents "la Parque," the Fates, busily sewing the destiny of the two women. The wedding ring, reproduced in the gesturing fingers of the two women, is held in Gabrielle's left hand, a sure sign that neither Gabrielle's nor Henriette's marriage will ever take place. The catafalque, covered in Gabrielle's favorite color green, represents her sad end.

CHAPTER 5

The Mistresses of the Sun King

La Vallière, Montespan, Maintenon

Such a triumph at Versailles! such renewed pride!
such a solid institution! such [a] Duchess of
Valentinois! such [a] stew, with these distractions and
absence! such a retaking of possession!

—MADAME DE SÉVIGNÉ, letter to her daughter,
Madame de Grignan, 11 June 1677

Although Henri IV's son, Louis XIII (b. 1601), had no official royal
mistress, the role remained in the social imaginary throughout the years
of his reign, 1610–43. Author and historiographer Charles Sorel, sieur
de Souvigny (1602–1674), pretended to be related to Agnès, although he
was not, apparently attempting to assume some of her glory for himself.
Sorel's biographer, Émile Roy, recounts how Sorel researched Agnès's
family, collecting all the texts that he could find relative to his "héroïne"
and traveling to Loches to copy the inscription on her tomb. He published
his findings in a book of philosophical musings, *La solitude et l'amour
philosophique de Cléomède*, in which the narrator pairs Agnès and Joan
of Arc as two renowned women of the time of Charles VII, each of
whom served France in her own way.[1] The pairing, picked up by Voltaire,
was renewed in the nineteenth century by historian Jules Michelet.[2]
Sorel's Agnès inspires Charles VII's courage in the way made popular by
Brantôme and Haillan, whom Sorel cites. He also alludes to the pencil
portrait of Agnès in the Aix album, which he had seen.

Agnès's legend also circulated among the networks of the mistresses explored in this chapter. But the court of Louis XIV (b. 1638; r. 1643–1715) was utterly different from the one that Agnès had occupied. Increasingly a site of elaborate spectacle and performance, the royal court reached its apogee under the Sun King. Every act was a carefully calibrated display, performed for spectators from various countries. Many contemporaries wrote about the court of Louis XIV, sources that underline the extent to which observers saw the court as theater and the courtiers as performers. The letters of Madame de Sévigné (1626–1696) and Roger de Bussy-Rabutin (1618–1693) breathlessly narrate the events at court like the unfolding of a play. Reports from ambassadors such as the Savoyard representative, Thomas-François Chabod, the Marquis de Saint-Maurice (1624–1682), and the Great Elector of Brandenburg's agent, Ézéchiel Spanheim (1629–1710), demonstrate a keen awareness of the performative nature of court life. Memoirs from both members of the French royalty, such as Anne Marie Louise of Orléans, Duchess of Montpensier (better known as La Grande Mademoiselle) (1627–1693), and fascinated foreigners, such as the Piedmontese chronicler Primi Visconti (1648–1713), paint the theater that was the Sun King's court with dramatic flair. Constantly aware of being observed, courtiers responded by adopting often artificial manners and dress, enhanced by elaborate clothing and cosmetics, all part of the dissimulation that court actors now took for granted.[3] The many festivals, theatrical productions, and ballets in which Louis and his male and female companions performed, especially early in his reign, were a natural progression from theatricality to literal theater. The splendor and magnificence that were characteristic of the court also served as a display of the monarch's power; the courtiers played an important role in this.[4]

Among these courtiers, the most important were the king's mistresses. The theatricality that had opened new spaces for women at court in the sixteenth century continued to shape possibilities at the court of Louis XIV. The prominence of the official mistress's role had increased dramatically since the reign of Anne de Pisseleu d'Heilly, becoming fully recognizable with the self-fashioning Diane de Poitiers and Gabrielle d'Estrées. Olivier Chaline suggests that under Louis XIV, the position of royal mistress "constituted a particular feminine variant on the concept of royal service."[5] The position required a woman skilled in self-presentation, whose presence at the king's side would be a source of honor for him. She was expected to participate in the festivities that punctuated court life throughout the 1660s and 1670s; Louis XIV's early mistresses, including Louise de La Vallière and Madame de Montespan, would take part in the ballets in which he also danced. In private conversation, the royal mistress would lobby the king on behalf of her supporters and offer advice on conducting affairs of state; Montespan and Madame de Maintenon in particular were key players in the cabals that dominated court politics.[6]

Louis XIV's first love, Marie Mancini (1639–1715), helped develop his predilection for festivals and display, shaping the flavor of his court in the early decades of his reign.[7] Louis XIII had notoriously shown little interest in women, leaving a void that was filled by male advisers and friends as well as women other than official mistresses. This would not, however, be the case for his son. For Louis XIV, writes Simone Bertière, women were "much more than mistresses." They shared his leisure activities and adorned his court.[8] Madame de La Fayette (1634–1693) commented that court ladies had noted Louis XIV's infatuation with Marie Mancini, and "for themselves they hoped that, surpassing her in charms, they might gain at least an equal credit, and many had already chosen for their model the fortunes of [Gabrielle d'Estrées]."[9] When Louise de La Vallière emerged as Louis's first official mistress, a precedent existed for "the delicate problem of her place at court. . . . The tradition of royal mistresses was long-standing, and the memory of Agnès Sorel, of Diane de Poitiers, of Gabrielle d'Estrées, was very much alive."[10] Indeed, in the *chambre Sévigné* in Bussy-Rabutin's chateau hung a portrait of Agnès Sorel along with the portraits of twenty-five women, including *maîtresses déclarées*. An inscription above the painting, probably written by Bussy-Rabutin himself, notes that Agnès assured the deliverance of France from the English by reviving the courage of the king.[11] In a letter to his cousin Madame de Sévigné of 23 February 1678, he compares Louis XIV's love for Montespan favorably to Charles VII's for Agnès, noting that despite Montespan's recent bout of the *tierce fièvre*, the king was out on the battlefield, where he belonged, in contrast with Charles VII, who had remained with Agnès while his kingdom fell apart.[12]

By the reign of Louis XIV, then, the royal mistress was an expected and recognized presence. Her romantic relationship with the king was known to all, including the queen, and her role as political adviser an open secret.[13] Louis XIV's two most prominent mistresses, Françoise Louise de La Baume Le Blanc de La Vallière, Duchess of Vaujours (1644–1710), and Françoise-Athénaïs de Rochechouart de Mortemart, Marquise de Montespan (1640–1707), fulfilled the office in distinctive ways, Montespan the more successfully according to contemporary opinion. The attitude of eyewitness observers vis-à-vis La Vallière was dismissive. Because members of the court did not recognize her as an adroit political player, she was unable to realize the possibilities available to the skilled royal mistress. Montespan was far more widely admired even as many grew to resent her imperiousness over time. The king's last mistress, Françoise d'Aubigné [Scarron], Marquise de Maintenon (1635–1719), was also widely recognized as an adept political adviser. However, we consider her tenure in less detail; Maintenon became the king's morganatic wife (although secretly), and for this reason she is in a category apart from the other official mistresses.[14] In addition to reports from ambassadors, our principal sources are memoirs and personal letters detailing court gossip. These sources allow us to add a sort of immediacy to the narratives of the royal mistresses of the courts of Louis XIV and XV that we can only dream of for their earlier colleagues.

REVISITING LOUISE DE LA VALLIÈRE

Cardinal Mazarin served as Louis XIV's chief minister until his death in 1661. At that point, Louis declared himself his own prime minister, which allowed him to weigh advice from a number of individuals, including his mother and former regent, Anne of Austria (1601–1666).[15] The queen mother's powerful presence at court left no space for a strong official mistress. It is not surprising that Louise de La Vallière, Louis's first recognized mistress, a woman willing to remain in the shadows at court, was not one who would satisfy the mature king after his mother's death.

The traditional narrative of Louis XIV's mistresses is a rather simplistic one. The young and innocent La Vallière, passion of Louis XIV's youth, supposedly cared little for the trappings of kingship and loved Louis for himself alone. Eventually, however, her guilt over their illicit relationship, as well as her despair at losing her position to a more glamorous woman, sent her to the convent of the Carmelite nuns in 1674. Montespan, imperious and stunningly beautiful, filled the role of official mistress during the prime years of Louis XIV's reign, her presence at his side filling him with pride. Capricious, ambitious, and demanding, she battled on multiple fronts to hold on to her position as long as possible, leaving court only in 1691, more than ten years after her sexual relationship with the king had ended. She was eventually supplanted by the intelligent and religious Maintenon, whose calm and devout demeanor was a balm to Louis in his

middle and old age. The pious Maintenon would preside over the stultifi-
cation of court life and the eventual decline of France's dominant position
in Europe.[16]

This contrast between the saintly La Vallière and the gorgeous but
grasping Montespan requires nuance.[17] Certainly history has been kinder
to Louise, the ideal woman—at least, according to later commentators—
as well as the ideal penitent, than it has been to Montespan. However, in
La Vallière's own time, observers were not always so generous, especially
about her decision to leave the king and enter the religious life in 1674.
While Mademoiselle d'Armentières pronounced that she "was never so
beautiful nor so content" as the day she became became a Carmelite nun,
Bussy-Rabutin's view of the affair was a bit more jaded: "The conversion
of mademoiselle de la Vallière confirms for me more and more that God
attracts people to himself by all sorts of paths. He would have experienced
difficulty, if one dares to speak thusly, drawing this penitent from the arms
of her lover, or even if [the king] had left her for reasons other than another
lover; but jealousy brought about this miracle."[18]

We cannot know whether La Vallière would have been so devoted to
Louis in the first place had he not been surrounded by the trappings of
kingship, but we do know that she benefited from her association with
him. And while she affected an air of docile passivity, it does not appear
that she willingly ceded her position as the king's lover to Montespan,
fighting a rearguard action, but less successfully than the more socially
accomplished Montespan. While her religiosity made La Vallière uncomfortable with the sinfulness of her position, she did, at times, try to situate
herself in the pantheon of official mistresses. Like her predecessors, she
sat for a portrait as the huntress Diana, which made sense for a young
woman adept at hunting at the same time that it drew on the by-now-
commonplace association.[19] But Montespan was the more successful even
at this symbolic effort; her portrayal as Diana was far more evocative than
that of La Vallière. Elise Goodman describes Pierre Mignard's portrait of
Montespan as Diana in its sensual glory: "The ravishing consort reclines
languorously before a landscape, her quiver and arrows resting at her side,
the hunt ended, Louis captured."[20]

Nor did La Vallière perform the role of official mistress with the panache
and brilliance that Montespan brought to the role. As Louis grew into his
position as the most powerful monarch in western Europe, it was imperative that the woman at the center of the court demonstrate a profound
sensitivity to the nuances and demands of its political machinations so

that she could serve as an effective adviser to the king and patron to her friends. It was a performance beyond La Vallière's capabilities.

The early story of La Vallière's romance with Louis is well known. Recently married to the dull and unattractive Infanta of Spain, Marie-Thérèse (1638–1683), for whom he had abandoned his first love, Marie Mancini, Louis found amusement and passion with his sister-in-law, Henriette (1644–1670), sister of Charles II of England. Marie-Christine Moine argues that Henriette, "refined and cultivated," exercised considerable, although discreet, influence on the early court life of Louis's reign, given the inadequacies of his wife in that regard.[21] However, this relationship distressed the queen mother, who was also the aunt of the new queen, and Henriette's mother, Henrietta Maria, former queen of England. Cowed by the queen mothers but unwilling to break off their relationship, Louis and Henriette seem to have plotted to find a new "love interest" for the young king: a member of Henriette's household, who would serve as a decoy for Louis and his sister-in-law. Their choice was La Vallière.[22]

La Vallière, born in 1644, came from the minor nobility of the Touraine. Her stepfather was the *premier maître d'hôtel* in the household of Louis XIV's disgraced uncle, Gaston of Orléans, in Blois. La Vallière became a *demoiselle d'honneur* to the princesses of Orléans. On the death of Gaston in 1660, La Vallière and her family followed his widow to Paris. A distant relative helped her obtain a position as *fille d'honneur* in the household of Henriette of England, new bride of the king's brother, Philippe of Orléans (1640–1701).[23]

But to everyone's surprise, the cover story soon became Louis XIV's new passion. The pretty, blond La Vallière, just seventeen years old, seemed an ideal mistress for the young king. She adored him and had little interest in drawing attention to herself and to her position. Her family was happy to encourage the king's interest, allowing him to carry on a quiet (although far from secret) love affair. Versailles was still a relatively modest royal residence at this point; the king would take La Vallière there to enjoy private moments with her.[24]

It is clear that Louis XIV remained attached to La Vallière for a number of years. It was less clear to his courtiers, however, why he remained devoted to her as long as he did.[25] La Vallière was not universally acclaimed as a beauty. Although Madame de Motteville wrote that she was "pleasant, and her beauty had great appeal because of the striking white and crimson of her complexion, because of her blue eyes that had much sweetness, and because of the beauty of her silvery hair, which increased that of her face,"

Ézéchiel Spanheim, the diplomat from Brandenburg, described her as a woman of "mediocre birth and beauty, and a fairly limited mind."[26] The Marquis de Sourches (1645–1716), grand prévôt of France, wrote that she was "a girl of mediocre quality; she was not a usual beauty; she was a little too thin, but blond, very well put-together, and perfectly agreeable with gentle and attractive manners."[27] La Vallière was reticent and lacked the wit and esprit of the more popular ladies of the court; in a cruel comparison, Savoyard ambassador the Marquis de Saint-Maurice wrote that Montespan, who would supplant Louise, had "much more charm than madame de La Vallière and infinitely more spirit and playfulness in her conduct."[28] Profoundly religious, La Vallière experienced sometimes crushing guilt over her relationship with the king, at one point running away to a convent from which the king came to fetch her, although John B. Wolf suggests that such behavior was a ploy, "one of the ways this sweet, simple, gentle young woman used to dominate her lover; she could not stage a scene, but running away was just as effective. She was the 'clinging vine' type and her methods worked well when their love was still young."[29]

The king wanted to honor and recognize his young mistress, and even while soft-pedaling her role out of respect for his mother and wife, he encouraged her participation in the spectacles of court life. Despite her slight lameness, she was skilled on horseback, attending hunting parties, and she also took part alongside the king in the ballets that were so popular in the early years of his reign. Most famously, "The Pleasures of the Enchanted Island," a sumptuous three-day pageant held at Versailles in 1664, was ostensibly dedicated to the two queens, Louis XIV's wife and mother, but everyone knew that it was for La Vallière.[30] This "open secret" harked back to the royal entry of Henri II and Catherine de Médicis into Lyon in 1549, with the festivities that obliquely rendered homage to Diane de Poitiers. La Vallière's timidity affected the nature of courtly spectacle in these early years. The guest list for the festival was limited to six hundred favored courtiers, and the setting—Versailles before it was the immense palace it would become—was natural and intimate. At a later date, when Montespan was the reigning favorite, the guest list would expand significantly, and the events would reflect her splendor.[31]

La Vallière's limitations as royal mistress were manifest early on. However, her willingness to remain in the shadows when Anne of Austria discovered a lump in her breast in 1664 and slowly succumbed to breast cancer served Louis's purposes. He could continue his relationship with his loyal and accommodating mistress while acting as a devoted son until his mother's death in January 1666. Anne's death freed Louis to structure the social and ceremonial life of the court as he wished, with a new favorite at its center.

Louis's voracious love of women and sexual pleasure linked him with the virility of his grandfather, Henri IV, the Vert Galant; indeed, Wolf notes that he had the blood of "a Henry IV in his veins."[32] There was certainly no shortage of women competing to fill the role of official mistress, especially in the wake of his mother's death. Still, Louis showed loyalty to his first mistress, showering her and their children (only two of whom survived infancy) with honors, culminating in the creation of the duchy of Vaujours in her name in 1667. However, he already had his eye on another woman, the Marquise de Montespan, whose beauty and wit had taken the court by storm.

THE RISE OF MONTESPAN

Montespan possessed the qualities that La Vallière lacked and that would make her uniquely suited to play the role of unofficial queen at Louis's court. Noble birth and cultivation of the already celebrated "esprit Mortemart" meant that she brought éclat to the royal court.[33] Descriptions of her in action recall Castiglione's "sprezzatura." According to Maintenon's biographer, the Abbé de Berthier, when Montespan appeared at the court, she "eclipsed all that had appeared there before her. . . . A natural nonchalance . . . made her words, her smallest movements, charming, creating the most harmonious & most sensual beauty. The appeal of features & mind seemed to be hereditary in the Mortemart family."[34]

Born in October 1640 in Lussac-lès-Châteaux, Montespan studied at the convent Sainte-Marie des Saintes and was presented at court in 1660 as Mademoiselle de Tonnay-Charente.[35] At the request of the queen mother, she became a *demoiselle d'honneur* to the new queen, Marie-Thérèse.[36] On marrying the Marquis de Montespan (1640–1691) in January 1663, a spouse of good family but little wealth, she lost her position as *fille d'honneur*. However, her husband's cousin, the Maréchal d'Albret, opened his home and salon to the young marquise.

This salon training was essential, allowing Montespan to refine her manners and wit. She adopted the classical Greek name "Athénaïs."[37] Her older sister, the Marquise de Thianges, introduced her to a useful ally, Philippe of Orléans, or Monsieur, the king's brother.[38] Despite her youth, her quick-witted participation in wordplay made a vivid impression on the other *salonniers*, as well as Monsieur.[39] He took a liking to her and helped her acquire a new position as one of the queen's six *dames d'honneur* in the winter of 1664.[40]

The queen and La Vallière also liked Montespan, and La Vallière, shy and reticent, got into the habit of including the vivacious and amusing Montespan in her soirées with the the king. The Marquis de La Fare (1644–1712) describes how effectively Montespan used her friendship with the queen, as well as the king's mistress, to draw attention to herself:

> At a time when the King was dreaming of madame de Monaco, madame de Montespan began to focus on him, and was clever enough to do two things at the same time: first, to provide the Queen with an extraordinary opinion of her virtue, by receiving communion in her presence weekly; then, to curry favor with mademoiselle de La Vallière, whom she never left, so that she was spending all her time with the King, and did everything she could to please him, which was not difficult to do with [her] great wit, next to La Vallière who had little.[41]

The Abbé de Berthier also suggests that Louis XIV grew bored with the diffidence of La Vallière, a fact that Montespan used to her advantage.[42] Court observer Primi Visconti insinuates that La Vallière was naive in bringing such a beautiful and vivacious woman to the attention of the king and suggests that she herself was to blame for the course of events; Montespan's grace and wit so pleased La Vallière "that she could not go without having her around or speaking well of her to the king. Hearing of her so often, and in such positive terms, made him curious to get to know her better and consequently he rapidly preferred [Montespan] to her friend." Visconti had little sympathy for La Vallière's complaints about the course of events, since "she was herself responsible for what happened."[43]

It is not certain when the affair between Montespan and Louis XIV began. Evidence suggests that Montespan had replaced Louise as the king's favorite by May 1667, around the time that he created the duchy of Vaujours for La Vallière.[44] The Marquis de La Fare, enamored of Montespan but dissuaded from pursuing the relationship when he perceived the king's interest, reported that it was during the 1667 military campaign in Flanders, which the queen and her household accompanied, that "the King's passion for her erupted."[45] The king's cousin, La Grande

Mademoiselle, also made reference to Louis XIV's developing affair with Montespan during that campaign:

> The king would visit Mme de la Vallière. He often saw Mme de Montespan, so they say, in her room. During this trip, her lodgings were above his. One day, while dining, the queen complained about how late bedtime was, turned to me and said, "The king didn't come to bed until four o'clock; it was already daybreak. I don't know how he is entertaining himself." He said to her: "I read dispatches and write responses." She said to him: "But you could do it at another time." He smiled, and so that she would not see it, turned his head toward me. I wanted to do the same, but didn't lift my eyes from my plate.[46]

It was during this military campaign that La Vallière too must have become aware of the king's interest in Montespan. Newly raised to duchess and pregnant, La Vallière was left behind while other women of the court accompanied the king to Flanders. Realizing that her position might be in danger, she hurried to join the court, but the king was visibly displeased to see her, and Marie-Thérèse furious.[47] The purportedly modest and self-effacing La Vallière had planned a dramatic *beau geste* that fell flat in a way that must have been humiliating—a failed performance. She remained at court, painfully aware of her diminished standing.

There is ample evidence that courtiers agreed that La Vallière had been less than satisfactory as the king's mistress and that the glorious Montespan would be a more impressive choice. The Duke of Enghien had already reported to the queen of Poland in 1666 that court watchers believed that the king had taken an interest in Montespan and that "to speak the truth, she well deserves it, for no one can be wittier, nor more beautiful than she."[48] In contrast, La Vallière's "gentle and self-effacing" manner did not suit the needs of court life.[49] By the end, it appears that the king found her dull; the Marquis de Saint-Maurice reported in 1673 that while Montespan was giving birth to her fourth child with the king, Louis "was extremely bored in the coach, because, I am assured, he no longer speaks to madame de la Vallière," who was in the carriage with him.[50]

Still, Montespan had to be careful about stepping onto center stage. There were many reasons that her role had to remain an "open secret." Unlike La Vallière, Montespan was married, and her husband showed little appetite for playing the role of dupe. A man with a theatrical flair himself, the Marquis de Montespan staged a "funeral" for his wife to demonstrate that she was dead to him once her relationship with the king was established.[51] For this reason, it was convenient to keep La Vallière at court as his officially recognized mistress, although most courtiers—and the king's subjects outside the court—recognized that Montespan was now the favorite. Their temporary shared tenure represents the exception that proves the rule. The Duke of Saint-Simon (1675–1755), writing long after the fact, described the situation that ensued with distaste, noting that the king "provided a new spectacle to the world of two mistresses at the same time. He travels with them to the borders, to camps, when he is with the army, both of them in the Queen's coach. People come running from all around to see the three queens and ask others simply if they had seen them [as well]."[52] La Vallière's pain over this humiliating situation, and perhaps a desire to bring Louis's attention back to herself, led her to flee the court again in early 1671. The king did not seek her out this time; rather, he sent others to bring her back, first the Marquis de Bellefonds, and, when he failed to persuade her to return, his contrôleur-général, Jean-Baptiste Colbert (1619–1683).[53] Bussy-Rabutin, who claimed that he had predicted that she would flee for months, pronounced himself baffled at the course of events, suggesting that Montespan, despite her forced delight at La Vallière's return, would not long tolerate the course of events.[54]

> I knew about the duchess de la Vallière's despair in love, the efforts
> of the king to see her again, and the joy when she returned. The
> behavior of the duchess seems quite natural to me, but I under-
> stand not at all the king's actions, because it is clear that he feels
> great passion for madame de Montespan. If he were simply content
> to bring madame de la Vallière back [to court], I would assume
> that he had been obliged to do so for political [reasons], so that
> he would have a pretext for madame de Montespan. But the tears
> of sorrow and of joy that he shed when the duchess left and at her
> return showed extraordinary tenderness. However, he is going to
> have to make up his mind, because madame de Montespan will
> demand her place, and my sense is that he will declare himself for
> her, and that he will separate himself from madame de la Vallière.
> I also believe that this will lead to a furor at the court and maybe
> considerable change.[55]

The tenderness that the king felt for his first mistress lingered a long time, even as Montespan assumed first place both at the court and in his heart. Ever cynical, Bussy-Rabutin wrote to Madame de Scudéry that "you will never get me to agree that he merits praise for showing respect for the mistresses he abandons. He is not trying to soothe them for the pain he caused them in ending their relationship, and I would even maintain that it is in his own interest, and for political [reasons] that he has brought madame de la Vallière back [to court]."[56]

THE REIGN OF MONTESPAN

Over time, the complicated dance between Montespan and La Vallière became intolerable to all concerned. Somehow, Montespan's personal situation had to be resolved to make her presence at court as the king's recognized mistress less fraught. If divorce was impossible, a separation could be arranged. However, even this king could not make it happen immediately. It was not until 1674 that the separation of Madame and the Marquis de Montespan was finalized—probably not coincidentally, the same year that La Vallière left the court for good and became a Carmelite nun. By this point, court watchers such as the Marquis de Saint-Maurice had observed that while "Mesdames de La Vallière and de Montespan are [both] at Court . . . they no longer live together, and the King goes every day as usual to the rooms of the latter without visiting the duchess."[57] That the king no longer even pretended that La Vallière interested him was undoubtedly the final push in her decision to leave. She did so in a dramatically staged ceremony designed to show her penitence over her sinful affair with the king, but also perhaps a not-so-subtle dig at his current mistress.[58] If La Vallière was incapable of occupying the role of royal mistress with panache, she excelled at the role of martyr, not necessarily the part that Louis wanted for his sexual partner and the ornament of his court, and not one that previous, more successful royal mistresses had embraced. Montespan, for her part, was happy to accept the public homage of the magnificent festival at Versailles that summer that was only ostensibly to celebrate the king's victory in the Franche-Comté.[59]

Montespan's success was the result of a number of personal factors. Her renowned beauty was certainly key: Saint-Simon wrote that she was "beautiful as the day until the last moment of her life,"[60] while Primi Visconti elaborated that she "had blond hair, big blue eyes the color of the sky, an aquiline nose, but very nicely shaped, a small rosy mouth, beautiful teeth, in one word, a perfect face."[61] When Louis in July 1668 organized his second great festival at Versailles after "The Pleasures of the Enchanted Island," "The Royal Entertainment of Versailles," Montespan was central to the festivities.[62] This pageant represented a shift in the nature of royal festivities, influenced by the presence of the new mistress: "With Madame de Montespan, festivals experience additional pomp, magnificence, and innovation, such as waterworks and floodlights for the walking paths and gondolas."[63] With her separation from her husband finalized and La Vallière departed from court, Montespan could more openly help organize the "Royal Entertainment" of 1674.[64]

Montespan was indeed a woman of whom Louis could be proud, a woman who contributed to the *gloire* that was so important to him. Her celebrated good taste extended to art, literature, music, and architecture. She sponsored some of the most talented and celebrated artists, writers, and musicians of the time, including Boileau, Corneille, Racine, La Fontaine, Lully, and Mignard (who painted her several times), as well as the architect Mansart and the famous gardener Le Nôtre.[65] She was also a fashion trendsetter whose noted beauty set off the stylized fashions of the court to perfection.[66] In 1673 she created a new style of dress, *la robe battante*, referred to mockingly as "l'innocente," with a looser cut of bodice that allowed her to endure her many pregnancies in greater comfort and achieved enormous popularity.[67] She wore the admired *hurluberlu* hairstyle, with curls around her face and cheeks, decorated with ribbons and pearls.[68] According to Joan DeJean, "in areas from fashion to architecture to interior decoration, the Marquise de Montespan invented a new category: the royal mistress as tastemaker."[69]

In spite of her celebrated beauty, Montespan was far from simply an "ornament of the court." The noted "esprit Mortemart" made not only Montespan but her equally lovely sisters, Madame de Thianges and Gabrielle, the abbess of Fontevrault, valued company.[70] She worked hard to elevate the intellectual life of the court. Orest Ranum highlights her central cultural role during her years as mistress, praising her as intelligent and well read, commissioning artistic and literary works that would honor the king, and fully capable of discussing literary and historical topics with the king and celebrated writers.[71] Montespan's successful performance as patron of the arts was one of the most important that a mistress could play. After all, part of the job of the royal mistress was to display not only her own charms but also the glories of France.[72] "A triumphant beauty who inspired the admiration of all the ambassadors," she served the monarchy well, ensuring that the French royal court was the most cultured and admired in the world.[73]

As a result of her aristocratic background and membership in the powerful Pardaillan-Rochechouart clan—but more importantly, because of her closeness to the king and position—Montespan was politically influential. Her skill at managing the subleties of polite behavior guaranteed her effectiveness as a patron to other clients at the court, in contrast with La Vallière. Wolf writes of the "myth" of La Vallière, who "is remembered as the girl who did not ask for anything but love, who even failed to tell the king that she had a brother until he stumbled on the fact by himself." In fact, La Vallière had been just as ready to request favors of the king as any of his mistresses or courtiers. Although often quite minor, the requests were constant. Wolf suggests that "Louis must finally have been tired of her requests and surprised that she used her influence so foolishly" and further notes that "neither Madame de Montespan nor Madame de Maintenon ever made such mistakes."[74] A woman skilled in the ways of court politics and sensitive to the appearance of greediness was far more useful to other courtiers than one who expended her capital unwisely.

We have underlined the more fluid definition of the political in the early modern court: the fact that female courtiers were significant political players would have surprised no one there. Emmanuel Le Roy Ladurie, in his influential work on court cabals, has emphasized how political influence operated through the activities of the various factions at court, centered on powerful players who helped place their allies into important positions.[75] The activities of an influential mistress, such as Montespan, were multifaceted. She sometimes acted as a patron, assisting and protecting her clients and their children, arranging marriages and finding offices for them. She would also act as a broker, bringing together people and opportunities, serving as intermediary, and helping facilitate negotiations.[76] She served as a conduit for pensions, gifts, emoluments for offices or military ranks, and commissions as well as honorary rewards, speculative opportunities, or simply the advantages of her friendship. It was not only the force of Montespan's personality and noted wit that brought individuals into her orbit; cultivation of the king's mistress could bring material advantages to individuals and families.[77] Her ability to effectively deploy her resources contributed to her unparalleled ascendancy at the court for nearly fifteen years. She used her credit to good effect, and all knew that she was a useful ally.[78] Bussy-Rabutin explicitly underlines this in a letter to Madame de Montmorency in 1670 enumerating the benefits that had come to Montespan's family and friends through her patronage: "You know about the governorship of Paris given to M. de Mortemart; the position of General of the Galleys to M. de Vivonne; the lieutenancy of the chevau-légers of Anjou to Thianges; the abbey of Fontevraud to madame de Mortemart, sister of madame de Montespan; the marriage of mademoiselle de Thianges with the duc de Nevers, and the governorship of Guienne to the maréchal d'Albret."[79] The Marquis de Sourches also made note of her success in rewarding her friends with powerful positions: "to the duchesse de Richelieu, the position of *dame d'honneur* to the Queen, and to the duc de Montausier, her friend, that of governor to Monseigneur le Dauphin."[80] The Maréchal de Bellefonds was named *premier écuyer* in the *maison de la Dauphine*, thanks to Montespan's efforts.[81] She reportedly helped procure the position of first physician for Antoine d'Aquin, previously physician to the queen, in 1672.[82] When the imminent death of the Duchess of Montausier promised a vacancy for the position of *dame d'honneur de la Reine*, there were numerous candidates for the position; however, according to the Marquis of Saint-Maurice, "we believe that madame de Montespan will win it for the duchesse de Richelieu, her good friend."[83] When the position of *premier président* in the Paris Parlement came open, Bussy-Rabutin was convinced that Montespan's wishes would carry the day.[84] In a court society, the ability to place allies into important positions was a display of genuine political power.

Montespan's family and most useful friends were the primary beneficiaries of her patronage. Those who had assisted in her rise to power also profited. The Maréchal d'Albret reaped the benefits of his earlier mentorship, while the efforts of Madame de Montausier, fellow *précieuse* and *dame d'honneur* to the queen, to facilitate the king's early relationship with Montespan brought favor to her family.[85] Madame de Richelieu was also rewarded for her faithful support. Even the queen turned to her for assistance. When her Spanish chambermaids were accused of spying and ordered out of the country, Montespan obtained permission to stay for one woman who was married to a Frenchman. "The queen is thrilled and says that she will never forget this intercession," wrote Madame de Sévigné.[86]

At a time when marriages were of great political significance for powerful families, arranging them was a primary activity of court women, especially queens.[87] Montespan took on this task as well, and she was instrumental in arranging the advantageous marriages of her children, nieces, and nephews. In 1670 Madame de Sévigné wrote to her son-in-law of the upcoming marriage between the Duke of Nevers and Montespan's niece, Mademoiselle de Thianges: "Madame de Montespan will be in charge of the wedding on Sunday; she will act as mother and receive all the credit. The king gives M. de Nevers all of his offices; so that this beauty, who hasn't a penny, is worth more than the greatest heiress in France. Madame de Montespan brings about wonders everywhere."[88] In 1677 she helped with the marriage of her niece to the Duke of Elbeuf; the king "takes care of everything" [pourvoit à tout] for the young spouses.[89] She played a key role in arranging the marriage of her nephew, Louis de Rochechouart, to the youngest daughter of contrôleur-général Jean-Baptiste Colbert, a move that cemented their already close relationship.[90] In her memoirs, La Grande Mademoiselle commented on Montespan's preoccupation with finding suitable spouses for her own children.[91] Montespan's three daughters with Louis who survived to adulthood were married to Princes of the Blood, while their two adult sons, the Duke of Maine and the Count of Toulouse, were married to princesses from the royal family, marriages that caused considerable outrage at court.[92] In 1686 her legitimate son with the Marquis de Montespan, the Marquis d'Antin, contracted a prestigious marriage with the eldest daughter of the Duke of Uzès; it was Montespan and the Duke of Montausier who provided generously for the young couple.[93] These marriages linked her with some of the most powerful families in France while improving the prestige and position of her children with the king.

In recent years some historians have been willing to acknowledge the influential role of aristocratic women in the maneuvering for favors and position in the early modern court, and even to credit these activities with political importance.[94] However, they have been more reticent about acknowledging mistresses as valued advisers to the king, undoubtedly influenced by the reluctance to believe that a man such as Louis XIV would turn to a woman for advice in the domain of "high politics," that is, affairs of state, domestic and foreign. And yet the Marquis de Feuquières (1648–1711) openly acknowledged Montespan's influence alongside that of Louis's powerful minister, Colbert, in changing the priorities of his reign— at the expense of the king's international standing, in Feuquières's opinion. He linked his analysis of the end of the war against Holland in 1672 to personal and political machinations at the court in which Montespan was involved, in particular the jealousy and conflict between Louis's minister of war, François-Michel Le Tellier, Marquis of Louvois, and Colbert, whose youngest daughter was married to Montespan's nephew: "[Colbert's] credit grew as a result & while at that time, it was easy to believe that one [military] campaign would suffice to achieve the conquest of the Netherlands, that clever Minister, in concert with the Mistress, was able to replace the King's glory and ambition to be the most powerful prince in Europe with a love of pleasure and building."[95] In Feuquières's disapproving narrative, Colbert's financial prudence dovetailed nicely with his ally Montespan's influence over Louis's military decisions.

We see Montespan's influence in military affairs, or at least her influence in the eyes of court chroniclers, in other instances as well. Her brother, the Duke of Vivonne (1636–1688), sought her help in 1676, writing her from Messina to ask that she intercede with the king to get him money, food, munitions, and better troops for a military campaign.[96] She was also instrumental in obtaining for him the *bâton de maréchal de France* against the desires of the king and, once again, the Marquis of Louvois, if the Abbé de Choisy is to be believed.[97] The Marquis of Puyguilhem (better known as Duke of Lauzun, his later title) was for a time a close friend of Montespan's, and he asked her to intercede with the king to help him obtain a regiment.[98]

We have already seen that Montespan accompanied Louis on his military campaigns. Evidence also suggests that councils of war were sometimes held in her chambers; Colbert's son, the Marquis of Seignelay, made note of this.[99] The imperial envoy to the Dutch Estates General, Franz Paul von Lisola (1613–1674), reported to the imperial chancellor, Johann Paul Hocher (1616–1683), that Spanish troops had intercepted several of Louis's couriers on their way to Paris and read four letters addressed to Montespan "in which extremely flattering love speeches alternated with detailed reports on the progress of the siege [of Maastricht], like a report for a high officer."[100] In his analysis of Louis's interactions with Montespan during the 1673 campaign, Carl J. Ekberg accepts Louis's assertion that he did not allow his mistresses to influence affairs of state, although he does believe that a "superb and demanding mistress like Montespan exercised a more subtle influence upon the king's policies." He suggests that Montespan's inclusion in these discussions was the result of "the king's need to demonstrate his virility to Montespan, and to himself."[101] However, it seems just as plausible that Louis regularly confided affairs of state and military matters to a woman whose intellect he respected and whose advice he valued. We hear echoes of Agnès Sorel credited with stiffening the king's martial resolve.

Once again, Montespan's role as key adviser to the king appears to have been an open secret at the court and among court observers such as Lisola.

The fact that Louis continued to visit Montespan's chambers most days after Mass or in the evening, and that they dined together frequently even after their sexual relationship had ended, suggests that he continued to value her counsel. In his journal, the Marquis of Dangeau (1638–1720) makes frequent reference to Louis's visits and dinners in Montespan's chambers, mentioning that the two discussed politics on occasion. For example, in August 1684 he reported that one evening, "after the king's dinner, M. de Croissy came to speak to H. M. in the rooms of madame de Montespan; he brought with him news of the signing of the truce, the Emperor and the Empire granting to the king all that he had asked for," going on to discuss the provisions in some detail. These visits were part of Louis's routine. At the end of the year 1684, Dangeau reported, "We usually left Mass between one and two o'clock, and the king went to visit madame de Montespan until his meat was brought to him."[102] The physical spaces that Montespan occupied at court were both a symbolic and a concrete representation of her influence. When the construction of Versailles was completed in 1676, Louis awarded Montespan twenty rooms on the first floor; in contrast, the queen received eleven on the second floor.[103] Still, in her frequent mentions in the *Mercure galant*, she is referred to only as Madame de Montespan. Even her obituary refers to her as Madame de Montespan Surintendante de la maison de la feuë Reine—with no mention of her relationship to the king.[104] The veil remained in place.

While Montespan served as an important adviser to the king, the pair shared an intense mutual attraction that was sometimes difficult to manage, despite Louis's legendary self-control. Attention to the dictates of honor was essential to aristocratic self-presentation in the emotional regime that dominated social practices in the seventeenth-century French court.[105] But court observers were well aware of the erotic tension and passion that made separation so difficult for this couple. Although Montespan's glorious beauty was a source of pride to the king, and he relished her place at the center of court life, their relationship was problematic. At combative moments in their relationship, Montespan even accused the king of simply wanting to display her like a prize rather than feeling genuine love for her.[106] More important, Montespan was married and her husband, as we have seen, was most unhappy about her love affair with the king. The king and his mistress were both in the uncomfortable and highly visible position of double adultery, presumably part of the reason he had tried to veil, if not conceal, his romantic relationship with Montespan by maintaining La Vallière as his official mistress

for so long.[107] While the king was unwilling to forego his sensual pleasures, he was sufficiently religious to feel guilty about the nature of his
relationship with Montespan. This came to a head in April 1675, when
the priest at the parish church of Versailles publicly refused Montespan
communion because she was living in a state of sin. Louis XIV confronted
Jacques-Bénigne Bossuet, then bishop of Condom (1627–1704), about
this affront to his mistress, but Bossuet urged the king to leave her and
to reconcile himself with his queen and God.[108] This public condemna-
tion was too much for the king, who agreed to send Montespan from the
court.[109] When informed of the king's decision, Montespan was unable to
control her anger and despair—at first. She fell into a rage and spent two
days locked in her apartments, refusing to see anyone. Bossuet, whom
Montespan blamed for the king's determination, tried to convince her
that the separation was for the best.[110] The king too suffered "in no less
despair. He did not take communion, as was customary, and appeared
with the queen, eyes red, 'like a man who had been crying.'" (This was
according to a letter that Bossuet wrote to the Maréchal de Bellefonds on
20 June 1675.) The king left for the military campaign in Flanders without telling his mistress goodbye.[111]

Few believed, however, that Louis would be able to resist returning to
Montespan once he allowed her to come back to Versailles.[112] And indeed,
the separation did not last for long, her triumphant return to court and her
position as official mistress of the king affirmed by court watchers a little
more than a year later.[113] Montespan's friends had fought for her return to
Versailles, arguing that she and the king should meet privately first so that
it would be less of a shock when they met in public. On that basis, the
king paid Montespan a visit; Madame de Caylus's poignant account of
their reunion underlines the passion between the two:

> So as not to give the least subject for gossip . . . the most respectable
> and serious ladies of the court would be present for the meet-
> ing, and the King would see madame de Montespan only in their
> company. So the King went to visit madame de Montespan, as he
> had decided; but gradually, he drew her near a window; they spoke
> for a while, cried, and said to each other the things one usually
> says in a similar case; next, they made a low bow to those venera-
> ble matrons, and went into another room, and [from the reunion]
> came madame la duchesse d'Orléans, and then M. le comte de
> Toulouse (their two next children).[114]

By August 1676 Madame de Sévigné was reporting to her daughter, "never has the sovereign power of *Quanto* [her nickname for Montespan] been so well established."[115] The king permitted unusual familiarity in public; in another letter Sévigné noted, "I was told that the other day, *Quanto* had her head resting intimately on the shoulder of her *friend* [the king]; it was believed that this affectation was to say, *I am better than ever*": an impressive performance of her power over the king.[116]

The relationship played out before the members of the court, who examined every move of their romance with fascination. According to Madame de Sévigné, "We followed the steps of Madame de Montespan; we hear everywhere what she says, what she does, what she eats, when she sleeps."[117] They also watched breathlessly for any sign of a diminution in her power. The correspondence of Bussy-Rabutin, though exiled since 1665, chronicled the growing influence of Madame de Ludre throughout the early months of 1677 as well as Montespan's efforts to undercut her.[118] As that drama ended, the report was that Montespan was "more the mistress than ever."[119] Madame de Sévigné made explicit reference to the legacy of Diane de Poitiers in writing to her daughter of Montespan's victory over Ludre: "Oh, my daughter! such a triumph at Versailles! . . . Such [a] Duchess of Valentinois!"[120] In 1678, perhaps thinking of the portrait of Agnès Sorel that hung in his chateau, Bussy-Rabutin drew a comparison between those earlier lovers, Agnès and Charles, and Louis XIV and Montespan in a letter to Madame de Sévigné we referred to earlier: "They inform me that Madame de Montespan suffered from two attacks of the tertian fever but that she is now well; she is not made for traveling, given her size. I notice, however, that the king loves her dearly and that he is right to do so, that he loves himself still more than he loves her, and he is not like Charles VII, who, rather than take the belle Agnès along with the army, stayed with her at Meun or at Bourges, while his kingdom was being attacked."[121]

THE WANING OF MONTESPAN

Guy Chaussinand-Nogaret suggests that by the late 1670s, given the king's wandering eye and need of "new flesh," "Montespan remained the favorite, but a favorite in name only."[122] Despite Montespan's playing her role to perfection during the prime of Louis's life and reign, the king's needs were changing as he matured into middle age. As more women challenged Montespan's position, her arrogance and capricious attitude, long noted by courtiers, became more pronounced. At the same time, her celebrated looks were beginning to fade as her weight increased dramatically.[123] Her relationship with the king, always combative, grew more so, and their heated disputes increased in number and intensity.[124] Court watchers noted that her hold on him had diminished. As time went on, her willfulness may have seemed less attractive. It was certainly at odds with the modesty and tranquility that he appreciated in his other mistresses, such as La Vallière in his youth, and Madame de Maintenon, who would become the companion of his old age.[125]

Louis's affair with the celebrated beauty Marie-Angélique de Scoraille de Roussille, the Duchess of Fontanges (1661–1681), in the late 1670s spelled the end of Montespan's reign. It is unlikely that the gorgeous Fontanges could have fulfilled Louis's expectations for long, the Abbé de Choisy snidely describing her as "beautiful as an angel and stupid as a basket."[126] Others also suggested that she was quite insipid.[127] Madame de Caylus wrote of her:

> Madame de Fontanges combined her lack of wit with romantic ideas that her provincial education and the praise for her beauty had inspired in her; and, in truth, the King was only attracted to her looks; he even looked ashamed when she spoke, and it was not just the two of them. One gets used to beauty, but one does not get used to stupidity . . . especially when, at the same time, one sees [her] around people with the wit and character of madame de Montespan, who notices any ridiculous behavior [*à qui les moindres ridicules n'échappoient point*], and who know how to point it out to others with that unique flair of the [members] of the house of Montemart.[128]

A woman so bereft of intelligence could not have satisfied Louis's need for a polished and clever companion by his side, nor could she have served as a respected adviser. Her death in childbirth at the age of twenty in 1681 ended her brief reign.

But Fontanges's demise did not lead to the return of Montespan as official mistress; the pious and sober Madame de Maintenon, governess of Montespan's children with the king, would replace her.[129] By 1682, Louis was offering Maintenon an honored place in his carriage instead of Montespan.[130] This slow loss of prestige, even while the king continued to visit her on a regular basis, caused Montespan immense pain. In a letter dated 6 April 1680, Madame de Sévigné wrote, "Madame de Montespan is enraged; she cried much yesterday; you can imagine the torture her pride is suffering, which is still more outraged by the high favor of Madame de Maintenon."[131] It seems that the reported involvement of Montespan in the Affair of the Poisons hastened her fall. While Montespan's name did not surface publicly during the notorious scandal as it unfolded in the late 1670s, Gabriel-Nicolas de La Reynie, the lieutenant general of police in Paris and the rapporteur-commissaire in the investigations associated with the affair, passed on word of her reported involvement to the king. Louis's ardor was already cooling, but undoubtedly the sordidness of the affair affected his feelings.[132]

THE ASCENDANCE OF MAINTENON

The Marquise de Maintenon would serve more openly as Louis's adviser on all matters, even if the king's passion for her never appeared as intense as it was for Montespan. By the time Louis XIV turned to Maintenon with romantic intent, she had been a member of the royal household for years; ironically, it was Montespan who had procured her a pension and eventually a position as governess to her children.[133] Montespan's relationship with the then Madame Scarron dated to their early years as *salonnières* at the Hôtel d'Albret.[134] Montespan had been so impressed by Maintenon's wit and tact that she remembered her later.[135] The king cared little for Scarron when Montespan first championed her but grew to appreciate her company over time.[136] Her capacity to please, her tact, and her psychological insight increasingly drew him into Maintenon's orbit; Wolf writes that "her favor with the king has to be found in her personal charm, her measured conversation, her emotional stability."[137] Maintenon ostentatiously presented herself as friend and religious confidant to Louis, persuading him to spend more time with his wife, Marie-Thérèse, in the years before the queen's death in July 1683. But the relationship between Montespan and Maintenon grew increasingly frigid as the former recognized the latter as a rival.[138]

Maintenon and Louis married secretly, probably late one night in January 1684. This marriage, like the one that Henri IV had proposed with Gabrielle d'Estrées, demonstrates how incompatible the ideas of queen and mistress were in the minds of contemporaries; the marriage with Maintenon could only be a morganantic marriage and discreetly ignored. Thus Maintenon's position, like that of Montespan in the early years of her relationship with Louis, was always ambiguous. Because this marriage could not be made public, Maintenon declined to appear beside the king at formal events. However, her place in the king's life was obvious to all and her role as his political adviser and unofficial prime minister became more evident over time, generating speculation, in the words of Mark Bryant, "that Maintenon was the evil genuis behind Louis XIV, and thus responsible for the numerous disasters that plagued the Bourbons and France during the Sun King's declining years."[139] Notably, many Protestant historians held Madame de Maintenon responsible for encouraging Louis's religious bigotry and especially the Revocation of the Edict of Nantes in 1685.[140] Louis XV's most famous mistress, Madame de Pompadour, subject of the next chapter, would play a similar role as adviser to that king. She might have done well to consider the negative aspects of Maintenon's reputation when she explicitly modeled herself on Maintenon after her sexual relationship with the king ended. According to Pierre Nolhac, she was one of the first subscribers to Maintenon's semifictitious memoirs, published by the Abbé de Berthier (and already cited), when they became available in the 1750s.[141]

CONCLUSION

Louis XIV is perhaps the French king best known to popular audiences, associated with the splendor of Versailles that he built, with the title of "The Sun King," and with the apogee of absolutism, all captured in that line he undoubtedly never uttered: "L'État, c'est moi" (I am the state). Television series such as *Versailles* have created an image of a licentious court controlled by scheming mistresses in the popular imagination. His theatrical court lends itself to modern theatrical representations.

It is at the court of Louis XIV that we see the most effective deployment of the myths and symbols that François I pioneered. Louis's appropriation of Apollo as his avatar reflected a "society that nourished its literary tastes with stories of pagan deities" and "expected him to pun and play on the theme, and to identify himself with the sun god."[142] The Sun King required a fitting consort, and the maladroit Spanish queen, relegated to her own lesser spaces, could not effectively fill that role. As Louis came to adulthood in the 1650s, he reveled in the theatricality of his court, with its festivals, plays, and ballets, surrounded by beautiful women competing to fill the role of his companion.[143] Jean Loret's glowing poems praising the women at court suggest just how many a young, handsome Louis had to choose among.[144] His first choice, the pretty La Vallière, performed gracefully in ballets but was too timid and conscience-stricken to make the position of royal mistress her own. Montespan, in her ebullient glory, stepped into the role and absorbed the attention of the court for close to fifteen years. Her beauty and effective use of her erotic capital made her a force to be reckoned with at court.[145] Minor players tried regularly to replace her,[146] but it was not until the late 1670s that she was nudged off the stage. And even then, the king continued to appreciate the "esprit Mortemart" and respected her position as mother to his many illegitimate children enough to continue his visits to her chambers long after their physical relationship had come to an end.

Even though the court was well aware of Montespan's relationship with the king and her influential role in court politics, her aristocratic background and other positions at the court—as lady-in-waiting to Marie-Thérèse and, from 1679 to 1683, as superintendent of the queen's household[147]—meant that, like previous mistresses, she occupied a variety of spaces, not all of which were defined by her relationship with the king. The same would be true of Maintenon, first governess to the king's children with Montespan, and later a wife whose actual relationship to the king was never openly acknowledged. As her position as chief political adviser to the king and his gatekeeper became more obvious with time, her reputation declined, along with that of Louis XIV. But it would be Louis XV's mistress, Madame de Pompadour, who ripped the veil from the polite fiction that the king's mistress played no real political role. The transparency that the public came to demand of its political rulers would render the position of royal mistress increasingly controversial and, eventually, untenable.

CHAPTER 6

Tearing the Veil
Pompadour and Du Barry

The demonstrations of respect and submission
shown her surpass all that one can imagine. The
days that the council [meets], she performs her
toilette in public. Anyone of importance is there.
The ambassadors do not miss it. Everyone remains
standing. To be fair, she plays her role there to
perfection.

—PRINCE VON KAUNITZ-RIETBERG, "Mémoire sur
la cour de France"

A member of one of the most ancient and celebrated aristocratic families in France, dating back to the eleventh century, les Rochechouart de
Mortemart, the future Madame de Montespan became a *demoiselle d'honneur* to the new queen Marie-Thérèse in 1660 at the personal request of the
queen mother. Montespan's origins were arguably as illustrious as those of
the king himself.[1] No one had to explain her presence at the court. Although
few had been of such lofty lineage as Montespan, all earlier royal mistresses
had also had a reason to be at court and therefore had not been required
to explain their presence there, with the result that their relationships with
the king had easily been accepted as open secrets.[2]

This tradition of choosing the official royal mistress from among the
ladies of the court came to an end when Louis XV (b. 1710, r. 1715–74) elevated
Jeanne-Antoinette Poisson (her last name, "Fish," caused considerable

merriment among her detractors), later the Marquise de Pompadour (1721–1764), to the position. The position's status as open secret immediately became difficult if not impossible to maintain.[3] Jeanne-Antoinette's father was the son of a weaver from Champagne who made a fortune working in finance. Jeanne-Antoinette's background, moreoever, was touched by scandal; her mother was notoriously accused of having a number of lovers, throwing her paternity into doubt.[4] Coming from the world of finance rather than the nobility, Jeanne-Antoinette could not appear at court until presented to the king and queen.[5] The formal presentation finally took place on 14 September 1745 when, in exchange for the payment of her debts, the Princess of Conti agreed to sponsor Jeanne-Antoinette.[6] But even installed at court, Jeanne-Anoinette occupied a lowly position relative to her predecessors, who had been able to point to their status as part of the queen's household or member of an illustrious family of courtiers. Despite her newly granted status as the Marquise de Pompadour, her presence at court was regarded with disapproval.[7]

The origins of Jeanne Bécu, Madame Du Barry (1743–1793), were yet more dubious. Her mother was a seamstress (later cook) from Lorraine, while her father was thought to be a monk. Although educated in a monastery, Du Barry spent time as a member of the Paris demimonde before she became Louis XV's last official mistress.[8] Louis XV, already madly in love, was visiting her on a regular basis by the fall of 1768, but he needed to arrange for her presentation at court so that she could live openly at Versailles. An additional complication was that she first had to be married, which was quickly arranged. As had been the case with Pompadour, ladies of the court were reluctant to sponsor a young woman with such a problematic background. Eventually, the Countess of Béarn agreed to do so when the king paid her debts and agreed to promote her two sons. Presented at court on 22 April 1769, Du Barry was now the royal mistress, with no reason for being at court other than to satisfy the king.[9]

Nineteenth-century French author Auguste Dietrich traces the devolution in the social status of mistresses under Louis XV: "The duchesse de Châteauroux [one of Louis's earlier mistresses] represents the noblewoman; madame de Pompadour, the bourgeois woman; la du Barry, the woman of the people. Each of these courtesans marks a new low in the progressive decline of the French monarchy and the Old Regime."[10] Despite his dyspeptic tone, Dietrich expresses a widely held perception: the royal mistress was required to carry out her political activity discreetly, out of public view, her honor guaranteed by her social standing. As long as appearances were maintained, her work received tacit acceptance. But in the face of such transgression, many courtiers and members of the public began to flout the long-standing convention of discretion.

DEVOLUTION OF THE POSITION

Perhaps even more than most kings, Louis XV depended on his mistresses; according to the Duke of Croÿ (1718–1784), "he believed that it was only his mistresses who loved him enough to tell him the truth."[11] Although Pompadour's sexual relationship with the king lasted only about six years, they were closely associated for twenty. Sometime around 1750, Pompadour began her transformation into the king's closest friend and adviser. Many have argued that by the mid-1750s, she was effectively the king's prime minister, her counsel on matters of state nearly as important to him as that of the Cardinal André-Hercule de Fleury (1653–1743) had been in Louis's youth.[12] As for Du Barry, when she made her appearance at court in 1769, powerful courtiers such as the Duke of Richelieu (1696–1788) and his nephew, the Duke of Aiguillon (1720–1788), relying on past experience, expected her to be a political player and adviser to the king as well, despite the fact that she was less equipped to do so (and far less interested in policy) than the intelligent and well-read Pompadour.

As we have seen, however, Pompadour and Du Barry were unhappily remarkable for their lack of social rank. This meant that their political activity was more visible than that of their predecessors, which meant, in turn, that they were more visible to the larger public, whose members were not sympathetic to them—which was consequently quite damaging to the king.[13] But the scrutiny that they attracted derived also from a shift in attitude toward the courtly ideal of "honest dissimulation" and the skillful mastery of one's emotions as a means of maintaining civility and politeness in conversation and conduct that had supported the role of political royal mistress.[14] No longer valued as a characteristic of aristocratic behavior, dissimulation became a typically feminine quality that undermined virtue in the public sphere.[15] Lisa Jane Graham suggests that royal mistresses "represented an older politics of secrecy in an age that demanded transparency and accountability from its rulers."[16] The new ideas that undergirded the Age of Enlightenment led to increased interest in and discussion of the machinations of the court to which both Pompadour and Du Barry were central. Their political activities caused outrage among the public, who blamed Pompadour for the Austrian alliance that ensnared the French in the disastrous Seven Years' War, while Du Barry's handiwork was seen in the fall of Étienne-François, Duke of Choiseul (1719–1785), and the attacks on the Parlements in the 1770s.[17] The details of their sexual relations with the king, especially in the case of Du Barry, became the stuff of the *libelles*.[18] The increased visibility, revealed in print and gossip, turned both Pompadour and Du Barry into focal points for the discontent brewing in France by the second half of the eighteenth century, hatred that bled into public sentiment toward the king.[19] Contemporaries took note of this new attitude toward the monarch, the Duke of Croÿ writing perceptively that "he allowed himself to be led by them, which contributed to losing [control] over finances, and that was the downfall of his reign."[20] An anonymous author who wrote a virulent biography of Madame Du Barry shortly after the death of Louix XV held that Louis himself was responsible for this disastrous rule by mistresses—he was too given over to pleasure, to which he devoted himself:

> Allowing himself to be ruled by all whom he believed deserved his trust, is it surprising that the mistresses also controlled him too much? isn't the heart the weakest part of a man in love? & even when the spirit is indomitable, doesn't the former often bend, even under the most tyrannical yoke? that of Louis XV, subjugated by Madame de Pompadour, had fallen into the unfortunate habit of slavery, [and he] could only live in chains; looking for a new master, he gave himself over entirely to Madame Du Barry, the woman the least deserving to have the honor to be his sovereign. This woman's deplorable destiny was to darken & tarnish the last years of a King.[21]

The institution of the royal mistress came under sustained attack, and the foundations of the absolutist monarchy in France began to shake at the same time.

Nineteenth-century authors accepted the narrative that by the reign of Louis XV, women operated the levers of government. The Goncourt brothers had a generally positve view of the impact of women during the era of Louis XV, celebrating it as "the century of woman and her caressing domination over manners and customs."[22] Still, it was their dominance that the brothers emphasized: "From the beginning to the end of the century, the government of women is the only visible and appreciable government,

having the succession and the qualifications, the reality and the employ-
ment of power, unflinchingly, without apathy, without interregnum."[23]
No one was more susceptible to this domination than Louis XV; as Jules
Michelet wrote in 1847, the king was tugged to the right by philosophers,
to the left by priests. Who would win? Neither. Women would, because
"this god [was] a god of flesh."[24]

From this belief that Louis XV's mistresses governed him, it was
a short step to blaming them for the downfall of the ancien régime.
Charles-Augustin de Sainte-Beuve asked, "Did Madame de Pompadour
contribute as much as people have said to the ruin of the monarchy?"
and answered himself: "She did not hinder it, certainly." Put off by the
stench of her bourgeois origins and the harsh actions that marred her
later years, he described her position as "eminent and little honorable
(much less honourable than she thought it)," concluding that "the world
saw the political system of Europe overthrown, the ancient alliances of
France interverted, and a whole series of great events undertaken at the
mercy of the inclinations, the antipathies, and the too fragile, too personal
good sense of an amiable woman."[25] He was still more contemptuous of
Madame Du Barry: "It is impossible to descend and enter with decency
into the history of the Du Barry."[26] In his three-volume account of the
life of Madame Du Barry, published in 1883, Charles Vatel emphasized a
dramatic decline in public willingness to tolerate the king's well-known
and flagrant "galanterie" over the course of the eighteenth century, with its
concomitant political implications: "Louis XV himself, young and victorious at Fontenoy, at Lawfeld, at Rocoux, had, for a long time, enjoyed
indulgence, almost encouragement, of his weaknesses, but that which
seemed natural in 1740 was no longer possible in 1769. A quarter of a
century had passed: social behavior had been reconsidered in the works
of Montesquieu, of J.-J. Rousseau, of Mably. The same practices, or let
us say, the same abuses tolerated under madame de Pompadour, would
arouse the public conscience against the subsequent royal offense with
madame du Barry."[27]

These nineteenth-century accounts make ample and sometimes uncriti-
cal use of the numerous memoirs (some forged), chronicles, correspondence,
and ambassadors' reports about intrigue at the court of Louis XV. Modern
historians make use of the same sources, although, we hope, more carefully, aware of the self-serving political agendas and misogynistic ideas that
shaped these accounts. Still, twentieth-century historians continued to
blame Louis XV's mistresses for bringing down the monarchy. The king's

biographer, Michel Antoine, writes of Pompadour, "she thought only to distract [the king] with theatrical performances (which she produced with rare talent) and with frivolities that quickly bored him, and which, furthermore, branded him as a frivolous and spendthrift prince. As for helping the king overcome his lack of confidence, Mme de Pompadour proved so incapable of doing so that the years of her favor were also those during which the conduct of policy appeared most unsteady."[28]

While recent historical assessments of Pompadour in particular are mixed, most take her seriously as a political actor.[29] However, it is clear that the contemporary narrative of the feminization of the French monarchy—a result of Louis's open reliance on his powerful mistresses—helped to delegitimize the ancien régime government. Previous kings had suffered criticism for their sinful behavior with mistresses. As we have seen, Bossuet shamed Louis XIV into renouncing his relationship with Montespan, at least temporarily. However, the graphic and sexually explicit attacks on the royal mistress represented something new in the public discourse. In complicated ways, the royal mistress had always served as a testament to the king's virility, proof of his assertive masculinity. The public took some pride in the exploits of Henri IV, the Vert Galant, and the beautiful Louis XIV in his prime. However, Louis's perceived submission to the controlling Pompadour, the salacious image of the Parc-aux-Cerfs, and the eventual elevation of a former courtesan to the position of official mistress came to represent the degradation of a king too susceptible to the sins of the flesh to tend to the good of the nation.

MADAME DE POMPADOUR

While much detail on Pompadour's background and her spectacular rise is obscure, we know the outlines of the story.[30] Born in 1721, she belonged to a family with connections to the Pâris brothers, noted bankers to the government, and the patronage of the wealthy Lenormant de Tournehem ensured her a good education and powerful connections, despite the absence of her father in her youth.[31] She learned all the important social skills to shine in Parisian society, and with the help of Tournehem, in 1741 she married his only nephew and heir, Charles-Guillaume Lenormant.[32] As a young married woman, polished, talented, intelligent, and very attractive, she made a splash in the salons of Paris among the wealthy and educated elite.

But the Parisian bourgeoisie also liked to spend time in the countryside. At the time of Jeanne-Antoinette's marriage to Lenormant, Tournehem provided them with the estate of Étiolles, a beautiful country home southeast of Paris. According to the Abbé de Bernis (1715–1794), who would soon serve as Pompadour's tutor in the ways of Versailles, the king often saw her while hunting in the forest of Sénart near Étiolles.[33] Told from childhood that she was "fit for a king" and by a fortune teller that she would be the king's mistress one day, Jeanne-Antoinette appears consciously to have sought to bring herself to the king's attention. Here are echoes of Agnès Sorel: as we have seen, in the sixteenth century, Brantôme had written that "an astrologer had predicted to [Agnès] that she would be loved and served by one of the most valiant and courageous kings in Christendom."[34] The narrative that emerged of the king and Jeanne-Antoinette's meeting in the woods also drew conveniently on the by-then-familiar association of the royal mistress with Diana the huntress. Pompadour would have Jean-Marc Nattier paint her as Diana around 1748, and the portrait hung in Fontainebleau.[35] By February 1745, reports of the king's romance with a beautiful young woman with whom he had danced at a masked ball at Versailles appear.[36] Courtiers heard that the king was pursuing the "young and lovely" Madame d'Étiolles, but, as we saw in the introduction, the Duke of Luynes (1695–1758) initially dismissed her, writing that, if the rumors were true, she was only a "fling [*galanterie*], not a mistress." It was inconceivable that a woman "whose mother is named Mme Poisson" could be the next *maîtresse déclarée* of the king.[37]

Nonetheless, during the summer of 1745, Jeanne-Antoinette, now the Marquise de Pompadour, prepared conscientiously to take her place at court while the king was on campaign.[38] She was already acquainted with some of the leading writers of Paris, whom she had met at the salons of Madame Geoffrin and occasionally Madame de Tencin; one of these was Voltaire (1694–1778), a frequent visitor that summer, who gave her a copy of the *Abrégé de l'histoire de France*.[39] Charles-Antoine, Marquis of Gontaut (1708–1798), provided counsel and support, and on the advice of her cousin by marriage, Elisabeth-Charlotte d'Estrades (1715–1784), she invited the Abbé de Bernis, a worldly cleric well versed in the ways of the aristocracy, to help her prepare for life at Versailles. It was a place foreign even to a woman as comfortable in salon society as she had been.[40] She applied herself to learning the particularities of language and the rigorous code of conduct that court life required, an education that prepared her for the dizzying elevation in status that she would experience in a short period of time.[41] Despite the controversy surrounding her presentation at court—few at Versailles were unaware of her bourgeois origins—she carried it off without incident, a consummate actress, and settled in to take her place,[42] although not without the occasional minor mistake of language and comportment.[43] Certainly, the king was pleased with her efforts: during the early years of their relationship, the Duke of Croÿ commented frequently on the king's devotion to his lovely young mistress.[44]

Many at court found Pompadour charming and tactful—most notably, unlike previous mistresses, she treated the king's wife, Queen Marie Lesczinska (1703–1768), with respect and deference.[45] The reports of her beauty were perhaps less effusive than those of Montespan or later Du Barry. The Abbé de Bernis, for example, suggested that she had "more sparkle than beauty."[46] Still, most reports acknowledged her loveliness and grace and understood why the king sought her out. Jean-Nicolas Dufort de Cheverny (1731–1802) praised her as a woman "every man would like to have as his mistress," a woman "very well-made," with "a round face, regular features, magnificent complexion, superb hands and arms, eyes more lovely than large, but with a fire, a brilliance that I have never seen in another woman."[47] The Austrian ambassador, Prince von Kaunitz-Rietberg (1711–1794), wrote that Pompadour was "unquestionably one of the most beautiful women of the City or the Court. Her eyes are blue, almond-shaped, large enough with a charming gaze. The shape of her face is oval, the mouth small, a lovely brow, and an especially agreeable nose."[48]

But many were hostile toward her, disparaging her origins and expressing surprise that the king was seduced by such a woman. The Marquis of Argenson (1694–1757), whose son would live among frescoes depicting a sympathetic history of past royal mistress Agnès Sorel, had nary a good thing to say about Pompadour.[49] In 1747 he wrote that she came "from the lowest background. She is blond and pale, without distinction [*sans traits*], but with gifts and talents; she is fairly tall and not particularly attractive." Further, "people who are respected at court assert that Mme de Pompadour will soon be dismissed; the reason will be the shame that the king is made to feel . . . for such a misplaced and lowly affection."[50] Kaunitz-Rietberg suggested that some women of the court snubbed Pompadour because of her social origins: "If she were well-born, they all would have bent the knee before her, but they are too proud to humble themselves before a woman [from the circle of] finance."[51] According to historian Danielle Gallet, myriad writings, including the notorious *poissonades*, along with various *nouvelles à la main*, viciously attacked Pompadour in the same vein:

"The king had lowered himself in choosing a *'femme obscure,'* a *'petite bour-geoise,'* a *'grisette,'* whose dizzying rise had upset the established order."[52]

Although it was her appearance that first drew the king to her, Pompadour's skill in keeping the king entertained made her essential. Louis seems to have disliked the confines of kingship.[53] Most notable was Pompadour's willingness to arrange dinners, ballets, and other performances to entertain the king.[54] Croÿ praised her unstinting efforts, saying that she "appears to have been born to fill this position. She takes on many things without seeming too busy. To the contrary, whether naturally or wisely, she acts as if more occupied with her little comedies and trifles rather than other things. She frequently teases the King and keeps his attention through the wittiest conversation [*l'art de la plus fine galanterie*]."[55] Louis XIV had made theatrical presentations central to court life in the early years of his personal reign, reifying the theatricalization of court life to which we have been referring. Pompadour, however, was the first actual actor to play the role of mistress. She had participated in theatrical productions at Étiolles, where Tournehem had built a private theater for her.[56] She now brought the theater to court to entertain Louis XV.[57] Appreciative of her skills as actor and singer, Luynes praised Pompadour for her "perfection of perfor-mance, taste, and voice."[58] She took pride in her productions, writing to the Duke of Richelieu in March 1748 that court performances were more brilliant than ever and would be even more so in the coming year.[59] Invi-tations to the small theater were a mark of favor, and courtiers eagerly petitioned for them.[60]

In addition to the amateur theatrical presentations, Pompadour also arranged with panache the small and intimate dinners that Louis loved.[61] She was willing to organize and accompany him on his frequent flights from Versailles to Compiègne and Fontainebleau, where she had small hermit-ages built on the grounds, as well as to her own properties of Crécy and Bellevue, which she furnished with skill and taste.[62] Dufort de Cherverny noted that she "had the great ability to distract the man in the realm the most difficult to entertain, whose preference was for privacy, and who real-ized that his position demanded the contrary; so much so that as soon as he could evade his kingly duties, he would go to her rooms via a secret staircase and dispense with the role of king."[63] Later in their relationship, she even encouraged him to try different crafts, such as woodworking and printing, taking the advice of her physician, the celebrated Dr. François Quesnay (1694–1774), that this could be a way "to amuse the King and give him some new recreations, to tear him away from the court."[64]

While Pompadour understood that her willingness to create endless diversions for the king made her indispensable for him, it also exhausted her, even in the early years, and underlay her constant complaints about life at court. In an oft-cited letter to her friend, the Countess of Lutzelbourg, Pompadour wrote, "The life I lead is dreadful, I hardly have a minute to myself: rehearsals and performances twice a week; constant trips to either the Petit Chateau or La Muette, etc. Considerable and indispensable obligations: Queen, Dauphin, Dauphine happily lounging on their couches, three daughters, two children, consider whether it is possible to take a breath; have pity on me and do not blame me."[65] In another to Richelieu, she complained, "I no longer wish to speak of this place where I live, the more I see, the more I detest and mistrust it."[66] Bernis reported in 1755 that Pompadour was "disgusted with the court."[67]

Moreover, she greatly feared the king's religiosity, which was intense. It could engender great guilt on his part, perhaps even greater than that of Louis XIV.[68] Struck by a serious illness while on campaign in Metz in 1744 and under pressure from his entourage, the king had confessed and sent away his then mistress, Madame de Châteauroux.[69] When he recovered, he was humiliated and angry with those who had pressured him rather than chastened by his near brush with death.[70] The danger of repudiation was particularly acute for Pompadour at the moment of royal daughter Madame Henriette's death in 1752, as well as after Robert-François Damiens's attempted assassination of the king in 1757. In response, Pompadour tried to reconcile with the church beginning in late 1755 and sought her confessor's approval for her continued role at court after her sexual relationship with the king ended.[71] Louis XV, however, continued to fear God's wrath at his irregular sex life, which led him to withdraw from traditional rituals that the public expected of its king, thereby disavowing the polite facade that usually cloaked a king's sinful behavior. This acknowledgment of guilt lifted the veil that usually protected the mistress, contributing to the public perception of scandalous behavior.[72]

Patronage of the arts and letters was a key way in which Pompadour followed in the footsteps of earlier mistresses, becoming a *mécène* every bit as important as Montespan.[73] Her friendship with Voltaire was legendary—she obtained for him his position as historiographer of France—as was their subsequent falling out.[74] Still, he remained supportive of her, deeply affected by her death.[75] She surrounded herself with philosophes in the 1740s and early 1750s, even reaching out to the skittish Rousseau for a time.[76] Her doctor, the physiocrat Quesnay, may have influenced her views on the French economy.[77] Pompadour very much liked to present herself as a *femme savante* and protector of men of letters.[78] As she aged, however, she became less open to what she saw as problematic elements of Enlightenment writings, withdrawing her protection from a number of bolder authors.[79] But her patronage of the arts and architecture continued throughout her reign at court. She was herself the subject of numerous paintings by Boucher, La Tour, and Nattier; she collected paintings and other *objets d'art* for her many homes.[80] She was also a printmaker of considerable skill.[81] Notably, she was an enthusiastic purchaser of delicate porcelain objects, and in 1756, on her initiative, the Manufacture Royale de Porcelaine at Vincennes was moved to Sèvres (from which it would take its name), near Pompadour's chateau of Bellevue.[82]

She shared a passion for building and architecture with the king, which put her in the tradition of previous mistresses Diane de Poitiers and Montespan. But it was an expensive hobby, and contemporaries and later historians excoriated her for the cost at a time of misery.[83] As Dietrich pointed out in his diatribe against the mistresses of Louis XV, this love of beauty and luxury could easily be used against her to explain the growing antimonarchical sentiments of the French people.[84]

We have seen that Montespan's relationship with Louis XIV continued long after their sexual activity had ceased. In Pompadour, we have more evidence that a physical relationship with the king was only one facet of the role of official mistress. Pompadour suffered from gynecological problems and supposedly acknowledged her "cold" nature, which she tried unsuccessfully to cure with various purported aphrodisiacs.[85] By 1750 she realized that the early passion between the two of them had attenuated and that it was time to shift to a new phase in their relationship, from lovers to friends. As she had drawn on the classical imagery of Diana earlier in their relationship, Pompadour made use of classical allegory, bidding farewell to Cupid, while making this transition as well.[86] However, there was no diminution in her importance. In May 1751 Pompadour moved to more prestigious new rooms at Versailles that "were about to become for Louis XV a sanctuary, and for the marquise a headquarters."[87] More comfortable and larger than her previous rooms, these had been occupied by Montespan when she was one of Louis XIV's most important advisers, underlining Pompadour's privileged role.[88] In 1752 she was awarded the *tabouret de grâce*: the right to sit in the presence of the king and queen, considered a great honor.[89] Indeed, the shift from mistress to best friend seems to have corresponded with Pompadour's increasing influence over the king.[90] Luynes affirmed in April 1754 that she had become the king's friend and "with that new title has perhaps more credit than with the former."[91] As was the case with many previous mistresses who served as advisers to kings, as well as regents, Pompadour asserted and demonstrated that her primary concern would always be the king; as she wrote to the Duke of Choiseul, "Personal interest has led me only [to work for] the glory of the King."[92]

Louis accepted the change in their relationship with good grace, as far as we can tell, and he began to turn to a series of young women famously maintained at the Parc-aux-Cerfs to satisfy his sexual urges.[93] While not particularly concerned about most of these young women, who presented no challenge to her position, Pompadour did worry about the possibility that a rival could supplant her at court.[94] As had been the case during previous reigns, young aristocratic women surrounded by a coterie of ambitious supporters were always eager to replace the reigning favorite, especially one who no longer enjoyed a sexual relationship with the king.[95] The greatest threat came from Charlotte-Rosalie, Countess of Choiseul-Romanet (1733–1753), in late 1752. Young and beautiful, she had the support of Pompadour's perfidious cousin by marriage, Elisabeth-Charlotte d'Estrades, and Estrades's lover, the Count of Argenson, a powerful actor at court and brother of the Marquis of Argenson, Pompadour's bitter critic. The king was clearly receptive to Choiseul-Romanet's advances, and she, along with her supporters, was confident that the king would replace Pompadour with her.[96] Observers drew on the stories of earlier mistresses to narrate the drama; Dufort de Cherverny compared the situation to that of Montespan confronted by Mademoiselle de Fontanges seventy years earlier.[97] Pompadour, alerted by the future Duke of Choiseul (then Marquis de Stainville), who was related to the countess by marriage (and who undoubtedly realized that Pompadour was more valuable to him than his young relative), persuaded the king to send the ambitious young woman away. Choiseul-Romanet died in childbirth not long afterward, once again echoing the fate of la belle Fontanges.[98]

With her change in status, Pompadour became increasing interested in representing her image as effectively as possible, something that had concerned her much less in the early years of her reign.[99] Various theatrical spaces at court outside those of the royal family were there for Pompadour to occupy; as was the case with previous mistresses, she drew on classical allegory in her self-fashioning, as well as the Enlightenment discourse that allowed her to position herself as a *femme savante* and protector of philosophes. A number of historians have treated at some length Pompadour's careful stewardship of her image in the many portraits by leading lights such as Boucher, Nattier, Van Loo, and others.[100] Even more than previous mistresses, Pompadour was aware that she was part of a lineage of royal mistresses, and she looked to their example.[101] Others were aware of that lineage as well. Louis-René, Marquis of Belleval (1741–1807), compared her influence on the king to that of her role model, Madame de Maintenon: "She was like another Maintenon, and if the council of ministers did not take place in her chambers, at least she met with them before the council [took place] and they kept her informed concerning their business."[102]

While royal mistresses were very often the king's political adviser of choice, never had this role been as public and explicit as it became with Pompadour, and never had the mistress so effectively acted as the king's gatekeeper.[103] Kaunitz-Rietberg admired her ability to insinuate herself into the king's confidence.[104] In time, she wisely sought an official title for herself at court other than that of mistress to buttress her position. This was, once again, somewhat problematic, given her bourgeois background. And yet in 1756 she was elevated to the position of *dame de palais* in the household of the queen. Even the jurisconsult and chronicler Edmond-Jean-François Barbier (1689–1771), who had a generally favorable attitude toward Pompadour, expressed surprise at her promotion, noting that "this seems remarkable. The marquise de Pompadour is the daughter of M. Poisson, and currently the wife of M. Lenormant, *fermier général*, and she is now close to the queen, among the most distinguished women of the kingdom. The queen has been very discerning about the personal background of the women presented for this honor, even women from the most prestigious families [*de grande condition*]."[105] Pompadour was clever at maneuvering and conscious of her carefully acquired dignity. Choiseul noted in his memoirs that "one is presented to her as to the Queen. I found that etiquette [in her presence] was more highly elevated than it had been around Mme de Châteauroux [Louis's previous mistress]."[106] The Prince de Ligne (1735–1814) made the same point, noting that after he had been taken to pay his respects to the various members of the royal family, "I was taken to a sort of second queen, who had a much more [queenly] air than the first."[107]

Pompadour's adversaries, like the Marquis of Argenson, criticized her viciously for what they saw as outsized ambition: "She is certainly ambitious; she wants to rule, and is pushed forward by those who would like to rule through her."[108] She took the long view in her battles with those who disrespected her or threatened her position at the court.[109] Her enemies, of course, were legion. The murmurings against her had started early on as she began to consolidate power, which in the eyes of some reflected badly on the king. Argenson noted that it may be "that finally the king realizes and feels the shame of her fetters; he reads in the secret mail all that is said against him, and he often sees mention of the *Poissonnaille*."[110] Over time, however, Pompadour was usually able to dispatch those who tried to undermine her. She helped persuade the king to fire the Count of Maurepas, minister of the navy (1701–1781), an enemy she suspected of authoring some of the scurrilous pamphlets circulating about her, including a reference to "fleurs blanches" (white flowers), a thinly veiled allusion to her gynecological difficulties.[111] The *mauvais discours* that circulated about her and the king—the notorious *poissonades*—caused her much pain, and she, even more so than the king, urged the Parisian police to track down the guilty parties and exact severe retribution.[112]

Other scalps followed that of Maurepas, and wise men eventually realized that it was more intelligent to court than to alienate Pompadour. Even the Duke of Richelieu, one of her most powerful enemies at court and her frequent challenger in his position as first gentleman of the bedchamber, trod more carefully after the king elliptically suggested that he might be facing another trip to the Bastille.[113] Particularly known for her implacable dislike of those who insulted her, she triumphed over the Marquis of Souvré. In November 1759 this *maître de la garde-robe*, much beloved by the king, was forced to sell his office and go into exile, all for making an indiscreet remark about Pompadour.[114] But it was not until after the Damiens affair in January 1757 that Pompadour was able to persuade the king to dispose of the Count of Argenson, long her enemy, as well as Jean-Baptiste de Machault d'Arnouville, a previous ally who had encouraged her to flee the court while the king was recovering from the assassination attempt.[115] Although these dismissals reflected other political intrigues at court beyond the machinations of Pompadour, they corresponded to the peak of her political power.[116]

As unforgiving as Pompadour could be of her enemies, she also worked hard to reward her allies and to place them in key positions at court. Like other mistresses, she was able to distribute favors and take care of her friends.[117] She made sure that her family members were well placed. Early on, she encouraged the king to dispatch Philibert Orry, who headed the department responsible for the maintenance of royal palaces.[118] Orry had irritated her powerful friends, the Pâris brothers, who were pleased by his dismissal.[119] Pompadour wanted a friend in control of the royal palaces;

the position went to Lenormant de Tournehem, with Pompadour's brother, Abel Poisson, later Marquis of Marigny (1727–1781), as his designated successor. Her father also received noble title.[120] She managed to acquire the position of *dame d'atours* for her then confidante, Madame d'Estrades.[121] When the wife of the dauphin suddenly died, Pompadour lent her support to the interests of her friend, the Maréchal of Saxony, and lobbied for the Princess of Saxony as the dauphin's next wife, with success.[122] The Marquis of Argenson, undoubtedly guilty of exaggeration in all things related to Pompadour, noted in June 1748 that "Mme de Pompadour and her family are taking control of everything."[123] However, as Cécile Berly notes, politics was an "affair of friendship" for Pompadour, "a pledge of confidence, of loyalty, and of dedication to the king."[124] Over time, a number of ministers had Pompadour's friendship and patronage to thank, at least in part, for their professional success.[125]

In fact, her influence was such that Pompadour was able to elevate even friends that the king disliked. Most notable among these was the future Duke of Choiseul. After the affair of Madame de Choiseul-Romanet, she managed to secure for him the position of ambassador to Rome, despite the king's aversion to him.[126] There is no doubt that her continued support was key to Choiseul's career.[127] However, he was one of the more skilled courtiers whom she sponsored; one of the frequent criticisms leveled at her by contemporaries and historians was her tendency to elevate mediocrities. Neither the Abbé de Bernis, who served as minister of foreign affairs during the Seven Years' War, nor the Marquis of Paulmy and Peyrenc de Moras (whom Pompadour championed to replace the Count of Argenson and Machault after they were exiled in 1757) demonstrated much aptitude for their important positions.[128]

Like Montespan before her, Pompadour also arranged marriages for family members and those close to her, working hard to find spouses for the large Baschi family.[129] In addition, she arranged the marriages of Marie-Anne de Chaumont Quitry with the Count of Amiblimont (a cousin of the Lenormants) and that of Henriette de Baschi with François de Monteynard.[130] Luynes reported that "Mme de Pompadour arranged this marriage" when the son of Champcenetz, *valet de chambre* of the king, married a Mademoiselle Pernon, daughter of a *député de commerce* of Lyon.[131] Her brother Marigny, however, apparently resisted all efforts to find him a wife and married only after the death of his sister.[132] Ironically, the marriage of Charlotte-Rosalie de Romanet to Francois-Martial de Choiseul-Beaupré took place at Pompadour's chateau of Bellevue in 1751.[133]

In many ways, then, Pompadour operated discreetly behind the scenes to influence policy and to aid her friends. But for the king, her willingness to assume some of the burdens of kingship was her greatest gift to him, and she could not do this covertly. Over time, audiences with members of the court became an important service that she rendered a king who disliked dealing with courtiers petitioning for favors.[134] True, not all court observers were aware of the enormous influence that Pompadour would exert over foreign policy, sometimes to their great disadvantage. The representative of Frederick the Great of Prussia in France, the baron Jean Le Chambrier, dismissed concerns about her influence in 1751:

> The marquise de Pompadour is all-Powerful when it comes to favors and benefits in cash, in offices, military as well as those at Court and in the Judiciary, [la Robe] and in general, anything connected to domestic affairs in the Kingdom. She has no influence over political affairs, except for placing ministers in foreign courts, something that she is working on, along with the marquis de Puisieux; but the marquise de Pompadour does not interfere in negotiations between foreign powers and France.[135]

The viciously misogynistic Frederick the Great was perhaps all too ready to believe his minister, although as he came to realize how powerful Pompadour was, he worked hard to discredit her.[136]

But Julian Swann sees Pompadour's political influence as greater even than that of Madame de Maintenon. He notes that while government business was not conducted in Pompadour's chambers, "ministers discussed their affairs with her before presenting them to the council."[137] By the early 1750s, she was moving openly into the realm of diplomacy and would play an important role in the pressing political crises facing the monarchy, including one of the most contentious political imbroglios of Louis's reign: his efforts to manage the quarrel between the Parlement and the church hierarchy over the Jansenist affair.[138] Dufort de Cheverny, responsible for introducing ambassadors at the court, writes of bringing Kaunitz-Rietberg to meet with her, along with a group of prominent men at court.[139] Kaunitz-Rietberg was well aware of Pompadour's potential and carefully solicited her favor—in his opinion, with great success: "If Mad. de Pompadour were to take an interest in foreign affairs, she would not serve us badly. She has much goodwill for and confidence in me." He was convinced that his personal relationship with Pompadour and the king would serve Austria well.[140] At her daily toilette, Pompadour would receive courtiers, listen to their requests for favors, and intercede with the king, sparing him the need to handle that job on his own. This was a highly theatrical demonstration of power, a performance on which the curtain rose each day. The Marquis of Argenson noted with some contempt, "The toilette of that lady is a grand ceremony at the court these days. . . . In the evening, all the most important people come running to show themselves."[141] Kaunitz-Rietberg, however, expressed admiration for Pompadour's performance at this daily ritual, observing that "she plays her role there to perfection."[142] The Duke of Croÿ, among others, was frequently in attendance, noting that "she has knowledge of everything."[143]

As one who frequently sought her assistance in his affairs, Croÿ wrote in 1754 that "it was quite agreeable to have done business with such a pretty prime minister," a recognition of her powerful role, which is underlined by the fact that provincial governors and commandants reported directly to her.[144] Acknowledging her central role in foreign affairs, Croÿ remarked that "Mme de Pompadour was doing absolutely everything, never had her credit extended so far."[145] As Kaunitz-Rietberg worked toward solidifying Austria's relations with France, he had good reason to hope that Pompadour would maintain her position. In his correspondence with imperial secretary Ignaz von Koch destined for the eyes of Empress Maria Theresa (1717–1780), he noted that, as a bourgeoise, Pompadour had no relatives to please in either powerful positions at court or the army, which could work to Austria's advantage.[146] His careful courtship of Pompadour would serve Maria Theresa well in the years leading up to the Renversement des alliances—the shift from an alliance with Frederick the Great's Prussia to a treaty of friendship and alliance with Austria—and the outbreak of the Seven Years' War. Choiseul, who came to worry about France's increasingly close and, in his view, problematic relationship with the Holy Roman Empire, glumly agreed that the Austrians had successfully appealed to Pompadour's vanity to solidify their relationship with France, crafting personal letters from the Empress Maria Theresa: "These letters flattered l'amour-propre of Mme de Pompadour, very easy to flatter."[147]

Presumably, Pompadour could have more carefully veiled her role as political adviser to the king on diplomatic affairs, as had previous mistresses. Diplomatic relations were, by their very nature, ambiguous and hidden. Pierre Nolhac writes of the many secret operators in foreign affairs who worked alongside officially recognized ambassadors and, in particular, those of whom Louis XV made use.[148] In fact, throughout the mid-1700s, Louis XV was involved in an extremely complex and secret channel of diplomacy through the Prince of Conti and the Count of Broglie referred to as "Le Secret du roi," an intrigue that was fully exposed only after the king's death.[149] Pompadour was excluded from these particular machinations, although she was certainly suspicious of Conti, an enemy.[150] But her visibility in other affairs created real problems. To act so publicly seemed to move beyond the traditional limits of the official royal mistress.[151] Previous mistresses had encouraged and applauded the king's military prowess, offering private advice and counsel, but Pompadour actively participated in the direction of foreign and military matters, moving beyond the role that even Maintenon had played. Even those who accepted that women could play a political role at court expressed unease as Pompadour took an increasingly visible part in the negotiation of foreign affairs. In general, Barbier was more positive about Pompadour than was the Marquis of Argenson. However, he also conveyed careful discomfort with her political activities by 1758, a year into what would become the Seven Years' War: "The influence of madame la marquise de Pompadour is said to be at an all-time high. Ministers keep her informed on all matters, before they come before the council; she meddles in military affairs, and all the affairs of State. She has much intelligence, it's true, but isn't she taking on too much? In a court like this, one makes many enemies, and consequential ones, and cannot ward them off."[152]

Despite the fact that she had played little role in foreign affairs in the late 1740s, anonymous writers blamed her for Louis XV's perceived failures, including the consequences of the less-than-glorious peace settlement at Aix-la-Chapelle (1748) ending the War of the Austrian Succession.[153] But it was her role in promoting and celebrating the Renversement des alliances that would most damage Pompadour's reputation among historians as well as contemporaries. This shift drew France into the Seven Years' War, a war that not only involved France's soldiers in central Europe, defending Austria's claim to Silesia, which Austria lost to Frederick the Great during the War of the Austrian Succession, but also intensified French conflicts with the British. The war was a disaster for the French, who would not only lose all of their North American colonies to the British but would also be saddled with an enormous debt, a financial catastrophe that started them on the path to revolution in 1789. And because public opinion blamed Pompadour, and later Choiseul, for promoting the Austrian alliance, the *parti dévôt*, which was associated with the queen and her children, turned against it, shaping French court politics and public opinion throughout the 1770s.[154]

Historians have criticized Pompadour's decision to abandon France's long-established foreign policy priorities to pursue an alliance with Austria, as did critics at the time. In retrospect, we know that the French decision to ally so closely with Austria had disastrous consequences, because the long war was politically and financially devastating for the monarchy. Evidence suggests that the king was even more invested in the alliance with Austria than was Pompadour.[155] Still, Auguste Dietrich wrote:

> Madame de Pompadour broke abruptly with this traditional policy (the containment of the Habsburgs). Because of her feminine self-love, because of her ambition to inaugurate a new state of affairs, because of an excessive deference to, and poor understanding of, the views of Maria Theresa and her minister, the cunning and unscrupulous Kaunitz, who flattered both . . . the favorite threw herself, with the usual enthusiasm of women, into an extremely serious situation, which she did not really understand well. We know the results: for France, the legendary defeats of Rosbach and Krefeld, the loss of her colonies in India and America, the death of three hundred thousand men, financial disaster by the end of the century; for Germany, the annihilation of entire lineages . . . for Europe, two billion [livres] wasted and nearly a million men killed! These are the fruits of the noble marquise's interference in the political sphere.[156]

This disapproving narrative continued into the twentieth century; Pierre Nolhac suggested that Pompadour's political choices were shaped by the wily Kaunitz-Rietberg, who played on her feminine vanity and social uncertainty.[157] While Michel Antoine accords less influence to Pompadour than many other historians, he notes her importance to Count von Starhemberg, the imperial representative, during the negotiations that led to the Renversement des alliances.[158]

As with other royal mistresses, the reign of Pompadour was never an easy one. Despite her efforts to charm and win over her adversaries, from the very beginning of her tenure as official royal mistress, a long line of courtiers and court watchers anticipated her fall, many with glee. Nearly every few months, her implacable enemy, the Marquis of Argenson, weighed in to assert that the king was on the verge of sending Pompadour away.[159] He was not the only one. In 1757 General du Fontenay, minister of the Polish king, was certain that Pompadour had lost favor after Damiens's assassination attempt, writing as much to King Stanislaw on 30 January. By April, however, he conceded that this would not be the case, admitting that her influence was stronger than ever.[160] Having supported the diplomatic revolution, Pompadour eagerly followed the course of the war once it started. Her influence was such that Richelieu found it prudent to involve her in discussions about the choice of generals and war maneuvers.[161] Her correspondence with him reveals her intense interest in the details of the war.[162] Her feverish epistolary activity throughout the seven years of accumulating military disaster records her growing anxiety; it seems likely that the stress of the war contributed to her premature death.[163] The confident mien of the favorite, despite the pressures at court that constantly gnawed at her, could not hide her declining physical condition. Pompadour had never enjoyed good health, but the ignominious course of the war with England and Prussia contributed to its worsening, leading to her death in April 1764 at the age of forty-two.[164] The mood at Versailles was somber at the time of her passing; Croÿ wrote: "In general, she was missed, being decent [bonne] and having done well by almost all those who asked her [for favors]."[165]

Most who knew the Marquise de Pompadour considered her lovely, intelligent, and charming. In the pantheon of royal mistresses, her name is one of the best known. However, her legacy demonstrates the increasingly negative view of the royal mistress as an institution and refusal to accept it quietly. Pompadour's willingness to act as mistress and political adviser in such a highly visible fashion, minus the ambiguity that had cloaked the machinations of earlier royal favorites, engendered criticism that was perhaps not new but was strikingly venomous. Both contemporary and later critics argued that her beauty and many talents were insufficient to counterbalance her "unfeminine" qualities, in many ways the qualities that would make her such a useful adviser to Louis XV. Dietrich painted the image of Pompadour that resonated for many: "But beneath that ravishing and poetic countenance, the young woman hid a cold and dry heart, perfect mistress of herself and in no way romantic [tournée au roman]. Ambitious, with an indomitable and unscrupulous tenacity that, in her sex, is evil, an 'idée fixe' had her in its grip almost since her infancy: still a little girl, she planned resolutely to be 'un morceau du roi'"—fit for a king.[166]

The announcements of her death in the Mémoires secrets pour servir à l'histoire de la République des Lettres en France illustrate a perhaps reflexive instinct to both guard the open secret of Pompadour's position and acknowledge the vicious gossip that circulated as that open secret turned into public knowledge. The entry for 15 April 1764 notes her death but makes no mention of her relationship to the king: "This evening Madame la marquise de Pompadour died. The brilliant protection with which she had honored letters, the taste that she had for the arts make it impossible to let such a sad event pass in silence." A few entries later, however, all sign of respect disappears, as the topic turns to some clever but extremely unflattering epigraphs dedicated to her memory.[167]

Pompadour built on the existing model of the royal mistress, and yet she shaped it in a way that would be difficult for any future mistress to sustain and that would become emblematic of all that was wrong with the French monarchy. Stripped of its former right to discretion, the open secret exposed, the position could not long continue.

MADAME DU BARRY

The question of who would be Louis XV's next official mistress became even more urgent after the death of Queen Marie Lesczinska in June 1768, around the same time that he also lost his daughter, known as Madame Infante; his grandson; and finally, his son the dauphin and his daughter-in-law. As Dufort de Cheverny noted after Pompadour's death, "Every woman at court was ready to catch the glove if the King wanted to toss it; but none satisfied him, no one had earned the same trust."[168]

Rivalries at Versailles meant that factions of courtiers sought to find a suitable mistress, Pompadour's death "fan[ning] the flames of intrigue at Versailles, where courtiers engaged in what was effectively a competition to replace her."[169] According to Madame Campan, future *première femme de chambre* of Marie Antoinette, an anti-Choiseul faction "wanted to find a mistress for the king . . . in whose salon they could triumph over the old attachment of the king for the duc de Choiseul through the power of daily innuendo."[170] The evidence suggests that it was Richelieu who brought to the king's attention a beautiful Parisian woman of shady background, Jeanne Bécu.[171] Born in 1743, she was educated in the convent of the Adoratrices du Sacré-Coeur de Jésus. After leaving the convent at the age of fifteen, she worked as a domestic servant, and then at a *boutique de mode* where her beauty drew many admirers. She eventually styled herself by the more impressive last name Vaubernier and was sometimes referred to as Mademoiselle Lange, or "l'Ange," apparently a reference to her angelic appearance.[172] A dissolute provincial nobleman, Jean-Baptiste Du Barry (nicknamed "le Roué"), took her under his wing around 1764; in addition to being her lover, he introduced her to a sumptuous and sociable lifestyle and to men who could help her maintain it. According to many biographers, he also trained her in the sexual arts that would prove so enticing to the king.[173] Thus Jeanne had acquired a reputation in the libertine Parisian circles to which le Roué had introduced her by the time she caught the attention of Richelieu.[174] Du Barry had already determined that Jeanne was ideal to serve as the king's next mistress, and Richelieu was the man who could help place her before the eyes of the king. With the help of the king's *valet de chambre*, Le Bel (who also helped manage the Parc-aux-Cerfs), she was introduced to Louis XV.[175]

Jeanne and the king began their torrid romance in the summer of 1768. This was apparently the king's first encounter with a woman trained in the arts of love.[176] Contemporary accounts suggest she captivated the king with her skill: "She had learned so much from her teacher and pleased the nearly sexagenarian monarch immensely, captivating him to such an extent that Le Bel justly took umbrage."[177] In addition, her good spirits seem to have suited the melancholic king.[178] All agreed that Louis was besotted.

Her supporters sought to arrange her presentation at court so that she could live at Versailles and assume the more powerful and stable position of official mistress. This required marriage and title on her part, swiftly arranged by her "handler" Du Barry. He provided her with a convenient spouse: his brother, Guillaume, Count Du Barry. She now had the necessary title.[179] The official presentation of the new countess would not be without complication, however, although the queen was no longer around to register her disapproval. Court observers, not surprisingly, considered the new Madame Du Barry's origins considerably more suspect than even those of Madame de Pompadour. Madame Campan observed acidly: "It's true that Mme Du Barry was chosen from a truly vile class. Her origins, her education, her habits, all gave rise to her vulgar and shameful character, but she was married off to a man [whose family origins were] from the fifteenth century, and they believed that scandal had been avoided."[180]

As had been the case with Pompadour, the king had to find a sponsor willing to introduce Du Barry at Versailles. The Marquis of Belleval commented on the gossip this caused as early as December 1768; in January 1769 he reported that an introduction "is not easy to arrange" given her circumstances. On 22 April the "long-awaited presentation finally took place. . . . It was Mme la comtesse de Béarn who introduced Mme du Barry to the king, to Mesdames, to M. le Dauphin and to the Enfants de France.

They say that Mme de Béarn was promised that she would win a major lawsuit she had been involved in for quite a while and upon which part of her fortune depended. They also say that, in addition, she has already been paid in cash."[181] The Duke of Croÿ pronounced Du Barry's presentation "one of the strangest and most remarkable events that ever took place at court," but he acknowledged that the court might see significant changes if the young woman "took on the same dominant role at Court that Mme de Pompadour had played."[182]

According to nearly all reports, her beauty was remarkable, considerably more so than that of Pompadour.[183] In his laudatory description of her, the Count of Espinchal (1748–1823) compared her to an illustrious predecessor: "The portrait of Agnès Sorel that Voltaire created for us is perfectly suited to her: 'love never formed anything like it, etc., etc. / She possessed everything: she would have enchained / The heroes, the sages and the kings, etc., etc.'"[184] The Prince de Ligne left a frequently cited written portrait of her: "She is tall, well-made, ravishingly blond, a clear brow, beautiful eyes, eyebrows to match, oval face with little beauty marks on her cheeks making her like no other, aquiline nose, a laughing mouth [*leste*], fine skin, an unfashionably [large] bosom, leading many to hide their breasts to avoid comparison."[185] Belleval affirmed that in addition to being "one of the loveliest women at court," she was also "the most seductive because of her complete perfection."[186] Choiseul appears to have been the only man unimpressed by her looks.[187]

The assumption, overt since the reign of Madame de Pompadour, that the king's mistress was his closest adviser and a useful political ally to others drew her inexorably into the political intrigues simmering among courtiers at Versailles. Charles Vatel suggests that early in her reign, when her "favor was far from as secure as that of the marquise," Du Barry tried to "slavishly imitate her [Pompadour]."[188] As Pompadour had looked to her predecessors, especially Maintenon, as models, Du Barry would consider hers in consolidating her position, despite the fact that most assumed she was more interested in clothing and jewelry than influencing policy.[189] During her early months at court, Croÿ observed that "she did not appear to be interested in intrigue, she liked finery, to be everywhere, [but] without the desire to meddle in business."[190] This changed over time. While not interested in foreign and domestic politics per se, she became important to those who sought power for themselves, especially Richelieu and his nephew the Duke of Aiguillon, with their links to the *parti dévot*, who had promoted her as royal mistress.[191] Significantly, both Richelieu and

Aiguillon had despised Pompadour and Choiseul, who had continued as the king's most influential secretary of state since the death of Pompadour. As Du Barry's allies, they were assumed by court observers to be planning the fall of Choiseul through the new mistress's rise.[192] Croÿ suggested that her political maneuvering was starting to imitate that of Pompadour, to the benefit of the Aiguillon faction.[193]

Had Choiseul tried to cooperate with Du Barry, it appears that she would have been amenable. His faction, however, was unwilling.[194] Choiseul and his sister, the Duchess of Gramont, both refused to pay court to her and treated her with open contempt.[195] Swann writes that Du Barry "was persistantly snubbed and subjected to a campaign of vilification, much of it in print, that spared none of the tawdry details of her earlier life as a courtesan."[196] In addition, recognizing the key role a mistress could play in controlling the king, the Choiseul faction tried unsuccessfully to replace Du Barry with another young woman in January 1769.[197] The result was that Du Barry was more than willing to promote against Choiseul her own supporters, who, in addition to Richelieu and Aiguillon, also included Choiseul's rivals, the chancellor Maupeou and the Abbé Terray. Thus she found herself, in the words of Croÿ, "at the head of a new party."[198] Consequently, Belleval reported that autumn that "the influence of the minister [Choiseul] diminishes day by day, while that of M. le duc d'Aiguillon, who has the support of Mme la comtesse du Barry, grows in proportion."[199]

Although political configurations at court were extremely complicated, the anonymous author of the venomous tract on Du Barry pronounced that she had become the sole channel to access the king's favor and that she, like Pompadour, was responsible for the appointment of ministers, always her cronies, and usually at the behest of Aiguillon.[200] She served her supporters in two ways. She was a conduit for criticisms of Choiseul, passing on complaints directly to the king, but she also exercised increasing control over the distribution of patronage, securing the post of lieutenant general of the *chevaux-légers*, her favored military company, for Aiguillon in September 1769.[201] In a letter to the Empress Maria Theresa in December 1771, Florimond Claude, Count of Mercy-Argenteau (1727–1794), wrote that Du Barry's control "over the thinking of the king is almost without limits; it obviously affects everything concerning the royal family, and the more the favorite is mortified by mistreatment, the more she takes actions to show her resentment."[202] However, the lines of battle that broke out in the court were not simply the result of her maneuvering.[203] Robert Darnton affirms that historians of France see the last five years of Louis XV's reign as the most politically catastrophic in that country before the French Revolution. The humiliating defeat in 1763 at the hands of the British and Prussia, continuing foreign entanglements that bound them to Bourbon Spain in what was called the "Family Compact," in addition to France's unwillingness to defend Poland against the aggression of eastern European powers, led to controversy over France's foreign policy decisions.[204] The ongoing struggle with the Parlements meant that the domestic scene was equally chaotic.[205]

While she was skillful at maintaining the adoration of the aging king and serving as a conduit to him for her allies, courtiers considered Du Barry less politically adept than her predecessors. Madame Campan mocked her efforts to insinuate herself into policy discussions, writing that she "neglected propriety to the extent that one day she wanted to attend the Council of State. The King foolishly consented to it; she remained there, ridiculously perched on the arm of his throne, indulging in all the little childish antics that seem to appeal to old [men]."[206] The royal mistress would be implicated in the breakdown of relations between the king's ministers and his judges that led to the Maupeou Parlement.[207] The anonymous tract viciously criticizing the reign of Du Barry compared her lack of political acumen with that of the savvier Pompadour, claiming that her sponsors at court recognized this fact: "M. Du Barry [her brother-in-law and patron], who knew that she did not have talent necessary to manage the affairs of State honorably, & to replace the Marquise de Pompadour in this respect, strongly recommended that she not interfere in any way." For the most part, the author suggests, she followed this advice, although, for personal reasons, she used her influence to take down Choiseul.[208] This did not mean that Du Barry was unintelligent. In fact, she apparently deduced the nature of the "Secret du roi" that had been hidden from Pompadour.[209] However, her interest in policy was shallow and tied to the politics of friendship and her desire for respect at the court. Espinchal would assess her as "in no way suited to the game of intrigue at court" and "an instrument used to gain influence over the king during her [period of] favor."[210]

Du Barry faced a personal and painful fight with the woman who would eventually replace her as the most powerful female actor at court, Marie Antoinette (1755–1793), future queen of France, who married the dauphin, Louis-Auguste (1754–1793), in April 1770.[211] The union between the future Louis XVI and the daughter of Maria Theresa, engineered by Choiseul, was a great victory on his part. Consequently, the dauphine saw Choiseul as an important supporter, which set her implacably against the king's mistress and her allies.[212] Predictably, the dauphine's dislike for Du Barry was characterized as jealousy; Espinchal wrote of her spite when she "perceived a favorite sharing with her the honors of the court when she believed that those [good] wishes should naturally be addressed to her alone."[213] Certainly, Marie Antoinette was appalled by the idea that she was expected to associate with a woman whom she considered a whore, although her mother, Maria Theresa, and the Austrian minister at Versailles, Mercy-Argenteau, encouraged flexibility.[214] Mercy-Argenteau suggested that the dauphine could make use of Du Barry because the favorite "appears to have little wit, much vanity, [and] is a bit of a lightweight, without indicating a nasty or hateful character. It would be very easy to get her to talk, and, in that case, we could make great use of her indiscretion."[215] Du Barry tried at first to follow the model of Madame de Pompadour vis-à-vis Marie Lesczinska, demonstrating respect and deference to the dauphine. Her partisans, however, entered the fray, which they saw as a proxy for the fight between the Barriens and the Choiseulists.[216]

This infighting meant that the court in the last six years of Louis XV's reign was a "shrunken, factional place, as Madame du Barry and the duc d'Aiguillon—the king's final, detested favourite and the leading figure in the ministry in the early 1770s—packed the court with those they could both rely on."[217] The Barriens were victorious in the first round, as Choiseul went into exile in December 1770, and Aiguillon, Maupeou, and Terray, Du Barry's allies, became Louis's chief ministers. This meant a modification of Choiseul's foreign policy, while domestically the king's ministers launched the governmental coup known as the Maupeou Revolution. In the long run, however, this was a disaster, the Maupeou Parlement and the ministers—and mistress—who engineered it remaining deeply unpopular as symbols of a despotic, rapacious government.[218] This opinion attached itself to the king. At the time of Louis XV's death, the commander of the Swiss Guard, the Baron of Besenval (1722–1794), reported: "The people, overburdened with taxes to make up for the embezzlement of funds wasted on luxuries and squandered because of the cupidity of the mistress and the intriguers who surrounded her, in addition to [being] indignant at the disorder in which this prince lived, considered the moment of his death the only way out from under oppression and proclaimed it loudly in the streets."[219]

Still, while the king lived, Du Barry appeared even more powerful than Pompadour had been at her peak: "Throughout the summer, the prodigious credit of Mme de Barry only grew, and rose to such a height that there is no [other] example and [it] surpassed the most brilliant era of Mme de Pompadour. She determined all favors and offices; they were only for her protégés and fervent admirers."[220] In the end, however, the death of Louis XV of smallpox in May 1774 would bring down the Barriens. Louis XVI, who brought in as his adviser the elderly Count of Maurepas, was persuaded to abandon his grandfather's attempted reforms and soon dismissed the ministers associated with Maupeou.[221] Neither Louis XVI nor his wife had any love for Du Barry, ordering her to withdraw to a convent.[222]

While few would argue that Du Barry demonstrated the acumen of Pompadour, contemporaries universally reported that she was a far nicer individual, similar to the contemporary assessment of Gabrielle d'Estrées. According to Belleval, she was "different in that way from Mme de Pompadour, who never forgot insults and who did not know what it was to forgive." Indeed, Du Barry, he continues, was "the first to laugh at all the songs about her."[223] Notably, she used her influence to ask for favors of mercy.[224] For example, in 1769 she persuaded the king to commute the death sentence of a young woman, Appoline Grégeois, who had been condemned for infanticide. Another case that aroused her interest was that of the Count and Countess of Loüesme, a couple who had gone bankrupt and, in the course of defending their chateau from confiscation for debt, had killed two officers and were sentenced to execution. The Countess of Béarn, who had presented Du Barry at court, turned to her to ask for a pardon for the couple from a king who was notoriously reluctant to grant one in most cases. "Madame du Barry threw herself to her knees, and declared that she would not get up until His Majesty granted her request. The king raised her up, crying out: 'Madame, I am delighted that the first favor you pressure me for is an act of humanity.'"[225] Belleval recounted that she also obtained a pardon for a soldier named Carpentier who deserted in 1769.[226] In the end, her pleasant nature may not have done her much good; Espinchal noted that "many whom she had obliged had forgotten."[227]

In the end, both Du Barry and Pompadour were criticized for the same thing: supporting their friends and helping place them in positions of influence rather than considering the good of France. In general, however, contemporaries and subsequent historians were less critical of Du Barry for her political intrigues than they were for her sexual excesses, chronicled in many *libelles*, and for her extravagant expenditures on jewels and clothing.[228] Dietrich was more sympathetic to Du Barry than Pompadour, because, according to him, "she loved neither vengeance nor spite, did not silence [her enemies] with *lettres de cachet*, did not send jokers to the

Bastille. She did not attempt to exercise any influence over the destinies of France and Europe." On the other hand, he did outline her expensive tastes with horror: she "could with both hands take from the royal treasury, and it cost her nothing to make generous gifts. She was a ridiculous spend-thrift, [showing] luxurious extravagance reminiscent of the insane whims of that other dangerous siren, Cleopatra." He noted that four volumes of accounts at the Bibliothèque nationale de France showed that she spent 12,500,000 livres in six years on ridiculously expensive luxuries, including, among other items, two sugar spoons for 2054 livres, earrings for 120,000, and a 12,000-livre dress. "Nothing more instructive and more lamenta-ble than this inventory. While people died of hunger, a brazen trollop purchased objects at this price."[229] Du Barry was also the recipient of the domain of Louveciennes, where, after the death of Louis XV, she would live until her execution in 1793 at the hands of a republican government that associated her with the worst abuses of the ancien régime.[230]

For this reason, contemporaries as well as subsequent historians dwelled on the increasing degradation of the court during her time as royal favor-ite.[231] Pamphleteers charged that the life that Du Barry led at court was totally corrupt: "Madame Du Barry brought to the Court a life of constant debauchery, & gave herself over to the outrageous ectasy of a spoiled and corrupt heart. . . . Wealth, luxury, pleasure, surrounded her. . . . Scarcely having the time to ask herself what she desired, her dishonor, like her triumph, was complete."[232] In the eyes of many, Du Barry symbolized the debasement of the monarchy at the hands of a woman. This would be her legacy to Marie Antoinette.[233]

CONCLUSION

Contemporaries were well aware of the long genealogy of the official royal mistress and explicitly linked the mistresses of Louis XV with those who had gone before. Pompadour had tried to do so, in a positive way, care-fully modeling herself on her predecessors and making use of the classical imagery on which previous mistresses had drawn to carve out a space for themselves. However, Pompadour's lack of noble pedigree made her posi-tion more difficult than that of earlier mistresses. Not even her elevation to *dame de palais* in 1756 could obscure the fact that she was at court only because of her relationship with the king. Madame Du Barry's position was even less ambiguous, as scurrilous *libelles* made clear. Du Barry would be the last royal mistress, and, in a vicious comparison, she was proclaimed the worst of them: "Madame Du Barry made a striking contrast with the Gabrielles d'Etrées [*sic*], the Maintenons, the Montespans, the La Valière [*sic*], & the Pompadours . . . much less beautiful than the Mistress of Henri IV, possessing none of the merit, the sensitivity, the birth, nor the real tenderness of the Mistresses of Louis XIV, much inferior in every respect to her predecessor."[234] The disasters of Louis XV's reign—the Seven Years' War, the quarrels with the Parlements, and the infighting among court factions followed with such interest by the public—were increasingly connected with his very visible and powerful favorites.

Others were more sympathetic toward Louis XV and his mistresses, seeing splendor in their performances. In his memoirs, the Prince de Ligne, who spent time at Versailles, wrote nostalgically, "I have seen Louis XV with the grand air of Louis XIV, and Mme. de Pompadour assuming that of Mme. de Montespan."[235] The Count of Espinchal made reference to the "brilliant reign" of Du Barry that ended with the death of the king.[236] Louis XV himself saw in his mistresses the continuation of a genealogy, and he paid respect to their predecessors. In 1772 the canons of Notre-Dame de Loches asked to move the body of Agnès Sorel from the choir of their church, where the large black marble tomb got in the way during services. After doing some research into Agnès, the king refused the request, writing that the tomb was to be left where it was. Surely he thought of Madame de Pompadour, whom he had buried four years earlier. Louis XVI, in contrast, had no particular sympathy for the royal tradition of official mistresses. When the canons made the same request in 1777, he granted it. Amelot, minister and secretary of state, announced to the canons of the Collegiate of Notre-Dame de Loches that His Majesty would allow them "to remove the tomb of Agnès Seurelle from the choir of their church where it gets in the way of the divine service." The exhumation took place on 5 March 1777; the tomb was moved and reinterred.[237]

The tradition of the official royal mistress ended with Louis XV. But the unfortunate queen of Louis XVI would be attributed with the worst of the roles of both wife and mistress, facing French xenophobia toward the foreign wives of monarchs as well as hatred toward the mistress.

Epilogue

Mistress-Queen and the End of a Tradition

MARIE ANTOINETTE

In ancien régime France, queen and mistress performed different functions. Too important to be left to the king to choose himself, the queen was selected in consultation with his advisers, and, in many cases, without meaningful participation on his part. The queen embodied ties of alliance and friendship between two countries, and she was charged first and foremost with giving birth to an heir. She was expected to be pious and charitable. Under certain circumstances, she might serve as intermediary between the country of her birth and her adopted country. Finally, the queen was a foreigner whose loyalties were always suspect, even after many years in the country and even after bearing heirs to the throne. In contrast, the official mistress, whom the king chose for himself, exuded a sexuality that would have been unseemly in a queen. She was beautiful and glamorous in a way that queens seldom were. Most important, the mistress, always a French woman, represented France. Her family was never a competing dynasty, member of the caste of ruling royal families. Because the king chose her, he also trusted her always to have his interests in mind.

This is not to say that the people of France were automatically and universally hostile toward young queens who arrived in the country to great pomp and circumstance. Many French men and women were charmed by the young Habsburg princess Marie Antoinette when she arrived at the Île des Épis near Strasbourg in May 1770 for the *remise*—her transfer to French authorities—and jubilant crowds lined the streets as she made her way to Compiègne to meet the king and the dauphin, her new husband.[1]

But her popularity waned, and by the time revolution broke out in 1789, Marie Antoinette was one of the most hated symbols of the ancien régime. Although the public had always mistrusted queens, in most cases these women were not sufficiently powerful to evoke real hatred from the French—unless they were regents, that is. The public directed vitriol against regents Catherine de Médicis, Marie de Médicis, and Anne of Austria, who wielded legal authority as they ruled in the name of their sons. Queens, however, resided at court, where they did not preside, drawing little attention unless their clothing and pastimes became the subject of ridicule. It was the royal mistress, rather, who was fashion icon and cultural arbiter, playing the starring role with the king at the theater of the court. It was she who whispered in his ear, who placed her allies in powerful positions, who served as primary political adviser, discreetly and cloaked in ambiguity. However, by the eighteenth century, as we have seen, this discretion was dissipating. Madame de Pompadour openly met with ministers and directly influenced policy, while Madame Du Barry allied visibly with court factions who fought over the direction of French foreign policy and the Parlements. The open secret of the mistress's political influence was no longer a secret in this new era.

Marie Antoinette was, in the words of Chantal Thomas, "exceptional in the history of France . . . both queen and favorite simultaneously." Worse, she "combined the faults of the first role (arrogance, the arbitrariness of absolute sovereignty) with those of the second (duplicity, obsession with appearances)."[2] Over the course of her reign, cut short by the Revolution and definitively ended by her execution in October 1793, Marie Antoinette, playing both roles, became the target of those who distrusted the queen for her divided loyalties as well as those who loathed mistresses for their extravagance and their illegitimate influence over the king. Louis XVI, timid and ill at ease with women, was able to consummate his marriage with his wife only after a long delay and with much difficulty; their first child was born eight years after their marriage.[3] Despite the difficult beginnings of their own, both he and Marie Antoinette preferred the idea of a companionate marriage. And yet Marie Antoinette's behavior might well have escaped such close scrutiny had her husband established a mistress at the court.[4] As Carolyn Harris writes, "During the reigns of Louis XIV and Louis XV, the king's mistress served as counterpoint to his consort, often allowing the sovereign's wife to develop a reputation for virtue and fidelity. . . . Despite the personal distress the presence of a royal mistress at court might cause for the queen, the counterpoint between the two women had the potential to deflect criticism from the sovereign's wife."[5]

Marie Antoinette herself rejected the role usually assigned the queen, a formal, regal, and public role as pious and obedient spouse, largely uninvolved in politics unless acting on behalf of her son as regent. Instead, she embraced the theatricality usually associated with the mistress and tried to carve out spaces where she could play different roles. Writes Thomas,

> Marie-Antoinette at Versailles, and even more so at the Trianon, was the first queen of France to break with the tradition of self-effacement to which the wives of Louis XIV or Louis XV had submitted before her. She was the first to lend to Versailles her style, to impose her imprint on it, and to promulgate the dictates of fashion. Such visibility placed Marie-Antoinette in line with the great courtesans. It was first under this title (leaving aside the detested title of "Austrian" to a people for whom Austria had been a hereditary enemy) that she drew the arrows of the lampoonists.[6]

Like Montespan and Pompadour, she embraced the role of Queen of Fashion and set new styles at the court and for the public at large. These styles were often eagerly copied (as with the "pouf" hairdo), but they could also cause shock, as when Elisabeth Vigée-Lebrun painted her *en chemise*—a simple and natural gown made of white muslin with a sash—a style condemned as unsuitably informal for a queen of France.[7] But more generally, it was highly unusual, and potentially dangerous, for a queen to show such an interest in fashion, a point that Caroline Weber makes:

> Because she was neither a king nor a king's mistress, Marie Antoinette's sartorial posturing represented a striking departure from established court custom. For a French consort to modify the conventions of royal appearance, or to seek attention or empowerment on her own terms, was virtually unheard of. But this is exactly what Marie Antoinette did, in ways that became even more daring after she became queen in 1774. Her stature unchallenged by a competing royal mistress, the young queen promptly jettisoned the stagnant and dowdy royal style that had long functioned to evoke the timelessness of the Bourbon reign and set out in heady new directions.[8]

In addition to seeming inappropriate to many, Marie Antoinette's sartorial extravagance left her vulnerable to accusations of financial profligacy at the expense of the French people, especially at a time when France was heavily in debt as a result of the disastrous Seven Years' War, as well as the more successful, but also very expensive, assistance to the fledgling American colonies in their war for independence from Great Britain. This recalled, for many, the extravagance of previous mistresses, especially Pompadour and Du Barry, all too fresh in the mind of the public.[9] Her nickname, Madame Déficit, reflected this image.

Marie Antoinette, whose first years at the court overlapped with Louis XV's last mistress, became associated with Du Barry, the greedy fashionista.[10] Even the great scandal of 1786, the Diamond Necklace affair, linked Marie Antoinette to Du Barry, because the necklace at the center of the affair was originally intended for Du Barry.[11] The connection to Pompadour, the friend and political adviser to the king, seems to have been less insistent and explicit in the *libelle* literature, even though Marie Antoinette tried—and came—to play that role as well. Still, Marie Antoinette would be reviled for interfering in politics, in part because all assumed that she would represent the interests of her country of origin. Certainly her mother, Maria Theresa of Austria, believed that her daughter would defend Habsburg interests. In a number of early battles at the French court, Marie Antoinette openly allied herself with those committed to Austrian priorities: in her support for Choiseul when she first arrived at Versailles, in the dismissal of ministers she opposed once her husband became king, and in her open (although unsuccessful) lobbying on behalf of Austria during the Bavarian Crisis of 1778.[12] Like royal mistresses, she relied on her personal relationship with the king to exert political influence. "The most satisfying thing for Mme la Dauphine," wrote the Austrian ambassador to France and confidante of the queen, the Count of Mercy-Argenteau, "is that she gains ascendancy daily over the mind of the dauphin. With a bit of care she will no doubt manage to subjugate him completely."[13] Perhaps with better advice, the queen would have behaved more circumspectly; her companion, Madame Campan, mourned the fact that Marie Antoinette was left without useful guidance after the departure of Choiseul, writing that the "fall of this minister took place in November 1770, six months after his long influence in the council had brought about the alliance with the Austrian house and the arrival of Marie Antoinette at the French court. This princess, young, fresh, flighty, inexperienced, found herself with no guide other than the abbé de Vermond . . . among people who hated Austria and who detested any alliance with the Empire."[14]

A contemporary wrote of the queen that "although she spoke constantly of her love for the French nation, at the bottom of her heart she always remained an Austrian, always disposed to sacrifice the interests of her husband to those of her brother the emperor Joseph II."[15] As Austrophobia became increasingly potent among the French, who blamed that empire for their own diplomatic decline, Marie Antoinette was an easy target— especially as, over time, she seemed to be choosing the interests of Austria over those of the French.[16] By the time of the Revolution, Marie Antoinette was part of the political faction that actively opposed the demands of revolutionary legislators and favored royal interests.[17]

Many scholars of the French Revolution have argued that the attacks on Marie Antoinette were emblematic of a deeply misogynistic vein in France's developing political culture that would lead to revolution in 1789 and to the violent elimination of female participation in the new polity.[18] While not denying the reality of that misogyny, Thomas Kaiser suggests that Austrophobia—a persistent theme in French political culture since at least the sixteenth century and exacerbated by the disaster of France's alliance with the Austrians during the Seven Years' War—may actually have been more damaging to Marie Antoinette's image than generalized misogyny.[19] This potent blend—the xenophobia often directed at queens, especially regents, combined with the hatred for mistresses who meddled in court politics to benefit themselves and their allies and who exhausted government coffers with their excessive spending on luxuries of all sorts— came together in explosive outrage directed at the Austrian queen.

Historians have exhaustively examined the performances of Marie Antoinette in a variety of roles over the course of her reign. From innocent princess to frivolous queen to shepherdess at Le Hameau to domesticated and obedient wife to dignified martyr, her life was as theatrical as any royal mistress. Some of her best-known roles were those invented for her: the dissolute queen, the licentious tigress, "the Austrian woman" with its implication of "the Austrian bitch" ("l'Autrichienne") emerged in the vicious pamphlet literature of the prerevolutionary and revolutionary years. In the minds of many, "frivolous, extravagant, libertine, orgiastic, lesbian, incestuous, and bloodthirsty, a poisoner and an infanticide, Marie-Antoinette tried her hand at every crime. Through her wickedness she caused the Revolution. She ruined the country, brought the people to despair, drove them to revolt."[20]

With the outbreak of the French Revolution, the impossible contradictions in the position of the royal mistress were laid bare. The mistress was the privileged emblem of theatricality and secrecy in politics, which only worked in a polity based on both of those elements. The new political order reviled secrecy and dissimulation, instead prizing transparency and "natural" behavior. Earlier mistresses had thrived in the culture of dissimulation at court; now, this was one of the most serious charges against Marie Antoinette: "Most threatening, of course, was her influence on the king; she was charged not only with the crime of having had perverse ministers named to office, but more significantly and generally with having taught the king how to dissimulate—that is, how to promise one thing in public and plan another in the shadows of the court." This kind of secrecy was expected under the old regime but untenable in the new one; the new republican polity saw dissimulation as a quintessentially feminine quality, one that they rightly associated with female power in the ancien régime.[21] It was antithetical to the values of the new republican government of France. The mistress and now Marie Antoinette became the focal point of all that was wrong with the polity of the old regime. Central in the rise of a French court perceived as theater and a French state conceived as absolutist, the royal mistress—now, merged with an unpopular queen—fell with it.

INTRODUCTION

1. Frederick II, *Anti-Machiavel*, part 2, 6. Frederick later had reason to acknowledge the genuine importance of the royal mistress, as he tried unsuccessfully to flatter and manipulate the powerful Madame de Pompadour into rejecting the French alliance with Austria as the Seven Years' War was breaking out. See Algrant, *Madame de Pompadour*, 91, and Kaiser, "Austrian Alliance," 173–74.

2. Wieland, *Miroir d'or*, 23.

3. Luynes, *Mémoires*, 6:354.

4. Translation of the modern "maîtresse en titre," which we adopt for convenience even though the term is anachronistic for much of the time covered in the study and contradictory given that the role was never actually "official." In keeping with its status as an open secret, the position had no fixed name: "favorite," "amie," "maîtresse" (Brantôme, *Œuvres complètes*, 5:244, refers to Anne de Pisseleu d'Heilly as François I's "principalle dame et maistresse"), and, especially in the eighteenth century, *maîtresse en titre* were common designations, although none of these terms referred uniquely to the position. We understand the situation somewhat differently from Knecht, who writes: "[François I] had several [mistresses] in the course of his reign, but only two were *maîtresses en titre*, or official mistresses. They were official in the sense that no attempt was made to conceal their existence: known to everyone, they were given an honourable place at court" (*French Renaissance Court*, 10). As we discuss in detail in chapter 2, the Duchess of Étampes was powerful in a way that was completely unprecedented. Françoise de Foix, one of the two mistresses to whom Knecht refers, never worked with diplomats. We differ also in regarding the official mistress as an open secret rather than simply as an openly acknowledged phenomenon.

5. A recent dissertation that considers the institution of the royal mistress in eighteenth-century France and England appeared too late for us to consider in this study. See Kauppinen, "Power, Politics and Pillowtalk." We thank Karen Offen for the reference. We also discovered art historian Sigrid Ruby's excellent *Mit Macht verbunden. Bilder der Favoritin im Frankreich der Renaissance* (Freiburg i. Br.: FWPF, 2010) too late for this study. Thanks to Kathleen Wilson-Chevalier for the reference.

6. For a study of French queenship, see Cosandey's magisterial *Reine de France*; for one of female regents, see Crawford, *Perilous Performances*. The mignons have attracted copious scholarship; we mention just Jouanna, "Faveur et favoris," and Le Roux, *Faveur du roi*. As for studies of individual royal mistresses, see, for example, Potter, "Anne de Pisseleu" and "Politics and

Faction"; Goodman, *Portraits of Madame de Pompadour*; Kaiser, "Madame de Pompadour"; Bardon, *Diane de Poitiers*.

7. We discuss the exception that proves the rule in chapter 5. For a time, Louis XIV's mistresses La Vallière and Montespan overlapped as the former was transitioning out. As we will see, the situation offended the courtiers' sensibilities.

8. Hufton, "Reflections on the Role of Women," 1.

9. For a succinct description of the schema that Braudel developed over the course of his career, see his "Histoire et sciences sociales," 725–53.

10. For Louis, see *Ordonnances*, 7:535; for Isabeau, see 7:530–31.

11. The ordinance, promulgated on 26 April 1403, states that if the king dies leaving a minor heir, the kingdom will have no regent. See *Ordonnances*, 8:582. However, the king acknowledged that some recent ordinances might have been damaging to his brother, Louis of Orléans, and rescinded any part of these ordinances that deprived Louis of his power, but the ordinances were reinstated after the assassination of Louis in November 1407, the Royal Council on 23 December passing an ordinance to this effect. See ibid., 9:267–69.

12. The queen mother's role was not specifically designated "regent" until the reign of Marie de Médicis beginning in 1610. See, for example, the pamphlet "Au Roy et a la Royne regente sa mere."

13. *Ordonnances*, 7:530; Masselin, *Journal des états généraux*, 142.

14. Louis VII responds to a letter of 1164 that a knight who refuses to appear before the Viscountess of Narbonne because of her sex is wrong: when there is no member of the strong sex, it is permissible that a woman administer the heritage. Cited in Contamine, "Le Royaume de France," 79n30. For examples of inheritance, see Beaumanoir, *Coutumes de Beauvaisis*, 1:222–43. The males inherit first, but females inherit where there is no male heir. Ableiges, *Grand coutumier de France*, 290–308, on fiefs, shows the same; see 373

on guardianship, which the surviving parent assumes. See also Wood, *French Apanages and the Capetian Monarchy*, which discusses how, when Louis X became king, his brother Philippe asked him to change the laws regarding apanage so that Philippe's daughters could inherit. Misogynistic writings, mostly clerical, denigrated female intelligence. But the participation of women in noble feudal society proves that, among many, women were seen as being as capable and competent as men.

15. Christine de Pizan, *Mutacion*, 1:51–52, lines 1337–65.

16. Ibid., 1:21, lines 413–19.

17. Ibid., 1:20, line 396.

18. Leschassier, *Du droit de nature*, 98.

19. Dupuy, *Traité de la majorité de nos rois*, 35–36.

20. Luyt, *Sceptre de France en quenouille*, cited in Cosandey, "Reine dans l'état modern," 815–16.

21. Bély, *Art de la paix*, 43.

22. Crawford, *Perilous Performances*, especially 34–50.

23. Christine de Pizan, *Città delle dame*, 92–94.

24. Christine de Pizan, *Livre des trois vertus*, 34–35.

25. Christine de Pizan, *Ditié de Jehanne d'Arc*, translated by Kennedy and Varty, 42–43, stanzas 13–14.

26. Autrand, "'Hôtel de seigneur ne vaut rien sans dame,'" 51.

27. See, for example, Cosandey, *Reine de France*, 66–72.

28. Le Roux, *Faveur du roi*, 22–23.

29. Jouanna, "Faveur et favoris," 155–57.

30. Adamson, "Introduction," 19. On the rise of the favorite, see also Elliott and Brockliss's introduction to *World of the Favourite*, which dates the onset of the phenomenon to the sixteenth century, when it came forcefully to consciousness, although recognizing its earlier existence.

31. Elliott and Brockliss, *World of the Favourite*, through essays on the rise of the favorite in different countries, makes this clear.

32. Zmora, *Monarchy, Aristocracy, and the State*, 86.

33. Jouanna, "Faveur et favoris," 159.

34. Le Roux, *Faveur du roi*, 12.

35. Akkerman and Houben make this point in the introduction to *Politics of Female Households*, 13. According to Moine, "Their influence was considerable, and not only with regard to the king's mistresses" (*Fêtes à la cour*, 141). Duindam has underlined the continued political importance of the court nobility, male and female, over the course of the early modern era: "In Europe, there has been a shift in attention from 'modern' state institutions and the sources generated by policy-making boards and councils to the social setting of dynastic power, the court. A closer look at state archives and private collections suggested that the domestic world around rulers stood at the heart of the early modern state. This was no 'gilded cage' captivating once powerful nobles through expensive luxury and endless squabbles, and allowing the state to develop without their interference. *In most European countries, high-placed nobles in domestic court offices retained political power, sometimes formalised and direct, sometimes through their proximity and intimacy with the ruler*" (emphasis added). This included women. See Duindam, *Dynasties*, 16.

36. Le Roux, *Faveur du roi*, 11.

37. Contamine, "Pouvoir et vie de cour," 544–45.

38. Basin, *Histoire des règnes*, 1:313. For the names of the mignons and citations of the accounts that name them, see Fresne de Beaucourt, *Histoire de Charles VII*, 4:177–81.

39. According to Kathleen Wellman, Anne had sixteen women and eighteen girls in her court in 1492; the numbers grew to fifty-nine and forty-one, respectively, by 1498 (*Queens and Mistresses*, 100).

40. Akkerman and Houben, introduction to *Politics of Female House-holds*, 11. On the duties associated with female offices, see Mallick, "Clients and Friends," 234–36.

41. On the key role of women in patronage networks, see Chapman, "Patronage as Family Economy."

42. Hufton described their role as follows: "They form networks associating themselves with other women and through them build bridges to other men to achieve specific ends" ("Reflections on the Role of Women," 1).

43. Davis writes: "Women took part in court ceremonial and joined in the relations of patronage and faction; they petitioned for posts, pensions, and pardons for members of their families and their clients as did men" ("Women in Politics," 174–75). See also Wellman's *Queens and Mistresses*.

44. Chastellain, *Œuvres*, 4:365, italics added.

45. See Hamilton, "Première description de Fontainebleau," 45. The king's apartments lay directly between those of the queen and his mistress.

46. Catherine de Médicis, *Lettres*, 8:36.

47. Van Krieken, *Celebrity Society*, 22.

48. Craveri, *Age of Conversation*, 256–57.

49. Budé, *Livre de l'institution du prince*, 25–26.

50. MaAS Cart. inv. e div. 638, 12 January 1539 from Antonio Bendidio.

51. Castiglione, *Book of the Courtier*, 67. See the discussion of "sprezzatura," translated as "nonchalance," 67–68. On the work in France, see Clough, "Francis I and the Courtiers," 23–25.

52. On the history of French collections of love poetry, see Alduy, *Politique des "amours."* For the history of the ballets de cour, see Nordera, "Ballet de cour"; on their political significance, see Gough, *Dancing Queen*.

53. Egginton, *How the World Became a Stage*, 2, 105, 108.

54. Féral and Bermingham, "Theatrical-ity," 99–100.

55. From the Renaissance on, writes Alastair Fowler, "stories have been conceived as events observed or reported, not experienced by participating viewers or listeners," which is to say as events

consciously reflected on via an authorial surrogate (*Renaissance Realism*, 84).

56. Marvick writes that it was "a series of young men (and, less intensely and more briefly, two young women) who were the objects of Louis's love" (*Louis XIII*, 223). Moote also writes of Louis's apparent bisexuality and strong attachment to beautiful young men (something that the gossipy Tallemant des Réaux noted in his *Historiettes*, 3:74); see *Louis XIII, the Just*, 148–50, 282–86.

57. Braudel's "histoire événementielle."

58. See Offen, *Woman Question in France*, 31–37.

59. Ozouf, *Mots des femmes*, 70. Ozouf is a well-known proponent of sexual difference as the basis for harmony between the sexes. More generally, see Fassin, "Purloined Gender."

60. See Fassin, "Purloined Gender," for a discussion of the debate on both sides of the Atlantic. See Bruckner and Finkielkraut, *Nouveau désordre amoureux*, esp. 196–97, for a representative example of this vision of gender in recent scholarship, and Fontenay and Finkielkraut, *En terrain miné*, 153–59, for a recent lament over the effacement of sexual difference.

CHAPTER I

1. Herman, *Sex with Kings*, 2.
2. Wellman, *Queens and Mistresses*, 25, 29.
3. Champion lays out what is known of Agnès's family in *Dame de beauté*, 34–35.
4. La Marche, *Mémoires*, 9:403–4.
5. Jean Chartier, *Chronique de Charles VII*, 2:181–86, quotation on 183.
6. Basin, *Histoire des règnes*, 1:313.
7. Chastellain, *Œuvres*, 4:365–66.
8. Du Clercq, *Mémoires*, 175.
9. Gaguin, *Croniques de France*, fol. CLXIX verso; Piccolomini, *Pii secundi pontificis maximi commentarii*, 160.
10. For Marie de Breuillet, see Van Kerrebrouck, *Capétiens*, 83, 91. Although Biette Cassinel has been attached occasionally to Charles V, no concrete evidence for a relationship exists. See Merlet, "Biographie

de Jean de Montagu," 248–84, and Van Kerrebrouck, *Capétiens*, 92n52. As for Charles VI, the mad king was given a mistress to take care of his needs during his periods of insanity when the queen feared him. See Vallet De Viriville, "Odette ou Odinette de Champdivers," 171–81.

11. On contemporary perceptions of Charles VII's sex drive, see Collard, "Excès débilitants," 397–409.

12. Some examples: popes accused Philip I of France of lust, although it is clear that he wanted to bolster his line with male heirs. See Duby on the story of this king and Bertrade in *The Knight, the Lady, and the Priest*, 11–17. The intermittent insanity of King Charles VI of France was attributed to his youthful debauchery. See Pintoin, *Chronique du Religieux de Saint-Denys*, 2:406. The failure of Anne of Brittany's father to produce sons was attributed to his lust. See L'Estrange, "Penitence, Motherhood, and Passion Devotion," 86.

13. La Marche, *Mémoires*, 9:403–4.
14. Chastellain, *Œuvres*, 4:366–68; Du Clercq, *Mémoires*, 90–91.
15. Du Clercq, *Mémoires*, 91.
16. On Yolande's career, see Rohr, *Yolande of Aragon*, esp. 167–96.
17. Vallet de Viriville, "Étude morale," 263.
18. Fresne de Beaucourt, "Charles VII et Agnès Sorel," 224.
19. Ibid., 221.
20. Ibid., 222.
21. Broomhall, introduction to *Women and Power*, 12.
22. Bourdigné, *Chroniques d'Anjou et du Maine*, 2:199. See the pertinent section of the list in Vallet de Viriville, "Recherches historiques sur Agnès Sorel," 304. The list is also printed in Champion, *Dame de beauté*, pièces justificatives, 173.
23. Fresne de Beaucourt details the itineraries to show the overlap (*Histoire de Charles VII*, 3:290–91).
24. For the donation documents, see Vallet de Viriville, "Recherches historiques sur Agnès Sorel," 312–18.

25. For Agnès's donations, see ibid., 318–22.

26. Fresne de Beaucourt, *Histoire de Charles VII*, 4:174n4.

27. See Vallet de Viriville, "Étude morale," 259–62. Fresne de Beaucourt disputes Agnès's authorship of some of the letters in *Histoire de Charles VII*, 4:440–43. However, he simply cites Étienne Chavaray, who in a personal letter to Fresne de Beaucourt asserts that three of the letters in question are false, based on his viewing of them. The letters are no longer available for view, and there is no way today of following up on Chavaray's assessment as reported by Fresne de Beaucourt, in which the former offers no real detail to support his assessment.

28. For Agnès in the service of Queen Marie, see Jean Chartier, *Chronique de Charles VII*, 2:181. For the complaint, see Chastellain, *Œuvres*, 4:365–66.

29. Du Clercq, *Mémoires*, 175.

30. Fresne de Beaucourt cites accounts showing that the king left Agnès in Loches under the care of one of his favorites, Guillaume Gouffier. Fresne de Beaucourt, *Histoire de Charles VII*, 4:217nn2, 3. For a description of the Jumièges abbey church and the house in which Agnès died, see Black, *Normandy and Picardy*, 39–40.

31. Green, "Bodies, Gender, Health, Disease," 1–46.

32. Jean Chartier, *Chronique de Charles VII*, 2:181.

33. See Fresne de Beaucourt, *Histoire de Charles VII*, 4:217.

34. Jean Chartier, *Chronique de Charles VII*, 2:184–85. The black marble plaque under which Agnès's heart once lay in the cathedral at Jumièges gives the date of death as 9 February. See Champion, *Dame de beauté*, 64.

35. Jean Chartier, *Chronique de Charles VII*, 2:184. He does actually mention a baby girl who did not live long but does not connect this to Agnès's death. Instead, he mentions the baby in a discussion of rumors about the king and Agnès, insisting that the child was not the king's.

36. For the baby, see Philippe Charlier, "Qui a tué la dame de Beauté?," 261; for Agnès's age, see Philippe Charlier, "Les dents d'Agnès Sorel."

37. Philippe Charlier, "Qui a tué la dame de Beauté?," 259.

38. Email communication with Philippe Charlier, October 2014. His conclusions about Agnès's death have been challenged: ingested mercury is not particularly toxic because it is not absorbed, and mercury was not popular with poisoners during the Middle Ages. However, although mercury in its liquid "quicksilver" form is not absorbed, in its "medicinal" form—that is, as mercuric chloride—it is highly toxic. See Warrell et al., *Oxford Textbook of Medicine*, 1:903. If mercuric chloride was not the poison most commonly used to commit murder, it was known to be toxic and used in assassinations. See Trestrail, *Criminal Poisoning*, 6.

39. Philippe Charlier, "Qui a tué la dame de Beauté?," 262.

40. On Poitevin, see Vallet de Viriville, "Notes biographiques sur Robert Poitevin," 488–99; Favreau, "Robert Poitevin," 141–51.

41. See Coward and Swann's introduction to *Conspiracies and Conspiracy Theory*, 3.

42. On accusations of poisoning during the Middle Ages, see Collard, *Crime de poison*. According to some chroniclers, Charles VII died malnourished, afraid to eat during his last years for fear of being poisoned by the dauphin Louis. See Fresne de Beaucourt, *Histoire de Charles VII*, 6:241–42. See also Commynes, *Mémoires*, 2:42.

43. See Clément, *Jacques Cœur et Charles VII*, 1:85, 133–35. As for Brézé, see Bernus, "Rôle politique de Pierre de Brezé," 303–4.

44. On the Praguerie, see Contamine, *Charles VII*, 251–55; Vale, *Charles VII*, 70–86; Fresne de Beaucourt, *Histoire de Charles VII*, 3:116–64.

45. For a discussion of the documents, see Fresne de Beaucourt, "Caractère de Charles VII," 92–103; for a summary, see Contamine, *Charles VII*, 284–85. The entire

deposition is edited in the pièces justificatives of Bueil, *Jouvencel*, 2:335–47.

46. See Bueil, *Jouvencel*, 2:342.

47. Escouchy, *Chronique de Mathieu
d'Escouchy*, 3:265–341. Guillaume confesses
to having actually enacted the script before
the Duke of Burgundy (3:306).

48. Chastellain, *Œuvres*, 3:347.

49. Escouchy, *Chronique de Mathieu
d'Escouchy*, 1:137. Subsequent references to
this work will be given parenthetically
within the text.

50. Guillaume explains this in ibid.,
3:307, referring back to items XLVIII and
XLXIX on 3:282.

51. Guillaume explains this in ibid.,
3:308, referring back to item LXXVIII on
3:288.

52. See Duclos, *Histoire de Louis XI*, 3,
preuves: 78.

53. For a discussion of the accusations
and Pierre de Brézé's defense of himself, see
Escouchy, *Chronique de Mathieu d'Escouchy*,
1:135–37.

54. *Journal d'un bourgeois de Paris
(1405–1449)*, 387–88.

55. For the letter exonerating Brézé, see
Duclos, *Histoire de Louis XI*, 3, preuves:
74–82.

56. Bernus, "Rôle politique de Pierre de
Brézé," 319.

57. See Chastellain's lament for the
imprisoned Pierre in *Œuvres*, 7:37–65. As
much as Chastellain may have disapproved of
Agnès, he has nothing but praise for Pierre.

58. Among the many examples one
could cite, the marriage between fourth
cousins Eleanor of Aquitaine and Louis VII
of France was annulled in 1152 after fifteen
years of marriage and two children. Both
then married spouses who were more
closely related.

59. See Fresne de Beaucourt, *Histoire de
Charles VII*, 4:102–4; Vale, *Charles VII*, 97–98.

60. Vallet de Viriville, "Recherches
historiques sur Agnès Sorel," 308.

61. For chasing a young woman with a
sword, see Piccolomini, *Pii secundi
pontificis maximi commentarii*, 160. On 163
the young woman is revealed to be Agnès.

62. Aliénor de Poitiers, *Honneurs de la
cour*, 2:165.

63. Le Clerc, *Cronique Martiniane*, 97.

64. Ibid., xviii–xix.

65. Du Clercq, *Mémoires*, 91, 95.

66. On Antoine de Chabannes, see Vale,
Charles VII, 100–102, 167–73; Fresne de
Beaucourt, *Histoire de Charles VII*, 4:189–93.

67. Clément, *Jacques Cœur et Charles VII*,
2:334–35.

68. See Vallet de Viriville, "Notes
biographiques sur Robert Poitevin," 496.

69. It is important to note that no
contemporary document states unequivo-
cally that Poitevin was present at Agnès's
death. The assumption that he was there is
based on the fact that she named him one
of the executors of her will and that the
Coeur children would not have called on
him as witness to the live birth of Agnès's
fourth baby had he not been present.

70. See Jean Chartier, *Chronique de
Charles VII*, 2:185, for those who were
present at her death.

71. On the development of Agnès's
legend, see Champion, *Dame de beauté*,
114–18. Also very useful is Philippe, *Agnès
Sorel*, 199–229.

72. On why the Virgin's features are
believed to reflect Agnès's, see Lombardi,
Jean Fouquet, 129–30, who suggests that the
Virgin's strikingly white skin symbolizes her
recent death, and Champion, *Dame de
beauté*, 138–48.

73. For these details, see Avril, *Jean
Fouquet*, 121, and Schneider, *Portrait*, 42.

74. On the fate of the diptych, see Avril,
Jean Fouquet, 125, and Champion, *Dame de
beauté*, 140–42.

75. Cavailler, "Compte des exécuteurs
testamentaires," 109. Two large ermines for
borders for capes and sleeves of dresses were
valued at thirteen livres and fifteen sous.

76. Christine de Pizan, *Trois vertus*,
175–76.

77. Holmes, "Disrobing the Virgin," 179.

78. Inglis, *Jean Fouquet*, 159.

79. Rubin, *Mother of God*, 310; Miles,
Complex Delight, 47.

80. Avril, *Jean Fouquet*, 129–30, 382–85.

81. Hérold, "Aux sources de l' 'invention,'" 51.

82. See, for example, Syson, "Belle," 246–48.

83. *Journal d'un bourgeois de Paris (1405–1449)*, 388.

84. Chavarnay, *Archives des missions scientifiques et littéraires*, 467–68.

85. See Champion, *Dame de beauté*, 64.

86. Vallet de Viriville, "Recherches historiques," 318. For more detail, see the published fragments of Agnès's will in Cavailler, "Compte des exécuteurs testamentaires," 101–4. On the request to move her tomb, see Champion, *Dame de beauté*, 91–94; see also Moréri, *Grand dictionnaire historique*, 9:502, which was first published in 1674.

87. Vallet de Viriville, "Recherches historiques," 477–88, and Durrieu, "Les filles d'Agnès Sorel."

88. Doüet d'Arcq, "Procès criminel," 211–39.

89. See Kren, "Bathsheba in French Books of Hours," 169–82, quotation on 178. We thank Cynthia Brown for pointing us to this reference.

90. For the date of composition, see Bueil, *Jouvencel*, 1:cccix.

91. Ibid., 136–37.

92. For the article, see "Histoire d'Agnès Sorel," 115–206. The author is not named. The periodical ran from 1775 to 1789. For more information, see Poirier, *Bibliothèque universelle des romans*.

93. The Château de la Guerche was owned by Antoinette's married family, the Villequiers. For more information, see Roy, *La vie et les œuvres de Charles Sorel*, 424–29.

94. "Histoire d'Agnès Sorel," 129–30.

95. Chastellain, *Œuvres*, 4:365.

96. Collard, "Excès débilitants, passions énergisantes," 408.

97. Dispatch of Prospero da Camogli to the Duke of Milan in Kendall and Ilardi, *Dispatches*, 2:345.

98. See Vallet de Viriville, "Recherches historiques," 319.

99. Jean Chartier, *Chronique de Charles VII*, 2:184.

100. See Miles, *Complex Delight*, referring to a sixteenth-century version of the Melun Virgin: "The child is absent, and Sorel holds a book in which she marks her place with a finger. Perhaps the artist sought to show that despite her physical beauty, Sorel was to be esteemed for her intelligence" (83).

101. Liepe, "On the Epistemology of Images," 424–25.

CHAPTER 2

1. "Uniform and homogeneous work by a single artist of mediocre talent, with the names of the models and their devices written by a single hand, the *Recueil d'Aix* . . . can be dated exactly to 1525–26, that is, between the Battle of Pavia, which forced Marguerite d'Angoulême . . . to don widow's weeds, indeed, the return of the king in March 1526 (if he was the author of the original annotations) and January 1527, date of the disgrace of Guillaume de Beaune Semblançay" (Zvereva, *Portraits dessinés*, 63). Agnès's portrait is based on an original by Fouquet. See also Zvereva, "Louise de Savoie," 203–4nn42–50.

2. "Executed during the terrible period of the king's captivity, [the album] is like a miniature of the court of François I as it was during the happy and almost carefree time before the dreadful defeat: the king himself is followed first by his family, then by the gentlemen and ladies of his immediate entourage from the captains of Marignan to the ladies-in-waiting of Louise de Savoy, by the connétable of Bourbon and three famous ladies of past courts, Agnès Sorel, Anne de France, dame de Beaujeu, and Mary Tudor" (Zvereva, *Portraits dessinés*, 64).

3. Zvereva, "Louise de Savoie," 190.

4. Sources of information about Françoise are few. Her liaison with the king took place during the lifetime of Louise, from roughly 1516 to the time of his captivity, and her power therefore was never in any way comparable to Anne's or Diane's: she is never mentioned as a political player

by foreign diplomats. The only in-depth study about Françoise was written in 1948 by novelist and popular historian Georges Toudouze, but the history it recounts is virtually unfootnoted. On her brothers, see Brousillon, *Maison de Laval*, 4:106–7. This cartulary gives a brief description of each of the charters that it records.

5. Anne's portrait did not figure in any of the three earliest collections, including Louise's, created 1525–30. See Zvereva, *Portraits dessinés*, 420. However, it seems that when the king returned he had a hand in choosing the portraits, Zvereva writes, keeping only about thirty of the old ones and adding new ones, including the new queen Eleonore, the king of Navarre, and the Duchess of Étampes. The new albums, created between 1535 and 1540, had a wider diffusion than the first (ibid., 68–69).

6. Zvereva explains that five portraits, including Louise's, have been lost from the Aix collection (ibid., 63).

7. This is the name she gives her son in her journal. See, for example, Louise de Savoie, *Journal*, 12.

8. Beatis, *Voyage*, 137.

9. *Letters and Papers*, 3:566–67, doc. no. 1404.

10. Ibid., 3:688–89, doc. no. 1651.

11. Ibid., 3:1068–69, doc. no. 2522.

12. On the challenge, see the Registers of the Parlement of Paris, printed in Champollion-Figeac, *Captivité*, 393–402.

13. Ibid., 396–97.

14. Brantôme, *Œuvres complètes*, 9:512.

15. *State Papers*, 6:599. In this passage, Brown describes Anne as being part of the household of Marie of Luxembourg, Countess of Vendôme, although other sources put her in the household of Louise of Savoy.

16. The standard biography in English of François I is Knecht, *Renaissance Warrior and Patron*. On François I's interest in Milan, see 62–68. We cite this work for what follows, but the same information is available in any of the major biographies of the king by, for example, Jacquart or, most recently, Michon.

17. Knecht, *Renaissance Warrior and Patron*, 67–83, 218–36, 243–48.

18. Sainte-Marthe and Sainte-Marthe, *Histoire généalogique*, 1:751.

19. See Potter, "Anne de Pisseleu," 537–38.

20. Potter, *War and Government in the French Provinces*, 135.

21. Knecht, *Renaissance Warrior and Patron*, 272–86. For Anne's presence, see Potter, "Anne de Pisseleu," 538, citing Paris, *Étude sur François premier*, 2:240, who cites a report on the festivities after the treaty's signing, but without bibliographical information.

22. For her position, see Paris, *Étude sur François premier*, 2:244, 251, citing the letter patent awarding the County of Étampes to Anne and her husband. The letter is printed in Fleureau, *Antiquités de la ville*, 224–26. However, to be precise, the letter does not actually state, as Paris claims it does, that Anne is the girls' governess, just that she is in their entourage ("à l'entour des personnes").

23. *State Papers*, 7:291.

24. See Robert, *Cabinet historique*, 12.2:96n10430.

25. Rentet, "Anne de Montmorency," 282, 304.

26. Knecht, *Renaissance Warrior and Patron*, 331, 329–30.

27. The rivalry is attested by such writings as Jean Du Bellay's warning to Montmorency's secretary in March 1530 that Brion was doing everything possible to discredit Montmorency. Letter cited in Knecht, "Philippe Chabot de Brion," 469. For the details of Montmorency's temporary loss of favor to Brion, see Decrue de Stoutz, *Anne de Montmorency*, 244–52.

28. Decrue de Stoutz, *Anne de Montmorency*, 260.

29. For detail on the military campaigns, see ibid., 254–338.

30. On the king's negative attitude toward the dauphin, see Lorenzo Contarini's 1551 report of what he had heard about the situation in Albéri, *Relazioni*, 4:64. Bernardo Navager reports to the doge of Venice that he had been told by a reliable source that the king had said to Charles on

the occasion of the Treaty of Crépy, "the wars that I have fought and the dangers that I have put myself in were for you and for the love that I have for you." Rozet and Lembey, *Invasion de la France*, 723.

31. Knecht, *Renaissance Warrior and Patron*, 386–89.

32. Ibid., 395–97.

33. On the development of the resident ambassador, see Mattingly, *Renaissance Diplomacy*, 132–39.

34. Bély, *Art de la paix*, 62–63.

35. Welch, *Theater of Diplomacy*, 2. See also Hampton, *Fictions of Embassy*, 14–44.

36. Lundell, "Renaissance Diplomacy," 208–9.

37. Mattingly, *Renaissance Diplomacy*, 97.

38. Snyder, *Dissimulation*, 6, 7.

39. Feminist scholarship on early modern women suggests that women with access to the king and his intimates along with intelligence and a knack for drama and dissimulation could participate in this type of politics as effectively as men. See, for example, Barbara Harris, "Women and Politics in Early Tudor England." Although the piece deals with the Tudor court, the mechanisms it describes are equally applicable to the French royal court.

40. Van Krieken, *Norbert Elias*, 54.

41. Cox-Rearick, *Collection of Francis I*, 32.

42. Wilson-Chevalier, "Women on Top at Fontainebleau," 34.

43. Still, a "project to construct an image of Louis XII as a new Caesar, restorer of Roman grandeur," did not bear significant results. See Hochner, *Louis XII*, 98, 101.

44. Cholcman, *Art on Paper*, 21.

45. Lecoq describes a spectacle in Rouen in 1517 in *François Ier imaginaire*, 269.

46. Ibid., 35–52.

47. Bibliothèque nationale de France (hereafter BnF) fr 2082, fol. 4.

48. Österreichische Nationalbibliothek 2645. See also Lecoq, *François Ier imaginaire*, 404–5. Lecoq notes that the attribution to a single person of the shared capacities of the Olympian gods became a Renaissance topos.

49. Although François I instigated renovations in other palaces, he preferred Fontainebleau above all others, spending there about half of the total time that he resided in palaces from 1527 to 1546, and it is here that his program is most clearly visible. Cox-Rearick, *Collection of Francis I*, 36.

50. Ibid., 47.

51. Lagerlöf, *Fate, Glory, and Love*, 21.

52. See Marguerite's letter to the king in Marguerite de Navarre, *Lettres*, 382.

53. See Zerner, *Renaissance Art in France*, 78–89.

54. Wilson-Chevalier, "Femmes, cour, pouvoir," 207. Wilson-Chevalier makes the point that the paintings suggest the king's sovereignty still more strongly in "Déboires," 412–13.

55. Wilson-Chevalier, "Femmes, cour, pouvoir," 207–8.

56. Wilson-Chevalier, "Women on Top at Fontainebleau," 36–37.

57. Cox-Rearick, *Collection of Francis I*, 264. After the mid-seventeenth century, much of the erotically themed work was sold or neglected.

58. Ibid., 272, 263.

59. Zerner, *Renaissance Art in France*, 92.

60. For detail, see Cox-Rearick, *Collection of Francis I*, 292–93; Marsengill, "Identity Politics."

61. Wilson-Chevalier, "Feminising the Warrior," 26.

62. Lagerlöf, *Fate, Glory, and Love*, 79.

63. Cited in Cox-Rearick, *Collection of Francis I*, 326. The original has been edited by Venturi, "Nuovi documenti," 377–78.

64. See Wilson-Chevalier, "Déboires," 420–21.

65. Marsengill, "Identity Politics," 39.

66. See Cellini, *Autobiography*, esp. 284–85.

67. With François I's death and Henri II's succession, Montmorency returned to the apartments. See Hamilton, "Première description de Fontainebleau," 46.

68. Wilson-Chevalier, "Femmes, cour, pouvoir," 208, quoting Claude Chappuys.

69. Tracing the origins of the concept of "favor," Nicolas Le Roux dates the notion of

178

178

sovereign authority crystallized in the figure of the royal favorite to around the mid-sixteenth century (*Faveur du roi*, 23). Although Le Roux refers primarily to male favorites, the concept is the same.

70. See, for example, Carlo Sacrati to the Duke of Ferrara, 7 June 1540, Modena Archivio di Stato (hereafter MoAS), Cancellaria, Sezzione Estero Carteggio di Ambasciatori, Francia 16.

71. See, for example, Marnol to Charles V, 22 October 1541, Österreichisches Staatsarchiv, Haus-, Hof- und Staatsarchiv (hereafter ÖStHHS) Fr B and W 9, 35v.

72. *Letters and Papers*, 6: June 1533, 306–13, no. 692.

73. See *Acta Nuntiaturae Gallicae* (hereafter *ANG*), 3:13.

74. Although discussing the court of Louis XIV, Le Roy Ladurie's discussion of court factions is instructive (*Saint-Simon ou le système de la Cour*, 181–235). Also very useful for understanding factionalism more generally is Pollack-Laguschenko, "Armagnac Faction," 1–94.

75. See Knecht, "Philippe Chabot de Brion," 476–77.

76. *Letters and Papers*, 15:70–82, doc. no. 223. On her legendary wiliness, see Brantôme, *Œuvres complètes*, 8:117.

77. *Letters and Papers*, 15:70–82, doc. no. 223.

78. Ibid., 15:82–118, doc. no. 253.

79. Ibid., 15:181–209, doc. no. 459.

80. Ibid., 15:82–118, doc. no. 480.

81. Ibid., 15:209–51, doc. no. 543.

82. *Calendar of State Papers, Spain*, 6.1:244–59, doc. no. 117.

83. Ibid. *Calendar of State Papers, Spain* gives Jean de St. Mauris as the author, but Potter, "Politics and Faction," 131n18, corrects this.

84. Decrue de Stoutz, *Anne de Montmorency*, 400.

85. Potter, "Politics and Faction," 132, citing *State Papers*, 8:461. See also Knecht, "Philippe Chabot de Brion," 476.

86. *State Papers*, 8:501.

87. *ANG*, 3:11.

88. Knecht, "Philippe Chabot de Brion," 478, citing Nawrocki, *Amiral Claude d'Annebault*, 1:202, citing a letter from Carlo Sacrati to the Duke of Ferrara.

89. Knecht, "Philippe Chabot de Brion," 478. Through the favor of Anne, "l'amie du Roy," Annebault had become a lieutenant general in 1536, writes Saulx-Tavannes, "Mémoires," 82.

90. Ultimately he was forced to work for the Cleves marriage.

91. See Decrue de Stoutz, *Anne de Montmorency*, 1:401. For Decrue, Montmorency begins to support the king's plans for Jeanne, knowing that he was drastically losing credit.

92. *ANG*, 3:13.

93. Rentet, "Anne de Montmorency," 296.

94. Potter, *Henry VIII and Francis I*, 52. See Reid, *King's Sister*, 2:502ff. for details. More generally, see Reid, "Imagination and Influence."

95. Jourda, *Marguerite d'Angoulême*, 1:252. See also Stephenson, *Power and Patronage*, 130–31.

96. Ruble, *Mariage de Jeanne d'Albret*, 70.

97. *State Papers*, 8:497ff.

98. Cited in Ruble, *Mariage de Jeanne d'Albret*, 107.

99. Cited by Potter, *Henry VIII and Francis I*, 51, citing an "advis" from Frotté of October 1540.

100. Ruble, *Mariage de Jeanne d'Albret*, 117–18, whose narration is based on that of Juan Martinez Descurra, an agent of the emperor.

101. Brantôme, *Œuvres complètes*, 8:117.

102. Ibid., 8:118; Decrue de Stoutz, *Anne de Montmorency*, 403.

103. *Letters and Papers*, 14.2:122–28n353.

104. Ibid., 14.2:170–76n492.

105. *Calendar of State Papers, Spain*, 8:217–30, doc. no. 115.

106. *ANG*, 3:220.

107. Ibid., 3:13.

108. This often-cited anecdote can be traced through Varillas, *Histoire de François Ier*, 2:277–82, back to Haillan, *Histoire générale*, 2:406–7. However, Haillan's own

work stops at the end of the reign of Charles VII. After the historian's death, his history was continued by booksellers, who drew on, among other texts, Arnoul le Ferron's (1515–1563) *De rebus gestis Gallorum*.

109. *Letters and Papers*, 17:46–62, doc. no. 128.

110. For the most recent discussion of Anne's life after the king's death, see Potter, "Life and After-Life," 321–31.

111. Potter, "Marriage and Cruelty," 10–11, citing a letter from Anne to the archbishop of Rheims, Amiens, in Potter, *War and Government*, 297.

112. Reid, *King's Sister*, 2:499.

113. Ibid., 2:499n4, citing *Letters and Papers*, 21.2:188–203, doc. no. 406.

114. On the costs of the wars, see Knecht, *Renaissance Warrior and Patron*, 503–4.

115. Potter, "Politics and Faction," 143, although in his more recent articles he has become more sympathetic to her.

116. Marnol to Charles V, 2 May 1542, ÖStHHS Fr B and W 10, 4r.

117. *Calendar of State Papers . . . Venice*, 5:132–33, doc. no. 327.

118. On the tensions, see Nawrocki, *Amiral Claude d'Annebault*.

119. Potter, *Henri VIII and Francis I*, 84, 147.

120. On the decision to continue the fight in Italy, which led to the battle of Ceresole, see the vivid discussion of Nawrocki, *Amiral Claude d'Annebault*, 294–99.

121. Knecht, *Renaissance Warrior and Patron*, 493–94.

122. For the text of the secret appendix, see Hasenclever, "Geheimartikel," 420–22. See also Nawrocki, *Amiral Claude d'Annebault*.

123. A dispatch to Henry VIII on French attitudes toward peace with England following the Treaty of Crépy notes that the "Dolphin desireth ernestly, that this peace may be concluded; for he feareth his brothers advancement." *State Papers*, 10:521–22.

124. For the protestation, see *Recueil des traitez de paix*, 2:449–50.

125. See Paris, *Étude sur François premier*, 2:301–4, who traces the accusation to an addition to Du Bellay by Beaucaire.

126. *Letters and Papers*, 17:46–62, doc. no. 128.

127. See Marguerite de Navarre, *Nouvelles Lettres*, 250–52, 283–85.

128. For Marguerite, see her enthusiastic letter to the king, in ibid., 250–52.

129. Reid, *King's Sister*, 2:499.

130. Ibid., 2:505, citing *Letters and Papers*, 20.1:583–614, doc. no. 1205.

131. Reid, *King's Sister*, 2:509–11.

132. See Le Glay, *Négociations diplomatiques*, 2:676–91.

133. Knecht, *Renaissance Warrior and Patron*, 502–3. For the treaty, see *Letters and Papers*, 21.1:505–18n1014.

134. Reid, *King's Sister*, 2:510, citing *Letters and Papers*, 21.2:108–21, doc. no. 248.

135. See Cloulas, *Diane de Poitiers*, 107–9; Decrue de Stoutz, *Anne, duc de Montmorency*, 3–4; Diane de Poitiers, *Lettres*, liv–lix. For a description of the women's rivalry and hatred, see Baumgartner, *Henry II*, 35, while Wellman, *Queens and Mistresses*, sees the factions as growing out of the mistresses' rivalry: "Their supporters polarized the court" (201).

136. Mézeray, *Histoire de France*, 3:1300; Potter, "Politics and Factions," 130 (Potter has become significantly more sympathetic to Anne in his more recent articles); Pollitzer, *Règne des favorites*, 24.

137. Desgardins, "Rivalité," 106, and *Anne de Pisseleu*, 56–57.

138. Decrue de Stoutz, *Anne, duc de Montmorency*, 3. See also Le Roux's analysis of the court factionalism (*Faveur du roi*, 34–36). Le Roux too sees a generational conflict, but in the opposite direction, with Henri's followers representing the new court with its economy of favor. Needless to say, he does not attribute the conflict to a rivalry between Anne and Diane.

139. Decrue de Stoutz, *Anne, duc de Montmorency*, 3–4.

140. Paris traces it to Varillas, *Histoire de François Ier*, 291n4. Wellman (*Queens and Mistresses*, 201) cites Paillard, "Mort de

François I," 89, but Paillard gives no footnote for the claim.

141. On the growing dislike, see Nawrocki, *Amiral Claude d'Annebault*, 199–202.

142. *Letters and Papers*, 16:553–60, doc. no. 1199.

143. *ANG*, 3:13, 25–26.

144. See Nawrocki, "Dauphin Henri," 591n3. Archives générales de Belgique, Papiers d'État et d'Audience, 1610, fols. 14–15.

145. Marnol to Charles V, 3 March 1542, ÖStHHS Fr B and W 10, 46v.

146. For the anecdote, see Thierry, *Diane de Poitiers*, 60. Thierry cites a dispatch of Alvarotti in the State Archives of Modena, giving the source as "Dispacci dalla Francia, Busta 24," by which he must mean MoAS, Cancellaria, Sezzione Estero Carteggio di Ambasciatori, Francia, 24. However, we have thus far been unable to locate the dispatch in this source. Still, the document that Thierry cites surely exists somewhere. We have located two documents that support the dates he gives. A letter from Alvarotti to the Duke of Ferrara of 7 November 1544 in MoAS, Cancellaria, Sezzione Estero Carteggio di Ambasciatori, Francia 20 reports in cipher that the dauphin had gone to visit Diane in secret (*con questa coperta*) because she was gone from court at one of her own residences; a letter of 19 December, also from Alvarotti, reports that Diane was back at court, seated across the table from Anne. Thanks to the staff of the State Archives of Modena for helping us try to locate Thierry's source.

147. The letter from Henri II to Diane, which points out that he no longer fears losing the good grace of his father (who has recently died) on Diane's behalf, is printed in Diane de Poitiers, *Lettres*, 219–20.

148. Marot, *Œuvres poétiques*, 2:371, 372.

149. Diane was of course the inspiration for much laudatory poetry as well, as was her chateau. See Gorris Camos, "Diane de Guindaye," and Balsamo, "Poètes d'Anet."

150. Desgardins, *Anne de Pisseleu*, 50.

151. Thierry, *Diane de Poitiers*, 130. Thierry offers no source.

152. Diane de Poitiers, *Lettres*, lv.

153. Reid notes that Visagier wrote to Jean Du Bellay, asking him to work for Marot's return from exile, in *King's Sister*, 2:460n11; see also 2:458n8 and 2:477n48 for Visagier's savaging of Béda. For Visagier more generally, see the introduction to Arlier, *Correspondance*, and Arlier's three letters to him (128, 169), and Visagier's poems to Arlier (230). Guiffrey, "Correspondant provençal," 178–81, discusses him as well.

154. For the story of Sainte-Marthe's strategic decision to dedicate his work to Anne and his informing Marot that he had done so, see Ruutz-Rees, *Charles de Sainte-Marthe*, 117–26.

155. Cottret, "Reines étrangères," 107.

156. Almost immediately after the marriage, her kinsman, Pope Clement VII, died. The whole point of the union had been to ally the French king with the pope against the emperor, and with the pontiff's death many concluded that the marriage had been a *mésalliance*. For perceptions of the young woman as a foreigner, see Dodu, "Drame conjugal," especially 122–24.

157. See Cloulas, *Catherine de Médicis*, 110.

158. *Calendar of State Papers, Spain*, 5.2:479–95, doc. no. 206.

159. Anne does not figure among the list of the ladies in the hotel of the queen at any time during her reign. The list is found in BnF NA 9175, fols. 372r–373. We have seen that she was in the household of the king's daughters: Madeleine, who died in 1537, and Marguerite, who remained in France until her marriage in 1559 to the Duke of Savoy. But Anne is often mentioned in the queen's company.

160. *Calendar of State Papers, Spain*, 8:427–46, doc. no. 293.

CHAPTER 3

1. On the details of the king's death, see Paillard, "Mort de François I."

2. On the changes in administration, see Nawrocki, *Amiral Claude d'Annebault*, 609–14.

3. Potter's transcription of Jean de St. Mauris's report is available at https://courdefrance.fr/article2750.html.

4. Reporting to Cosimo I of Florence in February 1548, Ricasoli claims to have heard that Anne was being held in prison in Brittany by her husband (Canestrini and Desjardins, *Négociations diplomatiques*, 3:224). See also Potter's transcription of Jean de St. Mauris's report.

5. Canestrini and Desjardins, *Négociations diplomatiques*, 3:189–90. See also Albéri, *Relazioni*, 4:65.

6. Alvarotti to the Duke of Ferrara, 8 July 1547, MoAS, Cancellaria, Sezzione Estero Carteggio di Ambasciatori, Francia 18.

7. Marnol to Charles V, 11 February 1542, ÖStHHS Fr B and W 10, 14–14v.

8. *State Papers*, 8:501.

9. Albéri, *Relazioni*, 4:79.

10. See Carroll, *Martyrs and Murderers*, 50–79, on the Guises' rise under Henri II and their rivalry with the connétable.

11. See *ANG*, 6:35.

12. Paillard, "Mort de François I," 110, citing a dispatch from St. Mauris to Mary of Hungary, 15 April 1547.

13. Ibid., citing a dispatch from St. Mauris, June 1547.

14. Act printed in Baudouin-Matuszek et al., *Catalogue des actes d'Henri II*, 2:396n3755.

15. No document attesting the date of her birth exists. Le Fur, *Diane de Poitiers*, 54.

16. For what follows on Diane's background, see any of the standard biographies, such as Cloulas or Thierry. Guiffrey's introduction to her collected letters is also useful and better footnoted than either Cloulas or Thierry. Also useful are Thompson's two articles, "De nouveaux aperçus" and "Diane de Poitiers." I have not been able to verify Diane's presence with Anne of France, but biographers routinely make the claim. See Le Fur, *Diane de Poitiers*, 16–17, who puts the claim into his chapter on the mythology surrounding

Diane titled "Il était une fois" (Once upon a time).

17. *Journal d'un bourgeois de Paris sous le règne*, 9–10, and note 4 on the same pages.

18. Le Franc and Boulenger, *Comptes de Louise de Savoie*, 8, 12.

19. Charles would die in 1527, helping sack Rome along with the emperor's troops.

20. Cloulas, *Diane de Poitiers*, 52. Cloulas cites from the records of the trial held today in the BnF as Dupuy 484 and français 5109. See his 377n1.

21. See the detailed defense in Guiffrey's introduction to Diane de Poitiers, *Lettres inédites*, ix–xxxii.

22. *Journal d'un bourgeois de Paris (1405–1449)*, 192.

23. Albéri, *Relazioni*, 4:77.

24. Brantôme, *Œuvres complètes*, 9:104.

25. See Godefroy, *Cérémonial françois*, 1:501, 773–74.

26. Le Laboureur, *Mémoires*, 1:270.

27. Baschet, *Diplomatie vénitienne*, 431.

28. Frieda, *Catherine de Medici*, 30–31.

29. Jean II d'Auvergne, maternal grandfather of Catherine, was the brother of Diane's paternal grandmother, Jeanne de La Tour d'Auvergne.

30. Albéri, *Relazioni*, 4:78.

31. Broomhall, "'King and I,'" 339.

32. Saulx-Tavannes, "Mémoires," 137.

33. *Calendar of State Papers, Spain*, 9:130–33.

34. See, for example, Dandino, writing on 31 March 1547. *ANG*, 6:176.

35. Saulx-Tavannes, "Mémoires," 137, 138.

36. Carloix, *Memoires de Vieilleville*, 1:200. See also Mézeray, *Histoire de France*, 2:1060–61.

37. Desgardins, *Anne de Pisseleu*, 67–70.

38. De Thou, *Histoire*, 1:260.

39. Baumgartner, *Henry II*, 60–61.

40. De Thou, *Histoire*, 1:260–61.

41. For the connétable's preference for peace, see Romier, *Origines politiques*, 1:37–39; for the Guises, see 1:42–46, 51.

42. See Carroll, *Martyrs and Murderers*, 78–79. On the details of the rivalry, see Decrue de Stoutz, *Anne, duc de Montmorency*, 22–44.

43. For the anecdote and references for the sources, see Romier, *Origines politiques*, 1:44–45.

44. Albéri, *Relazioni*, 4:78–79.

45. Broomhall, "'King and I,'" 343–45.

46. Brantôme, *Œuvres complètes*, 9:356.

47. Henry Samuel, "French King's Mistress Poisoned by Gold Elixir," Telegraph, 22 December 2009, https://www.telegraph.co.uk/news/worldnews/europe/france/6865939/Frenchkingsmistress poisonedbygoldelixir.html.

48. Persels, "Bragueta Humanística," 81–89.

49. Brantôme, *Œuvres complètes*, 9:211–12.

50. Berger, *Absence of Grace*, 87; Chappuys, *Discours de la court*, n.p.

51. So says Gaspare (Castiglione, *Book of the Courtier*, 209).

52. Ibid., 212.

53. See, for example, Mathieu-Castellani, "Figure de Diane."

54. Bardon, *Diane de Poitiers*, 3, 12.

55. A substantial body of research has been devoted to the phenomenon. See, for example, Lawrence Bryant, *The King and the City*; Cooper, "Theme of War"; Cosandey, *Reine de France*, 163–205; Guenée and Lehoux, *Entrées royales françaises*; Jackson, *Vive le roi!*; Jacquiot, "De l'entrée de César à Rome"; Jacquot, "Joyeuse et triomphante entrée"; Kipling, *Enter the King*.

56. Kipling, *Enter the King*, 28.

57. On Scève's description of the entry, see Chang, "Spectacle, Sublimation, and Civic Pride."

58. Scève, *Entry of Henri II*, n.p.

59. Surely Le Fur goes too far in denying that the spectacle was understood as a reference to Diane because Brantôme was the first to make the connection. We would not expect contemporaries to make the connection in writing. See Le Fur, *Diane de Poitiers*, 242.

60. Karagiannis-Mazeaud, "Diane chez les 'Antiquaires,'" 235.

61. Ibid.; Lecoq, *François Ier imaginaire*, 52.

62. Scève, *Entry of Henri II*, 312.

63. Brantôme, *Œuvres complètes*, 9:321.

64. See, in particular, Zalamea, "Subject to Diana," and Bardon, *Diane de Poitiers*.

65. "The emblems of Henri II, spread throughout the monuments and art of his reign, respond to a concept of the monarchy consistent with the mentality of the period: the contradiction is to conclude that the king adopted the emblems of his mistress." Crépin-Leblond, "Sens et contresens," 85. See also Wintroub, *Savage Mirror*, 15, 18–19, 111–12.

66. See Scève's illustrated description of Henri II's entry into Lyon, which notes that the *obelisque* was decorated with Henri II's "cipher" (*chiffre*), a crowned H interlaced with two Ds. Scève, *Entry of Henri II*, n.p. See also Giovanni Capello's description of Henri II's gold crescents embroidered in such a way as to look like an H interwined with two Ds, signifying the double initial of Madame de Valentinois. Baschet, *Diplomatie vénitienne*, 443. Jules de Pétigny makes the case that the emblem initially belonged to the Valois and that the portrait of Catherine de Médicis at Beauregard shows that she too used the moon as an emblem ("Emblèmes monétaires," 83–84).

67. Rothstein, *Reading in the Renaissance*, 29–30, 116.

68. Gorris Camos, "Diane de Guindaye," 295.

69. Balsamo, "'Dire le paradis d'Anet,'" 340, 341.

70. Marsengill, "Identity Politics," 38n22.

71. Zalamea, "Subject to Diana," 9. See Zerner, "Diane de Poitiers," esp. 336–38, and Plogsterth, "Institution of the Royal Mistress," who argues that Diane de Poitiers can be identified with only two of the images commonly associated with her.

72. *ANG*, 3:viii.

73. Albéri, *Relazioni*, 4:78.

74. Baumgartner, *Henry II*, 146–59; Cloulas, *Henri II*, 300–315.

75. Baumgartner, *Henry II*, 160–74; Cloulas, *Henri II*, 387–408.

76. Baumgartner, *Henry II*, 174; Cloulas, *Henri II*, 412.

77. Baumgartner, *Henry II*, 185–96; Cloulas, *Henri II*, 455–66.

78. See Carroll, *Martyrs and Murderers*, 80–99.

79. Baumgartner, *Henry II*, 221–30; Cloulas, *Henri II*, 569–94.

80. Broomhall, "'King and I,'" 347, citing BnF fr 3139, fol. 26v. Guiffrey prints the letter in Diane de Poitiers, *Lettres inédites*, 161–62, 162n1.

81. Broomhall, "'King and I,'" 348.

82. *Calendar of State Papers . . . Venice*, 6:1540–46, doc. no. 1281.

83. *ANG* 14:155–56.

84. In addition to the primary sources cited, see Baumgartner, *Henry II*, 218–30, for more context, and Romier, *Origines politiques*, 2:312–15.

85. Cited in Romier, *Origines politiques*, 2:314.

86. Baumgartner, *Henry II*, 250–54, citing *ANG* 14:212–18; Romier, "Mort de Henri II"; Romier, *Origines politiques*, 2:284–90.

87. Machiavelli, *Prince*, chap. 18, 61.

CHAPTER 4

1. *Calendar of State Papers . . . Venice*, 7:107, doc. no. 85.

2. For the contest for control between the Guises and the queen mother, see Crawford, *Perilous Performances*, 24–31.

3. Carroll, *Martyrs and Murderers*, 101.

4. On Marie Touchet and for a summary of chronicle accounts of Charles IX's love life, see Bayle, *Dictionnaire historique et critique*, 4:389–91.

5. Sully relates the story in *Mémoire des sages et royales oeconomies d'estat*, 1:319–20; the king's letter is printed in Henri IV, *Lettres d'amour*, 94.

6. Sully, *Mémoire des sages et royales oeconomies d'estat*, 1:319–20. Henriette's intermittent affair with the king was filled with action and danger. See especially De Thou, *Histoire universelle*, 14:427–29, on her narrow escape with her life after taking part in a plot to supplant the little dauphin

Louis, later Louis XIII, with her own son by the king.

7. Brantôme, *Œuvres complètes*, 9:449.

8. Henri IV's claim derived from Louis IX's sixth son, Robert, heir through marriage to the duchy of Bourbon.

9. For a review of the claimants, see Pitts, *Henri IV of France*, 157–59.

10. On the assassination attempts, including Chastel's, see ibid., 192.

11. Marguerite de Valois, *Mémoires*, 92–101.

12. Ibid., 129–30 (as an example).

13. Although Viennot calls her a "league member ('Ligueuse')" by accident, not design" (*Marguerite de Valois*, 163).

14. Crawford, "Politics of Promiscuity," 225.

15. Ibid., 230–31.

16. Montaigne, *Essais*, 2:90.

17. See Reid, "Marguerite de Navarre," 41–45.

18. Guiffrey, *Cronique du roy Françoys*, 238.

19. *Discours merveilleux*, 20–21. On this period of negative publicity, see Le Fur, *Diane de Poitiers*, 210–38.

20. Avril, *Jean Fouquet*, 151. The album said to have been Catherine's has since been disassembled. Avril believes that the crayon portraits descend from a Fouquet original sketched during Agnès's lifetime (152). Other have suggested the portrait is based on the Melun Virgin, pointing to an otherwise inexplicable decoration on the headdress, which seems to refer to a similar decoration on the Virgin's headdress.

21. Baïf, *Œuvres en rime*, 2:92, 93–94.

22. For Brantôme, see *Œuvres complètes*, 9:393–94. For Brantôme's shorter version of the same story, see 3:242.

23. Haillan, *Histoire générale des roys de France*, 1:1055–56.

24. Avril, *Jean Fouquet*, 151, 130. Avril cites pièce 663v of BnF fr. 8224, which is vol. 9 of *Épitaphes de Paris et ses environs*, collected in 1887. Pièce 663 describes the tomb of Chevalier and his wife. The verso records the presence of the diptych with Chevalier praying on one side and a

portrait of "la Belle Agnès" on the other, over the door of the sacristy, adding that "it is said that Henri IV wanted to give 10,000 livres for it."

25. Héroard, *Journal*, 1:323.

26. Gassot, *Sommaire mémorial*, 232.

27. For details, see Desclozeaux, "Le mariage et le divorce," 54–56.

28. See Anselme de Sainte-Marie, *Histoire généalogique*, 4:598–99.

29. See Ritter, *Charmante Gabrielle*, 56–57.

30. See Gustave Charlier, "Amour de Ronsard."

31. Tallemant des Réaux, *Historiettes*, 1:7–8.

32. For Bellegarde's service to Henri III, see Knecht, *Hero or Tyrant?*, 75–76, 160–61.

33. As for how the princess of Conti came to compose her stories, see DeJean, *Tender Geographies*, 22–23.

34. Louise-Marguerite de Lorraine, *Histoire*, 8–9, 12–13, 27.

35. Unton, *Correspondence*, 106. Sully too notes the king's affection for Gabrielle in 1591 (*Mémoire des sages et royales oeconomies d'estat*, 1:84). Antoine d'Estrées was governor of La Fere, Paris, and Ile de France (Anselme, *Histoire généalogique*, 4:599). See Desclozeaux for what is known about the king and Gabrielle's whereabouts in the first two years after their meeting ("Le mariage et le divorce," 60–62). In the same article, Desclozeaux argues that their intimate relationship began only in 1593, after Gabrielle's marriage to Liancourt (72–75).

36. Aubigné, *Histoire universelle*, 3:368.

37. See Babelon, *Henri IV*, 503–17; Pitts, *Henri IV*, 161.

38. Louise-Marguerite de Lorraine, *Histoire*, 27–28.

39. See, for examples, Henri IV, *Recueil des lettres missives*, 3:722–27, 754–60, 804–5, 808, 811, 818–21; 4:283–84, 289–91, 292, 983, 998–99; or read them collected and edited by Françoise Kermina in Henri IV, *Lettres d'amour*, 66–90.

40. See Desclozeaux, *Gabrielle d'Estrées*, 383–84. Desclozeaux gives his

source as "Unton to the queen, 3 February 1596 [o S] public record office. State Paper France, liasse 120. (Extrait de la mission du sire de Boissise, par M. de Kermaingant.)" Murat cites the same letter at length but gives no source (*Gabrielle d'Estrées*, 210–12). We have been unable to locate the document and cite here from Desclozeaux.

41. Aubigné, *Histoire universelle*, 3:462.

42. Louise-Marguerite de Lorraine, *Histoire*, 55.

43. Sully, *Mémoire des sages et royales oeconomies d'estat*, 1:296–97.

44. Ritter, *Charmante Gabrielle*, 164.

45. Sully, *Mémoire des sages et royales oeconomies d'estat*, 1:297.

46. Desclozeaux, "Gabrielle d'Estrées et Sully," 246, 247–51.

47. On Ravaillac, see Pitts, *Henri IV*, 324–29.

48. See Desclozeaux, *Gabrielle d'Estrées*, 383.

49. Desclozeaux lays out this argument of Jules Berger de Xivrey in "Le mariage et le divorce," 66–68. This is also what Louise-Marguerite de Lorraine suggests (*Histoire*, 10).

50. For the story of the marriage and annulment, see Desclozeaux, "Le mariage et le divorce."

51. Henri IV writes to Gabrielle that he is happy that she is getting along with her father, writing: "You will have no more occasion to reproach me that your father is angry on account of me" (*Recueil des lettres missives*, 3:811, cited by Desclozeaux, "Le mariage et le divorce," 62). For the annulment proceedings, see Desclozeaux, "Le mariage et le divorce," 76.

52. Tallemant des Réaux, *Historiettes*, 1:8–16. For more detail on the religious stakes, see Imberdis, *Histoire des guerres religieuses*, 2:408–13.

53. See Desclozeaux, "Le mariage et le divorce," 104. Gabrielle states that her father forced her to marry Liancourt and that Liancourt was unable to "render the conjugal duty."

54. Babelon, *Henri IV*, 630.

55. Pitts, *Henri IV*, 216.

56. Ritter, *Charmante Gabrielle*, 107–10.

57. Henri IV, *Recueil des lettres missives*, 4:291. The volume's editor, Berger de Xivrey, dates the letter to 1594; Ritter, in *Charmante Gabrielle*, 580n68, 20 July 1593.

58. Henri IV, *Recueil des lettres missives*, 4:867. Berger de Xivrey gives 1597 as the date, but Kermina convincingly argues for 1595 (Henri IV, *Lettres d'amour*, 121).

59. He had originally converted in the wake of the Saint Bartholomew Day's Massacre, shortly after his marriage to Marguerite in 1572, but he abjured in 1576. See Wolfe, *Conversion of Henri IV*, 24–29.

60. Mézeray, *Histoire de France*, 3:1067. Mézeray uses Sully's *Mémoire des sages et royales oeconomies d'estat* as a source. For Sully's version, which includes an attenuated version of Gabrielle's influence (the king was finally convinced by his "confidants and most tender servants, among whom may be counted his mistress"), see 1:117.

61. Aubigné, *Histoire universelle*, 3:409. For a Catholic reaction, see Ritter, *Charmante Gabrielle*, 190–95.

62. Aubigné, *Histoire universelle*, 3:409.

63. Not everyone was pleased about her surveillance. According to L'Estoile, the Protestants watching grew angry, muttering that the "vilaine" wanted to keep the king from singing God's praises (*Mémoires-Journaux*, 7:82–83). On singing the psalms as the very heart of Protestant worship, see Manetsch, *Calvin's Company of Pastors*, 234.

64. The offer is reported in De Thou, *Histoire universelle*, 12:425.

65. On the reconciliation and ceremony at Monceaux, see l'Estoile, *Mémoires-Journaux*, 7:47–9; Ritter, *Charmante Gabrielle*, 287–93; Babelon, *Henri IV*, 615–16.

66. See Rittter, *Charmante Gabrielle*, 383–85. Ritter's erudite study is nonetheless difficult to use because although he lists his sources, he very rarely footnotes and does not specify which editions he used or page numbers. I have been unable to trace his

source for Mercoeur's approaching Gabrielle.

67. See Rittter, *Charmante Gabrielle*, 401–5. Duplessis-Mornay's important letter soliciting Gabrielle's mediation, cited by Ritter on 402, can be found in Mornay, *Mémoires et correspondances*, 7:428.

68. De Thou, *Histoire universelle*, 13:202, 205. The agreement is printed in Goulart, *Mémoires de la Ligue*, 6:578–92.

69. L'Estoile, *Mémoires-Journaux*, 7:158.

70. See the document in Anselme, *Histoire généalogique*, 4:90, 85–87. See also Babelon, *Henri IV*, 643; Ritter, *Charmante Gabrielle*, 370.

71. On her pensions, see Babelon, *Henri IV*, 634, 642. See Fréville, "Notice historique sur l'inventaire," on the amazing wealth of possessions she accumulated during her tenure. On her regency for César, see Ritter, *Charmante Gabrielle*, 393.

72. Cosandey, *Reine de France*, 79–82.

73. Murat, *Gabrielle d'Estrées*, 143.

74. Carmona, *Marie de Médicis*, 12–14.

75. For the letter, see Anselme, *Histoire généalogique*, 4:90.

76. Ibid. Whether Henri IV intends César to inherit the throne is quite ambiguous.

77. Henri IV, *Recueil des lettres missives*, 4:961.

78. Ibid., 4:307.

79. As they would later of Henri IV's own family. For the story of the former queen's trips to visit the brood, see Viennot, *Marguerite de Valois*.

80. According to Chiverny's memoir, Gabrielle's fertility was the principal reason that the king wanted to marry her (*Mémoires*, 78). For Sully, see *Mémoire des sages et royales oeconomies d'estat*, 1:242.

81. See, for example, Sancy, *Discours*, 102. He describes his duty to speak the truth to the king about his proposed marriage. He claims that his only concern was the "good of the state," and that he could not fail in his duty, as an honorable man worried about the "honor of his master and the salvation of his fatherland." He also notes that he was not the only one

who felt this way, although Gabrielle herself saw him as her chief obstacle (116). Sully also lays out the problems in *Mémoires*, although, as we noted above, this work can only be used with caution. Still, the work can be understood to reflect a retrospective view of the situation by highly placed courtiers (*Mémoires*, 2:373–87).

82. Pitts, *Henri IV*, 131. See also Babelon, *Henri IV*, 646–48.

83. See, for example, Pitts, *Henri IV*, 275–79.

84. L'Estoile, *Mémoires-Journaux*, 6:227.

85. Canestrini and Desjardins, *Négociations diplomatiques*, 5:294, 301.

86. See Henri IV, *Recueil des lettres missives*, 4:999–1000. Ritter dates the poem to 21 May 1593 (*Charmante Gabrielle*, 142–44). Henri IV probably did not write the poem himself. See Henri IV, *Recueil des lettres missives*, 4:1000.

87. The painting may be a copy of the original that hung over the chimney in Gabrielle's apartment in the Pavillon de Poêles, just above the king's apartments at Fontainebleau. See the *Revue du Louvre et des musées de France* 51 (2001): 93. On the Diana gallery, see Zalamea, "Subject to Diana," 277–83. Zalamea suggests that in the seventeenth century the goddess came to be associated with France (284).

88. See the first part of Reinach's two-part article, "Diane de Poitiers et Gabrielle d'Estrées."

89. The medal is described at https:// www.britishmuseum.org/research/collec tion_online/collection_object_details.aspx ?objectId=895474&partId=1&subject=147 &page=1.

90. L'Estoile, *Mémoires-Journaux*, 122.

91. Canestrini and Desjardins, *Négociations diplomatiques*, 5:319–21.

92. De Thou, *Histoire universelle*, 13:25.

93. See Ritter, *Charmante Gabrielle*, 349–56, 371–75.

94. L'Estoile, *Mémoires-Journaux*, 7:99, 178.

95. De Thou, *Histoire universelle*, 13:223–24. De Thou gives the date as autumn 1598; other sources give January 1599.

96. L'Estoile, *Mémoires-Journaux*, 7:186–87.

97. Chiverny, *Mémoires*, 80.

98. A number of contemporary accounts of Gabrielle's death exist. See ibid., 79–86; Bassompierre, *Journal de ma vie*, 1:70–72; Sully, *Mémoire des sages et royales oeconomies d'estat*, 1:311–14 (containing the account of La Varenne, 313); Aubigné, *Histoire universelle*, 3:463; and what is often considered the most definitive, unbiased version, that of Jean de Vernhyès, member of the Council of Navarre, close friend of the king and Mornay as well as leader of the Royalist party in Auvergne. See Loiseleur, "Mort de Gabrielle d'Estrées," 199–213.

99. On Zamet and his tastes for the sumptuous, see Grodecki, "Sébastien Zamet."

100. Sully, *Mémoire des sages et royales oeconomies d'estat*, 1:313. La Varenne explains that Gabrielle was so disfigured that he did not want the king to see her.

101. It did receive at least one positive review in *Revue du nord* 37 (April–June 1955): 186–87. The format of Bolle's work is so strange that we wondered at first whether it was work of fiction. Recently historians studying Gabrielle—for example, Murat— have begun paying attention to it.

102. Bolle, *Pourquoi tuer Gabrielle d'Estrees?*, 118–19. Subsequent references to this work will be given parenthetically within the text.

103. On Guicciardini, see Zeller, "Le divorce et le second mariage," 223–24.

104. It is interesting to note that Sully describes the same scene in *Mémoire des sages et royales oeconomies d'estat*, 1:295, then again at 317 with the word *bagasse*, which places the event sometime between September and December 1598. Desclozeaux dismisses Sully's report of the conversation as false because Marguerite was in fact happy with her end of the deal, financially speaking ("Gabrielle d'Estrées et Sully," 260–65).

105. De Thou, *Histoire universelle*, 13:389.

106. Wellman, *Queens and Mistresses*, 356.

107. Sully, *Mémoires*, 2:378.

108. Fleischhauer, *Ligne pourpre*, 422.

CHAPTER 5

1. Sorel, *Solitude*, 325.
2. Michelet, *Histoire de France*, 5:226.
3. According to Margaret McGowan, the authors of memoirs agreed "on the theatrical character of the Court to which festival(s) contributed substantially" ("Fonction des fêtes," 37). As noted earlier, many historians, drawing on Norbert Elias, have written about the elaborate attention to etiquette and codes of honor that crystallized in the seventeenth-century court. Duindam agrees that the nobility increasingly emphasized polite behavior and etiquette in the seventeenth-century French court, although he disagrees with Elias's analysis of the reasons for these changes (*Myths of Power*, 13–19, 159–80). On dissimulation as an element of court life, see ibid., 157–58. On dress and cosmetics, see Martin, *Selling Beauty*, 1; Jennifer M. Jones, *Sexing* La Mode, 18–25; Perrot, *Travail des apparences*, 33–35; Matthews-Grieco, "Body, Appearance, and Sexuality," 3:63; Ribeiro, *Facing Beauty*, chap. 1.
4. Duindam, *Myths of Power*, 133–36.
5. Chaline, "Kingdoms of France and Navarre," 76.
6. Le Roy Ladurie, *Saint-Simon and the Court of Louis XIV*, 121–23, 127.
7. Moine, *Fêtes à la cour*, 143–44; Bertière, *Reines de France*, 2:27–28. Although the two were deeply in love, Wolf writes that "no shred of evidence has appeared that she ever had had the intention of becoming Louis' mistress" (*Louis XIV*, 112).
8. Bertière, *Reines de France*, 2:9.
9. La Fayette, *Secret History of Henrietta*, 8.
10. Bertière, *Reines de France*, 2:91.
11. Sarcus, *Notice historique et descriptive*, 52.
12. Bussy-Rabutin, *Correspondance*, 4:48–49.
13. See Adams, "'Belle comme le jour.'"

14. A morganatic marriage is one between two persons of unequal social rank, usually a high-ranking man with a lower-ranking woman. In this context, neither the spouse of lower social standing nor any children of the marriage have rights to the titles, precedence, or entailed property of the higher-status partner. The marriage, however, is a legitimate one.
15. Louis discusses this in his memoirs, addressed to his son. See Louis XIV, *Mémoires*, 24, 31–32.
16. We see this narrative repeated again and again in later histories of Louis's court. For example, in the early nineteenth century, Craufurd wrote, "Madame de Montespan was a more perfect beauty than madame de la Vallière; but far from having that gentleness, that goodness, that indifference to the splendors of this world, that disinterestedness in all things, that love for Louis alone and not for the brilliance of his throne, virtues that characterized madame de la Vallière, she was haughty, imperious and full of ambition" (*Notices*, 47–48). In her *Mémoires*, Madame Gacon-Dufour takes a similar tone, constrasting the "gentleness" of La Vallière, "who only wanted to continue to please him," with the "fierté" of Montespan, who "took pride in having subjugated the king" (1:18–19). H. Noel Williams writes of La Vallière, "What, however, has rendered her personality so irresistibly attractive is that there never has been the least question as to the disinterestedness of her affection. With her Louis XIV tasted, probably for the first and last time in his life, the happiness so rarely vouchsafed to a monarch of being loved for himself alone" (*Madame de Montespan*, 28). Modern historians repeat the same story: "[Madame de Montespan] differed in all ways from Mlle de la Vallière. She was as gentle and modest, distressed by the illicit love that she did not have the strength to fight, as Montespan was haughty, calculating and imperious" (Chaussinand-Nogaret, *Vie quotidienne*, 144).
17. Wolf also questions this narrative (*Louis XIV*, 291–93).

18. The letter from Mademoiselle Armentières was dated 30 May 1674, while that of Bussy-Rabutin to Madame de Scudéry was written on 14 June 1674. See Bussy-Rabutin, *Correspondance*, 2:353, 361.

19. The painting by Claude Lefebvre, *Louise-Françoise de La Baume Le Blanc, duchesse de la Vallière et de Vaujours* (1644–1710), is at the Musée national du château et des Trianons de Versailles. It is dated 1667, meaning it was painted as La Vallière's star was waning.

20. Goodman, *Portraits of Madame de Pompadour*, 14.

21. Moine, *Fêtes à la cour*, 144.

22. Madame de Motteville (1621–1689), Anne of Austria's friend and private secretary, recounts the story in *Mémoires*, 510–16.

23. Lair, *Louise de La Vallière*, 1–77; Craveri, *Reines et favorites*, 160–66;.Bertière, *Reines de France*, 2:92–93.

24. Newton, *Espace du roi*, 78.

25. La Beaumelle, the Abbé de Berthier (1726–1773), biographer of Madame de Maintenon, suggests that "women, lords, princes, ministers, all conspired against la Vallière" (*Mémoires*, 1:264).

26. Motteville, *Mémoires*, 10:516; Spanheim, *Relation de la cour de France*, 41.

27. Sourches, *Mémoires*, 1:87.

28. See Saint-Maurice, *Lettres*, 2:6.

29. Wolf, *Louis XIV*, 292.

30. Wine, "Honored Guests." See also Solnon, *Cour de France*, 302; Wolf, *Louis XIV*, 278; Moine, *Fêtes à la cour*, 145.

31. Moine, *Fêtes à la cour*, 146.

32. Wolf, *Louis XIV*, 94; Solnon, *Cour de France*, 281.

33. Van Elden, *Esprits fins et esprits géométriques*, 44–72. We thank Orest Ranum for the reference.

34. La Beaumelle, *Mémoires*, 265.

35. The general details of Madame de Montespan's early life are well known. See, for example, Petitfils, *Madame de Montespan*, 7–20.

36. In his work on the French court at Versailles, Newton discusses the importance of these many and varied female officials. See *L'espace du roi*, 43.

37. Lisa Hilton writes that "Athénaïs was conjuring a powerfully symbolic image ideally suited to the classical playfulness of the Parisian salons." She suggests that Montespan's intellectual and social formation among the *précieuses* was key to her education and preparation for life at court. See *Athénaïs*, 27. Madame de Montausier, Montespan's close friend who helped facilitate her relationship with the king, was a *précieuse* and daughter of celebrated *salonnière* Madame de Rambouillet.

38. Bertière, *Reines de France*, 2:195–96.

39. In his memoirs, Bussy-Rabutin noted that the young Françoise/Athénaïs was extremely quick-witted in responding to the Maxims d'Amours, a favorite salon game: "First I read the question, & before giving the answer, Monsieur, & then the Ladies responded according to their sentiments. After that, I read the Maxim. But I noticed that Madame de ***, young as she was, already demonstrated common sense concerning love, & quite rightly, which led her always to decide the question as I had determined, I, who had thought about it for quite a while." *Mémoires*, 235. Craveri indicates in *Art of Conversation* that this young woman was Montespan (120).

40. Bertière, *Reines de France*, 2:196. In February 1664 the Duke of Enghien wrote to the queen of Poland about the competition among the women at court, including Montespan, to be named to the queen's household, noting that "the King will choose six among them, but I believe that the Queen would be glad if there were none among them with whom he could fall in love." Condé and Condé, *Le Grand Condé et le duc d'Enghien*, 2–3.

41. See La Fare, *Mémoires et réflexions*, 264.

42. La Beaumelle, *Mémoires*, 271–72.

43. Visconti, *Mémoires*, 16.

44. Spanheim, *Relation de la cour de France*, 41n.

45. La Fare, *Mémoires et réflexions*, 264–65.

46. Montpensier, *Mémoires*, 4:52.

47. There are numerous embellished accounts of this incident, which come originally from the memoirs of La Grande Mademoiselle. Bertière summarizes it in *Reines de France*, 2:116–18; see also Petitfils, *Madame de Montespan*, 49–51. Montespan famously and hypocritically opined at the time of La Vallière's faux pas: "God forbid that I should be the mistress of the king! But if I were wretched enough to do so, I would never be so shameless as to stand before the queen." Montpensier, *Mémoires*, 4:49.

48. Condé and Condé, *Le Grand Condé et le duc d'Enghien*, 309.

49. Chaussinand-Nogaret, *Vie quotidienne*, 26, 144, 165–66.

50. Saint-Maurice, *Lettres*, 2:534.

51. Visconti writes: "The Marquis de Montespan, aggrieved by the love of the King for his wife, whom he loved very much, went to his properties in Gascony, went into mourning and made their children and all his servants do so [as well]. He had a funeral as if the marquise were dead." *Mémoires*, 16.

52. Saint-Simon, *Mémoires*, 1:374.

53. Madame de Sévigné describes the drama in a letter to her daughter written on 12 February 1671. See Sévigné, *Lettres*, 1:322.

54. In a letter to Madame du Bouchet dated 7 February 1671, Bussy-Rabutin wrote, "It has been more than four months since I predicted the retirement of madame de la Vallière, because I saw her decline; each in her turn." *Correspondance*, 1:371.

55. Ibid., 1:382.

56. From 13 March 1671. Ibid., 1:388.

57. Saint-Maurice, *Lettres*, 2:540.

58. The newspapers described La Vallière's theatrical departure from the court for the Convent of the Carmelites, noting that "all the Ladies of the Court came to bid her adieu & they were all seen with tears in their eyes" (*Gazette d'Amsterdam*, 17 April 1674; see also 27 April 1674). In a comment on a letter from the duc de Saint-Aignan (dated 19 April 1674),

Bussy-Rabutin suggested that Montespan was less than thrilled by the extended goodbye: "All these adieux, however, fatigued madame de Montespan greatly, whether she feared that pity in the king's heart would awaken love, [or] whether for some other reason; it appears that she was extremely impatient for the duchess to be in a convent." *Correspondance*, 2:344.

59. See Solnon, *Cour de France*, 305.

60. Saint-Simon, *Mémoires*, 2:87.

61. Visconti, *Mémoires*, 16.

62. Solnon, *Cour de France*, 302.

63. Moine, *Fêtes à la cour*, 146.

64. Du Crest, *Fêtes à Versailles*, 38–39.

65. Wolf, *Louis XIV*, 304–5; Clément, *Madame de Montespan et Louis XIV*, 1; 24.

66. Madame de Sévigné wrote of her stunning appearance in a dress of gold, "the most divine fabric that could ever have been imagined." Sévigné, *Lettres*, 6 November 1676, 5:197. Yarwood notes that "the court of Versailles was the arbiter of the European fashionable world" and that "the undisputed leader of feminine fashion was the current mistress of the king and every nuance of her toilette was carefully studied and copied." See *Fashion in the Western World*, 50–51. Jennifer M. Jones concurs that the "official mistress of the king became unofficial mistress of *la mode* as well" (*Sexing* La Mode, 11).

67. DeJean, *Age of Comfort*, 188–90; DeJean, *Essence of Style*, 44; Jennifer M. Jones, *Sexing* La Mode, 50, 55. It was the Duchess of Orléans, Louis XIV's sister-in-law, better known as Liselotte, who wrote that Montespan invented the *robes battantes* to hide her pregnancies. Élisabeth-Charlotte, *Mémoires*, 60.

68. DeJean, *Essence of Style*, 29; Challamel, *History of Fashion in France*, 133.

69. DeJean, *Age of Comfort*, 23.

70. Van Elden, *Esprits fins et esprits géometriques*, 45–49.

71. Ranum, *Artisans of Glory*, 294.

72. See Chaussinand-Nogaret, *Vie quotidienne*, 17–18.

73. Sevigné, *Lettres*, 29 July 1676, 5:45.

74. Wolf specifies some of the requests La Vallière made: "And this nearly worthless brother, who stupidly offended the king by trying to act like a brother-in-law, was high on the list of those who benefited by her station. There was a host of people who asked her to intercede for them, often enough for petty affairs, and she did not know how to say no. She asked for the property of a deceased bastard, the right to salt fish, the right to control commerce in this or that port, the right to inspect merchandise, for little pensions and gratuities." Wolf, *Louis XIV*, 293.

75. Le Roy Ladurie, *Saint-Simon and the Court of Louis XIV*, chap. 4.

76. Kettering's work is the authoritative study of patrons, clients, and brokers and their networks. See *Patrons, Brokers, and Clients*, 3–4. Mallick also discusses the role of women in patron/clientage relationships in "Clients and Friends." See also Le Roy Ladurie, *Saint-Simon and the Court of Louis XIV*, 154–55.

77. For more on this, see Adams, "'Belle comme le jour,'" 171–72.

78. As Hufton notes, "The mistress is often the creation of a domestic faction and her support network expects rewards as well as the rewards she gains herself" ("Reflections on the Role of Women," 6).

79. Bussy-Rabutin, *Correspondance*, 1:343.

80. Sourches, *Mémoires*, 88.

81. Visconti, *Mémoires*, 152.

82. O'Malley, "Medical History of Louis XIV," 147–48.

83. Saint-Maurice, *Lettres*, 2:182. When Madame de Montausier died ten days later, Saint-Maurice reported that "as soon as the King was at Versailles, he appointed madame la duchesse de Richelieu to be lady-in-waiting to the queen. There is no doubt that madame de Montespan procured these positions for her; but her merit certainly had a lot to do with it." Ibid., 2:185–86.

84. Bussy-Rabutin, *Correspondance*, 4:55. See also the letter from Le P. Rapin to Bussy, 4:52.

85. Petitfils, *Madame de Montespan*, 50–51, 72–73.

86. Sévigné, *Lettres*, 10 November 1673, 3:216; Bertière, *Reines de France*, 2:209.

87. Wellman, *Queens and Mistresses*, 100–101, 249; McIlvenna, "'Stable of Whores,'" 197–98; Kleinman, *Anne of Austria*, 14, 19–20, 266–69, 278–79. Duindam notes that "marriages were a major factor in the power balances among families at court as well as in the country at large": see *Vienna and Versailles*, 286. Le Roy Ladurie also accords weight to the importance of marriages in solidifying political cabals: see *Saint-Simon and the Court of Louis XIV*, chap. 4, passim.

88. Sévigné, *Lettres*, 10 December 1670, 1:280–81.

89. *Gazette d'Amsterdam*, 4 February 1677.

90. Dessert, *Royaume de Monsieur Colbert*, 194. Colbert's family constituted the core of one of the most important political cabals during the reign of Louis XIV. Le Roy Ladurie, *Saint-Simon and the Court of Louix XIV*, 144–47, 157–58.

91. Montpensier, *Mémoires*, 4:52.

92. Gerber, *Bastards*, 83; Wolf, *Louis XIV*, 343–44.

93. *Le Mercure galant*, August 1686, 301–2; Petitfils, *Madame de Montespan*, 342–43.

94. Wellman, for example, does so explicitly; see *Queens and Mistresses*, 5–6.

95. Feuquières, *Mémoires*, 2:31.

96. The letter was dated 24 August 1676; see Clément, *Madame de Montespan et Louis XIV*, 233.

97. Choisy, *Mémoires*, 174.

98. This effort did not end well and damaged Montespan's relationship with Lauzun. Visconti, *Mémoires*, 17–18.

99. Ekberg, *Failure of Louis XIV's Dutch War*, 44–45, 191–92n110.

100. This is drawn from a letter sent by Lisola to Hocher on 3 July 1673. Klopp, *Fall des Hauses Stuart*, 341. For the original Latin letter, see 394.

101. Ekberg, *Failure of Louis XIV's Dutch War*, 45.

102. Dangeau, *Journal*, 1:46, 87, and vol. I, passim.

103. Clément, *Madame de Montespan et Louis XIV*, 45–46. Ronald Asch emphasizes the political implications in the spaces provided courtiers: "the decision to grant or deny access to a courtier—by giving him or her lodgings near the royal apartments, for example, or by not doing so—had serious political implications." "Patronage," 179.

104. References to her are frequent. See, for example, *Mercure galant*, August 1679, 171, 316; August 1682, 51, 78; October 1689, 281, and so on. Her obituary is in the June 1707 issue, 238.

105. Reddy, *Navigation of Feeling*, 141–42, 145–49. Bell has written of the high premium that early modern French aristocrats placed on their ability to control their emotions (*First Total War*, 33–35). Even among these individuals, Louis's self-control was legendary. See Bluche, *Louis XIV*, 487.

106. According to Madame de Caylus, "[S] reproached him once for not being in love with her, but simply to believe that he owed it to the public to be loved by the most beautiful woman in his kingdom." Caylus, *Souvenirs et correspondance*, 54.

107. Wolf, *Louis XIV*, 300–304; Clément, *Madame de Montespan et Louis XIV*, 12–18.

108. Wolf, *Louis XIV*, 306.

109. Visconti recounts the story in his *Mémoires*, 66–67. Wolf suggests that the religious imprint of his mother intensified Louis's feelings of guilt about this relationship. See "Formation of a King," 111.

110. Desnoiresterres, *Cours galantes*, 2:201–2 [83–84] (facsimile with both the original and a new set of page numbers).

111. Cited by Desnoiresterres in ibid., 2:202 [85].

112. See the letter from Madame de Scudéry written on 16 April 1675. Bussy-Rabutin, *Correspondance*, 3:22.

113. Indeed, Madame de Scudéry confirmed in July, "Madame de Montespan resumed living at Versailles the day before the king arrived there; he went to see her as soon [as he got back] and thereafter

continued as before." Bussy-Rabutin, *Correspondance*, 3:50. See also Bertière, *Reines de France*, 2:201–12.

114. Caylus, *Souvenirs et correspondance*, 46.

115. Sévigné, *Lettres*, 7 August 1676, 5:66.

116. Underlined in original. Ibid., 2 September 1676, 5:108.

117. Ibid., 15 May 1676, 4:436.

118. Bussy-Rabutin, *Correspondance*, 3:205–84.

119. From Le P. Rapin to Bussy-Rabutin, in ibid., 3:302.

120. Sévigné, *Lettres*, 11 June 1677, 5:237.

121. Bussy-Rabutin, *Correspondance*, 4:48–49.

122. Chaussinand-Nogaret, *Vie quotidienne*, 152. Louis had short-term love affairs with a wide variety of women well into his forties; Montespan appears to have worried only about those who posed a threat to her official position.

123. So suggests her biographer Jean-Christian Petitfils: "Her taunts were more biting, more cruel" (*Madame de Montespan*, 64–65). Visconti wrote of her increasing girth in 1678: "She has recently had two more children, and her stoutness was such that, one day, as she was getting down from her carriage, I could see one of her legs, which was almost as large as me; I must say, in fairness, that I have lost a lot of weight since you last saw me." Visconti, *Mémoires*, 117. See also Bertière, *Reines de France*, 2:215. Madame de Caylus (who as the niece of Madame de Maintenon is perhaps not the most disinterested reporter) suggests that Maintenon's calm conversation was a balm for the king after the mockery and reproaches of Montespan. Caylus, *Souvenirs et correspondance*, 50–54.

124. Madame de Sévigné recorded their arguments in her letters to her daughter. See, for example, Sévigné, *Lettres*, 6:510, written on 25 May 1680. Primi Visconti asserts that by the late 1670s, "The King was tired of Mme de Montespan; she had an ascendancy over him that had become a kind of domination." Visconti, *Mémoires*, 117.

125. Bertière, *Reines de France*, 2:199–200; Chaussinand-Nogaret, *Vie quotidienne*, 165–66.

126. Choisy, *Mémoires*, 174. See also Spanheim, *Relation de la cour de France*, 43–44.

127. See, for example, Sévigné, *Lettres*, 7 July 1680, 7:91; Spanheim, *Relation de la cour de France*, 43; Sourches, *Mémoires*, 1:90.

128. Caylus, *Souvenirs et correspondance*, 29.

129. Bertière, *Reines de France*, 2:16–40.

130. The Marquis of Dangeau reported that Madame de Montespan was relegated to her own carriage with her children, while the dauphine and Maintenon rode with the king in the back of his carriage. *Journal*, 1:55 (entry from 11 September 1684). Dangeau also noted that during the absence of Montespan in February 1685, the king was spending the after-dinner hours in Madame de Maintenon's apartments. *Journal*, 4 February 1685, 1:117. See Spanheim, *Relation de la cour de France*, 45–46; Choisy, *Mémoires*, 134–35.

131. Sévigné, *Lettres*, 6:412. In another dated 22 March 1680, she wrote of the growing rancor between Montespan and Maintenon (6:439).

132. Historians disagree on the extent of Madame de Montespan's involvement in the Affair of the Poisons; see Mollenauer, *Strange Revelations*; Bertière, *Reines de France*, 2:266–69; Bluche, *Louis XIV*, 277–80; Petitfils, *Madame de Montespan*, 243–312; Mossiker, *Affair of the Poisons*.

133. Petitfils outlines Maintenon's history in *Madame de Montespan*, chap. 6.

134. Craveri, *Reines et favorites*, 225; Conley, *Suspicion of Virtue*, 126.

135. Craveri, *Age of Conversation*, 223.

136. This story is well documented. See, for example, Petitfils, *Madame de Montespan*, 157–58; Caylus, *Souvenirs et correspondance*, 52. La Beaumelle, in his partisan *Mémoires*, provides an account of their relationship particularly favorable to Maintenon. See vol. 2.

137. Wolf, *Louis XIV*, 326. For more on Maintenon's personality, see Craveri, *Age of Conversation*, 222–23, and *Reines et favorites*, 217–40.

138. Caylus makes this clear (*Souvenirs et correspondance*, 59–62, 75).

139. Mark Bryant has meticulously laid out the parameters of Maintenon's role as the king's political adviser in "Partner, Matriarch, and Minister." While he notes that, in the twentieth century, "absolutist historians dismissed the marquise as a devout and powerless but dutiful wife, whose only concerns were her finishing school at Saint-Cyr and the king's salvation," this position is unsustainable (77 and passim). See also Duindam, *Vienna and Versailles*, 230.

140. See, for example, Prével, "Questions et réponses," 260–61; McCloy, "Persecution of the Huguenots," 56.

141. Nolhac notes that Pompadour "was passionately interested in the *Mémoires sur la vie de madame de Maintenon* that La Beaumelle would publish and would be among the first subscribers. She would gather a number of valuable lessons from that biography" (*Études sur la cour de France*, 21). See also Goodman, *Portraits of Madame de Pompadour*, 58.

142. Wolf, *Louis XIV*, 269.

143. In *Le ballet de cour de Louis XIV*, Christout lists the women of the court who appeared in the numerous ballets during Louis's reign and notes that the "gracious, if not always expert, presence of this bevy of beauties certainly had to enhance the brilliance of these ballets [scheduled] regularly to please the sovereign and to give French and foreign guests an idea of the pleasures one experiences at Court" (165).

144. Loret, *Muse historique*, vol. 4, passim.

145. Adams, "'Belle comme le jour,'" 167.

146. As the correspondence of both Bussy-Rabutin and Sévigné makes clear.

147. Spanheim, *Relation de la cour de France*, 42. The *surintendante de la reine* was extremely powerful. It was the only position that could be held either by a woman or a man, and it was the best-paid position in the queen's household that a woman could hold.

CHAPTER 6

1. Montespan came from one of the oldest families of Poitou, indeed of France. Barnavi et al., *Journal de la France et des Français*, 836; Petitfils, *Madame de Montespan*, 8–10. Wolf notes that Montespan performed "with an insolent air that proclaimed her own ancient lineage: the Mortemarts had the blood of Spanish kings in their veins; to their daughter, being mistress of the king was a sort of 'marriage by left hand' that she earned by her blood, as well as by her beauty and brains" (*Louis XIV*, 304).

2. In a review of Colin Jones's book *Madame de Pompadour: Images of a Mistress*, written to accompany the National Gallery exhibit on Madame de Pompadour, Orr notes, "Most often a mistress belonged to an already powerful aristocratic clan" ("Rococo Queen," 246).

3. Duindam underlines this point, noting that "while previous mistresses had usually come from the group of noble ladies already present at court, attending princesses or taking care of children, Mme de Pompadour—the other inescapable model—was an outsider in all respects" (*Vienna and Versailles*, 240).

4. The many biographies of Madame de Pompadour—the best of which include Algrant, *Madame de Pompadour*; Lever, *Madame de Pompadour*; and the earlier work by Gallet, *Madame de Pompadour*— all cover her family background in some detail.

5. Duindam, *Dynasties*, 125–26.

6. Lever, *Madame de Pompadour*, 48.

7. Louis XV arranged for purchase of the estate of Pompadour in the Limousin for Jeanne-Antoinette and conferred the title of Marquise de Pompadour on her in the summer of 1745 (ibid., 42).

8. While there are some rather fanciful biographies of Madame du Barry from the twentieth century, including Loomis, *Du Barry*; Levron, *Destin de Madame du Barry*; and Haslip, *Madame du Barry*, the most

detailed is still the old standard by Charles Vatel, *Histoire de Madame Du Barry*.

9. Levron, *Destin de Madame du Barry*, 25–32.

10. Dietrich, *Maîtresses de Louis XV*, foreword, n.p.

11. Croÿ-Solre, *Journal de Cour*, 5:57.

12. See, for example, Swann, *Politics and the Parlement of Paris*, 52–55, and Colin Jones, *Madame de Pompadour*, 122–23.

13. Graham writes about the pivotal role of the royal mistress in shaping perceptions of the king, and especially how, by the eighteenth century, she was identified with royal weakness and licentiousness. See *If the King Only Knew*, 58–59. Maza notes that Louis XV's "notorious debauchery, the power wielded by his mistresses Madame de Pompadour and later Madame du Barry, and the existence of a house of pleasure called the Parc-aux-Cerfs, where the monarch was provided with an unending series of nubile young women, were widely known secrets long before his death. Many a subject of Louis 'le Bien-Aimé' shared the feelings of Jean-François Le Clerc, a veteran soldier arrested in 1757 for calling the king a 'bugger' and complaining that the kingdom was governed 'by two whores'" ("Diamond Necklace Affair Revisted," 76).

14. Snyder writes: "The discourse on honest dissimulation, as I will call it here, was instead most prominent in the late sixteenth and early seventeenth centuries. During these years interest was extremely keen in the individual management of the ebb and flow of passions and emotions, as well as their expression" (*Dissimulation*, 43). With Reddy, I would argue that this mastery of emotions remained important through the reign of Louis XIV, shifting perceptibly in the eighteenth century; see *Navigation of Feeling*, chap. 5.

15. Hunt, "Many Bodies of Marie-Antoinette," 121.

16. Graham, *If the King Only Knew*, 59.

17. Kaiser, "Austrian Alliance," 170. As for Du Barry, among many accounts, see Swann, *Exile, Imprisonment, or Death*, 156–57, 214–16. Certainly, the Duke of

Choiseul held her responsible as the tool of the Duke of Aiguillon and the *dévôt* faction at court. See Choiseul, *Mémoires*, 260–97.

18. See Darnton, *Forbidden Best-Sellers*, esp. chap. 5.

19. This topic has been treated at length. See, for example, Roger Chartier, *Cultural Origins of the French Revolution*, chap. 6; Darnton, *Forbidden Best-Sellers*, 236–37; Graham, *If the King Only Knew*, 56–65; Colin Jones, *Great Nation*, chap. 6; Maza, *Private Lives and Public Affairs*, 177–79; Merrick, *Desacralization of the French Monarchy*, esp. 19–22.

20. Croÿ-Solre, *Journal de Cour*, 5:58.

21. *Précis historique*, 70–71 (in some databases attributed to the Dutch bookseller J. F. Bernard; second run of those pages). The pamphlet is similar in tone to the *Anecdotes sur Mme la comtesse du Barry* described by Darnton and ascribed to Mathieu-François Pidansat de Mairobert. See *Forbidden Best-Sellers*, chap. 5; for the translation of the *Anecdotes*, see 337–89.

22. Quoted in Silverman, *Art Nouveau*, 25.

23. Goncourt and Goncourt, *Femme aux dix-huitième siècle*, 292.

24. Michelet, *Histoire de la révolution française*, 59. Also quoted in Maza, "Diamond Necklace Affair Revisited," 76.

25. Sainte-Beuve, introduction to *Memoirs and Letters of Cardinal de Bernis*, 1:33, 37–38. Lewis makes reference to this slight in the subtitle of her review article on recent biographies of Madame de Pompadour ("Madame de Pompadour: Eminence without Honor," 303–14). A review of Saint-Beuve's translation, in *Spectator* 88 (31 May 1902): 845–46, is more damning of Pompadour: "These are painful years to read of, those typical middle years of the eighteenth century, when the spirit of immorality rotted everything in France, and when Madame de Pompadour, assisted by Bernis and Choiseul, governed the nation and hurried it on its downward way."

26. Sainte-Beuve, *Memoires and Letters of Cardinal de Bernis*, introduction, 48.

27. Vatel, *Histoire de Madame Du Barry*, 1:170.

28. Antoine, *Louis XV*, 498.

29. See reviews of the historical literature on Pompadour, including Orr, "Rococo Queen"; Gordon, "Searching for the Elusive Madame de Pompadour"; Lewis, "Madame de Pompadour." There has been much less scholarly interest in Madame Du Barry.

30. The information that follows draws primarily on Lever, *Madame de Pompadour*, and Algrant, *Madame de Pompadour*, which both examine Jeanne-Antoinette Poisson's young life in detail.

31. He was accused of speculation and forced into exile for almost ten years under rather mysterious circumstances.

32. Kaiser writes that "the young Mlle Poisson was instructed in dance and music by such luminaries as Guibaudet and Jéllyotte; and having gained entry into the most prestigious salons of Paris—most notably that of Mme de Tencin—by way of her mother's influence, she received a literary education through contact with such figures as Montesquieu, Fontenelle, and Marivaux" ("Madame de Pompadour," 1027).

33. Bernis, *Mémoires et lettres*, 1:110.

34. Colin Jones, *Madame de Pompadour*, 21. Both Jones and Lever assure us that the story of the fortune teller appears to be true, citing the 600 livre pension that Pompadour provided for Mme Lebon "for having predicted for Mme de Pompadour that one day she would be the mistress of Louis XV" (Lever, *Madame de Pompadour*, 270n4). She continued to be compared to Agnès, sometimes in a positive way, sometimes negative. The Marquis of Argenson mentions that she was being compared favorably in an epigramme (Argenson, *Journal et mémoires* [April 1752], 9:214). However, Voltaire's secretly circulated poem about Joan of Arc, "La Pucelle d'Orléans," paints Pompadour, through the figure of Agnès, as a frivolous distraction. See *Œuvres de Voltaire*, 11:17–23, 269–73, 328–29.

35. Goodman, *Portraits of Madame de Pompadour*, 13–14. Goodman also underlines this genealogy, noting that "Pompadour, a serious student of French history and art, situated herself squarely in a long lineage of royal mistresses disguised as Diana."

36. The information on the early days of their affair is scattered and inconsistent. See Algrant, *Madame de Pompadour*, 35–36.

37. Luynes, *Mémoires*, 6:354.

38. "She requested excerpts from the memoirs of Dangeau and Saint-Simon, [and] asked Clairambault to make an illuminated album with the arms of the great families of the kingdom" (Gallet, *Madame de Pompadour*, 50). She and the king kept in close touch. Luynes noted that already by July, the king had written more than eighty letters addressed to the new Marquise de Pompadour, "sealed with a gallant motto, around which was written, 'Discret et fidèle'" (Luynes, *Mémoires*, 7:5).

39. Algrant, *Madame de Pompadour*, 18–19, 40; Gallet, *Madame de Pompadour*, 50. Gallet notes that Voltaire spoke of Pompadour with admiration: "She has read more at her age than any old lady of the country where she will reign [meaning Versailles] and where it is well to be desired that she will reign."

40. Algrant, *Madame de Pompadour*, 39–44. The Abbé de Bernis wrote of his attentions to Pompadour that summer in his memoirs (Bernis, *Mémoires et lettres*, 1:110–15).

41. Both Snyder and Duindam argue that mastery of this code was the key to social promotion in the early modern court. Snyder quotes Duindam, who argued that court life involved "both the presentation and legitimation of power. Paradoxically, the noble code of behavior served simultaneously as an impediment and as a vehicle for social mobility: those who could crack it found the way open to higher status." See Snyder, *Dissimulation*, 70, and Duindam, *Myths of Power*, 194–95.

42. Luynes reported that she was placed in the apartment of the late

Madame de Châteauroux, the king's former mistress (*Mémoires*, 7:60).

43. See Nicolle, *Madame de Pompadour*, 118–20, and Lever, *Madame de Pompadour*, 47–49.

44. Croÿ-Solre, *Journal de Cour*, 1:69, 76, 79.

45. Luynes made a favorable report: "It appears that everyone finds Mme de Pompadour extremely polite; not only is she not wicked and speaks ill of no one, but she will not even allow it in her home. She is cheerful and willingly speaks" (*Mémoires*, 7:110, 126). He later reported that "the Queen treats Mme de Pompadour in a very appropriate manner, and she is very pleased with the kindess of the Queen. The Queen often says that since there must be a mistress, she prefers Mme de Pompadour to any other" (10:170). See also Nicolle, *Madame de Pompadour*, 120; Antoine, *Louis XV*, 497; Lever, *Madame de Pompadour*, 66–67.

46. Bernis, *Mémoires et lettres*, 1:109. According to Marwick, the testimony on Pompadour's looks is varied and contradictory; he suggests that her expressivesness and vivacity were perhaps more striking than her looks, and that she was attractive rather than beautiful (*Beauty in History*, 112–17).

47. Dufort de Cheverny, *Mémoires*, 1:68.

48. Kaunitz-Rietberg, "Mémoire," 447.

49. See chapter 1.

50. Argenson, *Journal et mémoires*, 4:179, and 28 February 1747, 5:75. Argenson was secretary of state for foreign affairs from 1744 to 1747, and brother of the Count of Argenson (1696–1764), who served as minister of war from 1743 to 1757. Both despised Pompadour.

51. Kaunitz-Rietberg, "Mémoire," 449. In contrast, Luynes was impressed that she did not affect "de la hauteur" but spoke frequently of her relatives, even in the presence of the king; on the other hand, he also noted that she "often made use of terms and expressions that seemed

extraordinary at Versailles [*dans ce pays ci*]," a relic of her upbringing (*Mémoires*, 7:110).

52. Gallet, *Madame de Pompadour*, 94.

53. All of Pompadour's biographers, as well as many contemporaries, write of Louis's melancholic and easily bored personality. See, for example, Hooper-Hamersley, *Hunt After Jeanne-Antoinette de Pompadour*, 101–3; Kaiser, "Madame de Pompadour," 1035; Craveri, *Reines et favorites*, 289. However, Antoine suggests that, in her efforts to amuse the king, Pompadour fundamentally misunderstood the king's personality and needs; that in addition to hunting, this highly educated man would have preferred "serious distractions such as drawing and talking with architects, conversing with scientists, and applying himself to mathematics" (*Louis XV*, 497). Croÿ-Solre noted that she was "full of amusing talents, the kind that the king appeared to like more than any others, and he was right: as mistress, she was the most pleasant" (*Journal de Cour*, 1:59).

54. Craveri, *Age of Conversation*, 256–57.

55. Croÿ-Solre, *Journal de Cour*, 1:95. The Marquis of Argenson took a typically peevish view of her efforts, writing of "her taste for spectacles, which bore the king and only amuse this lady [Pompadour] born among street performers" (Argenson, *Journal et mémoires*, 15 November 1748, 5:274).

56. Kaiser, "Madame de Pompadour," 1034; Algrant, *Madame de Pompadour*, 22.

57. Hooper-Hamersley, *Hunt After Jeanne-Antoinette de Pompadour*, 111–14.

58. Luynes, *Mémoires*, 9:2. Throughout his memoirs, Luynes describes a number of plays, operas, concerts, and other amusements that Pompadour arranged and performed for the king, esp. in vols. 8–9.

59. In the collection of "Lettres inédites de Mme de Pompadour et du roi Louis XV" in the French publication of Lever's *Madame de Pompadour*, 347.

60. As Luynes makes clear (*Mémoires*, 8:86–88).

61. Algrant, *Madame de Pompadour*, 55; Colin Jones, *Madame de Pompadour*, 51.

62. Colin Jones, *Madame de Pompadour*, 89. Luynes wrote of Crécy: "It's a very beautiful chateau, well furnished, with a terrace said to have cost 100,000 écus" (*Mémoires*, 7:303).

63. Dufort de Cheverny, *Mémoires sur les règnes*, 1:319.

64. Du Pont de Nemours, *Autobiography*, 242–43.

65. Pompadour, letter to the Countess of Lutzelbourg dated 1749 (in Berly, *Lettres de Madame de Pompadour*, 132).

66. Letter written on 29 September 1748, in Lever, *Madame de Pompadour*, 349.

67. Bernis, *Mémoires et lettres*, 1:207.

68. Antoine writes, "Edified by the precedent of Mme de Mailly, the marquise de Pompadour was fiercely determined not to let anyone dislodge her from the place that she had conquered, and to make every effort to occupy it indefinitely. To that end, it was necessary to tirelessly deploy an indomitable energy, for she was threatened by the attitude of a faction of courtiers and the royal family as well as by the scruples of Louis XV" (*Louis XV*, 495–96).

69. Prior to the installation of Madame de Pompadour, Louis took several women of the same family as mistresses consecutively. See Craveri, "Les soeurs Mailly-Nesle: Amour en famille," in *Reines et favorites*, 253–80.

70. Antoine, *Louis XV*, 372–78; Algrant, *Madame de Pompadour*, 30–31; Lever, *Madame de Pompadour*, 10–11. He was particularly distraught when Madame de Châteauroux died shortly thereafter at the age of twenty-seven.

71. Lever, *Madame de Pompadour*, 200–204; Algrant, *Madame de Pompadour*, 188–90, 203–4. There was considerable debate at court (and among historians) as to whether her conversion and newfound devotion were sincere or one more performance. Ultimately, the Jesuit Father de Sacy withheld his absolution from Pompadour, and she asked him to leave the

court; her displays of devotion waned thereafter.

72. Algrant writes, "Most importantly, by withdrawing from some of the public rites of kingship, he compromised the sacred role the king played in the life of the kingdom. Since 1738 Louis XV, acknowledging his adultery, had found it impossible to confess and take communion at Easter; he then discontinued the age-old rite of touching those affected by scrofula, as his ancestors had done; he considered himself a sinner living in adultery, and he would not be dishonest" (*Madame de Pompadour*, 58). See also Merrick, *Desacralization of the French Monarchy*, 20.

73. Hooper-Hamersley covers this extensively in chaps. 4 and 5 of *Hunt After Jeanne-Antoinette de Pompadour*.

74. Gallet, *Madame de Pompadour*, 180; Algrant, *Madame de Pompadour*, 105. Voltaire, considering her an important patron, mentions her frequently in his correspondence. See *Œuvres*, 55:51–52, 54–70. Relations had cooled considerably by 1750. Marmontel writes that "since that time, Voltaire was received coldly and ceased going to court," as the writer Crébillon attained increasing favor and as Voltaire flirted with Frederick the Great of Prussia, offending both Louis XV and Pompadour (Marmontel, *Mémoires*, 1:288). See also Hooper-Hamersley, *Hunt After Jeanne-Antoinette de Pompadour*, 76n25.

75. Hooper-Hamersley, *Hunt After Jeanne-Antoinette de Pompadour*, 28. In a letter to d'Alembert, Voltaire wrote, "Have you grieved for Mme de Pompadour? Yes, no doubt, as she was at the bottom of her heart one of us; she was a patron of letters as much as she could be: behold the end of a beautiful dream. They say that she died with a courage worthy of your praises; at court such courage is rare, for there they cling more to life. . . . Believe that Mme de Pomadour never persecuted anyone. I am very affected by her death." Quoted in Algrant, *Madame de Pompadour*, 291.

76. Lever, *Madame de Pompadour*, 175.

77. Du Pont de Nemours writes that Quesnay "restored life and beauty to Madame de Pompadour, and, with two such important services, had acquired her entire confidence, which he used with circumspection, with ability, sometimes with courage, never for himself, always for the public good." He goes on to say that "Quesnay's discourses began to direct her ambition toward the glory and utility of a good government" and inspired in her an interest in agriculture and free trade (*Autobiography*, 237, 245).

78. Goodman, *Portraits of Madame de Pompadour*, esp. chap. 2, and Colin Jones, *Madame de Pompadour*, 62–66. Gallet notes, "She had too often frequented Parisian salons not to be charmed by the spirit that sparkled in their words" (*Madame de Pompadour*, 179).

79. Hooper-Hamersley suggests that a careful and nuanced position was inevitable given Pompadour's position at the court. See *Hunt After Jeanne-Antoinette de Pompadour*, chap. 5. However, she was still willing to offer patronage to some writers, finding a position in the civil service (he eventually became manager of *Le Mercure*) for Marmontel in 1758. He writes of his solicitation for a *survivance* from her in 1757 in his *Mémoires*, followed by his work for the Abbé Bernis (2:38–59). See Algrant, *Madame de Pompadour*, 138–39, 149–50.

80. Hooper-Hamersley, *Hunt After Jeanne-Antoinette de Pompadour*, chap. 4; Colin Jones, *Madame de Pompadour*, esp. chap. 4; Goodman, *Portraits of Madame de Pompadour*.

81. Pompadour's etchings were on display at the Walters Art Museum in Baltimore, Maryland, in 2016: https://thewalters.org/news/rareetchingsbymadamedepompadouronviewatthewalters.

82. Craveri, *Reines et favorites*, 295. Hooper-Hamersley notes that her taste influenced artistic shifts in the production of porcelain at Sèvres even if she did not personally direct them (*Hunt After Jeanne-Antoinette de Pompadour*, 267).

83. Argenson, *Journal et mémoires*, 31 May 1753, 8:4, and 28 July 1753, 8:86; Barbier, *Journal historique et anecdotique*, 3:183–84; Nicolle, *Madame de Pompadour*, 176–81; Algrant, *Madame de Pompadour*, 91.

84. Dietrich, *Maîtresses de Louis XV*, 31. Nicolle agrees that "it would be futile to deny that all of this was very expensive. She had no inhibitions about it, convinced that she worked for the glory of the king, and thus of France. A balance sheet of her expenses from the time of her arrival at court until her death can be found among her papers. The total is certainly impressive: 36,924,140 livres, 8 sols and 9 deniers" (Nicolle, *Madame de Pompadour*, 181).

85. Lever, *Madame de Pompadour*, 130–31; Craveri, *Reines et favorites*, 296–7; Colin Jones, *Madame de Pompadour*, 60. Most biographers draw on the suspect memoirs of Madame de Hausset when quoting Pompadour herself, but her gynecological issues were common knowledge and the subject of *poissonades*. On the problems with these memoirs, see Gordon, "Longest-Enduring Pompadour Hoax."

86. Gallet, *Madame de Pompadour*, 153–54; Colin Jones, *Madame de Pompadour*, 70–72.

87. Algrant, *Madame de Pompadour*, 125.

88. Gallet, *Madame de Pompadour*, 138.

89. Argenson, *Journal et mémoires*, 20 and 15 October 1752, 7:327–28; Algrant, *Madame de Pompadour*, 140. Duindam writes, "The tabourets were the consequence of princely or ducal rank: they could not be withheld, but the king rarely could grant a *tabouret de grâce*. If a lady received this right by the king's personal favour, however, she would henceforth hold ducal rank, as did Mme de Pompadour after 1752, although she still styled herself *marquise*" (Duindam, *Vienna and Versailles*, 213).

90. According to Gallet, "She acquired an ascendancy over the king through business that she had not obtained through pleasure. She knew Louis XV better than anyone. . . . Because of her ability to listen, through a reflection complementary to his own, she gently led him toward solutions,

leaving him with the feeling that he had made the choice himself. No prime minister had been able to play this subtle role" (*Madame de Pompadour*, 218). See also Lever, *Madame de Pompadour*, 141–43.

91. Luynes, *Mémoires*, 13:430.

92. From a letter to the Count of Stainville, future Duke of Choiseul, 28 June 1755, in Berly, *Lettres de Madame de Pompadour*, 254.

93. Many contemporaries and subsequent historians have written about the Parc-aux-Cerfs, by its nature a fascinating and salacious topic, as well as the degree of Pompadour's complicity in helping locate the young women provided for Louis's pleasure. Kaiser suggests that "there is little evidence to connect her directly with its operations, although she was undoubtedly well aware of its existence" ("Madame de Pompadour," 1037n41); in a review of the recent biographies of Pompadour, Lewis concurs ("Madame de Pompadour," 308). Luynes wrote knowledgeably about various women associated with the Parc-aux-Cerfs in 1756, but he did not suggest that Pompadour was involved (*Mémoires*, 15:325).

94. Bertière suggests that, in this fashion, Pompadour once again followed in the footsteps of her predecessors: "She reacts as had all the previous declared royal mistresses, who barred the path of dangerous rivals while letting the king search for pleasure among the women whose condition was too humble to aspire to replace her. Precedents are not lacking. For example, during the many pregnancies that left Mme de Montespan unavailable, she supplied the king with one or another of her chambermaids" (*Reines de France*, 3:382).

95. Already in February 1749, when rumors started that Pompadour planned to miss a masked ball, Luynes wrote, "As we like to think about it, we have already considered a large number of young women who greatly desire to achieve the same position" (*Mémoires*, 10:97–98).

96. The most frequently cited and thorough (although secondhand) contemporary account of this conspiracy comes from

Marmontel, *Mémoires*, 2:24–27. For a detailed (and somewhat breathless) narrative, see Nolhac, *Études sur la cour de France*, 1–11.

97. "Finally la marquise was greatly vexed. The comtesse de Choiseul-Romanet, beautiful as an angel, tender, wise, faithful, was fit for a king. One could compare her to mademoiselle de Fontanges under Louis XIV" (Dufort de Cheverny, *Mémoires sur les règnes*, 1:138).

98. Choiseul presents his self-serving version of the related events in his *Mémoires*, 92–105. Butler uses these memoirs along with additional sources to paint a rather more complex account of the intrigues in *Choiseul*, chap. 7.

99. Colin Jones, *Madame de Pompadour*, 61.

100. Goodman, *Portraits of Madame de Pompadour*, and Colin Jones, *Madame de Pompadour*, provide the most useful analyses of Pompadour's efforts to shape her image.

101. The title of chapter 3 in Elise Goodman's book is "The New Montespan / The New Maintenon."

102. Belleval, *Souvenirs d'un Chevau-Léger*, 9. Nolhac suggests that she drew explicitly on the example of Madame de Maintenon (*Études sur la cour de France*, 20–21).

103. Craveri, *Reines et favorites*, 297.

104. Kaunitz-Rietberg, "Mémoire," 448.

105. Barbier, *Journal historique et anecdotique*, 4:117. Luynes also discusses some of the delicate negotiations involved in obtaining this position for Pompadour, which were part of Pompadour's larger efforts to reconcile with the church while still remaining at court. *Mémoires*, 15:321–25.

106. Choiseul, *Mémoires*, 63.

107. Nicolle, *Madame de Pompadour*, 121.

108. Argenson, *Journal et mémoires*, 15 November 1748, 5:274.

109. Gallet, *Madame de Pompadour*, 104.

110. Argenson, *Journal et mémoires*, 28 September 1748, 5:253. The king's spies kept an eye on the mail. Algrant, *Madame de Pompadour*, 130–31.

111. Kaiser, "Madame de Pompadour," 1030; Lever, *Madame de Pompadour*, 120.

Barbier made note of Maurepas's firing for his complicity in the "nasty verses" (méchants vers) circulating at Versailles and in Paris, and he suggested that because "he did not pay court to madame de Pompadour she did not have reason to like him" (Barbier, *Journal historique et anecdotique*, April 1749, 3:74–75). In his memoirs, Choiseul mentions that "M. de Maurepas helped a bit with the intrigues of his enemies by assisting with the composition of songs that were written about Mme de Pompadour, and, in those songs, the King was also held up to ridicule" (*Mémoires*, 87).

112. Kaiser, "Drama of Charles Edward Stuart"; Lewis, "Madame de Pompadour," 304; Gallet, *Madame de Pompadour*, 95–96; Hooper-Hamersley, *Hunt After Jeanne-Antoinette de Pompadour*, 338–43.

113. On 19 January 1749 Argenson reported: "The other day, the king asked M. de Richelieu, taking him by surprise, how many times he had been in the Bastille. 'Three times,' said the maréchal. With that, His Majesty discussed the causes. It is said that question is a very bad omen" (Argenson, *Journal et mémoires*, 5:362). See also Algrant, *Madame de Pompadour*, 84.

114. According to Belleval, "It was because of Mme de Pompadour. An imprudent remark by M. de Souvré was reported to her, and that was enough to lose her and to deprive him of the king's favor and friendship. He is said to be in despair, but the marquise will not forgive him. If it is good to be among her friends, it is not good to be one of her enemies. Still, if only M. de Souvré had spoken ill of just the king!" (Belleval, *Souvenirs d'un Chevau-Léger*, 28).

115. The Baron of Besenval recounts in detail these intrigues during the king's convalescence in Besenval, *Mémoires*, 1:208–15.

116. Swann, *Politics and the Parlement of Paris*, 143–44. While the hand of Pompadour was visible in the machinations, Louis's decision to dismiss his ministers was not simply to please her; in the case of Argenson and Machault, he had other

reasons to be frustrated with both men, although he had been loyal to them for a long time. See Swann, *Exile, Imprisonment, or Death*, 146–52, and *Politics and the Parlement of Paris*, 141–43; Lever, *Madame de Pompadour*, 216–17.

117. "Indeed, positions, offices, pensions, honors, all were in her hands. With the love of the king, her *crédit* grew, and with *crédit*, courtiers surged around her. . . . She liked to be of service, was delighted to win over the nobility, made obliging offers, and granted audiences immediately" (Gallet, *Madame de Pompadour*, 73–74). Swann suggests that "Pompadour's power lay in her ability to persuade Louis XV to appoint her candidates to key offices, even when it was against his better judgement" (*Politics and the Parlement of Paris*, 54).

118. Nicolle, *Madame de Pompadour*, 122.

119. Lever, *Madame de Pompadour*, 60–61.

120. Algrant, *Madame de Pompadour*, 53–54; Nicolle, *Madame de Pompadour*, 147–49.

121. Algrant, *Madame de Pompadour*, 91.

122. Pompadour alludes to this in a letter to the Maréchal of Saxony, dated 1746 (in Berly, *Lettres de Madame de Pompadour*, 228). Choiseul makes reference to her successful efforts in his memoirs, noting that "le maréchal of Saxony persuaded Mme de Pompadour that it was infinitely better for the Dauphin to marry a Saxon princess" (*Mémoires*, 72). He also wrote that he heard frequently about the machinations at court of Pompadour and her friend Mme d'Estrades, but he claimed, with his typical effort at insouciance, that he was not really interested in court intrigues at this point in his career.

123. Argenson, *Journal et mémoires*, 27 June 1748, 5:229.

124. Berly, *Lettres de Madame de Pompadour*, 220.

125. Swann, *Politics and the Parlement of Paris*, 54.

126. Choiseul, *Mémoires*, 110.

127. A point that Swann also makes (*Politics and the Parlement of Paris*, 54).

128. Swann recounts Bernis's rise to power and his eventual fall in *Exile, Imprisonment, or Death*, 300–309. He writes: "The Seven Years War is now viewed almost unanimously as a disaster for the monarchy, and Bernis has come to serve as a symbol for the shambles into which French arms and diplomacy had fallen both before and after Rossbach. That the cardinal was diplomatically out of his depth seems beyond doubt, although his disgrace owed more to his astute assessment of France's plight" (302). The Abbé de Bernis, not surprisingly, saw things differently; see vol. II of his *Mémoires et lettres*. See also Algrant, *Madame de Pompadour*, 210–12. In his bitter memoirs, reflecting on the aftermath of the disgrace and exile of the Count of Argenson and Machault, Choiseul wrote that no one would have missed them "if they had been replaced by at least a mediocrity; but I believe that there was never a more ridiculous Council than that of the King after the dismissal of MM. d'Argenson and de Machault" (*Mémoires*, 146).

129. They were related to her by marriage; François de Baschi, Count of Saint-Estève, was married to Pompadour's sister-in-law.

130. Nicolle, *Madame de Pompadour*, 151–52.

131. Luynes, *Mémoires*, 14:163.

132. Nicolle, *Madame de Pompadour*, 148; Algrant, *Madame de Pompadour*, 150.

133. The Marquis of Argenson noted that "she is the cousin of the marquise, it is the marquise who had her married." *Journal et mémoires*, 17 November 1751, 7:20. Luynes noted that Pompadour had loaned the couple Bellevue for their wedding and wedding night (*Mémoires*, 11:110).

134. One can find examples of these favors scattered throughout the memoirs of various courtiers. For example: "The brother of Mme de Rochambeau is very rich; he is in business; he is under the protection of Mme de Pompadour who is a relative. Mme de Pomadpour also arranged for a regiment for the son of Mme de Rochambeau, who married Mlle Thelés who is very rich" (Luynes, *Mémoires*,

13:297). He also provides examples of her acting as intermediary between the king and his courtiers (15:331–32). Croÿ-Solre pressed Pompadour to use her influence with the king to grant him a variety of favors, so much so that she was occasionally irritated by him (*Journal de Cour*, 1:86, 100).

135. This letter from Le Chambrier was written to Frederick the Great on 11 January 1751. He goes on to argue dismissively that Pompadour was interested in amusing the king and maintaining her position, not foreign affairs. See Flammermont, *Correspondances*, 17–18.

136. Craveri, *Reines et favorites*, 303.

137. Swann draws on the memoirs of Bernis, Robert de Saint-Vincent, and the Duke of Croÿ to support this assertion (*Politics and the Parlement of Paris*, 54–55).

138. Swann emphasizes the role she played in the parlementaire crisis of 1756–57; Pompadour's lack of sympathy with the Jesuits, especially after the failed efforts with Père de Sacy, undermined their position in conflicts with the Parlement. See ibid., esp. 211–12. For more on this crisis, see Van Kley, *Jansenists*.

139. Dufort de Cheverny, *Mémoires sur les règnes*, 1:84.

140. Kaunitz-Rietberg to Koch, Paris, 22 August 1751, in Schlitter, *Correspondance secrète*, 113–14.

141. Argenson, *Journal et mémoires*, 29 November 1748, 5:291.

142. Kaunitz-Rietberg, "Mémoire," 449. Kiernan writes that Pompadour's toilettes were "a means of displaying both her beauty and her influence" ("Absolutely Beautiful?," 194).

143. Croÿ-Solre, *Journal de Cour*, 1:62.

144. Ibid., 1:219; Swann, *Politics and the Parlement of Paris*, 55.

145. Croÿ-Solre, *Journal de Cour*, 2:130.

146. Broglie, *Alliance autrichienne*, 57–58.

147. Choiseul, *Mémoires*, 156.

148. Nolhac, *Études sur la cour de France*, 24.

149. See Bauer, "Fate of Secrets," and Antoine, *Louis XV*, 645–48, 727–31, on "Le Secret du roi." Swann provides a useful

discussion of its ramifications in *Exile, Imprisonment, or Death*, 203–13.

150. Algrant, *Madame de Pompadour*, 61–62, 151. Ironically, Madame Du Barry reportedly became aware of this secret correspondence when she noticed a large package on Louis's table and read some of the king's correspondence from the Count of Broglie (Vatel, *Histoire de Madame Du Barry*, 1:322–23).

151. As Berly writes, "The interventions of Madame de Pompadour in the foreign policy of the kingdom were frequent, and most often decisive" (*Lettres de Madame de Pompadour*, 293).

152. Barbier, *Journal historique et anecdotique*, 4:256.

153. Gallet, *Madame de Pompadour*, 93. This was especially true of those who supported Charles Edward Stuart, pretender to the English throne, whom the French abandoned in the Treaty of Aix-la-Chapelle (Kaiser, "Drama of Charles Edward Stuart," 372–74).

154. See Kaiser, "Who's Afraid of Marie-Antoinette?," 245.

155. Kaiser, "Austrian Alliance," 169; Bertière, *Reines de France*, 3:504–5; Nolhac, *Études sur la cour de France*, 132–35. The king deeply admired the Empress Maria Theresa. Bernis, *Mémoires et lettres*, 1:232–33; Bertière, *Reines de France*, 3:499–500.

156. Dietrich, *Maîtresses de Louis XV*, 36.

157. Nolhac, *Études sur la cour de France*, 42.

158. Antoine, *Louis XV*, 672–75.

159. Argenson, *Journal et mémoires*, e.g., 30 April 1747, 5:79; 27 May 1747, 5:80; 28 September 1748, 5:252; 23 November 1748, 5:282 and passim. This continued until shortly before his death: on 15 January 1757 he wrote with satisfaction that Pompadour was clearly on her way out in the wake of the Damiens affair (9:390). On 17 January, however, he finally acknowledged that "the King went to visit the Marquise, whose fate is no longer uncertain" (9:392).

160. Flammermont, *Correspondances*, 176.

161. Luynes, *Mémoires*, 17:96–97.

162. Lever, "Lettres inédites," in *Madame de Pompadour*, 343–76. See also chap. 6 of Berly, *Lettres de Madame de Pompadour*.

163. Berly, *Lettres de Madame de Pompadour*, 296.

164. Algrant, *Madame de Pompadour*, 254, 282–88; Lever, *Madame de Pompadour*, chap. 25.

165. Croÿ-Solre, *Journal de Cour*, 3:100–101.

166. Dietrich, *Maîtresses de Louis XV*, 25.

167. Petit de Bachaumont, *Mémoires secrets*, 2:45, 46.

168. Dufort de Cheverny, *Mémoires sur les règnes*, 1:324.

169. Swann, *Politics and the Parlement of Paris*, 260.

170. Campan, *Mémoires*, 25.

171. The information that follows is drawn primarily from Vatel's *Histoire de Madame Du Barry* and Craveri, "Madame Du Barry: L'ange des bas-fonds," in *Reines et favorites*, 311–28.

172. Vatel suggests that she modified her name several times (*Histoire de Madame Du Barry*, 1:84–85).

173. This is certainly the implication in the scandalous *Anecdotes sur Mme la comtesse du Barry*. See Darnton, *Forbidden Best-Sellers*, 351–55.

174. Swann writes, "Du Barry's journey to the royal bed had included many stops along the way, and she had been guided by, among others, the king's fellow rake and long-time crony, the duc de Richelieu, who was acting in conjunction with his ambitious nephew the duc d'Aiguillon" (*Exile, Imprisonment, or Death*, 214). See also Graham, *If the King Only Knew*, 216; Levron, *Destin de Madame du Barry*, 22.

175. Precisely how she came to the king's attention is a matter of debate. Vatel notes that "it must be said, the beginnings of madame du Barry's favor have remained quite obscure" (*Histoire de Madame Du Barry*, 1:110–11, 168).

176. Craveri, *Reines et favorites*, 315.

177. Espinchal, *Journal d'émigration*, 148.

178. Vatel, *Histoire de Madame Du Barry*, 121–22.

179. Swann, *Politics and the Parlement of Paris*, 317–18.

180. Campan, *Mémoires*, 25.

181. Belleval, *Souvenirs d'un Chevau-Léger*, 117, 120.

182. Croÿ-Solre, *Journal du Cour*, 4:81–82.

183. Marwick writes that "the earlier portraits [of Du Barry], taken with the wealth of written testimony, suggest that, of her own particular type, Du Barry was quintessentially beautiful" (*Beauty in History*, 120).

184. Espinchal, *Journal d'émigration*, 148.

185. Quoted in Vatel, *Histoire de Madame Du Barry*, 1:82n.

186. Belleval, *Souvenirs d'un Chevau-Léger*, 129.

187. Vatel, *Histoire de Madame Du Barry*, 1:114. Vatel also cites a rather lukewarm appraisal by Choiseul's friend Horace Walpole, who only saw her from a distance, but who still acknowledged that "she is pretty." Quoted in ibid., 1:287–88.

188. Ibid., 1:165.

189. See Levron, *Destin de Madame du Barry*, 60.

190. Croÿ-Solre, *Journal de Cour*, 4:160.

191. Duindam, in his analysis of court factions, argues that "the chances of parties at court, we may infer, depended on their connections in the ministry, as well as among the courtiers in the king's proximity—with the mistress in Louis XV's later days as the most significant factor" (*Vienna and Versailles*, 252).

192. Already in January 1769, Belleval reported, "It seems that the disgrace of M. le duc de Choiseul would be the first and natural consequence." Belleval himself was not necessarily convinced of this: "I don't believe it, because the new favorite does not yet have a firm enough foothold here to lead such a major affair" (*Souvenirs d'un Chevau-Léger*, 117).

193. Croÿ-Solre, *Journal du Cour*, 4:171.

194. Swann, *Politics and the Parlement of Paris*, 320–21.

195. Croÿ discusses the unwillingness of Choiseul and his sister to treat Du Barry

with respect. See Croÿ-Solre, *Journal du Cour*, 4:175–76.

196. Swann, *Exile, Imprisonment, or Death*, 215. See also Vatel, *Histoire de Madame Du Barry*, 1:171–86.

197. Belleval, *Souvenirs d'un Chevau-Léger*, 117–18; Vatel, *Histoire de Madame Du Barry*, 1:183–84.

198. Croÿ-Solre, *Journal du Cour*, 4:176.

199. Belleval, *Souvenirs d'un Chevau-Léger*, 125.

200. *Précis historique*, 70–71. This was also the perspective presented in the *Anecdotes sur Mme la comtesse du Barry*. See Darnton, *Forbidden Best-Sellers*, chap. 5, esp. 51–52, and the corresponding primary source on 337–89. Swann agrees that Du Barry lent full support to Aiguillon, who had backed her so strongly ("From Servant of the King," 73).

201. Swann, *Politics and the Parlement of Paris*, 320. Belleval asserted that the *chevaux-légers* were strong supporters of Du Barry, whom they found to be someone "kind and who loved to oblige," and her faction, especially Aiguillon, called themselves "Barriens." In contrast, they hated Choiseul and his sister (Belleval, *Souvenirs d'un Chevau-Léger*, 131–32).

202. Arneth and Geffroy, *Correspondance secrète*, 1:251.

203. Swann, "From Servant of the King," 67.

204. Choiseul was the architect of the "Family Compact," which committed the French to defending Spain's claim to the Falklands and thus threatened to drag them into war against the British once again, a war that they could ill afford, due to continuing financial woes (Darnton, *Forbidden Best-Sellers*, 147–48). Vatel also stresses Choiseul's commitment to war against England, which Louis XV absolutely did not want (*Histoire de Madame Du Barry*, 1: chap. 27). The abandonment of Poland was deeply resented, especially by those associated with "Le Secret du roi." Kaiser's forthcoming book on French relations with Austria will be an invaluable guide to understanding this complicated period. I thank him for sharing with me his work in progress.

205. Swann, *Politics and the Parlement of Paris*.

206. Campan, *Mémoires*, 26.

207. *Précis historique*, 67–68; Swann, *Politics and the Parlement of Paris*, 346–47, 351.

208. *Précis historique*, 67–68.

209. Swann, *Exile, Imprisonment, or Death*, 204.

210. Espinchal, *Journal d'émigration*, 149.

211. On this, see Vatel, *Histoire de Madame Du Barry*, 1: chap. 24.

212. Swann, *Exile, Imprisonment, or Death*, 422.

213. Espinchal, *Journal d'émigration*, 149.

214. For excerpts of the correspondence between the empress and Mercy-Argenteau on this matter, see Vatel, *Histoire de Madame Du Barry*, 2: chap. 8.

215. Arneth and Geffroy, *Correspondance secrète*, 1:215.

216. Vatel, *Histoire de Madame Du Barry*, 1:343, 345–49.

217. Rowlands, "Maison militaire du roi," 247.

218. Jacques Necker, future director general of finances under Louis XVI, would praise statesmen of virtue who acted in the public interest, and he obliquely critiqued Louis XV's triumvirate of ministers "whose rise owed far more to the influence of courtly intrigue and Louis XV's mistress, the comtesse du Barry, than to any selfless desire to advance the public good" (Swann, *Exile, Imprisonment, or Death*, 419).

219. Besenval, *Mémoires*, 1:291–92.

220. Croÿ-Solre, *Journal de Cour*, 4:237.

221. Swann, *Politics and the Parlement of Paris*, 361.

222. Levron, *Destin de Madame du Barry*, 67; Lever, *Marie Antoinette*, 60.

223. Belleval, *Souvenirs d'un Chevau-Léger*, 131.

224. Vatel discusses the two cases that follow in *Histoire de Madame Du Barry*, 1: chaps. 17 and 18.

225. Ibid., 1:250.

226. Belleval, *Souvenirs d'un Chevau-Léger*, 128–31. Vatel recounts the

same story in *Histoire de Madame du Barry*, 1: 299–307.

227. Espinchal, *Journal d'émigration*, 149.

228. See Darnton, *Forbidden Best-Sellers*, chap. 5; Maza, "Diamond Necklace Affair Revisited," 77–79; Levron, *Destin de Madame du Barry*, 60–64.

229. Dietrich, *Maîtresses de Louis XV*, 50, 51–52.

230. On the details of her conviction and execution, see Levron, *Destin de Madame du Barry*, 197–242.

231. Vatel, *Histoire de Madame Du Barry*, 1:221. Robert Darnton notes that the tone of the *Anecdotes sure Mme la comtesse du Barry* underscored the total corruption of the court during her time as maîtresse officielle (*Forbidden Best-Sellers*, 162–63).

232. *Précis historique*, 82.

233. Maza, "Diamond Necklace Affair Revisited," 79.

234. *Précis historique*, 76–77.

235. Ligne, *Old French Court Memoirs*, 2:244.

236. Espinchal, *Journal d'émigration*, 149.

237. Champion, *Dame de beauté*, 92–95. Agnès's tomb was destroyed during the Revolution and later restored. It remains today in the same church, which has been renamed Saint-Ours de Loches.

EPILOGUE

1. See Lever, *Marie Antoinette*, 16–21.

2. Thomas, *Wicked Queen*, 97–98.

3. Lever, *Marie Antoinette*, 40–41, 92–94, 107–14, 119–20.

4. "In a court environment with neither a dowager queen nor an acknowl-edged royal mistress to serve as an alternate source of court patronage, the sovereign's wife attracted intense scrutiny from both courtiers and members of the public who were able to visit Versailles." Carolyn Harris, *Queenship and Revolution*, 110.

5. Ibid.

6. Thomas, *Wicked Queen*, 22.

7. The term "Queen of Fashion" comes from the title of Weber, *Queen of Fashion*, who in turn borrowed it from a chapter in

Chantal Thomas's *Wicked Queen*. On the portraits of Marie Antoinette, her choice of dress in them, and their impact on the public, see Sheriff, "Portrait of the Queen."

8. Weber, *Queen of Fashion*, 5.

9. Thomas, *Wicked Queen*, 98.

10. "As a vulnerable target of calumny, Marie-Antoinette merely took over from Mme du Barry, King Louis XV's last favorite" (Thomas, *Wicked Queen*, 13). Carolyn Harris quotes from a 1781 pamphlet that directly compared the two women, "similar again in the art of deceit and degrading those who should respect her" (*Queenship and Revolution*, 112).

11. Thomas, *Wicked Queen*, 47; Maza, "Diamond Necklace Affairs Revisited," 81.

12. Swann, *Exile, Imprisonment, or Death*, 257–58, 420–22; Kaiser, "Who's Afraid of Marie-Antoinette?," 253–55.

13. Quoted in Thomas, *Wicked Queen*, 38.

14. Campan, *Mémoires*, 37–38.

15. Kaiser, "From the Austrian Committee," 586.

16. Kaiser writes, "Although she was not the architect of her own situation, Marie-Antoinette, through her own political indiscretions, did little to improve it. In particular, she made herself vulnerable to the charge of disloyalty through her pronounced Austrian tastes and occasional advocacy of Austrian foreign interests before the king. Previous French queens had generally sought to submerge their foreign backgrounds upon marriage. By contrast, Marie-Antoinette flaunted her Austrian origins" ("From the Austrian Committee," 586).

17. Colin Jones, *Great Nation*, 440, 449.

18. For this perspective, see Hunt, "Many Bodies of Marie-Antoinette"; Maza, "Diamond Necklace Affairs Revisited"; Colwill, "Just Another Citoyenne?"

19. Kaiser, "From the Austrian Committee," and "Who's Afraid of Marie-Antoinette?," 242–43.

20. Thomas, *Wicked Queen*, 133.

21. Hunt, "Many Bodies of Marie-Antoinette," 118, 121.

MANUSCRIPT SOURCES

Archives nationales du Royaume de Belgique
Papiers d'État et d'Audience 1610

Bibliothèque nationale de France
Français 2082, 3139, 8224, 13429
Nouvelles acquisitions françaises 9175

Mantova Achivio di Stato
Archivio Gonzaga di Mantova, carteggio
d'inviati et diversi 638

Modena Archivio di Stato
Cancellaria, Sezzione Estero Carteggio di
Ambasciatori Francia 16, 17, 20, 24

Österreichische Nationalbibliothek
Codex 2645

Österreichisches Staatsarchiv, Haus-,
Hof- und Staatsarchiv
Staatenabteilungen, Diplomatische Korre-
spondenz Frankreich
        Berichte, Weisungen 9, 10

PERIODICALS

Gazette d'Amsterdam
Mercure galant
Revue du Louvre et des musées de France
Spectator, The

PRIMARY SOURCES

Ableiges, Jacques d'. *Le grand coutumier de*
France. Edited by Édouard

Laboulaye and Rodolphe Dareste de
    la Chavanne. Paris: A. Durand, 1868.
Acta Nuntiaturae Gallicae. 17 vols. Rome:
    Presses de l'Université Grégorienne /
    École française de Rome; Paris:
    Boccard, 1961–2002.
Albéri, Eugenio. *Relazioni degli ambasciatori*
    Veneti al Senato. Series I. 6 vols.
    Florence: Segna di Clio, 1839–63.
Aliénor de Poitiers. *Les honneurs de la cour:*
    Mémoires sur l'ancienne Chevalerie.
    Edited by Jean-Baptiste de La Curne
    de Sainte-Palaye. 3 vols. Paris: N.-B.
    Duchesne, 1759–81.
Argenson, René-Louis de Voyer. *Journal et*
    mémoires du marquis d'Argenson.
    Edited by Edmé-Jacques-Benoît
    Rathery. 9 vols. Paris: Renouard,
    1859–67.
Arlier, Antoine. *Correspondance d'Antoine*
    Arlier: Humaniste languedocien,
    1527–1545. Edited by Jan Noble
    Pendergrass. Geneva: Droz, 1990.
Arneth, Alfred von, and Auguste Geffroy,
    eds. *Correspondance secrète entre*
    Marie-Thérèse et le comte de
    Mercy-Argenteau. 3 vols. Paris:
    Firmin-Didot frères, fils, 1874.
Aubigné, Théodore Agrippa d'. *L'Histoire*
    universelle du sieur d'Aubigné. 3 vols.
    Amsterdam: pour les héritiers de
    Hier. Commelin, 1626.
Au Roy et a la Royne regente sa mere, sur
    l'execrable parricide, commis en la
    personne du deffunct roy, Henry le

Grand de tres-heureuse et tres louable
   mémoire. Pamphlet, 1611, n.p.
Baïf, Jean-Antoine de. *Œuvres en rime de*
   Jean-Antoine de Baïf. Edited by
   Charles Marty-Laveaux. 5 vols. Paris:
   Alphonse Lemerre, 1881–90.
Baschet, Armand. *La diplomatie vénitienne,*
   les princes de l'Europe au XVIe siècle
   d'après les rapports des ambassadeurs
   vénitiens. Paris: Plon, 1862.
Basin, Thomas. *Histoire des règnes de Charles*
   VII et de Louis XI. Edited by Jules
   Quicherat. 4 vols. Paris: Renouard,
   1855–59.
Bassompierre, François de. *Journal de ma*
   vie: Mémoires du maréchal de
   Bassompierre. Edited by Audoin de
   Chantérac. 4 vols. Paris: Renouard,
   1870–77.
Baudouin-Matuszek, Marie-Noëlle, ed.
   Catalogue des actes d'Henri II. 7 vols.
   Paris: Editions du CNRS,
   1978–2010.
Beatis, Antonio de. *Voyage du cardinal*
   d'Aragon en Allemagne, Hollande,
   Belgique, France et Italie (1517–1518).
   Translated by Madeleine Havard de
   la Montagne. Paris: Perrin, 1913.
Beaumanoir, Philippe de. *Coutumes de*
   Beauvaisis. Edited and introduction
   by Amédée Salmon. 2 vols. Paris:
   Picard, 1899–1900.
Belleval, Louis René de. *Souvenirs d'un*
   Chevau-Léger de la garde du roi.
   Edited by René de Belleval, son
   arrière-petit-fils. Paris: Aug. Aubry,
   1866.
Berly, Cécile, ed. *Lettres de Madame de*
   Pompadour: Portrait d'une favorite
   royale. Paris: Perrin, 2014.
Bernis, François-Joachim de Pierre de.
   Mémoires et lettres de
   François-Joachim de Pierre, Cardinal
   de Bernis (1715–1758). Edited by
   Frédéric Masson. Paris: Plon, 1878.
Besenval, Pierre-Victor de. *Mémoires du*
   Baron de Besenval, avec une notice sur
   sa vie, des notes et des éclaircissemens
   historiques. Edited by Saint-Albin

Berville et François Barrière. 2 vols.
   Paris: Baudouin Frères, 1821–23.
Bourdigné, Jean de. *Chroniques d'Anjou et*
   du Maine. Edited and introduction
   by Théodore de Quatrebarbes. 2
   vols. Angers: Cosnier & Lachèse,
   1842.
Brantôme, Pierre de Bourdeille, seigneur de
   Brantôme. *Memoires de Messire Pierre*
   de Bourdeille, Seigneur de Brantome:
   Contenans les vies des hommes illustres
   et grands capitaines estrangers de son
   temps. 2 vols. Leyden: Jean Sambix le
   Jeune, 1666.
———. *Œuvres complètes*. Edited by
   Ludovic Lalanne. 11 vols. Paris:
   Renouard, 1864–82.
Brewer, J. S., ed. *Letters and Papers, Foreign*
   and Domestic, Henry VIII. 21 vols.
   London: Her Majesty's Stationery
   Office, 1875–1910.
Budé, Guillaume. *Le Livre de l'institution du*
   prince . . . faict et composé par M.
   Guillaume Budé. Paris: J. Foucher,
   1547.
Bueil, Jean de. *Le Jouvencel par Jean de*
   Bueil, suivi du commentaire de
   Guillaume Tringant. Edited by Léon
   Lecestre. Introduction by Camille
   Favre. 2 vols. Paris: Renouard,
   1887–89.
Bussy-Rabutin, Roger, comte de. *Correspon-*
   dance de Roger de Rabutin, comte de
   Bussy avec sa famille et ses amis:
   1666–1693: Nouvelle Édition revue sur
   les manuscrits et augmentée d'un
   très-grand nombre de lettres inédites
   avec une préface, des notes et des tables.
   Edited by Ludovic Lalanne. 6 vols.
   Paris: Charpentier, Libraire-Éditeur,
   1858–59.
———. *Les Mémoires de messire Roger de*
   Rabutin, comte de Bussy. Paris:
   Rigaud, 1731.
Calendar of State Papers Relating to English
   Affairs in the Archives of Venice.
   Edited by Rawdon Brown. 38 vols.
   London: Her Majesty's Stationery
   Office, 1864–1947.

Calendar of State Papers, Spain. Edited by Pascual de Gayangos. 13 vols. London: Her Majesty's Stationery Office, 1879–1954.

Campan, Jeanne-Louise-Henriette. *Mémoires de Madame Campan, Première femme de chambre de Marie Antoinette*. Edited by Jean Chalon and Carlos de Angulo. Paris: Ramsay, 1979.

Canestrini, Giuseppe, and Abel Desjardins, eds. *Négociations diplomatiques de la France avec la Toscane*. 6 vols. Paris: Imprimerie impériale (then nationale), 1859–86.

Castiglione, Baldassare. *The Book of the Courtier*. Translated and introduction by George Bull. 1967; reprint, London: Penguin, 1976.

Catherine de Médicis. *Lettres de Catherine de Médicis*. Edited by Hector de la Ferrière and Gustave Baguenault de Puchesse. 11 vols. Paris: Imprimerie nationale, 1880–1943.

Caylus, Marthe-Marguerite Le Valois de Villette de Murçay, comtesse de. *Souvenirs et correspondance de Madame de Caylus*. Edited by Émile Raunié. Paris: G. Charpentier, 1881.

Cellini, Benvenuto. *The Autobiography of Benvenuto Cellini*. Translated and introduction by George Bull. London: Penguin Classics, 1999.

Chappuys, Claude. *Discours de la court*. Paris: André Roffer, 1543.

Chartier, Jean. *Chronique de Charles VII, roi de France*. Edited and introduction by Auguste Vallet de Viriville. 3 vols. Paris: P. Jannet, 1858.

Chastellain, Georges. *Œuvres de Georges Chastellain*. Edited by Joseph Kervyn de Lettenhove. 8 vols. Brussels: Heussner, 1863–66.

Chiverny, Philippe Hurault, comte de. *Mémoires de Chiverny, chancelier de France sous les rois Henri III et Henri IV*. 2 vols. The Hague: T. Johnson, 1720.

Choisy, François-Timoléon, l'abbé de. *Mémoires pour servir à l'histoire de Louis XIV par feu M. l'Abbé de Choisy: Mémoires de l'Abbé de Choisy habillé en femme*. Edited by George Mongrédien. Paris: Mercure de France, 1979.

Christine de Pizan. *La città delle dame*. Edited and translated by Patrizia Caraffi and E. J. Richards. Milan: Luni Editrice, 1997.

———. *Le ditié de Jehanne d'Arc*. Edited by Angus J. Kennedy and Kenneth Varty. Medium Aevum Monographs, New Series 9. 1977; reprint, Oxford: Society for the Study of Mediaeval Languages and Literature, 2003.

———. *Le livre de la mutacion de fortune*. Edited by Suzanne Solente. 4 vols. Paris: Picard, 1955–61.

———. *Le livre des trois vertus*. Edited by Charity Cannon Willard. Paris: Champion, 1989.

Commynes, Philippe. *Mémoires de Philippe Commynes*. Edited by Emilie Dupont. 3 vols. Paris: Renouard, 1840.

Condé, Henri Jules de Bourbon, and Louis de Bourbon Condé. *Le Grand Condé et le duc d'Enghien: Lettres inédites à Marie-Louise de Gonzague, reine de Pologne, sur la cour de Louis XIV (1660–1667)*. Edited by Émile Magne. Paris: Émile-Paul, Frères, 1920.

Croÿ-Solre, Emmanuel de. *Journal de Cour, 1718–1784*. Edited by Laurent Sortais. 6 vols. Paris: Paleo, 2004–5.

Dangeau, Philippe de Courcillon, marquis de. *Journal du marquis de Dangeau publié en entier pour la première fois par MM. Soulié, Dussieux, de Chennevières, Mantz, de Montaiglon, avec les additions du Duc de Saint-Simon, publiées par M. Feuillet de Conches*. 19 vols. Paris: Firmin Didot, Frères, 1854–60.

De Thou, Jacques Auguste. *Histoire universelle de Jacques Auguste de Thou, depuis 1543, jusqu'en 1607. Traduite sur l'édition latine de Londres*. Continued by Nicolas Rigault. 16 vols. London, 1734.

Diane de Poitiers. *Lettres inédite de Dianne de Poytiers.* Introduction and edited by Georges Guiffrey. Paris: Renouard, 1866.

Discours merveilleux de la vie, actions et desportemens de Catherine de Médicis. Pamphlet, 1575, n.p.

Du Clercq, Jacques. *Mémoires: Choix de chroniques et mémoires relatives à l'histoire de la France.* Edited by Jean-Alexandre Bûchon. Orléans: H. Herluison, 1875.

Dufort de Cheverny, Jean-Nicolas. *Mémoires sur les règnes de Louis XV et Louis XVI et sur la Révolution.* Edited by Robert de Crevecoeur. 2 vols. Paris: Plon, Nourrit, 1886.

Du Pont de Nemours, Pierre Samuel. *The Autobiography of Du Pont de Nemours.* Translated by Elizabeth Fox-Genovese. Wilmington, Del.: Scholarly Resources, 1984.

Dupuy, Pierre. *Traité de la majorité de nos rois, et des régences du royaume.* Paris: Mathurin Du Puis, 1655.

Du Tillet, Jean. *La chronique des roys de France, dupuis Pharamond jusques au Roy Henry second du nom.* Paris: Galiot de Pre, 1549.

Élisabeth-Charlotte, duchesse d'Orléans. *Mémoires sur la cour de Louis XIV et de la Régence.* Paris: Ponthieu, 1823.

Escouchy, Mathieu d'. *La Chronique de Mathieu d'Escouchy.* Edited by Gaston du Fresne de Beaucourt. 3 vols. Paris: Renouard, 1863–64.

Espinchal, Thomas, comte d'. *Journal d'émigration du comte d'Espinchal publié d'après les manuscrits originaux.* Edited by Ernest d'Hauterive. Paris: Perrin, 1912.

Ferron, Arnoul le. *De rebus gestis Gallorum.* Paris: Vascosanus, 1549.

Feuquières, Antoine de Pas, marquis de. *Mémoires sur la guerre écrits par feu Mons. Le Marquis de Feuquières, Lieutenant-Général des Armées de France, pour l'Instruction de son fils.* 2nd ed. 3 vols. Amsterdam: J. F. Bernard, 1735.

Flammermont, Jules. *Les correspondances des agents diplomatiques étrangers en France avant la Révolution conservées dans les archives de Berlin, Dresde, Genève, Turin, Gênes, Florence, Naples, Simancas, Lisbonne, Londres, La Hayes et Vienne.* Paris: Imprimerie nationale, 1896.

Frederick II, King of Prussia. *Anti-Machiavel, ou essai critique sur le Prince de Machiavel, publié par Voltaire.* Amsterdam: Jaques la Caze, 1741.

Gacon-Dufour, Marie Armande Jeanne. *Mémoires, anecdotes secrètes, galantes, historiques et inédites, sur Mesdames de La Vallière, de Montespan, de Fontanges, de Maintenon, et autres illustres personnages du siècle de Louis XIV.* 2 vols. Paris: Chez Léopold Collin, 1807.

Gaguin, Robert. *Les croniques de France, excellens faictz et vertueux gestes des très chrestiens roys et princes qui ont régné au dict pays, depuis l'exidion de Troye la grande jusques au règne du . . . roy Françoys premier.* Translated into French by Pierre Desrey. Paris: Galliot Du Pré, 1515.

Gassot, Jules. *Sommaire mémorial de Jules Gassot, secrétaire du roi, 1555–1625.* Edited by Pierre Champion. Paris: Champion, 1934.

Godefroy, Théodore. *Le Cérémonial françois.* 2 vols. Paris: Cramoisy, 1649.

Goncourt, Edmond de, and Jules de Goncourt. *La femme aux dix-huitième siècle.* 1862; reprint, Paris: Flammarion, 1982.

Goulart, Simon. *Mémoires de la Ligue.* 6 vols. Amsterdam: Arkstée & Merkus, 1758.

Guiffrey, Georges, ed. *Cronique du roy Françoys, premier de ce nom.* Paris: Renouard, 1860.

Haillan, Bernard Girard du. *Histoire générale des roys de France.* 2 vols. Paris: Sonnius, 1627.

Henri IV. *Lettres d'amour, 1580–1610.* Edited by Françoise Kermina. Paris: Tallandier, 2010.

————. *Recueil des lettres missives de Henri IV.* Edited by Jules Berger de Xivrey. 9 vols. Paris: Imprimerie royale (later impériale), 1843–58.

Héroard, Jean. *Journal de Jean Héroard sur l'enfance et la jeunesse de Louis XIII (1601–1628) extrait des manuscrits originaux.* Edited by Eudoxe Soulié and Edouard de Barthélemy. 2 vols. Paris: Firmin Didot, 1868.

"Histoire d'Agnès Sorel, tirée des meilleurs ouvrages historiques concernant le règne de Charles VII." *Bibliothèque Universelle du roman* (October 1778): 115–206.

Journal d'un bourgeois de Paris (1405–1449). Edited by Alexandre Tuetey. Paris: Champion, 1881.

Journal d'un bourgeois de Paris sous le règne de François Premier (1515–1536). Edited by Ludovic Lalanne. Paris: Renouard, 1854.

Kaunitz-Rietberg, Wenzel Anton, Fürst von. "Mémoire sur la cour de France." *Revue de Paris* 11 (1904): 441–54, 827–47.

Kendall, Paul Murray, and Vincent Ilardi, ed. and trans. *Dispatches with Related Documents of Milanese Ambassadors in France and Burgundy.* 3 vols. DeKalb: Northern Illinois University Press, 1971.

La Beaumelle, Laurent Angliveil de, l'abbé Berthier de. *Mémoires pour servir à l'histoire de Madame de Maintenon et à celle du siècle passé.* 6 vols. Amsterdam, 1755–56.

La Fare, Charles-Auguste. *Mémoires et réflexions sur le principaux événemens du règne de Louis XIV, et sur le caractère de ceux qui y ont eu la principale part; par le Marquis de La Fare. Nouvelle collection des mémoires pour servir à l'histoire de France,* 8, 3rd series. Edited by Joseph-François Michaud and Jean-Joseph-François Poujoulat. Paris: Ed. du commentaire analytique du Code civil, 1836–39.

La Fayette, Marie-Madeleine Pioche de La Vergne, Countess of. *The Secret History of Henrietta, Princess of England, first Wife of Philippe, Duc d'Orléans together with Memoirs of the Court of France for the Years 1688–1689.* Edited and translated by J. M. Shelmerdine. New York: Howard Fertig, 1993.

La Marche, Olivier de. *Les Mémoires de Messire Olivier de La Marche,* vol. 9–10 of *Des Mémoires relatifs à l'Histoire de France.* Edited by Claude Bernard Petitot. Paris: Foucault, 1825.

La Perrière, Guillaume. *Le théâtre des bons engins, auquel sont contenus cent emblèmes.* Paris: Janot, 1539.

Le Clerc, Jean. *Cronique Martiniane.* Edited by Pierre Champion. Paris: Champion, 1907.

Le Franc, Abel, and Jacques Boulenger, eds. *Comptes de Louise de Savoie (1515, 1522): Et de Marguerite d'Angoulême (1512, 1517, 1524, 1529, 1539).* Paris: Champion, 1905.

Le Glay, André, ed. *Négotiations diplomatiques entre la France et l'Autriche.* 2 vols. Paris: Imprimerie royale, 1845.

Le Laboureur, Jean. *Les mémoires de Messire Michel de Castelnau.* 3 vols. Brussels: Jean Leonard, 1731.

Leschassier, Jacques. *Du droit de nature.* Paris: Claude Morel, 1601.

L'Estoile, Pierrre de. *Mémoires-journaux, 1574–1611: Reproduction intégrale de l'édition Jouaust et Lemerre complétée des inédits découverts ultérieurement.* 12 vols. Paris: Tallandier, 1982.

Letters and Papers, Foreign and Domestic, Henry VIII. 21 vols. Edited by J. S. Brewer. London: Her Majesty's Stationery Office, 1875–1910.

Ligne, Charles Joseph. *Old French Court Memoirs: The Prince de Ligne: His Memoirs, Letters, and Miscellaneous Papers.* Edited by Katharine Wormeley Prescott. 2 vols. New York: Brentano's, 1899.

Loret, Jean. *La muze historique, ou Recueil des lettres en vers contenant les nouvelles du temps : écrites à Son Altesse Mademoizelle de Longueville, depuis duchesse de Nemours (1650–1665).* Paris: P. Jannet, P. Daffis, and H. Champion, 1857–91.

Louis XIV. *Mémoires for the Instruction of the Dauphin.* Edited and translated by Paul Sonnino. New York: The Free Press / London: Collier-Macmillan, 1970.

Louise de Savoie. *Louise de Savoie: Journal (1459–1522).* Edited by Pascal Dumaih. Paris: Paleo, 2006.

Louise-Marguerite de Lorraine, Princess of Conti. *L'histoire des amours de Henri IV avec diverses lettres écrites à ses maistresses, et autres pièces curieuses.* Leiden: Jean Sambyx, 1665.

Luynes, Charles-Philippe-Albert de. *Mémoires du duc de Luynes sur la Cour de Louis XV (1735–1758).* Edited by Louis Dussieux and Eudore Soulié. 17 vols. Paris: Firmin-Didot frères, 1860–65.

Marguerite de Navarre. *Lettres de Marguerite d'Angoulême, soeur de François Ier, reine de Navarre.* Edited by François Génin. Paris: J. Renouard, 1841.

———. *Nouvelles lettres de la reine de Navarre: Adressées au roi François Ier, son frère.* Edited by François Génin. Paris: J. Renouard, 1842.

Marguerite de Valois. *Mémoires et autres écrits, 1574–1614.* Edited by Eliane Viennot. Paris: Champion, 1999.

Marmontel, Jean-François. *Mémoires de Marmontel.* Edited by Maurice Toureaux. 3 vols. Paris: Librairie des bibliophiles, 1891.

Marot, Clément. *Œuvres poétiques de Clément Marot.* 2 vols. Edited by Gérard Defaux. Paris: Bordas, 1990–93.

Masselin, Jean. *Journal des états généraux de France tenus à Tours en 1484 sous le règne de Charles VIII.* Edited and translated into French by Adhelm

Bernier. Paris: Imprimerie royale, 1835.

Mézeray, François Eudes de. *Histoire de France depuis Faramond jusqu'au règne de Louis le juste.* 3 vols. Paris: Denys Thierry, 1685.

Montaigne, Michel de. *Essais.* Edited by Alexandre Micha. 3 vols. Paris: Garnier-Flammarion, 1979.

Montpensier, Anne-Marie-Louise d'Orléans, duchesse de. *Mémoires de Mademoiselle de Montpensier, petite-fille de Henri IV.* 4 vols. Paris: Charpentier, 1858–68.

Mornay, Philippe de. *Mémoires et correspondances: Pour servir à l'histoire de la réformation et des guerres civiles et religieuses en France.* Edited by A.-D. de La Fontenelle de Vaudoré and P.-R. Auguis. 12 vols. Geneva: Slatkine Reproductions, 1969.

Motteville, Françoise de. *Mémoires de Madame de Motteville. Nouvelle collection des mémoires pour servir à l'histoire de France*, 10, 2nd series. Edited by Joseph-François Michaud and Jean-Joseph-François Poujoulat. Paris: Ed. du commentaire analytique du Code civil, 1836–39.

Les Ordonnances des rois de France de la troisième race. Edited by Denis-François Secousse. 21 vols. Paris: L'Imprimerie nationale, 1723–1849.

Petit de Bachaumont, Louis. *Mémoires secrets pour servir à l'histoire de la République des Lettres en France, depuis MDCCLXII, ou Journal d'un observateur, contenant les analyses des pièces de théâtre qui ont paru durant cet intervalle, les relations des assemblée littéraires.* 18 vols. London: John Adamson, 1783–89.

Piccolomini, Enea Silvio. *Pii secundi pontificis maximi commentarii rerum memorabilium, quae temporibus suis contigerunt.* Frankfurt: Officina Aubriana, 1614.

Pintoin, Michel. *La Chronique du Religieux de Saint-Denys contenant le règne de*

Charles VI, de 1380–1422. Edited and translated by Louis Bellaguet. 2nd ed. 6 vols. Paris: Éditions du Comité des travaux historiques et scientifiques, 1994.

Précis historique de la vie de Madame la comtesse Du Barry avec son portrait. Paris, 1774.

Recueil des traitez de paix, de trève, de neutralité, d'alliance et de commerce, faits entre la France et les maisons de Bourgogne, d'Arragon et d'Autriche, depuis l'an 1435 jusqu'à l'an 1598. Edited by Frédéric Léonard. 6 vols. Paris, 1693.

Ribier, Guillaume. *Lettres et memoires d'Estat, des roys, princes, ambassadeurs, et autres ministres, sous les regnes de François premier, Henry II et François II.* Blois: J. Hotot, 1666.

Robert, Ulysse. *Le cabinet historique: Revue mensuelle contenant, avec un texte et des pièces inédites, intéressantes ou peu connues, le catalogue général des manuscrits que renferment les bibliothèques publiques de Paris et des départements, touchant l'histoire de l'ancienne France et de ses diverses localités.* 29 vols. Paris: Au bureau du Cabinet historique, 1854–83.

Sainte-Beuve, Charles-Augustin de, ed. *Memoirs and Letters of Cardinal de Bernis.* Translated by Katherine Prescott Wormeley. 2 vols. Boston: Hardy, Pratt, 1901.

Sainte-Marthe, Scévole, and Louis Sainte-Marthe. *Histoire généalogique de la maison de France . . . avec les illustres familles qui sortent des roynes et princesses du sang.* 2 vols. Paris: Cramoisy, 1647.

Saint-Maurice, Thomas-François Chabod, marquis de. *Lettres sur la Cour de Louis XIV.* Edited by Jean Lemoine. 2 vols. Paris: Calmann-Lévy, 1911–12.

Saint-Simon, Louis de Rouvroy, duc de. *Mémoires du duc de Saint-Simon.* Edited by Yves Coirault. 2 vols. Paris: Gallimard, 1990.

Sancy, Nicolas de Harlay de. *Discours sur l'occurrence de ses affaires.* Edited by Gilbert Schrenck. Paris: Champion, 2000.

Saulx-Tavannes, Jean de. *Mémoires de très noble et très illustre Gaspard de Saulx, seigneur de Tavannes. Nouvelle collection des mémoires pour servir à l'histoire de France,* 8, 1st series. Edited by Joseph-François Michaud and Jean-Joseph-François Poujoulat. Paris: Ed. du commentaire analytique du Code civil, 1836–39.

Scève, Maurice. *The Entry of Henri II into Lyon September 1548.* A facsimile with introduction by Richard Cooper. Tempe: Arizona State University Press, 1997.

Schlitter, Hans, ed. *Correspondance secrète entre le comte A. W. Kaunitz-Rietberg, ambassadeur impérial à Paris, et le baron Ignaz de Koch, secrétaire de l'Impératrice Marie-Thérèse, 1750–1752.* Paris: Plon, 1899.

Sévigné, Marie de Rabutin-Chantal, marquise de. *Lettres de Madame de Sévigné, de sa famille, et de ses amis.* Edited by Pierre Gault-de-St.-Germain. 12 vols. Paris: Chez Dalibon, 1823.

Sorel, Charles. *La solitude et l'amour philosophique de Cléomède, premier sujet des exercices moraux.* Paris: A. de Sommaville, 1640.

Sourches, Louis François de Bouschet, marquis de. *Mémoires sur le règne de Louis XIV.* Edited by Gabriel-Jules de Cosnac. 2 vols. Clermont-Ferrand: Éditions Paleo, 2010.

Spanheim, Ézéchiel. *Relation de la Cour de France en 1690.* Edited by Émile Bourgeois and Michel Richard. Paris: Mercure de France, 1973.

State Papers, Published Under the Authority of His Majesty's Commission . . . King Henry the Eighth. 5 parts in 12 vols. London: J. Murray, 1830–52.

Sully, Maximilien de Béthune, duc de. *Mémoire des sages et royales oeconomies d'estat. Nouvelle collection des mémoires pour servir à l'histoire de France*, 2, 2nd series. 2 vols. Edited by Joseph-François Michaud and Jean-Joseph-François Poujoulat. Paris: Ed. du commentaire analytique du Code civil, 1836–39.

———. *Mémoires du duc de Sully*. 6 vols. Paris: E. Ledoux, 1822.

Tallemant des Réaux, Gédéon. *Les historiettes de Tallemant Des Réaux: Mémoires pour servir à l'histoire du XVIIᵉ siècle*. Edited by Louis Jean Nicolas Monmerqué. 6 vols. Paris: A. Levavasseur, 1834–35.

Unton, Sir Henry. *Correspondence of Sir Henry Unton, ambassador from Queen Elizabeth to Henry IV King of France, in the Years MDXCI and MDXCII*. Edited by Joseph Stevenson. London: W. Nicol, 1847.

Varillas, Antoine. *Histoire de François Ier*. 2 vols. Paris: Barbin, 1685.

Venturi, A. "Nuovi documenti." *Archivio storico dell'arte* 2 (1890): 377–78.

Visconti, Primi. *Mémoires sur la Cour de Louis XIV, 1673–1688*. Introduction and notes by Jean-François Solnon. Paris: Librairie Académique Perrin, 1988.

Voltaire. *Œuvres de Voltaire*. Edited by Adrien-Jean-Quentin Beuchot. 72 vols. Paris: Firmin Didot frères and Werdet et Lequien fils, 1830–34.

———. *La Pucelle, or, the Maid of Orleans: A Poem in XXI Cantos*. Translated by Charles William Bury. 2 vols. London, 1796–97.

SECONDARY SOURCES

Adams, Christine. "'Belle comme le jour': Beauty, Power, and the King's Mistress." *French History* 29, no. 2 (2015): 161–81.

Adamson, John. "Introduction: The Making of the Ancien-Régime Court." In *The Princely Courts of Europe: Ritual, Politics, and Culture Under the Ancien Régime, 1500–1750*, edited by John Adamson, 7–41.

London: Weidenfeld & Nicolson, 1999.

Akkerman, Nadine, and Birgit Houben, eds. *The Politics of Female Households: Ladies-in-Waiting Across Early Modern Europe*. Leiden: Brill, 2014.

Alduy, Cécile. *Politique des "amours": Poétique et genèse d'un genre français nouveau (1544–1560)*. Geneva: Droz, 2007.

Algrant, Christine Pevitt. *Madame de Pompadour: Mistress of France*. New York: Grove Press, 2002.

Anselme de Sainte-Marie. *Histoire généalogique et chronologique de la maison royale de France, des pairs, grands officiers de la Couronne, de la Maison du Roy et des anciens barons du royaume*. 9 vols. Paris: La compagnie des libraires, 1726–33.

Antoine, Michel. *Louis XV*. Paris: Fayard, 1989.

Asch, Ronald. "Patronage, Friendship and the Politics of Access." In *The Key to Power? The Culture of Access in Princely Courts, 1400–1750*, edited by Dries Raeymaekers and Sebastiaan Derks, 178–201. Leiden: Brill, 2016.

Autrand, Françoise. "'Hôtel de seigneur ne vaut rien sans dame': Le marriage de Jean, comte de Poitiers, et de Jeanne d'Armagnac, 24 Juin 1360." In *Guerre, pouvoir et noblesse au Moyen Âge: Mélanges en l'honneur de Philippe Contamine*, edited by Jacques Paviot and Jacques Verger, 51–61. Paris: Presses de l'Université de Paris-Sorbonne, 2000.

Avril, François, ed. *Jean Fouquet: Peintre et enlumineur du XVᵉ siècle*. Paris: Bibliothèque nationale de France / Hazan, 2003.

Babelon, Jean-Pierre. *Henri IV*. Paris: Fayard, 1982.

Balsamo, Jean. "'Dire le paradis d'Anet': Les poètes français de la génération de 1550 et l'architecture." In *Travaux de littérature XII: Architectes et architecture dans la littérature française*, edited by Madeleine

Bertaud, 339–49. Paris: Klincksieck, 1999.

———. "Les poètes d'Anet." In *Henri II et les arts: Actes du colloque international, École du Louvre et Musée national de la Renaissance-Écouen, 25, 26 et 27 septembre 1997*, 417–25. Paris: École du Louvre, 2003.

Bardon, Françoise. *Diane de Poitiers et le mythe de Diane*. Paris: Presses universitaires de France, 1963.

Barnavi, Elie, Hélène Duccini, Yann Fauchois, Patrice Gueniffey, Frédéric Gugelot, François Lebrun, Guy Lobrichon, et al., eds. *Journal de la France et des Français: Chronologie politique culturelle et religieuse de Clovis à 2000*. Paris: Gallimard, 2001.

Bauer, Nicole. "The Fate of Secrets in a Public Sphere: The Comte de Broglie and the Demise of the *Secret du Roi*." *Journal of the Western Society for French History* 43 (2015): 51–65.

Baumgartner, Frederic J. *Henry II: King of France, 1547–1559*. Durham: Duke University Press, 1988.

Bayle, Pierre. *Dictionnaire historique et critique par Mr. Pierre Bayle avec la vie de l'auteur par Mr. Des Maizeaux*. 4 vols. Basel: Brandmuller, 1738.

Bell, David A. *The First Total War: Napoleon's Europe and the Birth of Warfare as We Know It*. Boston: Houghton Mifflin, 2007.

Bély, Lucien. *L'art de la paix en Europe: Naissance de la diplomatie modern, XVIᵉ–XVIIIᵉ siècle*. Paris: Presses universitaires de France, 2007.

Berger, Harry, Jr. *The Absence of Grace: Sprezzatura and Suspicion in Two Renaissance Courtesy Books*. Stanford: Stanford University Press, 2000.

Bernus, Pierre. "Le rôle politique de Pierre de Brezé au cours des dix dernières années du règne de Charles VII (1451–1461)." *Bibliothèque de l'École des Chartes* 69 (1908): 303–47.

Bertière, Simone. *Les reines de France au temps des Bourbons*. 4 vols. Paris: Éditions de Fallois, 1996.

Black, Charles Bertram. *Normandy and Picardy: Their Relics, Castles, Churches, and Footprints of William the Conqueror*. London: Adam & Charles Black, 1899.

Bluche, François. *Louis XIV*. Translated by Mark Greengrass. New York: Franklin Watts, 1990.

Bolle, Jacques. *Pourquoi tuer Gabrielle d'Estrées?* Florence: G. Barbèra, 1955.

Braudel, Fernand. "Histoire et sciences sociales: La longue durée." *Annales: Économies, Sociétés, Civilisations* 13, no. 4 (1958): 725–53.

Broglie, Albert, duc de. *L'Alliance autrichienne*. Paris: Calman-Levy, 1895.

Broomhall, Susan. "'The King and I': The Rhetoric of Power in the Letters of Diane de Poitiers." In *Women and Power at the French Court, 1483–1563*, edited by Susan Broomhall, 335–56. Amsterdam: University of Amsterdam Press, 2018.

———, ed. *Women and Power at the French Court, 1483–1563*. Amsterdam: University of Amsterdam Press, 2018.

Brousillon, Arthur Bertrand de. *La maison de Laval, 1020–1605*. 5 vols. Paris: Picard, 1895–1903.

Bruckner, Pascal, and Alain Finkielkraut. *Le nouveau désordre amoureux*. Paris: Seuil, 1977.

Bryant, Lawrence M. *The King and the City in the Parisian Royal Entry Ceremony: Politics, Ritual, and Art in the Renaissance*. Geneva: Droz, 1986.

Bryant, Mark. "Partner, Matriarch, and Minister: Mme de Maintenon of France, Clandestine Consort, 1680–1715." In *Queenship in Europe, 1660–1815*, edited by Clarissa Campbell Orr, 77–106. Cambridge: Cambridge University Press, 2004.

Butler, Rohan. *Choiseul: Father and Son, 1719–1754*. Oxford: Clarendon Press, 1980.

Carmona, Michel. *Marie de Médicis: Grandeur et chute d'une reine de France*. Paris: Fayard, 1981.

Carroll, Stuart. *Martyrs and Murderers: The Guise Family and the Making of Europe*. Oxford: Oxford University Press, 2009.

Cavailler, Paulette. "Le compte des exécuteurs testamentaires d'Agnès Sorel." *Bibliothèque de l'École des Chartes* 114 (1956): 97–114.

Chaline, Olivier. "The Kingdoms of France and Navarre: The Valois and Bourbon Courts, c. 1515–1750." In *The Princely Courts of Europe: Ritual, Politics and Culture Under the Ancien Regime, 1500–1750*, edited by John Adamson, 67–93. London: Weidenfeld & Nicolson, 1999.

Challamel, Augustin. *The History of Fashion in France; or, The Dress of Women from the Gallo-Roman Period to the Present Time*. Translated by Cashel Hoey and John Lillie. London: Sampson Low, Marston, Searle & Rivington, 1882.

Champion, Pierre. *La dame de beauté: Agnès Sorel*. Paris: Champion, 1931.

Champollion-Figeac, Aimé. *Captivité de François Ier*. Paris: Imprimerie royale, 1847.

Chang, Leah. "Spectacle, Sublimation, and Civic Pride in Scève's 'L'entree de la royne.'" *Romance Quarterly* 54, no. 2 (2007): 124–35.

Chapman, Sara. "Patronage as Family Economy: The Role of Women in the Patron-Client Network of the Phélypeaux de Pontchartrain Family, 1670–1715." *French Historical Studies* 24 (2001): 11–35.

Charlier, Gustave. "Un amour de Ronsard, Astrée." *Revue du seizième siècle* 7 (1920): 123–44.

Charlier, Philippe. "Les dents d'Agnès Sorel." *L'Information Dentaire* 25 (87) (June 22, 2005): 1512–13.

———. "Qui a tué la dame de Beauté? Étude scientifique des restes d'Agnès Sorel (1422–1450)." *Histoire des sciences médicales* 40, no. 3 (2006): 255–63.

Chartier, Roger. *The Cultural Origins of the French Revolution*. Translated by Lydia G. Cochrane. Durham: Duke University Press, 1991.

Chaussinand-Nogaret, Guy. *La vie quotidienne des femmes du roi d'Agnès Sorel à Marie Antoinette*. Paris: Hachette, 1990.

Chavarnay, Étienne ed. *Archives des missions scientifiques et littéraires: Choix de rapports et instructions publié sous les auspices du Ministère de l'Instruction publique et des Beaux-Arts*, 3rd series. Vol. 7, *Rapport sur les lettres de Louis XI et sur les documents concernant ce prince conservés dans les Archives de l'Italie*. Paris: Imprimerie nationale, 1881.

Choiseul, Étienne-François de. *Mémoires du duc de Choiseul*. Edited by Jean-Pierre Guicciardi. Notes by Philippe Bonnet. Paris: Mercure de France, 1987.

Cholcman, Tamar. *Art on Paper: Ephemeral Art in the Low Countries: The Triumphal Entry of the Archdukes Albert and Isabella into Antwerp, 1599*. Turnhout: Brepols, 2014.

Christout, Marie Françoise. *Le ballet de cour de Louis XIV, 1643–1672: Mises en scène*. Paris: Centre national de la danse, 2005.

Clément, Pierre. *Jacques Cœur et Charles VII, ou La France au XVᵉ siècle*. 2 vols. Paris: Guillaumin, 1853.

———. *Madame de Montespan et Louis XIV: Étude historique*. 2nd ed. Paris: Didier, 1868.

Clough, Cecil H. "Francis I and the Courtiers of Castiglione's *Courtier*." *European History Quarterly* 8 (1978): 23–70.

Cloulas, Ivan. *Catherine de Médicis*. Paris: Fayard, 1979.

———. *Diane de Poitiers*. Paris: Fayard, 1997.

———. *Henri II*. Paris: Fayard, 1985.

Collard, Franck. *Le crime de poison au Moyen Age*. Paris: Presses universitaires de France, 2003.

———. "Excès débilitants, passions énergisantes: La sexualité de Charles VII relève-t-elle de la pathologie politique?" In *La pathologie du pouvoir: Vices, crimes et délits des gouvernants*, edited by Patrick Gilli, 397–409. Leiden: Brill, 2016.

Colwill, Elizabeth. "Just Another *Citoyenne?* Marie-Antoinette on Trial, 1790–1793." *History Workshop* 28 (1989): 63–87.

Conley, John J. *The Suspicion of Virtue: Women Philosophers in Neoclassical France*. Ithaca: Cornell University Press, 2002.

Contamine, Philippe. *Charles VII: Une vie, une politique*. Paris: Perrin, 2017.

———. "Pouvoir et vie de cour dans la France du XVᵉ siècle: Les mignons." *Comptes rendus des séances de l'Académie des Inscriptions et Belles-Lettres* 138, no. 2 (1994): 541–54.

———. "Le Royaume de France ne peut tomber en fille: Fondements, formulation et implications d'une théorie politique." *Perspectives médiévales* 13 (1987): 67–81.

Cooper, Richard. "The Theme of War in French Renaissance Entries." In *Ceremonial Entries in Early Modern Europe: The Iconography of Power*, edited by J. R. Mulryne, 15–35. Farnham, UK: Ashgate, 2015.

Cosandey, Fanny. "La reine dans l'état modern." *Annales: Histoire, Sciences Sociale* 52 (1997): 799–820.

———. *La reine de France: Symbole et pouvoir*. Paris: Gallimard, 2000.

Cottret, Monique. "Les reines étrangères." In *Sociétés et idéologies des temps modernes: Hommage à Arlette Jouanna*, edited by Joël Fouilheron, Guy Le Thiec, and Henri Michel, 105–16. Montpellier: Université de Montpellier III, 1996.

Coward, Barry, and Julian Swann, eds. *Conspiracies and Conspiracy Theory in Early Modern Europe: From the Waldensians to the French Revolution*. Aldershot, UK: Ashgate, 2004.

Cox-Rearick, Janet. *The Collection of Francis I: Royal Treasures*. Antwerp: Fonds Mercator / New York: H. N. Abrams, 1996.

Craufurd, Quentin. *Notices sur Mesdames De La Vallière, De Montespan, De Fontanges, et De Maintenon extraites du catalogue raisonné de la Collection de portraits de M. Craufurd*. Paris: J. Gratiot, 1818.

Craveri, Benedetta. *The Age of Conversation*. Translated by Teresa Waugh. 2001; reprint, New York: New York Review of Books, 2005.

———. *Reines et favorites: Le pouvoir des femmes*. Translated into French by Éliane Deschamps-Pria. Paris: Édition France Loisirs, 2005.

Crawford, Katherine. *Perilous Performances: Gender and Regency in Early Modern France*. Cambridge: Harvard University Press, 2004.

———. "The Politics of Promiscuity: Masculinity and Heroic Representation at the Court of Henry IV." *French Historical Studies* 26 (2003): 225–52.

Crépin-Leblond, Thierry. "Sens et contresens de l'emblématique de Henri II." In *Henri II et les arts*, edited by Hervé Oursel and Julia Fritsch, 77–92. Paris: École du Louvre, 2003.

Darnton, Robert. *The Forbidden Best-Sellers of Pre-Revolutionary France*. New York: W. W. Norton, 1995.

Davis, Natalie Zemon. "Women in Politics." In *A History of Women in the West*. Vol. 3: *Renaissance and Enlightenment Paradoxes*, edited by Natalie Zemon Davis and Arlette Farge, 167–83. Cambridge: Belknap Press of Harvard University Press, 1995.

Davis, Tracy C., and Thomas Postlethwait. *Theatricality*. Cambridge: Cambridge University Press, 2003.

Decrue de Stoutz, Francis. *Anne de Montmorency, grand maître et connétable de France à la cour du roi François Ier.* Paris: Plon, 1885.

———. *Anne, duc de Montmorency, connétable et pair de France sous les rois Henri II, François II et Charles IX.* Paris: Plon, 1889.

DeJean, Joan. *The Age of Comfort: When Paris Discovered Casual—and the Modern Home Began.* New York: Bloomsbury, 2009.

———. *The Essence of Style: How the French Invented High Fashion, Fine Food, Chic Cafés, Style, Sophistication, and Glamour.* New York: Free Press, 2005.

———. *Tender Geographies: Women and the Origins of the Novel in France.* New York: Columbia University Press, 1991.

Desclozeaux, Adrien. *Gabrielle d'Estrées.* London: Arthur L. Humphreys, 1907.

———. "Gabrielle d'Estrées et Sully." *Revue Historique* 33 (1887): 241–95.

———. "Le mariage et le divorce de Gabrielle d'Estrées d'après des documents nouveaux." *Revue Historique* 30 (1886): 49–106.

Desgardins, E. *Anne de Pisseleu, duchesse d'Étampes et François Ier: Favorites des rois.* Paris: Champion, 1904.

Desnoiresterres, Gustave. *Les cours galantes.* 4 vols. Geneva: Slatkine Reprints, 1971.

Dessert, Daniel. *Le royaume de Monsieur Colbert (1661–1683).* Paris: Perrin, 2007.

Dietrich, Auguste. *Les maîtresses de Louis XV, la duchesse de Châteauroux et ses soeurs / Madame de Pompadour / La du Barry.* Vienna: Keisse, 1881.

Dodu, Gaston. "Le Drame conjugal de Catherine de Medicis." *Revue des études historiques* (1930): 89–128.

Doüet d'Arcq, Louis. "Procès criminel intenté à Jacques de Brézé, grand sénéchal de Normandie, au sujet du meurtre de sa femme (1467–1486)."

Bibliothèque de l'École des Chartes 10 (1849): 211–39.

Duby, Georges. *The Knight, the Lady, and the Priest: The Making of Modern Marriage in Medieval France.* Translated by Barbara Bray. New York: Pantheon, 1983.

Duclos, Charles. *Histoire de Louis XI.* 3 vols. Paris: Guérin, 1745.

Du Crest, Sabine. *Fêtes à Versailles: Les divertissements de Louis XIV.* Paris: Aux Amateurs de Livres / Éditions Klincksieck, 1990.

Duindam, Jeroen. *Dynasties: A Global History of Power, 1300–1800.* Cambridge: Cambridge University Press, 2016.

———. *Myths of Power: Norbert Elias and the Early Modern European Court.* Amsterdam: University of Amsterdam, 1994.

———. *Vienna and Versailles: The Courts of Europe's Dynastic Rivals, 1550–1780.* Cambridge: Cambridge University Press, 2003.

Durrieu, Paul. "Les filles d'Agnès Sorel." *Comptes rendus des séances de l'Académie des Inscriptions et Belles-Lettres* 3 (1922): 150–68.

Egginton, William. *How the World Became a Stage: Presence, Theatricality, and the Question of Modernity.* Albany: SUNY Press, 2003.

Ekberg, Carl J. *The Failure of Louis XIV's Dutch War.* Chapel Hill: University of North Carolina Press, 1979.

Elliott, John Huxtable, and L. W. B. Brockliss. *The World of the Favourite.* New Haven: Yale University Press, 1999.

Fassin, Eric. "The Purloined Gender: American Feminism in a French Mirror." *French Historical Studies* 22 (1999): 113–38.

Favreau, Robert. "Robert Poitevin, professeur à Paris, médecin des Princes, trésorier de Saint-Hilaire-le-Grand de Poitiers (v. 1390–1400 à 1474)." *Bulletin de la Société des*

antiquaires de l'Ouest et des musées de
Poitiers, 4th series, 6 (1961): 141–51.

Féral, Josette, and Ronald P. Bermingham.
"Theatricality: The Specificity of
Theatrical Language." SubStance 31
(2002): 94–108.

Fleischhauer, Wolfram. La ligne pourpre.
Translated into French by Olivier
Mattoni. Paris: Lattès, 2005.

Fleureau, Basile. Antiquités de la ville et du
duché d'Étampes. Paris: J.-B.
Coignard, 1683.

Fontenay, Elisabeth de, and Alain
Finkielkraut. En terrain miné: Une
amitié conflictuelle. Paris: Stock,
2017.

Fowler, Alastair. Renaissance Realism:
Narrative Images in Literature and
Art. Oxford: Oxford University
Press, 2003.

Fresne de Beaucourt, Gaston du. "Le
caractère de Charles VII: Troisième
partie." Revue des questions historiques
14 (1873): 61–128.

———. "Charles VII et Agnès Sorel." Revue
des questions historiques 1 (1866):
204–24.

———. Histoire de Charles VII. 6 vols.
Paris: A. Picard, 1881–91.

Fréville, Ernest de. "Notice historique sur
l'inventaire des biens meubles de
Gabrielle d'Estrées." Bibliothèque de
l'École des Chartes 3 (1842): 148–71.

Frieda, Leonie. Catherine de Medici.
London: Weidenfeld & Nicolson,
2003.

Gallet, Danielle. Madame de Pompadour ou
le pouvoir féminin. Paris: Fayard,
1985.

Gerber, Matthew. Bastards: Politics, Family,
and Law in Early Modern France.
Oxford: Oxford University Press,
2012.

Goodman, Elise. The Portraits of Madame de
Pompadour: Celebrating the Femme
Savante. Berkeley: University of
California Press, 2000.

Gordon, Alden R. "The Longest-Enduring
Pompadour Hoax: Sénac de Meilhan
and the Journal de Madame du

Hausset." In Art and Culture in the
Eighteenth Century: New Dimensions
and Multiple Perspectives, edited by
Elise Goodman, 28–38. Newark:
University of Delaware Press /
London: Associated University
Presses, 2001.

———. "Searching for the Elusive Madame
de Pompadour." Eighteenth-Century
Studies 37, no. 1 (2003): 91–111.

Gorris Camos, Rosanna. "Diane de
Guindaye, Pentasilée et les autres, ou
les Diane de Jacques Gohory." In "Le
mythe de Diane en France au XVIᵉ
siècle," edited by Jean-Raymond
Fanlo and Marie-Dominique
Legrand. Special issue, Albineana 14
(2002): 291–332.

Gough, Melinda J. Dancing Queen: Marie
de Médicis' Ballets at the Court of
Henri IV. Toronto: University of
Toronto Press, 2019.

Graham, Lisa Jane. If the King Only Knew:
Seditious Speech in the Reign of Louis
XV. Charlottesville: University Press
of Virginia, 2000.

Green, Monica. "Bodies, Gender, Health,
Disease: Recent Work on Medieval
Women's Medicine." Studies in
Medieval and Renaissance History:
Sexuality and Culture in Medieval
and Renaissance Europe. Edited by
Philip M. Soergel, 3rd series, 2
(2005): 1–46.

Grodecki, Catherine. "Sébastien Zamet,
amateur d'art." In Les arts au temps
d'Henri IV. Colloque de Fontainebleau 20 et 21 septembre 1990 organisé
par l'Association Henri IV 1989 et le
Musée national du Château de
Fontainebleau, edited by J. Perot and
P. Tucoo-Chala, 185–254. Pau:
Association Henry IV, 1992.

Guenée, Bernard, and Françoise Lehoux.
Les entrées royales françaises de 1328 à
1515. Paris: CNRS, 1968.

Guiffrey, Georges. "Un correspondant
provençal de Jean Du Bellay, Abbé
de Lérins: Denys Faucher." In

Melanges offerts à Abel Lefranc par ses élèves et ses amis. Paris: Droz, 1936.

Hamilton, Marc. "La première description de Fontainebleau." *Revue de l'Art* 91 (1991): 44–46.

Hampton, Timothy. *Fictions of Embassy: Literature and Diplomacy in Early Modern Europe.* Ithaca: Cornell University Press, 2009.

Harris, Barbara J. "Women and Politics in Early Tudor England." *Historical Journal* 33, no. 2 (1990): 259–81.

Harris, Carolyn. *Queenship and Revolution in Early Modern Europe: Henrietta Maria and Marie Antoinette.* New York: Palgrave, 2016.

Hasenclever, Adolf. "Die Geheimartikel zum Frieden von Crepy von 19. September 1544." *Zeitschrift für Kirchengeschichte* 45 (1926): 418–26.

Haslip, Joan. *Madame du Barry: The Wages of Beauty.* 1991; reprint, London: Tauris Parke Paperbacks, 2005.

Herman, Eleanor. *Sex with Kings: 500 Years of Adultery, Power, Rivalry, and Revenge.* New York: Harper Perennial, 2004.

Hérold, Michel. "Aux sources de l' 'invention': Gaultier de Campes, peintre à Paris au début du XVIᵉ siècle." *Revue de l'Art* 120 (1998): 49–57.

Hilton, Lisa. *Athénaïs: The Life of Louis XIV's Mistress, the Real Queen of France.* Boston: Little, Brown, 2002.

Hochner, Nicole. *Louis XII: Les dérèglements de l'image royale (1498–1515).* Seyssel: Champ Vallon, 2006.

Holmes, Megan. "Disrobing the Virgin: The Madonna Lactans in Fifteenth-Century Florentine Art." In *Picturing Women in Renaissance and Baroque Italy,* edited by Sara F. Matthews-Grieco and Geraldine A. Johnson, 167–95. Cambridge: Cambridge University Press, 1997.

Hooper-Hamersley, Rosamond. *The Hunt After Jeanne-Antoinette de Pompadour: Patronage, Politics, Art, and the French Enlightenment.* Lanham, Md.: Lexington Books, 2011.

Hufton, Olwen. "Reflections on the Role of Women in the Early Modern French Court." *Court Historian* 5 (2000): 1–13.

Hunt, Lynn. "The Many Bodies of Marie-Antoinette: Political Pornography and the Problem of the Feminine in the French Revolution." In *Marie-Antoinette: Writings on the Body of a Queen,* edited by Dena Goodman, 117–38. London: Routledge, 2003.

Imberdis, André. *Histoire des guerres religieuses en Auvergne, pendant les XVIᵉ et XVIIᵉ siècles.* 2 vols. Moulins: Desrosiers, 1840.

Inglis, Erik. *Jean Fouquet and the Invention of France: Art and Nation After the Hundred Years War.* New Haven: Yale University Press, 2011.

Jackson, Richard A. *Vive le roi! A History of the French Coronation from Charles V to Charles X.* Chapel Hill: University of North Carolina Press, 1984.

Jacquart, Jean. *François Ier.* Paris: Fayard, 1981.

Jacquiot, Josèphe. "De l'entrée de César à Rome à l'entrée des rois de France dans leurs bonnes villes." In *Italian Renaissance Festivals and Their European Influence,* edited by J. R. Mulryne and Margaret Shewring, 255–68. Lewiston, N.Y.: Mellen Press, 1992.

Jacquot, Jean. "Joyeuse et triomphante entrée." In *Les fêtes de la Renaissance,* edited by Jean Jacquot, 9–19. 2 vols. Paris: CNRS, 1956.

Jones, Colin. *The Great Nation: France from Louis XV to Napoleon.* London: Penguin Books, 2002.

———. *Madame de Pompadour: Images of a Mistress.* London: National Gallery / New Haven: Yale University Press, 2002.

Jones, Jennifer M. *Sexing La Mode: Gender, Fashion and Commercial Culture in*

Old Regime France. Oxford: Berg, 2004.

Jouanna, Arlette. "Faveur et favoris: L'exemple des mignons de Henri III." In *Henri III et son temps, études réunies par Robert Sauzet, actes du colloque international du Centre de la Renaissance de Tours, octobre 1989*, 155–65. Paris: J. Vrin, 1992.

Jourda, Pierre. *Marguerite d'Angoulême: Duchesse d'Alençon, reine de Navarre (1492–1549), étude biographique et littéraire*. 2 vols. 1930; reprint, Paris: Champion, 1968.

Kaiser, Thomas E. "The Austrian Alliance, the Seven Years' War, and the Emergence of a French 'National' Foreign Policy, 1756–1790." In *The Crisis of the Absolute Monarchy: France from Old Regime to Revolution*, edited by Julian Swann and Joël Félix, 167–79. Oxford: Oxford University Press, 2013.

———. "The Drama of Charles Edward Stuart, Jacobite Propaganda, and French Political Protest, 1745–1750." *Eighteenth-Century Studies* 30, no. 4 (1997): 365–81.

———. "From the Austrian Committee to the Foreign Plot: Marie-Antoinette, Austrophobia, and the Terror." *French Historical Studies* 26 (2003): 579–617.

———. "Madame de Pompadour and the Theaters of Power." *French Historical Studies* 19 (1996): 1025–44.

———. "Who's Afraid of Marie-Antoinette? Diplomacy, Austrophobia, and the Queen." *French History* 14, no. 3 (2000): 241–71.

Karagiannis-Mazeaud, Edith. "Diane chez les 'Antiquaires': Le discours sur les médailles." In "Le mythe de Diane en France au XVIᵉ siècle," edited by Jean-Raymond Fanlo and Marie-Dominique Legrand. Special issue, *Albineana* 14 (2002): 227–46.

Kauppinen, Elina. "Power, Politics and Pillowtalk: The Role of Royal Mistresses in British and French Discourses on the Legitimacy of Monarchical Rule, 1714–1774." PhD diss., University of Jyväskylä, 2019.

Kettering, Sharon. *Patrons, Brokers, and Clients in Seventeenth-Century France*. New York: Oxford University Press, 1986.

Kiernan, Linda. "Absolutely Beautiful? Madame de Pompadour and the Aesthetics of Power." In *Female Beauty Systems: Beauty as Social Capital in Western Europe and the United States, Middle Ages to the Present*, edited by Christine Adams and Tracy Adams, 187–205. Cambridge: Cambridge Scholars, 2015.

Kipling, Gordon. *Enter the King: Theatre, Liturgy, and Ritual in the Medieval Civic Triumph*. Oxford: Clarendon Press, 1998.

Kleinman, Ruth. *Anne of Austria: Queen of France*. Columbus: Ohio State University Press, 1985.

Klopp, Onno. *Der Fall des Hauses Stuart und die Succession des Hauses Hannover in Gross-Britannien und Irlande*. 14 vols. Vienna: W. Braumüller, 1875–88.

Knecht, Robert. *The French Renaissance Court, 1483–1589*. New Haven: Yale University Press, 2008.

———. *Hero or Tyrant? Henry III, King of France, 1574–89*. London: Routledge, 2014.

———. "Philippe Chabot de Brion (v. 1492–1543)." In *Les conseillers de François Ier*, edited by Cédric Michon, 463–80. Rennes: Presses universitaires de Rennes, 2011.

———. *Renaissance Warrior and Patron: The Reign of Francis I*. Cambridge: Cambridge University Press, 1994.

Kren, Thomas. "Bathsheba in French Books of Hours Made for Women, ca. 1470–1500." In *The Medieval Book: Glosses from Friends and Colleagues of Christopher de Hamel*, edited by James H. Marrow, Richard A.

Linenthal, and Andrew Noel. Houten: Hes and de Graf, 2010.

Lagerlöf, Margaretha Rossholm. *Fate, Glory, and Love in Early Modern Gallery Decoration: Visualizing Supreme Power*. Farnham, UK: Ashgate, 2013.

Lair, Jules. *Louise de La Vallière et la jeunesse de Louis XIV d'après des documents inédits*. 4th ed. Paris: Plon-Nourrit, 1907.

Lecoq, Anne-Marie. *François Ier imaginaire: Symbolique et politique à l'aube de la Renaissance française*. Paris: Editions Macula, 1987.

Le Fur, Didier. *Diane de Poitiers*. Paris: Perrin, 2015.

Le Roux, Nicolas. *La faveur du roi: Mignons et courtisans au temps des derniers Valois (vers 1547–vers 1589)*. Seyssel: Éditions Champ-Vallon, 2000.

Le Roy Ladurie, Emmanuel. *Saint-Simon and the Court of Louis XIV*. Translated by Arthur Goldhammer. Chicago: University of Chicago Press, 2001. Originally published as *Saint-Simon ou Le système de la Cour*. Paris: Le grand livre du mois, 1998.

L'Estrange, Elizabeth. "Penitence, Motherhood, and Passion Devotion: Contextualizing Anne de Bretagne's Prayer Book, Chicago Newberry Library MS 83." In *The Cultural and Political Legacy of Anne de Bretagne: Negotiating Convention in Books and Documents*, edited by Cynthia Brown, 81–98. Cambridge: D. S. Brewer, 2010.

Lever, Evelyne. *Madame de Pompadour: A Life*. 2000. Translated by Catherine Temerson. New York: Farrar, Straus & Giroux, 2002.

———. *Marie Antoinette: The Last Queen of France*. Translated by Catherine Temerson. New York: St. Martin's Griffin, 2000.

Levron, Jacques. *Le destin de Madame du Barry*. Paris: Éditions Berger-Levrault, 1961.

Lewis, Tess. "Madame de Pompadour: Eminence Without Honor." *Hudson Review* 56, no. 2 (Summer 2002): 303–14.

Liepe, Lena. "On the Epistemology of Images." In *History and Images: Towards a New Iconology*, edited by Axel Bolvig and Phillip Lindley, 415–30. Turnhout: Brepols, 2003.

Loiseleur, Jules. "La mort de Gabrielle d'Estrées d'après une relation contemporaine inédite." In *Questions historiques du XVIIème siècle: Ravaillac et ses complices*, 179–243. Paris: Didier, 1873.

Lombardi, Sandro. *Jean Fouquet*. Florence: Libreria editrice Salimbeni, 1983.

Loomis, Stanley. *Du Barry: A Biography*. London: Jonathan Cape, 1959.

Lundell, Richard. "Renaissance Diplomacy and the Limits of Empire: Eustace Chapuys, Habsburg Imperialisms, and Dissimulation as Method." In *The Limits of Empire: European Imperial Formations in Early Modern World History: Essays in Honor of Geoffrey Parker*, edited by Tonio Andrade and William Reger, 205–22. 2012; reprint, Abingdon, UK: Routledge, 2016.

Machiavelli, Niccolò. *The Prince*. Edited by Quentin Skinner and Russell Price. Cambridge: Cambridge University Press, 1988.

Mallick, Olivier. "Clients and Friends: The Ladies-in-Waiting at the Court of Anne of Austria (1615–66)." In *The Politics of Female Households: Ladies-in-Waiting Across Early Modern Europe*, edited by Nadine Akkerman and Birgit Houben, 231–64. Leiden: Brill, 2014.

Manetsch, Scott M. *Calvin's Company of Pastors: Pastoral Care and the Emerging Reformed Church, 1536–1609*. Oxford: Oxford University Press, 2013.

Marsengill, Katherine. "Identity Politics in Renaissance France: Cellini's Nymph of Fontainebleau." *Athanor* 19 (2001): 35–42.

Martin, Morag. *Selling Beauty: Cosmetics, Commerce, and French Society, 1750–1830.* Baltimore: Johns Hopkins University Press, 2009.

Marvick, Elizabeth Wirth. *Louis XIII: The Making of a King.* New Haven: Yale University Press, 1986.

Marwick, Arthur. *Beauty in History: Society, Politics, and Personal Appearance, c. 1500 to the Present.* London: Thames & Hudson, 1988.

Mathieu-Castellani, Gisèle. "La figure de Diane dans la poésie baroque et maniériste: De la dramatisation du mythe à sa décoloration." In "Le mythe de Diane en France au XVIᵉ siècle," edited by Jean-Raymond Fanlo and Marie-Dominique Legrand. Special issue, *Albineana* 14 (2002): 149–68.

Matthews-Grieco, Sara F. "The Body, Appearance, and Sexuality." In *A History of Women in the West.* Vol. 3: *Renaissance and Enlightenment Paradoxes*, edited by Natalie Zemon Davis and Arlette Farge, 46–84. Cambridge: Belknap Press of Harvard University Press, 1995.

Mattingly, Garett. *Renaissance Diplomacy.* Boston: Houghton Mifflin, 1955.

Maza, Sarah. "The Diamond Necklace Affair Revisted (1785–1786): The Case of the Missing Queen." In *Marie-Antoinette: Writings on the Body of a Queen*, edited by Dena Goodman, 73–98. London: Routledge, 2003.

———. *Private Lives and Public Affairs: The Causes Célèbres of Prerevolutionary France.* Berkeley: University of California Press, 1993.

McCloy, Shelby T. "Persecution of the Huguenots in the 18th Century." *Church History* 20, no. 3 (1951): 56–79.

McGowan, Margaret. "La fonction des fêtes dans la vie de cour au XVIIᵉ siècle." In *La cour au miroir des mémoiralistes, 1530–1682*, edited by Noémi

Hepp, 27–41. Paris: Klincksieck, 1991.

McIlvenna, Una. *Scandal and Reputation at the Court of Catherine de Medici.* London: Routledge, 2016.

———. "'A Stable of Whores'? The 'Flying Squadron' of Catherine de Medici." In *The Politics of Female Households: Ladies-in-Waiting Across Early Modern Europe*, edited by Nadine Akkerman and Birgit Houben, 181–208. Leiden: Brill, 2014.

Merlet, Lucien. "Biographie de Jean de Montagu, grand maître de France (1350–1409)." *Bibliothèque de l'Écoles des Chartes* 13 (1852): 248–84.

Merrick, Jeffrey W. *The Desacralization of the French Monarchy in the Eighteenth Century.* Baton Rouge: Louisiana State University Press, 1990.

Michelet, Jules. *Histoire de France.* 17 vols. Paris: Chamerot & Lauwereyns, 1833–67.

———. *Histoire de la révolution française.* 6 vols. Paris: Librairie internationale, 1869.

Michon, Cédric, ed. *Les conseillers de François I.* Rennes: Presses universitaires de Rennes, 2011.

———. *François Ier: Les femmes, le pouvoir et la guerre.* Paris: Belin, 2015.

Miles, Margaret R. *A Complex Delight: The Secularization of the Breast, 1350–1750.* Berkeley: University of California Press, 2008.

Moine, Marie-Christine. *Les fêtes à la cour du Roi Soleil, 1653–1715.* Paris: Fernand Lanore, 1984.

Mollenauer, Lynn Wood. *Strange Revelations: Magic, Poison, and Sacrilege in Louis XIV's France.* University Park: Pennsylvania State University Press, 2007.

Moote, A. Lloyd. *Louis XIII, the Just.* Berkeley: University of California Press, 1989.

Moréri, Louis. *Le grand dictionnaire historique, ou Le melange curieux de*

l'histoire sainte et profane. 10 vols.
Paris: Libraires Associés, 1759.

Mossiker, Frances. *The Affair of the Poisons: Louis XIV, Madame de Montespan, and One of History's Great Unsolved Mysteries*. New York: Knopf, 1969.

Murat, Ines. *Gabrielle d'Estrées*. Paris: Fayard, 1992.

Nawrocki, François. *L'amiral Claude d'Annebault, conseiller favori de François Ier*. Paris: Classiques Garnier, 2015.

———. "Le dauphin Henri (1519–1559)." In *Les Conseillers de François I*, edited by Cédric Michon, 591–97. Rennes: Presses universitaires de Rennes, 2011.

Newton, William R. *L'espace du roi: La cour de France au château de Versailles*. Paris: Arthème Fayard, 2000.

Nicolle, Jean. *Madame de Pompadour et la société de son temps*. Paris: Éditions Albatros, 1980.

Nolhac, Pierre de. *Études sur la cour de France: Madame de Pompadour et la politique d'après des documents nouveaux*. Paris: Clamann-Lévy, 1928.

Nordera, Marina. "Ballet de cour." In *The Cambridge Companion to Ballet*, edited by Marion Kant, 19–31. Cambridge: Cambridge University Press, 2011.

Offen, Karen. *The Woman Question in France, 1400–1870*. Cambridge: Cambridge University Press, 2017.

O'Malley, Charles D. "The Medical History of Louis XIV: Intimations of Mortality." In *Louis XIV and the Craft of Kingship*, edited by John C. Rule, 132–54. Columbus: Ohio State University Press, 1969.

Orr, Clara Campbell. "Rococo Queen." *History Workshop Journal* 56 (Autumn 2003): 245–50.

Ozouf, Mona. *Les mots des femmes: Essai sur la singularité française*. Paris: Fayard, 1995.

Paillard, C. "La mort de François Ier et les premiers temps du règne de Henri II

d'après Jean de Saint-Mauris, ambassadeur de Charles-Quint à la cour de France (avril–juin 1547)." *Revue historique* 5 (1877): 84–120.

Paris, Paulin. *Étude sur François premier, roi de France, sur sa vie privée et son règne*. 2 vols. Paris: Léon Techener, 1885.

Perrot, Philippe. *Le travail des apparences, ou Les transformations du corps féminin, XVIII–XIX siècles*. Paris: Éditions du Seuil, 1984.

Persels, Jeffery C. "Bragueta Humanística, or Humanism's Codpiece." *Sixteenth Century Journal* 28 (1997): 79–99.

Pétigny, Jules. "Emblèmes monétaires du règne de Henri II." *Revue numismatique* 14 (1848): 80–84.

Petitfils, Jean-Christian. *Madame de Montespan*. Paris: Fayard, 1988.

Philippe, Robert. *Agnès Sorel*. Paris: Hachette, 1983.

Pitts, Vincent J. *Henri IV of France: His Reign and Age*. Baltimore: Johns Hopkins University Press, 2009.

Plogsterth, Ann Rose. "The Institution of the Royal Mistress and the Iconography of Nude Portraiture in Sixteenth-Century France." PhD diss., Columbia University, 1991.

Poirier, Roger. *La bibliothèque universelle des romans: Rédacteurs, textes, public*. Geneva: Droz, 1976.

Pollack-Laguschenko, Timur. "The Armagnac Faction: New Patterns of Political Violence in Late Medieval France." PhD diss., Johns Hopkins University, 2004.

Pollitzer, Marcel. *Le règne des favorites*. Paris: Aubanel, 1973.

Potter, David. "Anne de Pisseleu (1508–80) maîtresse et conseillère de François I." In *Les Conseillers de François I*, edited by Cédric Michon, 535–56. Rennes: Presses universitaires de Rennes, 2011.

———. *Henry VIII and Francis I: The Final Conflict, 1540–1547*. Leiden: Brill, 2011.

———. "The Life and After-Life of a Royal Mistress, Anne de Pisseleu, Duchess of Étampes." In *Women and Power at the French Court, 1483–1563*, edited by Susan Broomhall, 311–36. Amsterdam: University of Amsterdam Press, 2018.

———. "Marriage and Cruelty Among the Protestant Nobility in Sixteenth-Century France: Diane de Barbançon and Jean de Rohan, 1561–7." *European History Quarterly* 20 (1990): 5–38.

———. "Politics and Faction at the Court of Francis I: The Duchesse d'Etampes, Montmorency and the Dauphin Henri." *French History* 21, no. 2 (2007): 127–46.

———. *War and Government in the French Provinces: Picardy, 1470–1560*. Cambridge: Cambridge University Press, 1993.

Prével, P. "Questions et réponses: Les conséquences morales de la révocation de l'Édit de Nantes. Madame de Maintenon en est-elle responsable aux yeux de l'histoire?" *Bulletin de la Société de l'Histoire du Protestantisme Français* 12 (1863): 260–61.

Ranum, Orest. *Artisans of Glory: Writers and Historical Thought in Seventeenth-Century France*. Chapel Hill: University of North Carolina Press, 1980.

Reddy, William M. *The Navigation of Feeling: A Framework for the History of Emotions*. Cambridge: Cambridge University Press, 2001.

Reid, Jonathan. "Imagination and Influence: The Creative Powers of Marguerite de Navarre at Work at Court and in the World." In *Women and Power at the French Court, 1483–1563*, edited by Susan Broomhall, 265–88. Amsterdam: University of Amsterdam Press, 2018.

———. *King's Sister—Queen of Dissent: Marguerite of Navarre (1492–1549) and Her Evangelical Network*. 2 vols. Leiden: Brill, 2009.

———. "Marguerite de Navarre and Evangelical Reform." In *A Companion to Marguerite de Navarre*, edited by Gary Ferguson and Mary B. McKinley, 29–58. Leiden: Brill, 2013.

Reinach, Salomon. "Diane de Poitiers et Gabrielle d'Estrées." *Gazette des Beaux Arts* (August–September 1920): 157–80, 249–66.

Rentet, Thierry. "Anne de Montmorency (1493–1567): Le conseiller mediocre." In *Les Conseillers de François I*, edited by Cédric Michon, 279–317. Rennes: Presses universitaires de Rennes, 2011.

———. *Anne de Montmorency: Grand maître de François Ier*. Rennes: Presses universitaires de Rennes, 2011.

Ribeiro, Aileen. *Facing Beauty: Painted Women and Cosmetic Art*. New Haven: Yale University Press, 2011.

Ritter, Raymond. *Charmante Gabrielle*. Paris: Albin Michel, 1947.

Roche, Aline. "'Une perle de pris': La maison de la reine Eléonore d'Autriche." 2010. https://courdefrance.fr/histoireetfonction/histoireetfonctionnement/structureetfonctionnement/etudesmodernes/article/uneperledeprislamaisondelareineeleonoredautriche?lang=fr.

Rohr, Zita E. *Yolande of Aragon (1381–1442). Family and Power: The Reverse of the Tapestry*. New York: Palgrave, 2016.

Romier, Lucien. "La mort de Henri II." *Revue du seizième siècle* 1 (1913): 99–152.

———. *Les origines politiques des guerres de religion*. 2 vols. Paris: Perrin, 1913–14.

Rothstein, Marian. *Reading in the Renaissance: Amadis de Gaule and the Lessons of Memory*. Newark: University of Delaware Press, 1999.

Rowlands, Guy. "The *Maison militaire du roi* and the Disintegration of the Old Regime." In *The Crisis of the Absolute Monarchy*, edited by Julian Swann and Joël Félix, 245–73. Oxford: Oxford University Press, 2013.

Roy, Émile. *La vie et les œuvres de Charles Sorel, sieur de Souvigny (1602–1674)*. Paris: Hachette, 1891.

Rozet, Albin, and J.-F. Lembey. *L'invasion de la France et le siège de Saint-Dizier par Charles-Quint en 1544, d'après les dépêches italiennes de Francesco d'Este, de Hieronymo Feruffino, de Camillo Capilupo et de Bernardo Navager*. Paris: Plon-Nourrit, 1910.

Rubin, Miri. *Mother of God: A History of the Virgin Mary*. New Haven: Yale University Press, 2009.

Ruble, Alphonse de. *Le mariage de Jeanne d'Albret*. Paris: Labitte, 1877.

Ruutz-Rees, Caroline. *Charles de Sainte-Marthe (1512–1555)*. New York: Columbia University Press, 1910.

Sarcus, Félix de. *Notice historique et descriptive sur le château de Bussy-Rabutin*. Dijon: Tracault, 1854.

Sheriff, Mary D. "The Portrait of the Queen." In *Marie-Antoinette: Writings on the Body of a Queen*, edited by Dena Goodman, 45–71. New York: Routledge, 2003.

Silverman, Deborah L. *Art Nouveau in Fin-de-Siècle France: Politics, Psychology, and Style*. Berkeley: University of California Press, 1989.

Snyder, Jon R. *Dissimulation and the Culture of Secrecy in Early Modern Europe*. Berkeley: University of California Press, 2009.

Solnon, Jean-François. *La cour de France*. Paris: Fayard, 1987.

Stephenson, Barbara. *The Power and Patronage of Marguerite de Navarre*. Aldershot, UK: Ashgate, 2004.

Swann, Julian. *Exile, Imprisonment, or Death: The Politics of Disgrace in Bourbon France, 1610–1789*. Oxford: Oxford University Press, 2017.

———. "From Servant of the King to 'Idol of the Nation': The Breakdown of Personal Monarchy in Louis XVI's France." In *The Crisis of the Absolute Monarchy*, edited by Julian Swann

and Joël Félix, 63–89. Oxford: Oxford University Press, 2013.

———. *Politics and the Parlement of Paris Under Louis XV, 1754–1774*. Cambridge: Cambridge University Press, 1995.

Syson, Luke. "Belle: Picturing Beautiful Women." In *Art and Love in Renaissance Italy*, edited by Andrea Bayer, 246–54. New York: Metropolitan Museum of Art / New Haven: Yale University Press, 2008.

Thierry, Adrien. *Diane de Poitiers*. Paris and Geneva: La Palatine, 1955.

Thomas, Chantal. *The Wicked Queen: The Origins of the Myth of Marie-Antoinette*. Translated by Julie Rose. New York: Zone Books, 1999.

Thompson, Patricia Z. "De nouveaux aperçus sur la vie de Diane de Poitiers." In "Le mythe de Diane en France au XVIe siècle," edited by Jean-Raymond Fanlo and Marie-Dominique Legrand. Special issue, *Albineana* 14 (2002): 345–60.

———. "Diane de Poitiers: A Re-assessment." *Stanford French Review* 13 (1989): 49–63.

Toudouze, Georges. *Françoise de Chateaubriant et François Ier*. Paris: Libraire Floury, 1948.

Trestrail, John H., III. *Criminal Poisoning: Investigational Guide for Law Enforcement, Toxicologists, Forensic Scientists, and Attorneys*. Totowa, N.J.: Humana Press, 2007.

Vale, Malcolm G. A. *Charles VII*. Berkeley: University of California Press, 1977.

Vallet de Viriville, Auguste. "Étude morale et politique sur le quinzième siècle." *Revue de Paris* 10 (1855): 43–49, 250–82.

———. "Notes biographiques sur Robert Poitevin, médecin des rois Charles VII et Louis XI, l'un des exécuteurs testamentaires d'Agnès Sorel." *Bibliothèque de l'École des Chartes* 11 (1850): 488–99.

———. "Odette ou Odinette de Champdivers était-elle fille d'un marchand de chevaux? Notes historiques sur ce personnage." *Bibliothèque de l'École des Chartes* 20 (1859): 171–81.

———. "Recherches historiques sur Agnès Sorel: Documents inédits ou restitués, relatifs à sa famille, à sa personne et à ses enfants." *Bibliothèque de l'École des Chartes* 11 (1849): 297–325, 477–98.

van Elden, D. J. H. *Esprits fins et esprits géometriques dans les portraits de Saint-Simon: Contribution à l'étude du vocabulaire et du style.* The Hague: Martinus Nijhoff, 1975.

Van Kerrebrouck, Patrick. *Les Capétiens, 987–1328.* Villeneuve d'Asq: Presses universitaires du Septentrion, 2000.

Van Kley, Dale. *The Jansenists and the Expulsion of the Jesuits from France, 1757–1765.* New Haven: Yale University Press, 1975.

van Krieken, Robert. *Celebrity Society.* London: Routledge, 2012.

———. *Norbert Elias.* London: Routledge, 1998.

Vatel, Charles. *Histoire de Madame Du Barry d'après ses papiers personnels et les documents des archives publiques: Précédée d'une introduction sur Madame de Pompadour, le Parc-aux-cerfs et Mademoiselle de Romans.* 3 vols. Versailles: Bernard, 1883.

Venturi, A. "Nuovi documenti." *Archivio storico dell'arte* 2 (1889): 377–78.

Viennot, Eliane. *Marguerite de Valois: Histoire d'une femme, histoire d'un mythe.* Paris: Payot, 1993.

Warrell, David A., Timothy M. Cox, and John D. Firth. *The Oxford Textbook of Medicine.* 3 vols. Oxford: Oxford University Press, 2003.

Weber, Caroline. *Queen of Fashion: What Marie Antoinette Wore to the Revolution.* New York: Picador, 2006.

Welch, Ellen R. *A Theater of Diplomacy: International Relations and the Performing Arts in Early Modern France.* Philadelphia: University of Pennsylvania Press, 2017.

Wellman, Kathleen. *Queens and Mistresses of Renaissance France.* New Haven: Yale University Press, 2013.

Wieland, Christoph Martin. *Le miroir d'or ou Les rois du Chéchian: Histoire veritable.* Neufchâtel: Société Typographique, 1774.

Williams, H. Noel. *Madame de Montespan.* London: Harper & Brothers, 1903.

Wilson-Chevalier, Kathleen. "Les déboires de Diane au château de Fontainebleau." In "Le mythe de Diane en France au XVIᵉ siècle," edited by Jean-Raymond Fanlo and Marie-Dominique Legrand. Special issue, *Albineana* 14 (2002): 409–41.

———. "Feminising the Warrior at Francis I's Fontainebleau." In *Masculinities in Sixteenth-Century France: Proceedings of the Eighth Cambridge French Renaissance Colloquium, 5–7 July 2003,* edited by Philip Ford and Paul White, 23–59. Cambridge: Cambridge French Colloquia, 2006.

———. "Femmes, cour, pouvoir: La chambre de la duchesse d'Étampes à Fontainebleau." In *Royaume de fémynie: Pouvoirs, contraintes, espaces de liberté de femmes, de la Renaissance à la Fronde,* edited by Kathleen Wilson-Chevalier and Eliane Viennot, 203–36. Paris: Champion, 1999.

———. "Women on Top at Fontainebleau." *Oxford Art Journal* 16 (1993): 34–48.

Wine, Kathleen. "Honored Guests: Wife and Mistress in 'Les plaisirs de l'île enchantée.'" *Dalhousie French Studies* 56 (2001): 78–90.

Wintroub, Michael. *A Savage Mirror: Power, Identity, and Knowledge in Early Modern France.* Stanford: Stanford University Press, 2006.

Wolf, John B. "The Formation of a King." In *Louis XIV and the Craft of Kingship,* edited by John C. Rule, 102–31. Columbus: Ohio State University Press, 1970.

———. *Louis XIV.* New York: W. W. Norton, 1968.

Wolfe, Michael. *The Conversion of Henri IV: Politics, Power, and Religious Belief in Early Modern France.* Cambridge: Harvard University Press, 1993.

Wood, Charles T. *The French Apanages and the Capetian Monarchy, 1224–1328.* Cambridge: Harvard University Press, 1966.

Yarwood, Doreen. *Fashion in the Western World, 1500–1990.* London: Batsford, 1992.

Zalamea, Patricia. "Subject to Diana: Picturing Desire in French Renaissance Courtly Aesthetics." PhD diss., Rutgers University, 2007.

Zeller, Berthold. "Le divorce et le second mariage de Henri IV." *Séances et travaux de l'Académie des sciences morales et politiques* 8 (1877): 221–70.

Zerner, Henri. "Diane de Poitiers, maîtresse de son image?" In "Le mythe de Diane en France au XVIᵉ siècle," edited by Jean-Raymond Fanlo and Marie-Dominique Legrand. Special issue, *Albineana* 14 (2002): 335–43.

———. *Renaissance Art in France: The Invention of Classicism.* Translated by Deke Dusinberre, Scott Wilson, and Rachel Zerner. Paris: Flammarion, 2003.

Zmora, Hillay. *Monarchy, Aristocracy, and the State in Europe, 1300–1800.* London: Routledge, 2001.

Zvereva, Alexandra. "Louise de Savoie et les recueils de portraits." In *Louise de Savoie (1476–1531)*, edited by Pierre Brioist, Laure Fagnart, and Cédric Michon. Tours: Presses universitaires François-Rabelais de Tours, 2015.

———. *Portraits dessinés de la cour des Valois: Les Clouet de Catherine de Médicis.* Paris: Arthena, 2011.

relationship with Anne de Montmorency,
39, 41–42, 48, 51, 53, 56, 89
relationship with Anne de Pisseleu, 39–41,
47, 48, 51, 56, 63, 65, 89
relationship with women, 36, 39, 44, 49
role in marriage of Jeanne of Navarre and
William of Cleves, 53–56
theatricalization of his court, 3, 9–11, 14, 36,
43–49, 132, 177n49
François II of France, 12, 85, 86
François (dauphin) of France, 40, 42
Frederick III, Holy Roman Emperor, 28
Frederick II (the Great) of Prussia, 1, 149, 150,
151, 169n1, 197n74
"French Singularity," 16–17
Fresne de Beaucourt, Gaston du, 22, 23, 25
Frotté, Jean de, 55

Gaston, Duke of Orléans, 115
Gaultier de Campes, 31
Gabrielle d'Estrées (Duchess of Beaufort), x,
2, 16, 85–86, 97, 111, 112, 131, 160
amiability of, 93–95, 160
beauty of, 93, 97
children with Henri IV, 96, 100–101, 103
death from possible poisoning, 15, 86,
104–7, 108–9
Estrées family, 92–93, 96
linked with Agnès Sorel, 14, 88, 91–92,
marriage and annulment, 95–96
as political adviser and diplomat, 14, 95
as potential queen, 15, 88–89, 95, 98–103,
108
relationship with Duke of Bellegarde, 92,
96, 109
Gaguin, Robert, 20
Gallet, Danielle, 141
Gassot, Jules, 91
Geoffrin, Marie-Thérèse Rodet, 140
Gohory, Jacques, 79
Goncourt, Edmond and Jules de, 137
Gontaut, Marquis of (Charles-Antoine), 140
Gonzaga, Frederico (Duke of Mantua), 65
Goodman, Elise, 114
Gouffier de Boisy, Charles de, 73
Graham, Lisa Jane, 136
Gramont, Duchess of (Béatrix de
Choiseul-Stainville), 157
Grandes Chroniques de France (by Jean
Chartier), 20
Grand dictionnaire historique, 32
Grégeois, Appoline, 160
Guerche, Château de la, 34
Guicciardini, Jacopo, 105

Guise, Duchess of (Antoinette de Bourbon),
69
Guise, Duchess of (Catherine of Clèves), 103
Guise, Duke of (Claude de Lorraine), 68, 73
Guise, Charles of Lorraine (Cardinal and
Archbishop of Reims), 51, 68, 74, 82
Guise, Charles of Lorraine (Duke of
Mayenne), 87, 88, 98
Guise, Claude of (Duke of Aumale), 72
Guise, Duke of (François de Lorraine, Prince
of Joinville), 74, 82, 87, 98
Guise, Duke of (Henri I), 87
Guise, Louise of, 107
Guise family, 5, 14, 59, 68, 69, 72, 73, 81, 82,
83, 86, 87

Haillan, Seigneur de (Bernard de Girard), 90,
91, 110
Harris, Carolyn, 16, 164
Heidegger, Martin, 12
Henri I, Duke of Guise, *See* Guise, Duke of
(Henri I)
Henri II (d'Albret) of Navarre, 49, 53, 54, 87,
176n5
Henri II of France, 14, 40, 41, 67, 68, 73–75,
77, 85, 87, 89, 98, 103, 116
child with Janet Fleming, 10, 74
difficult relationship with father, 42, 46,
and Anne de Pisseleu, 62
opposition to Treaty of Crépy, 59
relationship with Catherine de Médicis, 10,
65, 71–72
relationship with Diane de Poitiers, 14, 48,
61, 63, 65, 69, 71–72, 78–82, 84, 102
Henri III of France, 13, 85, 86, 87, 90, 92, 93, 98
and emergence of the mignons, 7–8
Henri IV of France and Navarre, 10, 94, 98,
110, 117, 139, 162
considers marrying Gabrielle d'Estrées, 15,
85, 95, 101–5, 107–8, 131
decision to marry Marie de Médicis, 15, 101,
105–6
falls in love with Gabrielle, 14, 86, 92–93,
96, 97
marriage and divorce, Marguerite of Valois,
87, 92, 97, 100, 101
need for an heir, 88, 99–101
and re-emergence of the royal mistress, 85,
86, 88, 91
relationship with Henriette Balzac
d'Entragues, 86, 109
Henrietta Maria of England, 115
Henriette (Anne-Henriette), daughter of Louis
XV, 143